Favorite Recipes

# Italian

Favorite Recipes

# Italian

p

This is a Parragon Publishing Book
This edition published in 2004

Parragon Publishing
Queen Street House
4 Queen Street
Bath BA1 1HE, UK

ISBN: 1-40540-486-8

Printed in China

**Notes**

This book uses imperial, metric, or US cup measurements. Follow the same units of
measurement throughout; do not mix imperial and metric.
All spoon measurements are level: teaspoons are assumed to be 5 ml and tablespoons
are assumed to be 15 ml unless otherwise stated.
Milk is assumed to be whole, eggs and individual vegetables such as potatoes are
medium, and pepper is freshly ground black pepper.
The preparation times include chilling and marinating, where appropriate.
The times given for each recipe are an approximate guide only because the
preparation times may differ according to the techniques used by different people and
the cooking times may vary as a result of the type of oven used.
Ovens should be preheated to the specified temperature. If using a fan-assisted oven,
check the manufacturer's instructions for adjusting the time and temperature.
Recipes using raw or very lightly cooked eggs should be avoided by infants, the
elderly, pregnant women, convalescents, and anyone suffering from an illness.

# Contents

Introduction   10

## Soups

## Appetizers

## Snacks & Light Meals

# Fish & Seafood

# Meat

# Poultry & Game

# Vegetables

# Salads

# Pasta

# Rice & Grains

# Pizzas & Breads

# Desserts

# Introduction

**Italian food, including the many pasta dishes, pizzas, and risottos, as well as the decadent desserts, are enjoyed all around the world. This inspirational cookbook aims to bring a little bit of Italy into your kitchen!**

Glorious sunlight, spectacular beaches, luscious countryside, rugged mountains, world-famous museums and art galleries, elegant designer shops, picturesque villages, and magnificent cities—if this were not enough, Italy also boasts one of the oldest and finest culinary traditions in the whole of Europe.

The ancient Romans loved good food and plenty of it, vying with each other to produce increasingly lavish and outlandish banquets. One of the earliest cookbooks, written by Apicius, a gourmet in the first century, includes a recipe for dormouse stuffed with walnuts! As the Roman Empire expanded, overseas trade brought new ingredients, and agriculture began to flourish at home. However, even then, wine production was just as prodigious as it is today.

With the collapse of the Roman Empire, the diet returned to plainer fare, relying on the wealth of cereals, fruit, and vegetables that could be cultivated on the fertile plains. However, with the Renaissance, an interest in and enthusiasm for fine food revived and, once again, there were wealthy families who presided over extravagant banquets.

Italian pastry cooks were valued throughout the courts of Europe and were generally acknowledged as the best in the world. When Catherine de' Medici went to Paris to marry the future King Henri II, she took an army of Italian cooks with her and changed French culinary traditions irrevocably. A new middle class developed who also took an interest in eating well, creating a bourgeois cuisine characterized by fresh flavors and simple, unsauced dishes. The poor, of course, continued with a peasant subsistence.

The very finest produce and freshest ingredients still characterize Italian cuisine as a whole.

# Introduction

Although modern transportation makes it possible for more exotic ingredients to travel across the world, Italian cooking still centers on home-grown produce. Over 60 percent of the land is devoted to crops and pasture. With a climate that ranges from very cold in the Alps and Apennines to semitropical along the coast of the Ligurian Sea, the range of produce is extensive: olives, oranges, lemons, figs, grapes, pomegranates, almonds, wheat, potatoes, tomatoes, sugar beet, corn, and rice.

Livestock includes cattle and buffalo, sheep, goats, pigs, and chickens. In a single year, Italy produces nearly 6.5 million tons of wine, nearly 2.5 million tons of olives, about 500,000 tons of olive oil, more than 4.5 million tons of tomatoes, and 120 million chickens. An impressive amount, you'll agree!

The introduction to this book continues to explore Italy, region by region, to discover the different types of food that are identified with specific areas of the country. Seasonal ingredients are also examined to provide the reader with an insight into the type of produce used by the very discerning people of Italy.

## Ragu Sauce

3 tbsp olive oil

3 tbsp butter

2 large onions, chopped

4 celery stalks, sliced thinly

6 oz/175 g lean bacon, chopped

2 garlic cloves, chopped

1 lb 2 oz/500 g ground lean beef

2 tbsp tomato paste

1 tbsp flour

14 oz/400 g canned chopped
    tomatoes

⅔ cup beef stock

⅔ cup red wine

2 tsp dried oregano

½ tsp freshly grated nutmeg

salt and pepper

1 Heat the oil and butter in a pan over medium heat. Add the onions, celery, and bacon and cook for 5 minutes, stirring.

2 Stir in the garlic and ground beef and cook, stirring until the meat has lost its redness. Lower the heat and cook for 10 minutes, stirring.

3 Increase the heat to medium, then stir in the tomato paste and the flour and cook for 1–2 minutes. Stir in the tomatoes, stock, and wine and bring to a boil, stirring. Season and stir in the oregano and nutmeg. Cover and simmer for 45 minutes, stirring. The sauce is now ready to use.

# Regional Cooking

**To talk about Italian cuisine is somewhat misleading, as it is not a single entity. The country has been united only since March 17, 1861, and Italians still have a powerful sense of their regional identity.**

Regional cuisine is a source of pride and considerable competition. Sicilians are dismissed as *mangimaccaroni* (pasta eaters), and they in turn express their contempt for Neapolitans with the term *mangiafoglie* (vegetable eaters). Each region bases its cuisine on local ingredients: the best ham comes from the area where pigs are raised; fish and seafood feature in coastal regions; butter is used in dishes from the north of Italy where there is dairy farming, while olive oil is characteristic of southern recipes.

## Abruzzi & Molise

Once a single region, this has now been divided into two separate provinces, although they remain closely associated. Located in northern Italy to the east of Rome, the area is well known for its high-quality cured meats and cheese. The cuisine also features lamb and fish, and seafood in the coastal areas. Pepperoncino is a tiny, fiery hot, dried red chile from Abruzzi.

## Basilicata

If the Italian peninsula looks like a boot, Basilicata is located on the arch of the foot. The landscape is rugged and inhospitable, with much of the region being over 6,500 feet/ 2,000 meters above sea level.

# Regional Cooking

It is hardly surprising, therefore, that the cuisine is warming and filling, featuring substantial soups in particular. Cured meats, pork, lamb, and game are typical ingredients and freshwater fish are abundant in the more mountainous areas.

## Calabria

In the south, on Italy's toe, Calabria is a region of dramatic contrasts—superb beaches and towering mountains. Excellent fish and seafood typify the local cuisine, which is well known for its swordfish and tuna dishes. Fruit and vegetables are abundant, particularly oranges, lemons, eggplants, and olives. Like other southern regions, desserts are a specialty, often based on local figs, honey, or almonds.

## Campania

Naples on the west coast is the home of pizza, now known across the world from Sydney to New York, and the region bases many of its other dishes on the wonderful sun-ripened tomatoes grown locally. Fish and seafood feature strongly in the Neapolitan diet and robust herb-flavored stews, redolent with garlic, are popular. Pastries and fruit desserts are also characteristic.

## Emilia–Romagna

Emilia-Romagna is a central Italian province, whose capital is the beautiful medieval city of Bologna. Nicknamed *la grassa*, "the fat city," it is home to some of the best restaurants in the country. A gourmet paradise, the region is famous for Parmesan cheese and prosciutto from Parma, balsamic vinegar from the area around Modena, cotechino, mortadella and other cured meats, and, of course, *spaghetti alla bolognese*. Butter, cream, and other dairy products

feature in the food
of the region and a wide range
of pasta dishes is popular.

## Lazio

Capital of the region and the country, Rome is a cosmopolitan and sophisticated city with some of the best restaurants—and ice-cream parlors—in Europe. Fruit and vegetables are abundant and lamb and veal dishes are characteristic of the region, which is famous for *saltimbocca*, which literally means "jump in the mouth." Here, they have perfected the art of preparing high-quality ingredients in simple, but delicious ways that retain the individual flavors. A Roman specialty is *supplì al telefono*—"telephone wires"—mozzarella cheese wrapped in balls of cooked rice and deep-fried. The mozzarella is stringy, hence the name of the dish.

## Liguria

A northern province with a long coastline, Liguria is well known for its superb fish and seafood. It is also said to produce the best basil in the whole of Italy and it is where pesto sauce was first invented. The ancient port of Genoa was one of the first places in Europe to import Asian spices, and highly seasoned dishes are still particularly characteristic of this area.

## Lombardy

An important rice-growing region in northwest Italy, this is the home of risotto, and there are probably as many variations of this dish as there are cooks. Dairy produce features in the cuisine, and Lombardy is credited with the invention of butter, as well as mascarpone cheese. Vegetable soups, stews, and pot roasts are characteristic of this region. Bresaola, cured raw beef, is a

# Regional Cooking

local specialty that is often served wrapped around soft goat cheese.

## Marche

With its long coastline and high mountains, this region is blessed with both abundant seafood and game. Pasta, pork, and olives also feature and methods of preparation are even more elaborate than those of neighboring Umbria.

## Piedmont

On the borders of France and Switzerland, Piedmont in the northwest is strongly influenced by its neighbors. A fertile, arable region, it is well known for rice, polenta, and gnocchi and is said to grow the finest onions in Italy. Gorgonzola, one of the world's greatest cheeses, comes from this region although, sadly, the little village that gave it its name has now

been subsumed by the urban sprawl of Milan. Piedmontese garlic is said to be the best in Italy and the local white truffles are a gourmet's dream.

## Puglia

On the heel of Italy, this region produces excellent olives, herbs, vegetables, and fruit, particularly melons and figs. Fish and seafood are abundant and the region is known for its oyster and mussel dishes. Calzone, a sort of inside-out pizza, was invented here.

## Sardinia

This Mediterranean island is famous for its luxurious desserts and extravagant pastries, many of them featuring honey, nuts, and home-grown fruit. Hardly surprisingly, fish and seafood—tuna, eel, mullet, sea

bass, lobster, and mussels—are central to Sardinian cuisine, and spit-roasted suckling pig is the national dish served on feast days. *Sardo* is a mild-tasting Romano cheese produced in Sardinia.

## Sicily

Like their southern neighbors, Sicilians have a sweet tooth, which they indulge with superb cakes, desserts, and ice cream, often incorporating locally grown almonds, pistachios, and citrus fruits. Pasta dishes are an important part of the diet, and fish and seafood, including tuna, swordfish, and mussels, feature prominently.

## Trentino Alto-Adage

A mountainous region in the north-east, Trentino has been strongly influenced by its Austrian neighbor. Smoked sausage and dumplings are characteristic of the cuisine, which is also well known for its filled pasta.

## Tuscany

The fertile plains of Tuscany are ideal for farming and the region produces superb fruit and vegetables. Cattle are raised here, and both steak and veal dishes feature on the Tuscan menu, together with a wide range of game. Tripe is a local specialty and *Panforte di Siena*, a traditional Christmas cake made with honey and nuts, comes from the city of Siena. A grain known as *farro* is grown almost exclusively in Tuscany, where it is used to make a nourishing soup.

## Umbria

Pork, lamb, game, and freshwater fish, prepared and served simply but deliciously, characterize the excellent cuisine of the region. Fragrant black truffles are a feature and Umbrian cooking makes good use of its high-quality olive oil. Umbria is also famous for *imbrecciata*, a hearty soup made with lentils, chickpeas, and navy beans.

## Veneto and Friuli

An intensively farmed area in the northeast of Italy, this region produces cereals and almost 20 percent of the country's wine.

Polenta and risotto feature in the cuisine, as well as an extensive range of fish and seafood. *Risi e bisi*, rice and peas, is a traditional dish that was served every year at the Doge's banquet in Venice to honor the city's patron saint, St Mark.

# Ingredients

**Whatever regional variations there may be, all the cuisines of Italy have one thing in common —the use of the freshest and highest-quality seasonal ingredients. Choosing and buying meat, fish, vegetables, and fruit are as important as the way they are prepared and cooked.**

## Cheese

### Bel Paese

Its name means "beautiful country" and it is a very creamy, mild-flavored cheese with a waxy yellow rind. It may be eaten on its own or used for cooking.

### Dolcelatte

This is a very creamy, delicate-tasting type of Gorgonzola. Its name means "sweet milk."

### Fontina

A mild, nutty-tasting cheese with a creamy texture, genuine fontina is produced from the unpasteurized milk of cattle grazed on alpine herbs and grass in the Val d'Aosta. When fresh, it is delicious eaten on its own and the mature cheese is excellent for cooking.

### Gorgonzola

Strictly speaking, this cheese should be called Stracchino Gorgonzola. It is a creamy cheese with green-blue veining and its flavor can range from mild to strong. Delicious on its own, it can also be used in pasta sauces and stirred into polenta.

### Mascarpone

From Lombardy, this is a triple cream cheese that can be used for making cheesecakes and other desserts. It also adds richness to risotto and pasta sauces.

### Mozzarella

No Italian kitchen would be complete without a supply of this moist, white, egg-shaped cheese. Traditionally made from buffalo milk, it is the ideal cheese for cooking and is also used in salads with tomatoes and fresh basil. It originated in the area around Naples, which still produces the best mozzarella, but it is now made throughout Italy, often from cow's milk.

### Parmesan

Probably the best-known Italian cheese, Parmesan is extensively used in cooking. Parmigiano Reggiano is produced under strictly controlled conditions in a closely defined area. It is always aged for a minimum of two years, but this may be extended up to seven years. A cow's milk cheese, it is hard with a granular, flaky texture and a slightly nutty flavor. It is best bought in a single piece and grated as required.

## Pecorino

A hard or semihard ewe's milk cheese, pecorino is widely used in cooking. It has a sharp flavor and a granular texture rather like Parmesan. Pecorino pepato from Sicily is studded with black peppercorns.

## Provolone

Eaten on its own when fresh, provolone is also perfect for cooking, as it has a stringy texture when melted. It is made from different types of milk—the strongest being made from goat's milk. Buffalo milk is often used in the south of Italy. Cylindrical or oval, it varies considerably in size and is often seen hanging from the ceiling in Italian delicatessens.

## Ricotta

Literally translated as "recooked," ricotta is a soft white curd cheese originally made from goat's or ewe's milk. It is more often made from cow's milk these days. It is widely used for both savory and sweet dishes and is classically paired with spinach.

## Cured Meats

## Bresaola

This salt-cured, air-dried beef is usually served in thin slices as an antipasto. It is similar to prosciutto in flavor, but not so salty.

## Mortadella

Considered to be one of the finest Italian sausages, mortadella is also the largest with a diameter that may reach 18 inches/45 cm. It has a smooth texture and a fairly bland flavor. It is usually eaten in

# Ingredients

sandwiches or as an antipasto, but may also be added to risottos or pasta sauces shortly before the end of the cooking time.

## Pancetta

Made from belly of pork, this resembles unsmoked bacon. It is very fatty and is used in a wide variety of dishes, particularly spaghetti alla carbonara. Smoked pancetta is also available.

## Prosciutto

This salted, air-dried ham does not need any cooking. The drying process may take up to two years.  Produced under strictly controlled conditions in a closely defined area between Taro and Baganza, Prosciutto di Parma, also known as Parma ham, is made from pigs fed on the whey from the process of making Parmesan cheese. San Daniele

is a leaner prosciutto with a very distinctive flavor, and is produced in Friuli. Prosciutto cotto is a cooked ham, often flavored with herbs. Prosciutto is traditionally served with melon or figs as an antipasto, but is also used in veal dishes, risottos, and pasta sauces.

## Salami

Salami are all made from pork, but there is an almost infinite variety of types, which vary according to how finely or coarsely the meat is ground, the proportion of lean meat to fat, the seasoning and spices; and the length of drying time. Some of the best known varieties are salame milano; salame sardo, a hotly spiced sausage from Sardinia; salame napoletano, flavored with black and red pepper; salame fiorentina, a coarse-cut Tuscan salame flavored with fennel seeds and pepper; and salame di

Felino from the Emilia-Romagna, a very lean salame flavored with garlic and white wine.

## Sausages

Most Italian sausages are made from pork, but both venison and wild boar are sometimes used. There must be hundreds of different varieties from every region of the country. Cotechino is a large, lightly spiced sausage, weighing about 2 lb 4 oz/ 1 kg. It is usually boiled and served hot with lentils or beans. Luganega is a mildly spiced, long, coiled sausage that is sold by the yard. Zampone is a pig's trotter stuffed with ground pork. Traditionally, it is boiled, then sliced into rings and served with lentils. It is one of the classic ingredients of bollito misto.

## Mushrooms

Collecting wild mushrooms is a national pastime and pharmacies throughout the country will identify species if there is any doubt whether they are edible varieties.

### Caesar's mushrooms

These are large mushrooms with orange caps and were once the favorites of Roman emperors. They are difficult to find outside Italy.

### Chanterelles

These slightly frilly, orange-yellow mushrooms have a delicate flavor and aroma. They are now cultivated and are widely available in supermarkets.

### Porcini

Also known as ceps or boletus mushrooms, these have a superb flavor. They can grow to be huge, weighing as much as 1 lb 2 oz/500 g each. Young mushrooms may be eaten raw and larger specimens are delicious broiled. Dried porcini are available from Italian delicatessens and although they are very expensive, you need only a small quantity.

## Pasta

### Plain & filled pasta

There are hundreds of different types of pasta and new shapes are being produced all the time. Basic pasta is made from hard durum wheat flour and water, while pasta all'uova is enriched with eggs. Additional ingredients, such as spinach, tomatoes, and squid ink, are used to flavor and color it.

It is worth buying fresh pasta, called *maccheroni* in Italy, if you have access to a good Italian delicatessen, and the stuffed varieties available in supermarkets are often quite good. Otherwise, commercially available, fresh, unfilled pasta is not really any better than the dried variety. There is no definitive list of names and the same shape may be called different things in various regions. Some have delightfully descriptive names: *capelli d'angelo,* angel's hair; *dischi volante,* flying saucers; *linguine di passeri,* sparrows' tongues; and *strozzapreti,* priest strangler, for example.

There are no hard-and-fast rules about which pasta should be served with which sauce. As a guide, long, thin types of pasta, such as fettuccine, tagliatelle, spaghetti and taglioni, are best for delicate, olive-oil-based and seafood sauces. Short, fat pasta shapes (such as lumache, conchiglie, and penne) or curly shapes (such as farfalle and fusilli)

# Ingredients

are best for meat sauces, as they trap the pieces. Tomato-based sauces go with virtually any pasta shape. Tiny pasta shapes (such as stellete, pepe bucato, and risi) are used for soups.

Pasta may be stuffed with cheese, meat, fish, chicken, sun-dried tomatoes, and various other fillings. Traditionally, ravioli are square, tortelli are round, and tortelloni resemble the shape of Venus's navel! Flat pasta is used to make baked dishes, such as lasagne al forno.

## Gnocchi

These are rather like little dumplings and are served as a first course in a similar way to pasta, either in soup or with a sauce. They are made from a variety of ingredients: milled durum wheat, potatoes, flour, or spinach and ricotta. They are available from Italian delicatessens and are easy to make at home.

## Basic Pasta Dough

Making your own pasta dough is time-consuming but immensely satisfying. You will need plenty of space for the rolled-out dough, and somewhere to hang it to dry.

### SERVES 4

### INGREDIENTS

1 cup all-purpose flour, plus extra for dusting

⅔ cup fine semolina

1 tsp salt

1 tbsp olive oil

2 eggs

2–3 tbsp hot water

1 Sieve the flour, semolina, and salt into a bowl and make a well in the center. Pour in the oil and add the eggs. Add 1 tablespoon of hot water and, using your fingertips, work to form a smooth dough. Sprinkle on a little more water if necessary to make the dough pliable.

2 Lightly dust a board with flour, then turn the dough out and knead it until it is elastic and silky. This could take 10–15 minutes. Dust the dough with more flour if your fingers become too sticky.

3 Alternatively, put the eggs, 1 tablespoon hot water, and the oil in the bowl of a food processor and process for a few seconds. Add the flour, semolina, and salt and process until smooth. Sprinkle on a little more hot water if necessary to make the dough pliable. Transfer to an electric mixer and knead using the dough hook for 2–3 minutes.

4 Divide the dough into 2 equal pieces. Cover a counter with a clean cloth or dish towel and dust it liberally with flour. Place one portion of the dough on the floured cloth and roll it out as thinly and evenly as possible, stretching the dough gently until the pattern of the weave shows through. Cover it with a cloth and roll out the second piece in a similar way.

5 Use a ruler and a sharp knife blade to cut long, thin strips for noodles, or small confectionery cutters to cut rounds, stars, or an assortment of other decorative shapes.

6 Cover the dough shapes with a clean cloth and leave them in a cool place (not the refrigerator) for 30–45 minutes to become partly dry. To dry ribbons, place a dish towel over the back of a chair and hang the ribbons over it.

## Olive Oil

Arguably the best olive oil in the world comes from Italy and each region produces an oil with a different flavor. The oil is made by pressing the pulp of ripe olives. The first pressing, with no additional processing, produces extra virgin olive oil. This is the highest quality and is carefully regulated. It is the best oil to use for salad dressings.

The next quality, virgin olive oil, may also be used for dressings and is good for cooking. It has a slightly higher level of acidity than extra virgin, but still has a good flavor.

Other types of olive oil are usually refined and may have been heat-treated. They can be used for cooking, but should not be used in dressings.

## Rice & Grains

### Polenta

A kind of cornmeal, polenta is a staple in northern Italy. There, it is available in an astonishing range of degrees of coarseness, but elsewhere there are two main types—coarse and fine. It is boiled to make a kind of porridge and can then be cooled and left to set, before being broiled, fried, or baked. It is very versatile and can be used for both savory and sweet dishes. Traditionally, polenta was cooked in a large copper pan and had to be stirred for at least 1 hour. Nowadays, quick-cook polenta is available.

### Rice

Italy produces a wide range of types of rice in greater quantities than any other European country. Superfino rice is a round grain used for risottos. It can absorb a large amount of liquid, swelling to three times its size during cooking, while still retaining its shape and texture. This is what gives the dish its unique and characteristic creaminess. Carnaroli, arborio, and vialone nano are especially fine varieties. Semifino rice is used for soups and salads. Italians never serve food on a bed of rice, but may sometimes serve plain boiled rice with butter and cheese as a separate dish.

## Vegetables & Pulses

### Artichokes

Globe artichokes are cultivated throughout Italy and grow wild on Sicily. Naples is credited with the first cultivation and, nowadays, they are regarded as a Roman specialty, being served twice deep-fried. Tiny plants may be eaten raw or braised

# Ingredients

with olive oil and fresh herbs. Larger artichokes are boiled and served with a dressing or stuffed.

## Arugula

Now enjoying a new popularity in the United States, arugula has never lost favor in Italy, where it grows wild. It is also cultivated, but the home-grown variety has a better flavor. It is usually served in salads or on its own with a dressing of balsamic vinegar and olive oil. It is sometimes cooked like spinach, but tends to lose some of its pungency.

## Beans

Navy, cannellini, borlotti, black-eye (known as *fagioli coll'occhio*), and fava beans, chickpeas, and other pulses are eaten all over Italy, although Tuscans in particular are renowned for being bean-eaters. Beans are incorporated in substantial stews and soups or

may be served as a simple side dish that has been dressed with a little olive oil.

## Bell Peppers

Capsicums, or sweet bell peppers, are invariably sun-ripened in Italy. While they do not always have the uniform shape of greenhouse-grown bell peppers, they have a depth of flavor that is unsurpassed. Bell peppers are served raw or roasted as an antipasto, and roasted or stuffed as a hot dish. They are classically partnered with anchovies, aubergines, capers, olives, or tomatoes.

## Eggplants

Originally regarded with great suspicion, eggplants are now integral to Italian cooking. This is especially true in the southern part of the country. They may be cooked in a wide variety of ways and add

depth of flavor and color to a range of different dishes.

## Fennel

Also known as Florence fennel, this anise-flavored bulb is one of the most important ingredients in Italian cooking. It is served raw with a vinaigrette or with cheese at the end of a meal and may be cooked in a variety of ways, including sautéing, braising, and baking.

## Onions

Sweet red onions are delicious raw and add color to cooked dishes. White onions also have a sweet flavor and yellow onions are mild-tasting. Baby white onions are traditionally cooked in a sour-sweet sauce—*agrodolce*—and usually served as an antipasto.

## Radicchio

This bitter-tasting, red-leafed

member of the chicory family is nearly always cooked in Italy, rather than being included in salads. It may be broiled or stuffed and baked and is quite often used as a pizza topping.

## Spinach

Spinach and its close relatives Swiss chard and spinach beet are used in a wide variety of Italian dishes. Anything described as *alla fiorentina* is likely to contain it. Young leaves are eaten raw in salads and spinach is typically paired with ricotta in pasta and pancake fillings. It is also classically combined with eggs, fish, chicken, and veal.

## Squash

A huge variety of squashes, from tiny butternuts to great pumpkins, are used in northern Italian cooking for both savory and sweet dishes, including soups, risottos, stuffed pasta, and dessert tarts. Deep-fried pumpkin flowers in batter are also served.

## Tomatoes

Many different varieties of tomatoes have been grown throughout Italy since the sixteenth century and it is difficult to imagine an Italian kitchen without them. Plum tomatoes are probably the most familiar and they have a firm texture that is less watery than other varieties, which makes them ideal for cooking. They may be served raw, typically partnering mozzarella cheese and fresh basil in an *insalata tricolore,* and are used to add both color and flavor to a range of dishes. Italian tomatoes are always sun ripened and have a truly unmistakable flavor.

Sun-dried tomatoes have an intense flavor and are sold dry in packages or preserved in oil. These days, commercially produced sun-dried tomatoes have, in fact, been air-dried by machine, although sometimes it is possible to obtain the genuine article. If dry ones are to be used for cooking, they should be soaked in hot water first.

Passata is a pulp made from strained tomatoes. It has a strong flavor and may be fine or coarse. It is useful for soups and sauces and can be used as a substitute for fresh tomatoes in slow-cooked dishes. Tomato paste has a less intense flavor than passata.

## Zucchini

Widely used in northern Italian cooking, zucchini combine well with many other typically Mediterranean ingredients, such as tomatoes and eggplants. They may be served cold as an antipasto, stuffed, or deep-fried. They are often sold with their flowers still attached.

# Basic Recipes

**These recipes form the basis of several of the dishes contained throughout this book. Many of these basic recipes can be made in advance and stored in the refrigerator until required.**

## Basic Tomato Sauce

2 tbsp olive oil

1 small onion, chopped

1 garlic clove, chopped

14 oz/400 g canned chopped tomatoes

2 tbsp chopped parsley

1 tsp dried oregano

2 bay leaves

2 tbsp tomato paste

1 tsp sugar

salt and pepper

1 Heat the oil in a pan over medium heat and cook the onion for 2-3 minutes or until translucent. Add the garlic and cook for 1 minute.

2 Stir in the chopped tomatoes, parsley, oregano, bay leaves, tomato paste, sugar, and salt and pepper to taste.

3 Bring the sauce to a boil, then simmer, uncovered, for 15–20 minutes, or until the sauce has reduced by half. Taste the sauce and adjust the seasoning if necessary. Discard the bay leaves just before serving.

## Béchamel Sauce

1¼ cups milk

2 bay leaves

3 cloves

1 small onion

¼ cup butter, plus extra for greasing

6 tbsp all-purpose flour

1¼ cups light cream

large pinch of freshly grated nutmeg

salt and pepper

1 Pour the milk into a small pan and add the bay leaves. Press the cloves into the onion, add to the pan and bring the milk to a boil. Remove the pan from the heat and set aside to cool.

2 Strain the milk into a jug and rinse the pan. Melt the butter in the pan and stir in the flour. Stir for 1 minute, then gradually pour on the milk, stirring constantly. Cook the sauce for 3 minutes, then pour on the cream and bring it to a boil. Remove from the heat and season with nutmeg, salt and pepper to taste.

## Lamb Sauce

2 tbsp olive oil

1 large onion, sliced

2 celery stalks, thinly sliced

1 lb 2 oz/500 g lean lamb, minced (ground)

3 tbsp tomato paste

5½ oz/150 g bottled sun-dried tomatoes, drained and chopped

1 tsp dried oregano

1 tbsp red wine vinegar

⅔ cup chicken stock

salt and pepper

1 Heat the oil in a skillet over medium heat and cook the onion and celery until the onion is translucent, about 3 minutes. Add the lamb and cook, stirring frequently, until it browns.

2 Stir in the tomato paste, sun-dried tomatoes, oregano, vinegar, and stock. Season with salt and pepper to taste.

3 Bring to a boil and cook, uncovered, for 20 minutes, or until the meat has absorbed the stock. Taste and adjust the seasoning if necessary.

## Cheese Sauce

2 tbsp butter

1 tbsp all-purpose flour

1 cup milk

2 tbsp light cream

pinch of freshly grated nutmeg

3 tbsp grated sharp Cheddar cheese

1 tbsp freshly grated Parmesan cheese

salt and pepper

1 Melt the butter in a pan, then stir in the flour and cook for 1 minute. Gradually pour on the milk, stirring all the time. Stir in the cream and season the sauce with nutmeg and salt and pepper to taste.

2 Simmer the sauce for 5 minutes to reduce, then remove it from the heat and stir in the cheeses. Stir until the cheeses have melted and blended into the sauce.

## Espagnole Sauce

2 tbsp butter

¼ cup all-purpose flour

1 tsp tomato paste

1⅛ cups hot veal stock

1 tbsp Madeira

1½ tsp white wine vinegar

2 tbsp olive oil

¼ cup diced bacon

¼ cup diced carrot

3 tbsp diced onion

2 tbsp diced celery

3 tbsp diced leek

2 tbsp diced fennel

1 fresh thyme sprig

1 bay leaf

1 Melt the butter in a pan, then add the flour and cook, stirring, until lightly colored. Add the tomato paste, then stir in the hot veal stock, Madeira, and white wine vinegar and cook for 2 minutes.

2 Heat the oil in a separate pan, then add the bacon, carrot, onion, celery, leek, fennel, thyme sprig, and bay leaf and cook until the vegetables have softened. Remove the vegetables from the pan with a slotted spoon and drain thoroughly. Add the vegetables to the sauce and leave to simmer for 4 hours, stirring occasionally. Strain the sauce before using.

## Italian Red Wine Sauce

⅝ cup Brown Stock (see page 30)

⅔ cup Espagnole Sauce (see left)

½ cup red wine

2 tbsp red wine vinegar

4 tbsp shallots, chopped

1 bay leaf

1 thyme sprig

pepper

1 First make a demi-glace sauce. Put the Brown Stock and Espagnole Sauce in a pan and heat for 10 minutes, stirring occasionally.

2 Meanwhile, put the red wine, red wine vinegar, shallots, bay leaf, and thyme in a pan, then bring to a boil and reduce by three-fourths.

3 Strain the demi-glace sauce and add to the pan containing the Red Wine Sauce, then leave to simmer for 20 minutes, stirring occasionally. Season with pepper to taste and strain the sauce before using.

# Basic Recipes

## Italian Cheese Sauce

2 tbsp butter

¼ cup all-purpose flour

1¼ cups hot milk

pinch of nutmeg

pinch of dried thyme

2 tbsp white wine vinegar

3 tbsp heavy cream

½ cup grated mozzarella cheese

½ cup Parmesan cheese

1 tsp English mustard

2 tbsp sour cream

salt and pepper

1 Melt the butter in a pan and stir in the flour. Cook, stirring, over a low heat until the roux is light in color and crumbly in texture. Stir in the hot milk and cook, stirring, for 15 minutes until thick and smooth.

2 Add the nutmeg, thyme, white wine vinegar and season to taste. Stir in the cream and mix well.

3 Stir in the cheeses, mustard, and sour cream and mix until the cheeses have melted and blended into the sauce.

## Fish Stock

2 lb/900 g non-oily fish pieces, such as heads, tails, trimmings, and bones

⅔ cup white wine

1 onion, chopped

1 carrot, sliced

1 celery stalk, sliced

4 black peppercorns

1 bouquet garni

7½ cups water

1 Put the fish pieces, wine, onion, carrot, celery, black peppercorns, bouquet garni, and water in a large pan and leave to simmer for 30 minutes, stirring occasionally. Strain and blot the fat from the surface with paper towels before using.

## Garlic Mayonnaise

2 garlic cloves, crushed

8 tbsp mayonnaise

chopped parsley

salt and pepper

1 Put the mayonnaise in a bowl. Add the garlic, parsley, and salt and pepper to taste and mix together well.

## Brown Stock

2 lb/900 g veal bones and shin of beef

1 leek, sliced

1 onion, chopped

1 celery stalk, sliced

1 carrot, sliced

1 bouquet garni

⅔ cup white wine vinegar

1 thyme sprig

7½ cups cold water

1 Roast the veal bones and shin of beef in their own juices in the oven for 40 minutes.

2 Transfer the bones to a large pan, then add the leek, onion, celery, carrot, bouquet garni, white wine vinegar, and thyme and cover with the cold water. Leave to simmer over very low heat for about 3 hours. Strain and blot the fat from the surface with paper towels before using.

# How to Use This Book

**Each recipe contains a wealth of useful information, including a breakdown of nutritional quantities, preparation, and cooking times, and level of difficulty. All of this information is explained in detail below.**

This amount of time represents the actual cooking time.

The nutritional information provided for each recipe is per serving or per portion. Optional ingredients, variations, or serving suggestions have not been included in the calculations.

The number of chef's hats represents the difficulty of each recipe, ranging from easy (1 chef's hat) to difficult (5 chef's hats).

This amount of time represents the preparation of ingredients, including cooling, chilling, and soaking times.

The ingredients for each recipe are listed in the order that they are used.

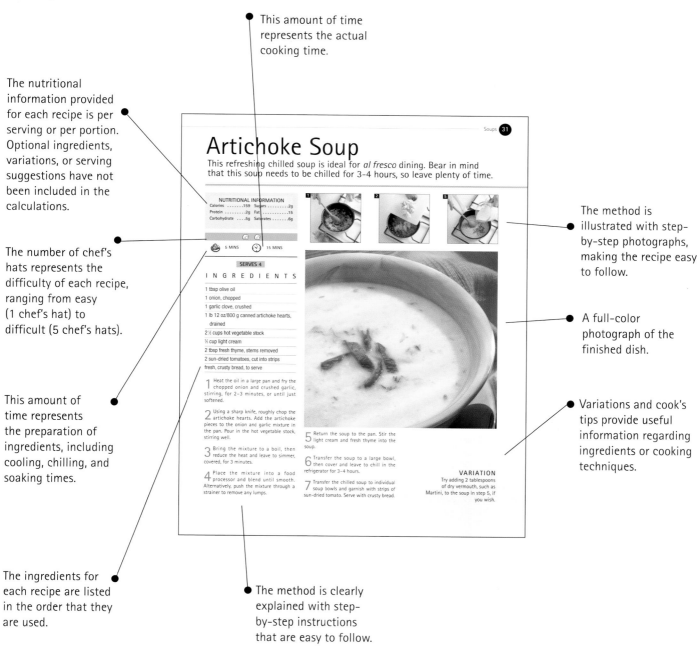

Soups **31**

## Artichoke Soup

This refreshing chilled soup is ideal for *al fresco* dining. Bear in mind that this soup needs to be chilled for 3-4 hours, so leave plenty of time.

**NUTRITIONAL INFORMATION**

Calories .......159  Sugars .........2g
Protein .........2g  Fat .............15
Carbohydrate ...5g  Saturates .......6g

5 MINS          15 MINS

**SERVES 4**

**INGREDIENTS**

1 tbsp olive oil
1 onion, chopped
1 garlic clove, crushed
1 lb 12 oz/800 g canned artichoke hearts, drained
2 ½ cups hot vegetable stock
½ cup light cream
2 tbsp fresh thyme, stems removed
2 sun-dried tomatoes, cut into strips
fresh, crusty bread, to serve

1 Heat the oil in a large pan and fry the chopped onion and crushed garlic, stirring, for 2-3 minutes, or until just softened.

2 Using a sharp knife, roughly chop the artichoke hearts. Add the artichoke pieces to the onion and garlic mixture in the pan. Pour in the hot vegetable stock, stirring well.

3 Bring the mixture to a boil, then reduce the heat and leave to simmer, covered, for 3 minutes.

4 Place the mixture into a food processor and blend until smooth. Alternatively, push the mixture through a strainer to remove any lumps.

5 Return the soup to the pan. Stir the light cream and fresh thyme into the soup.

6 Transfer the soup to a large bowl, then cover and leave to chill in the refrigerator for 3-4 hours.

7 Transfer the chilled soup to individual soup bowls and garnish with strips of sun-dried tomato. Serve with crusty bread.

**VARIATION**
Try adding 2 tablespoons of dry vermouth, such as Martini, to the soup in step 5, if you wish.

The method is illustrated with step-by-step photographs, making the recipe easy to follow.

A full-color photograph of the finished dish.

Variations and cook's tips provide useful information regarding ingredients or cooking techniques.

The method is clearly explained with step-by-step instructions that are easy to follow.

# Soups

Soups are an important part of the Italian cuisine. They vary in consistency from light and delicate to hearty main meal soups. Texture is always apparent—Italians rarely serve smooth soups. Some may be partially puréed, but the identity of the ingredients is never entirely obliterated. There are regional characteristics, too. In the north, soups

are often based on rice, while in Tuscany, thick bean- or bread-based soups are popular. Tomato, garlic, and pasta soups are typical of the south. Minestrone is known worldwide, but the best-known version probably comes from Milan. However, all varieties are full of vegetables and are delicious and satisfying. Fish soups also abound in one guise or another, and most of these are village specialties, so the variety is unlimited and always tasty.

# Tuscan Onion Soup

This soup is best made with white onions, which have a mild flavor.
If you cannot get hold of them, try using large Spanish onions instead.

## NUTRITIONAL INFORMATION

Calories .......390    Sugars .........0g
Protein .........9g    Fat ..........33g
Carbohydrate ...15g    Saturates ......14g

5–10 MINS    40–45 MINS

### SERVES 4

## I N G R E D I E N T S

½ cup pancetta ham, diced

1 tbsp olive oil

4 large white onions, sliced thinly into rings

3 garlic cloves, chopped

3½ cups hot chicken or ham stock

4 slices ciabatta or other Italian bread

3 tbsp butter

¾ cup grated Gruyère or Cheddar cheese

salt and pepper

1 Cook the pancetta in a large pan for 3–4 minutes until it begins to brown. Remove the pancetta from the pan and set aside until required.

2 Add the oil to the pan and cook the onions and garlic over high heat for 4 minutes. Reduce the heat, cover and cook for 15 minutes or until the onions are lightly caramelized.

3 Add the stock to the pan and bring to a boil. Reduce the heat and leave the mixture to simmer, covered, for 10 minutes.

4 Toast the slices of ciabatta on both sides, under a preheated broiler, for 2–3 minutes, until golden. Spread the ciabatta with butter and top with the Gruyère cheese. Cut the bread into bite-size pieces.

5 Add the reserved pancetta to the soup and season with salt and pepper to taste.

6 Pour into 4 soup bowls and top with the toasted bread.

## COOK'S TIP

Pancetta is similar to bacon, but it is air- and salt-cured for about 6 months. Pancetta is available from most delicatessens and some large supermarkets. If you cannot obtain pancetta, use unsmoked bacon instead.

# Pumpkin Soup

This thick, creamy soup has a wonderful, warming golden color.
It is flavored with orange and thyme.

## NUTRITIONAL INFORMATION

| | | | |
|---|---|---|---|
| Calories | ........111 | Sugars | .........4g |
| Protein | .........2g | Fat | ...........6g |
| Carbohydrate | ....5g | Saturates | .......2g |

  10 MINS     35–40 MINS

### SERVES 4

## INGREDIENTS

2 tbsp olive oil

2 medium onions, chopped

2 garlic cloves, chopped

2 lb/900 g pumpkin, peeled and cut into
    1-inch/2.5-cm chunks

6 ¼ cups boiling vegetable or chicken stock

finely grated rind and juice of 1 orange

3 tbsp fresh thyme, stalks removed

⅔ cup milk

salt and pepper

crusty bread, to serve

1 Heat the olive oil in a large pan. Add the onions to the pan and cook for 3–4 minutes or until softened. Add the garlic and pumpkin and cook for an additional 2 minutes, stirring well.

2 Add the boiling vegetable stock, orange rind and juice, and 2 tablespoons of the thyme to the pan. Leave to simmer, covered, for 20 minutes, or until the pumpkin is tender.

3 Place the mixture in a food processor and blend until smooth. Alternatively, mash the mixture with a potato masher until smooth. Season to taste.

4 Return the soup to the pan and add the milk. Reheat the soup for 3–4 minutes, or until it is piping hot but not boiling.

5 Sprinkle with the remaining fresh thyme just before serving.

6 Divide the soup among 4 warm soup bowls and serve with lots of fresh crusty bread.

### COOK'S TIP

Pumpkins are usually large vegetables. To make things a little easier, ask the sales clerk to cut a chunk off for you. Alternatively, make double the quantity and freeze the soup for up to 3 months.

# Cream of Artichoke Soup

A creamy soup with the unique, subtle flavoring of Jerusalem artichokes and a garnish of grated carrots for extra crunch.

## NUTRITIONAL INFORMATION

| Calories | ........19 | Sugars | .........0g |
|---|---|---|---|
| Protein | ........0.4g | Fat | ...........2g |
| Carbohydrate | ...0.7g | Saturates | .....0.7g |

10–15 MINS    55–60 MINS

### SERVES 6

## I N G R E D I E N T S

1 lb 10 oz/750 g Jerusalem artichokes

1 lemon, sliced thickly

¼ cup butter or margarine

2 onions, chopped

1 garlic clove, crushed

5½ cups chicken or vegetable stock

2 bay leaves

¼ tsp ground mace or ground nutmeg

1 tbsp lemon juice

⅔ cup light cream or mascarpone

salt and pepper

### TO GARNISH

coarsely grated carrot

chopped fresh parsley or cilantro

1 Peel and slice the artichokes. Put into a bowl of water with the lemon slices.

2 Melt the butter in a large pan. Add the onions and garlic and cook gently for 3–4 minutes, or until soft but not colored.

3 Drain the artichokes (discarding the lemon) and add to the pan. Mix well and cook gently for 2–3 minutes without letting it color.

4 Add the stock, seasoning, bay leaves, mace, and lemon juice. Bring slowly to a boil, then cover and simmer gently for 30 minutes, or until the vegetables are very tender.

5 Discard the bay leaves. Cool the soup slightly, then press through a strainer or blend in a food processor until smooth. If liked, a little of the soup may be only partially puréed and added to the rest of the puréed soup, to give extra texture.

6 Pour into a clean pan and bring to a boil. Adjust the seasoning and stir in the cream. Reheat gently without boiling. Garnish with grated carrot and chopped parsley or cilantro.

# Vegetable & Bean Soup

This wonderful combination of cannellini beans, vegetables, and vermicelli is made even richer by the addition of pesto and dried mushrooms.

## NUTRITIONAL INFORMATION

Calories . . . . . . .294   Sugars . . . . . . . . .2g
Protein . . . . . . . .11g   Fat . . . . . . . . . .16g
Carbohydrate . . .30g   Saturates . . . . . . .2g

 30 MINS    30 MINS

### SERVES 4

## INGREDIENTS

1 small eggplant

2 large tomatoes

1 potato, peeled

1 carrot, peeled

1 leek

15 oz/425 g canned cannellini beans

3 ¾ cups hot vegetable or chicken stock

2 tsp dried basil

½ oz/15 g dried porcini mushrooms, soaked for 10 minutes in enough warm water to cover

¼ cup vermicelli

3 tbsp pesto (see page 47 or use store-bought)

freshly grated Parmesan cheese, to serve (optional)

1 Slice the eggplant into rings about ½ inch/1 cm thick, then cut each ring into 4.

2 Cut the tomatoes and potato into small dice. Cut the carrot into sticks, about 1 inch/2.5 cm long and cut the leek into rings.

3 Place the cannellini beans and their liquid in a large pan. Add the eggplant, tomatoes, potatoes, carrot, and leek, stirring to mix.

4 Add the stock to the pan and bring to a boil. Reduce the heat and leave to simmer for 15 minutes.

5 Add the basil, dried mushrooms and their soaking liquid, and the vermicelli, then simmer for 5 minutes, or until all of the vegetables are tender.

6 Remove the pan from the heat and stir in the pesto.

7 Serve with freshly grated Parmesan cheese, if using.

  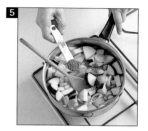

# Chickpea Soup

A thick vegetable soup that is a delicious meal in itself. Serve with Parmesan cheese and warm sun-dried tomato-flavored ciabatta bread.

## NUTRITIONAL INFORMATION

Calories .......297   Sugars .........0g
Protein ........11g   Fat ..........18g
Carbohydrate ...24g   Saturates .......2g

 5 MINS    15 MINS

## SERVES 4

## I N G R E D I E N T S

2 tbsp olive oil

2 leeks, sliced

2 zucchini, diced

2 garlic cloves, crushed

1 lb 12 oz/800 g canned chopped tomatoes

1 tbsp tomato paste

1 fresh bay leaf

3 ¾ cups chicken stock

14 oz/400 g canned chickpeas, drained and rinsed

8 oz/225 g spinach

salt and pepper

### T O   S E R V E

freshly grated Parmesan cheese

sun-dried tomato bread

1 Heat the oil in a large pan, then add the leeks and zucchini and cook briskly for 5 minutes, stirring constantly.

2 Add the garlic, tomatoes, tomato paste, bay leaf, stock, and chickpeas. Bring to a boil and simmer for 5 minutes.

3 Shred the spinach finely, then add to the soup. Cook for 2 minutes. Season.

4 Remove the bay leaf from the soup and discard.

5 Serve the soup with freshly grated Parmesan cheese and sun-dried tomato bread.

## COOK'S TIP

Chickpeas are used extensively in North African cuisine and are also found in Italian, Spanish, Middle Eastern, and Indian cooking. They have a deliciously nutty flavor with a firm texture and are an excellent canned product. Also known as garbanzo beans.

# Potato & Pesto Soup

Fresh pesto is a treat to the taste buds and very different in flavor from that available from supermarkets. Store fresh pesto in the refrigerator.

## NUTRITIONAL INFORMATION

| | | | |
|---|---|---|---|
| Calories | .......548 | Sugars | .........0g |
| Protein | ........11g | Fat | ..........52g |
| Carbohydrate | ...10g | Saturates | ......18g |

 5–10 MINS    50 MINS

### SERVES 4

### INGREDIENTS

3 strips rindless, smoked, fatty bacon

1 lb/450 g mealy potatoes

1 lb/450 g onions

2 tbsp olive oil

2 tbsp butter

2 ½ cups chicken stock

2 ½ cups milk

¾ cup dried conchigliette

⅔ cup heavy cream

chopped fresh parsley

salt and pepper

freshly grated Parmesan cheese and garlic
   bread, to serve

### PESTO SAUCE

1 cup finely chopped fresh
parsley

2 garlic cloves, crushed

⅔ cup pine nuts, crushed

2 tbsp chopped fresh basil leaves

⅔ cup freshly grated Parmesan cheese

white pepper

⅔ cup olive oil

1 To make the pesto sauce, put all of the ingredients in a blender or food processor and process for 2 minutes, or blend by hand using a pestle and mortar.

2 Finely chop the bacon, potatoes, and onions. Cook the bacon in a large pan over medium heat for 4 minutes. Add the butter, potatoes, and onions and cook for 12 minutes, stirring constantly.

3 Add the stock and milk to the pan, then bring to a boil and simmer for 10 minutes. Add the conchigliette and simmer for an additional 10–12 minutes.

4 Blend in the cream and simmer for 5 minutes. Add the parsley, salt and pepper, and 2 tbsp pesto sauce. Transfer the soup to serving bowls and serve with Parmesan cheese and fresh garlic bread.

# Creamy Tomato Soup

This quick and easy creamy soup has a lovely fresh tomato flavor.
Basil leaves complement tomatoes perfectly.

## NUTRITIONAL INFORMATION

| | | | |
|---|---|---|---|
| Calories | .218 | Sugars | 10g |
| Protein | 3g | Fat | 19g |
| Carbohydrate | 10g | Saturates | 11g |

5 MINS     25–30 MINS

### SERVES 4

## I N G R E D I E N T S

3 tbsp butter

1 lb 9 oz/700 g ripe tomatoes, preferably
    plum, coarsely chopped

3¾ cups hot vegetable stock

generous ½ cup ground almonds

⅔ cup milk or light cream

1 tsp sugar

2 tbsp shredded basil leaves

salt and pepper

1 Melt the butter in a large pan. Add the tomatoes and cook for 5 minutes, or until the skins start to wrinkle. Season to taste with salt and pepper.

2 Add the stock to the pan and bring to a boil, then cover and simmer for 10 minutes.

3 Meanwhile, under a preheated broiler, lightly toast the ground almonds until they are golden-brown. This will take only 1-2 minutes, so watch them closely.

4 Remove the soup from the heat, then place in a food processor and blend the mixture to form a smooth consistency. Alternatively, mash the soup with a potato masher until smooth.

5 Pass the soup through a strainer to remove any tomato skin or seeds.

6 Place the soup in the pan and return to the heat. Stir in the milk, toasted ground almonds, and sugar. Warm the soup through and add the shredded basil leaves just before serving.

7 Transfer the creamy tomato soup to warm soup bowls and serve hot.

## COOK'S TIP

Very fine bread crumbs can be used instead of the ground almonds, if you prefer. Toast them in the same way as the almonds and add with the milk or cream in step 6.

# Calabrian Mushroom Soup

The Calabrian Mountains in southern Italy provide large amounts of wild mushrooms that are rich in flavor and color.

## NUTRITIONAL INFORMATION

| | | | |
|---|---|---|---|
| Calories | .......452 | Sugars | .........5g |
| Protein | ........15g | Fat | ..........26g |
| Carbohydrate | ...42g | Saturates | ......12g |

 5 MINS  25–30 MINS

### SERVES 4

## INGREDIENTS

2 tbsp olive oil

1 onion, chopped

1 lb/450 g mixed mushrooms, such as
  cèpe, oyster, and white

1 ¼ cups milk

3 ¾ cups hot vegetable stock

8 slices of rustic bread or French stick

2 garlic cloves, crushed

3 tbsp butter, melted

¾ cup finely grated, Gruyère cheese

salt and pepper

1 Heat the oil in a large skillet and cook the onion for 3–4 minutes, or until soft and golden.

2 Wipe each mushroom with a damp cloth and cut any large mushrooms into smaller, bite-size pieces.

3 Add the mushrooms to the pan, stirring quickly to coat them in the oil.

4 Add the milk to the pan and bring to a boil, then cover and leave to simmer for 5 minutes. Gradually stir in the hot vegetable stock and season with salt and pepper to taste.

5 Under a preheated broiler, toast the bread on both sides until golden.

6 Mix together the garlic and butter and spoon generously over the toast.

7 Place the toast in the bottom of a large tureen or divide it among 4 individual serving bowls and pour over the hot soup. Top with the grated Gruyère cheese and serve at once.

### COOK'S TIP

Mushrooms absorb liquid, which can lessen the flavor and affect cooking properties. Therefore, carefully wipe them with a damp cloth rather than rinsing them in water.

# Tomato & Pasta Soup

Plum tomatoes are ideal for making soups and sauces as they have denser, less watery flesh than rounder varieties.

## NUTRITIONAL INFORMATION

| | | | |
|---|---|---|---|
| Calories | . . . . . . .503 | Sugars | . . . . . . . .16g |
| Protein | . . . . . . . . .9g | Fat | . . . . . . . . . .28g |
| Carbohydrate | . . .59g | Saturates | . . . . . .17g |

5 MINS     50–55 MINS

### SERVES 4

### INGREDIENTS

4 tbsp unsalted butter

1 large onion, chopped

2 ½ cups vegetable stock

2 lb/900 g Italian plum tomatoes, skinned
    and coarsely chopped

pinch of baking soda

2 cups dried fusilli

1 tbsp superfine sugar

⅔ cup heavy cream

salt and pepper

fresh basil leaves, to garnish

1 Melt the butter in a large pan, add the onion and cook for 3 minutes, stirring. Add 1¼ cups of vegetable stock to the pan, with the chopped tomatoes and baking soda. Bring the soup to a boil and simmer for 20 minutes.

## VARIATION

To make orange and tomato soup, simply use half the quantity of vegetable stock, topped up with the same amount of fresh orange juice, and garnish the soup with orange rind.

  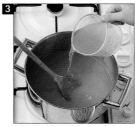

2 Remove the pan from the heat and set aside to cool. Purée the soup in a blender or food processor and pour through a fine strainer back into the pan.

3 Add the remaining vegetable stock and the fusilli to the pan, and season to taste with salt and pepper.

4 Add the sugar to the pan and bring to a boil, then lower the heat and simmer for 15 minutes.

5 Pour the soup into a warm tureen, then swirl the heavy cream around the surface of the soup and garnish with fresh basil leaves. Serve immediately.

# Artichoke Soup

This refreshing chilled soup is ideal for alfresco dining. Bear in mind that this soup needs to be chilled for 3-4 hours, so leave plenty of time.

## NUTRITIONAL INFORMATION

| | | |
|---|---|---|
| Calories .......159 | Sugars .........2g | |
| Protein .........2g | Fat ..........15g | |
| Carbohydrate ....5g | Saturates .......6g | |

 5 MINS      15 MINS

### SERVES 4

## I N G R E D I E N T S

1 tbsp olive oil

1 onion, chopped

1 garlic clove, crushed

1 lb 12 oz/800 g canned artichoke hearts, drained

2 ½ cups hot vegetable stock

⅔ cup light cream

2 tbsp fresh thyme, stems removed

2 sun-dried tomatoes, cut into strips

fresh, crusty bread, to serve

1 Heat the oil in a large pan and fry the chopped onion and crushed garlic, stirring, for 2–3 minutes, or until just softened.

2 Using a sharp knife, roughly chop the artichoke hearts. Add the artichoke pieces to the onion and garlic mixture in the pan. Pour in the hot vegetable stock, stirring well.

3 Bring the mixture to a boil, then reduce the heat and leave to simmer, covered, for 3 minutes.

4 Place the mixture into a food processor and blend until smooth. Alternatively, push the mixture through a strainer to remove any lumps.

5 Return the soup to the pan. Stir the light cream and fresh thyme into the soup.

6 Transfer the soup to a large bowl, then cover and leave to chill in the refrigerator for 3–4 hours.

7 Transfer the chilled soup to individual soup bowls and garnish with strips of sun-dried tomato. Serve with crusty bread.

## VARIATION

Try adding 2 tablespoons of dry vermouth, such as Martini, to the soup in step 5, if you wish.

# Minestrone & Pasta Soup

Italian cooks have created some very heart-warming soups and this is the most famous of all.

## NUTRITIONAL INFORMATION

| | | | |
|---|---|---|---|
| Calories | . . . . . . . .231 | Sugars | . . . . . . . . .3g |
| Protein | . . . . . . . .8g | Fat | . . . . . . . . . .16g |
| Carbohydrate | . . .14g | Saturates | . . . . . . .7g |

🍲 10 MINS    🕐 1¾ HOURS

### SERVES 10

### I N G R E D I E N T S

3 garlic cloves

3 large onions

2 celery stalks

2 large carrots

2 large potatoes

3½ oz/100 g green beans

3½ oz/100 g zucchini

4 tbsp butter

¼ cup olive oil

¼ cup finely diced rindless fatty bacon

6⅞ cups vegetable or chicken stock

1 bunch fresh basil, finely chopped

½ cup chopped tomatoes

2 tbsp tomato paste

3½ oz/100 g Parmesan cheese rind

3 oz/85 g dried spaghetti, broken up

salt and pepper

freshly grated Parmesan cheese, to serve

1 Finely chop the garlic, onions, celery, carrots, potatoes, beans, and zucchini.

2 Heat the butter and oil together in a large pan, then add the bacon and cook for 2 minutes.

3 Add the garlic and onion and cook for 2 minutes, then stir in the celery, carrots, and potatoes and cook for an additional 2 minutes.

4 Add the beans to the pan and cook for 2 minutes. Stir in the zucchini and fry for an additional 2 minutes. Cover the pan and cook all the vegetables, stirring frequently, for 15 minutes.

5 Add the stock, basil, tomatoes, tomato paste, and cheese rind and season to taste. Bring to a boil, then lower the heat and simmer for 1 hour. Remove and discard the cheese rind.

6 Add the spaghetti to the pan and cook for 20 minutes. Serve in large, warm soup bowls; sprinkle with freshly grated Parmesan cheese.

# Red Bean Soup

Beans feature widely in Italian soups, making them hearty and tasty. The beans need to be soaked overnight, so prepare well in advance.

## NUTRITIONAL INFORMATION

Calories .......184   Sugars .........5g
Protein .........4g   Fat ...........11g
Carbohydrate ...19g   Saturates .......2g

5–10 MINS      3¾ HOURS

### SERVES 6

### I N G R E D I E N T S

scant 1 cup dried red kidney beans, soaked overnight

7½ cups water

1 large ham bone or bacon knuckle

2 carrots, chopped

1 large onion, chopped

2 celery stalks, sliced thinly

1 leek, trimmed, washed, and sliced

1–2 bay leaves

2 tbsp olive oil

2–3 tomatoes, peeled and chopped

1 garlic clove, crushed

1 tbsp tomato paste

4½ tbsp arborio or Italian rice

4–6 oz/125–175 g green cabbage, shredded finely

salt and pepper

1 Drain the beans and place them in a pan with enough water to cover. Bring to a boil, then boil for 15 minutes to remove any harmful toxins. Reduce the heat and simmer for 45 minutes.

2 Drain the beans and put into a clean pan with the water, ham bone, carrots, onion, celery, leek, bay leaves, and olive oil. Bring to a boil, then cover and simmer for 1 hour, or until the beans are very tender.

3 Discard the bay leaves and bone, reserving any ham pieces from the bone. Remove a small cupful of the beans and reserve. Purée or liquidize the soup in a food processor or blender, or push through a coarse strainer, and return to a clean pan.

4 Add the tomatoes, garlic, tomato paste, rice, then season. Bring back to a boil and simmer for 15 minutes, or until the rice is tender.

5 Add the cabbage and reserved beans and ham, and continue to simmer for 5 minutes. Adjust the seasoning and serve very hot. If liked, a piece of toasted crusty bread may be put in the base of each soup bowl before ladling in the soup. If the soup is too thick, add a little boiling water or stock.

# Ravioli alla Parmigiana

This soup is traditionally served at Easter and Christmas in the province of Parma.

4½–5 HOURS    25 MINS

### SERVES 4

## INGREDIENTS

10 oz/280 g Basic Pasta Dough (see page 24)

5 cups veal stock

freshly grated Parmesan cheese, to serve

### FILLING

½ cup Espagnole Sauce (see page 29)

1 cup freshly grated Parmesan cheese

1 ⅔ cup fine white bread crumbs

2 eggs

1 small onion, finely chopped

1 tsp freshly grated nutmeg

## COOK'S TIP

It is advisable to prepare the Basic Pasta Dough (see page 24) and the Espagnole Sauce (see page 29) well in advance, or buy ready-made equivalents if you are short of time.

1 Make the Basic Pasta Dough (see page 24) and the Espagnole Sauce (see page 29).

2 Carefully roll out 2 sheets of the pasta dough and cover with a damp dish cloth while you make the filling for the ravioli.

3 To make the filling, place the freshly grated Parmesan cheese, fine white bread crumbs, eggs, Espagnole Sauce, finely chopped onion, and the freshly grated nutmeg in a large mixing bowl, and mix together well.

4 Place spoonfuls of the filling at regular intervals on 1 sheet of pasta dough. Cover with the second sheet of pasta dough, then cut into squares and seal the edges.

5 Bring the veal stock to a boil in a large pan.

6 Add the ravioli to the pan and cook for 15 minutes.

7 Transfer the soup and ravioli to warm serving bowls and serve, generously sprinkled with Parmesan cheese.

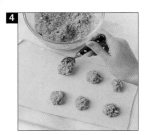

# Minestrone with Pesto

This version of minestrone contains cannellini beans—these need to be soaked overnight, so prepare in advance.

## NUTRITIONAL INFORMATION

| | | |
|---|---|---|
| Calories .......604 | Sugars .........3g |
| Protein ........26g | Fat ..........45g |
| Carbohydrate ...24g | Saturates ......11g |

10-15 MINS     1¾ HOURS

### SERVES 6

## INGREDIENTS

scant 1 cup dried cannellini beans, soaked overnight

10 cups water or stock

1 large onion, chopped

1 leek, trimmed and sliced thinly

2 celery stalks, sliced very thinly

2 carrots, chopped

3 tbsp olive oil

2 tomatoes, peeled and chopped roughly

1 zucchini, trimmed and sliced thinly

2 potatoes, diced

¾ cup cup elbow macaroni (or other small macaroni)

salt and pepper

4–6 tbsp freshly grated Parmesan cheese, to serve

### PESTO

2 tbsp pine nuts

5 tbsp olive oil

2 bunches basil, stems removed

4–6 garlic cloves, crushed

½ cup grated Romano or Parmesan cheese

1 Drain the beans, rinse and put in a pan with the water. Bring to a boil, then cover and simmer for 1 hour.

2 Add the onion, leek, celery, carrots, and oil. Cover and simmer for 4–5 minutes.

3 Add the tomatoes, zucchini, potatoes, macaroni, and seasoning. Cover again and continue to simmer for 30 minutes, or until very tender.

4 Meanwhile, make the pesto. Cook the pine nuts in 1 tablespoon of the oil until pale brown, then drain. Put the basil into a food processor or blender with the nuts and garlic. Process until well chopped. Alternatively, chop finely by hand and pound with a pestle and mortar. Gradually add the remaining oil until smooth. Turn into a bowl, then add the cheese and seasoning, and mix thoroughly.

5 Stir 1½ tablespoons of the pesto into the soup until well blended. Simmer for an additional 5 minutes and adjust the seasoning. Serve very hot, sprinkled with the cheese.

# Fish Soup

There are many varieties of fish soup in Italy, some including shellfish. This one, from Tuscany, is more like a chowder.

## NUTRITIONAL INFORMATION

| | | | |
|---|---|---|---|
| Calories | .......305 | Sugars | .........3g |
| Protein | ........47g | Fat | ...........7g |
| Carbohydrate | ....11g | Saturates | .......1g |

  5–10 MINS    1 HOUR

### SERVES 6

## I N G R E D I E N T S

2 lb 4 oz/1 kg assorted prepared fish
  (including mixed fish fillets, squid, etc.)

2 onions, sliced thinly

2 celery stalks, sliced thinly

a few sprigs of parsley

2 bay leaves

⅔ cup white wine

4 cups water

2 tbsp olive oil

1 garlic clove, crushed

1 carrot, chopped finely

14 oz/400 g canned peeled tomatoes, puréed

2 potatoes, chopped

1 tbsp tomato paste

1 tsp chopped fresh oregano or
  ½ tsp dried oregano

12 oz/350 g fresh mussels

6 oz/175 g peeled shrimp

2 tbsp chopped fresh parsley

salt and pepper

crusty bread, to serve

1 Cut the fish into slices and put into a pan with half the onion and celery, the parsley, bay leaves, wine, and water. Bring to a boil, then cover and simmer for 25 minutes.

2 Strain the fish stock and discard the vegetables. Skin the fish, remove any bones and reserve.

3 Heat the oil in a pan. Cook the remaining onion and celery with the garlic and carrot until soft but not colored, stirring occasionally. Add the puréed canned tomatoes, potatoes, tomato paste, oregano, reserved stock, and seasoning. Bring to a boil and simmer for 15 minutes, or until the potato is almost tender.

4 Meanwhile, thoroughly scrub the mussels. Add the mussels to the pan with the shrimp and leave to simmer for 5 minutes, or until the mussels have opened (discard any that remain closed).

5 Return the fish to the soup with the chopped parsley, then bring back to a boil and simmer for 5 minutes. Adjust the seasoning.

6 Serve the soup in warmed bowls with chunks of fresh crusty bread, or put a toasted slice of crusty bread in the bottom of each bowl before adding the soup. If possible, remove a few half shells from the mussels before serving.

# Mussel & Potato Soup

This quick and easy soup would make a delicious summer lunch, served with fresh crusty bread.

## NUTRITIONAL INFORMATION

Calories .......804   Sugars .........3g
Protein ........17g   Fat ..........68g
Carbohydrate ...32g   Saturates ......38g

10 MINS   35 MINS

### SERVES 4

## I N G R E D I E N T S

1 lb 10 oz/750 g mussels

2 tbsp olive oil

scant ½ cup unsalted butter

2 slices rindless fatty bacon, chopped

1 onion, chopped

2 garlic cloves, crushed

½ cup all-purpose flour

1 lb/450 g potatoes, thinly sliced

¾ cup dried conchigliette

1 ¼ cups heavy cream

1 tbsp lemon juice

2 egg yolks

salt and pepper

### TO GARNISH

2 tbsp finely chopped fresh parsley

lemon wedges

1 Debeard the mussels and scrub them under cold water for 5 minutes. Discard any mussels that do not close immediately when sharply tapped.

2 Bring a large pan of water to a boil, then add the mussels, oil, and a little pepper. Cook until the mussels open (discard any mussels that remain closed).

3 Drain the mussels, reserving the cooking liquid. Remove the mussels from their shells.

4 Melt the butter in a large pan, add the bacon, onion, and garlic and cook for 4 minutes. Carefully stir in the flour. Measure 5 cups of the reserved cooking liquid and stir it into the pan.

5 Add the potatoes to the pan and simmer for 5 minutes. Add the conchigliette and simmer for an additional 10 minutes.

6 Add the cream and lemon juice, and season to taste with salt and pepper, then add the mussels to the pan.

7 Blend the egg yolks with 1-2 tablespoons of the remaining cooking liquid, then stir into the pan and cook for 4 minutes.

8 Ladle the soup into 4 warm individual soup bowls. Garnish with the chopped fresh parsley and lemon wedges and serve immediately.

# Italian Fish Stew

This robust stew is full of Mediterranean flavors. If you do not want to prepare the fish yourself, ask your local supplier to do it for you.

## NUTRITIONAL INFORMATION

| | | | |
|---|---|---|---|
| Calories | ....236 | Sugars | .....4g |
| Protein | ....20g | Fat | .....7g |
| Carbohydrate | ...25g | Saturates | .....1g |

 5-10 MINS    25 MINS

### SERVES 4

## INGREDIENTS

2 tbsp olive oil

2 red onions, finely chopped

1 garlic clove, crushed

2 zucchini, sliced

14 oz/400 g canned chopped tomatoes

3 ½ cups fish or vegetable stock

¾ cup dried pasta shapes

12 oz/350 g firm white fish, such as cod,
    haddock, or hake

1 tbsp chopped fresh basil or oregano or
    1 tsp dried oregano

1 tsp grated lemon rind

1 tbsp cornstarch

1 tbsp water

salt and pepper

sprigs of fresh basil or oregano, to garnish

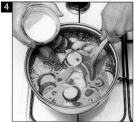

1 Heat the oil in a large pan and cook the onions and garlic for 5 minutes. Add the zucchini and cook for 2–3 minutes, stirring often.

2 Add the tomatoes and stock to the pan and bring to a boil. Add the pasta, then cover and reduce the heat. Simmer for 5 minutes.

3 Skin and bone the fish, then cut it into chunks. Add to the pan with the basil and lemon rind and cook gently for 5 minutes, or until the fish is opaque and flakes easily (take care not to overcook it).

4 Blend the cornstarch with the water and stir into the stew. Cook gently for 2 minutes, stirring, until thickened. Season with salt and pepper to taste and ladle into 4 warmed soup bowls. Garnish with basil sprigs and serve at once.

# Italian Seafood Soup

This colorful mixed seafood soup would be superbly complemented by a dry white wine.

## NUTRITIONAL INFORMATION

Calories .......668  Sugars .........3g
Protein ........48g  Fat ..........43g
Carbohydrate ...21g  Saturates ......25g

5 MINS     55 MINS

### SERVES 4

## INGREDIENTS

4 tbsp butter

1 lb/450 g assorted fish fillets, such as
  pompano and snapper

1 lb/450 g prepared seafood, such as squid
  and shrimp

8 oz/225 g fresh crabmeat

1 large onion, sliced

¼ cup all-purpose flour

5 cups fish stock

¾ cup dried pasta shapes, such as ditalini
  or elbow macaroni

1 tbsp anchovy extract

grated rind and juice of 1 orange

¼ cup dry sherry

1 ¼ cups heavy cream

salt and pepper

crusty brown bread, to serve

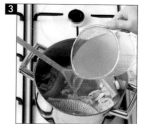

1 Melt the butter in a large pan, add the fish fillets, seafood, crabmeat, and onion and cook gently over low heat for 6 minutes.

2 Add the flour to the seafood mixture, stirring thoroughly to avoid any lumps from forming.

3 Gradually add the stock, stirring, until the soup comes to a boil. Reduce the heat and simmer for 30 minutes.

4 Add the pasta to the pan and cook for an additional 10 minutes.

5 Stir in the anchovy extract, orange rind, orange juice, sherry, and heavy cream. Season to taste with salt and pepper.

6 Heat the soup until completely warmed through.

7 Transfer the soup to a tureen or to warm soup bowls and serve with crusty brown bread.

# Lemon & Chicken Soup

This delicately flavored summer soup is surprisingly easy to make, and tastes delicious.

## NUTRITIONAL INFORMATION

| | | |
|---|---|---|
| Calories .......506 | Sugars .........4g | |
| Protein ........19g | Fat ..........31g | |
| Carbohydrate ...41g | Saturates ......19g | |

  5–10 MINS  1¼ HOURS

### SERVES 4

## I N G R E D I E N T S

4 tbsp butter

8 shallots, thinly sliced

2 carrots, thinly sliced

2 celery stalks, thinly sliced

8 oz/225 g boned chicken breasts,
 finely chopped

3 lemons

5 cups chicken stock

8 oz/225 g dried spaghetti, broken into
 small pieces

⅔ cup heavy cream

salt and white pepper

### TO GARNISH

fresh parsley sprig

3 lemon slices, halved

## COOK'S TIP

You can prepare this soup up to the end of step 3 in advance, so that all you need do before serving is heat it through before adding the pasta and the finishing touches.

1 Melt the butter in a large pan. Add the shallots, carrots, celery, and chicken and cook over low heat, stirring occasionally, for 8 minutes.

2 Thinly pare the lemons and blanch the lemon rind in boiling water for 3 minutes. Squeeze the juice from the lemons.

3 Add the lemon rind and juice to the pan, together with the chicken stock. Bring slowly to a boil over low heat and simmer for 40 minutes, stirring occasionally.

4 Add the spaghetti to the pan and cook for 15 minutes. Season to taste with salt and white pepper and add the cream. Heat through, but do not let the soup boil or it will curdle.

5 Pour the soup into a tureen or individual bowls. Garnish with the parsley and half slices of lemon and serve immediately.

# Chicken & Pasta Broth

This satisfying soup makes a good lunch or supper dish and you can use any vegetables you like. Children will love the tiny pasta shapes.

## NUTRITIONAL INFORMATION

Calories . . . . . . .185  Sugars . . . . . . . . .5g
Protein . . . . . . . .17g  Fat . . . . . . . . . . .5g
Carbohydrate . . .20g  Saturates . . . . . . .1g

5 MINS          15–20 MINS

### SERVES 6

## I N G R E D I E N T S

12 oz/350 g boneless chicken breasts

2 tbsp corn oil

1 medium onion, diced

1 ½ cups diced carrots

9 oz/250 g cauliflower florets

3 ¾ cups chicken stock

2 tsp dried mixed herbs

generous 1 cup small pasta shapes

salt and pepper

freshly grated Parmesan cheese (optional)
  and crusty bread, to serve

1 Using a sharp knife, finely dice the chicken, discarding any skin.

2 Heat the oil in a large pan and quickly sauté the chicken, onion, carrots, and cauliflower until they are lightly colored.

3 Stir in the chicken stock and dried mixed herbs and bring to a boil.

4 Add the pasta shapes to the pan and return to a boil. Cover the pan and leave the broth to simmer for 10 minutes, stirring occasionally to prevent the pasta shapes from sticking together.

5 Season the broth with salt and pepper to taste and sprinkle with Parmesan cheese, if using. Serve the broth with fresh crusty bread.

### COOK'S TIP

You can use any small pasta shapes for this soup—try conchigliette or ditalini or even spaghetti broken up into small pieces. To make a fun soup for children you could add animal-shaped or alphabet pasta.

# Veal & Wild Mushroom Soup

Wild mushrooms are available commercially and an increasing range of cultivated varieties is now to be found in many supermarkets.

## NUTRITIONAL INFORMATION

Calories . . . . . . . . .413    Sugars . . . . . . . . .3g
Protein . . . . . . . .28g    Fat . . . . . . . . . .22g
Carbohydrate . . .28g    Saturates . . . . . .12g

5 MINS        3¼ HOURS

### SERVES 4

### I N G R E D I E N T S

1 lb/450 g veal, thinly sliced

1 lb/450 g veal bones

5 cups water

1 small onion

6 peppercorns

1 tsp cloves

pinch of mace

5 oz/140 g oyster and shiitake mushrooms,
 coarsely chopped

⅔ cup heavy cream

¾ cup dried vermicelli

1 tbsp cornstarch

3 tbsp milk

salt and pepper

1 Put the veal, bones, and water into a large pan. Bring to a boil and lower the heat. Add the onion, peppercorns, cloves, and mace and simmer for 3 hours, until the veal stock is reduced by one-third.

2 Strain the stock, then skim off any fat on the surface with a slotted spoon, and pour the stock into a clean pan. Add the veal meat to the pan.

3 Add the mushrooms and cream. Bring to a boil over low heat and then leave to simmer for 12 minutes, stirring occasionally.

4 Meanwhile, cook the vermicelli in lightly salted boiling water for 10 minutes, or until tender but still firm to the bite. Drain and keep warm.

5 Mix the cornstarch and milk to form a smooth paste. Stir into the soup to thicken. Season to taste with salt and pepper, then just before serving, add the vermicelli. Transfer the soup to a warm tureen and serve immediately.

## COOK'S TIP

You can make this soup with the more inexpensive cuts of veal, such as breast or neck slices. These are lean and the long cooking time ensures that the meat is really tender.

# Veal & Ham Soup

Veal and ham is a classic combination, complemented here with the addition of sherry to create a richly flavored Italian soup.

## NUTRITIONAL INFORMATION

Calories . . . . . . . .501  Sugars . . . . . . . .10g
Protein . . . . . . . .38g  Fat . . . . . . . . . .18g
Carbohydrate . . .28g  Saturates . . . . . .10g

 5 MINS     5¼ HOURS

### SERVES 4

## I N G R E D I E N T S

4 tbsp butter

1 onion, diced

1 carrot, diced

1 celery stalk, diced

1 lb/450 g veal, very thinly sliced

1 lb/450 g ham, thinly sliced

½ cup all-purpose flour

4 cups beef stock

1 bay leaf

8 black peppercorns

pinch of salt

3 tbsp red currant jelly

⅔ cup cream sherry

¾ cup dried vermicelli

garlic croûtons (see Cook's Tip), to serve

1 Melt the butter in a large pan. Add the onion, carrot, celery, veal, and ham and cook over a low heat for 6 minutes.

2 Sprinkle over the flour and cook, stirring constantly, for an additional 2 minutes. Gradually stir in the stock, then add the bay leaf, peppercorns, and salt. Bring to a boil and simmer for 1 hour.

3 Remove the pan from the heat and add the red currant jelly and cream sherry, stirring to combine. Set aside for 4 hours.

4 Remove the bay leaf from the pan and discard. Reheat the soup over very low heat until warmed through.

5 Meanwhile, cook the vermicelli in a pan of lightly salted boiling water for 10-12 minutes. Stir the vermicelli into the soup and transfer to soup bowls. Serve with garlic croûtons.

## COOK'S TIP

To make garlic croûtons, remove the crusts from 3 slices of day-old white bread. Cut the bread into ¼-inch/5-mm cubes. Heat 3 tbsp oil over low heat and stir-fry 1–2 chopped garlic cloves for 1–2 minutes. Remove the garlic and add the bread. Cook, stirring frequently, until golden. Remove with a slotted spoon and drain.

# Appetizers

Appetizers are known as antipasto in Italy which translates as "before the main course." Antipasti usually come in three categories: meat, fish, and vegetables. There are many varieties of cold meats, including ham, invariably sliced paper-thin. All varieties of fish are popular in Italy, including inkfish, octopus, and cuttlefish. Seafood is also

highly prized, especially huge shrimp, mussels, and fresh sardines. Numerous vegetables feature in Italian cuisine and are an important part of the daily diet. They are served as an appetizer, as an accompaniment to main dishes, or as a course on their own. In Italy, vegetables are cooked only until "al dente" and still slightly crisp. This ensures that they retain more nutrients and the colors remain bright and appealing.

# Eggplant Rolls

Thin slices of eggplant are sautéed in olive oil and garlic, and then topped with pesto sauce and finely sliced Mozzarella.

## NUTRITIONAL INFORMATION

| | | | |
|---|---|---|---|
| Calories | .......278 | Sugars | .........2g |
| Protein | .........4g | Fat | ..........28g |
| Carbohydrate | ....2g | Saturates | .......7g |

15–20 MINS     20 MINS

### SERVES 4

## I N G R E D I E N T S

2 eggplants, sliced thinly lengthwise

5 tbsp olive oil

1 garlic clove, crushed

4 tbsp pesto

1½ cups grated mozzarella cheese

basil leaves, torn into pieces

salt and pepper

fresh basil leaves, to garnish

1 Sprinkle the eggplant slices liberally with salt and leave for 10–15 minutes to extract the bitter juices. Turn the slices over and repeat. Rinse well with cold water and drain on paper towels.

2 Heat the olive oil in a large skillet and add the garlic. Sauté the eggplant slices lightly on both sides, a few at a time. Drain them on paper towels.

3 Spread the pesto on one side of the eggplant slices. Top with the grated mozzarella and sprinkle with the torn basil leaves. Season with a little salt and pepper. Roll up the slices and secure with wooden toothpicks.

4 Arrange the eggplant rolls in a greased ovenproof baking dish. Place in a preheated oven, 350°F/180°C, and bake for 8–10 minutes.

5 Transfer the eggplant rolls to a warmed serving plate. Scatter with fresh basil leaves and serve at once.

# Leek & Tomato Timbales

Angel-hair pasta, known as cappellini, is mixed with fried leeks, sun-dried tomatoes, fresh oregano, and beaten eggs, and baked in ramekins.

## NUTRITIONAL INFORMATION

| | | | |
|---|---|---|---|
| Calories . . . . . . . .331 | Sugars . . . . . . . .10g |
| Protein . . . . . . . .10g | Fat . . . . . . . . . .21g |
| Carbohydrate . . .26g | Saturates . . . . . . .9g |

5–10 MINS    50 MINS

### SERVES 4

## I N G R E D I E N T S

3 oz/85 g angel-hair pasta (cappellini)

2 tbsp butter

1 tbsp olive oil

1 large leek, sliced finely

½ cup sun-dried tomatoes in oil, drained
   and chopped

1 tbsp chopped fresh oregano
   or 1 tsp dried oregano

2 eggs, beaten

scant ½ cup light cream

1 tbsp freshly grated Parmesan

salt and pepper

sprigs of oregano, to garnish

lettuce leaves, to serve

### S A U C E

1 small onion, chopped finely

1 small garlic clove, crushed

12 oz/350 g tomatoes, peeled and chopped

1 tsp mixed dried Italian herbs

4 tbsp dry white wine

1 Cook the pasta in plenty of boiling salted water for about 3 minutes, or until "al dente" (just tender). Drain and rinse with cold water to cool quickly.

2 Meanwhile, heat the butter and oil in a skillet. Gently cook the leek for 5–6 minutes, or until softened. Add the sun-dried tomatoes and oregano, and cook for an additional 2 minutes. Remove from the heat.

3 Add the leek mixture to the pasta. Stir in the beaten eggs, cream, and Parmesan. Season with salt and pepper. Divide between 4 greased ramekin dishes or dariole molds.

4 Place the dishes in a roasting pan with enough warm water to come halfway up their sides. Bake in a preheated oven, 350°F/180°C, for 30 minutes, or until set.

5 Meanwhile, make the tomato sauce. Cook the onion and garlic in the remaining butter and oil until softened. Add the tomatoes, herbs, and wine. Cover and cook gently for 20 minutes, or until pulpy. Blend in a food processor until smooth, or press through a sieve.

6 Run a knife or small spatula around the edge of the ramekins, then turn out the timbales onto 4 warm serving plates. Pour over a little sauce and garnish with oregano. Serve with the lettuce leaves.

# Baked Fennel Gratinati

Fennel is a common ingredient in Italian cooking. In this dish its distinctive flavor is offset by the smooth Béchamel Sauce.

## NUTRITIONAL INFORMATION

| | | |
|---|---|---|
| Calories .......426 | Sugars .........9g |
| Protein ........13g | Fat ..........35g |
| Carbohydrate ...16g | Saturates ......19g |

5-10 MINS     45 MINS

### SERVES 4

## INGREDIENTS

4 heads fennel

2 tbsp butter

⅔ cup dry white wine

Béchamel Sauce (see page 28),
   enriched with 2 egg yolks

½ cup fresh white bread crumbs

3 tbsp freshly grated Parmesan

salt and pepper

fennel fronds, to garnish

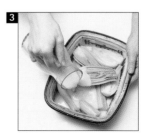

1 Remove any bruised or tough outer stems of fennel and cut each head in half. Put into a pan of boiling salted water and simmer for 20 minutes, or until tender, then drain.

2 Butter an ovenproof dish liberally and arrange the drained fennel in it.

3 Mix the wine into the Béchamel Sauce and season with salt and pepper to taste. Pour over the fennel.

4 Sprinkle evenly with the bread crumbs and then the Parmesan.

5 Place in a preheated oven, 400°F/200°C, and bake for 20 minutes, or until the top is golden. Serve garnished with fennel fronds.

# Stewed Artichokes

This is a traditional Roman dish. The artichokes are stewed in olive oil with fresh herbs.

## NUTRITIONAL INFORMATION

Calories .......129  Sugars .........0g
Protein .........4g  Fat ...........8g
Carbohydrate ...10g  Saturates .......1g

 5 MINS    50 MINS

### SERVES 4

## INGREDIENTS

4 small globe artichokes

olive oil

4 garlic cloves, peeled

2 bay leaves

finely grated rind and juice of 1 lemon

2 tbsp fresh marjoram

lemon wedges, to serve

1 Using a sharp knife, carefully peel away the tough outer leaves surrounding the artichokes. Trim the stems to about 1 inch/2.5 cm.

2 Using a knife, cut each artichoke in half and scoop out the heart.

3 Place the artichokes in a large heavy-based pan. Pour over enough olive oil to half cover the artichokes in the pan.

4 Add the garlic cloves, bay leaves, and half of the grated lemon rind.

5 Start to heat the artichokes gently, then cover the pan and continue to cook over low heat for 40 minutes. It is important that the artichokes should be stewed in the oil, not fried.

6 Once the artichokes are tender, remove them from the oil with a perforated spoon and drain thoroughly. Discard the bay leaves.

7 Transfer the artichokes to warm serving plates. Garnish the artichokes with the remaining grated lemon rind, fresh marjoram, and a little lemon juice. Serve with lemon wedges.

## COOK'S TIP

To prevent the artichokes from oxidizing and turning brown before cooking, brush them with a little lemon juice. In addition, use the oil used for cooking the artichokes for salad dressings—it will impart a lovely lemon and herb flavor.

# Eggplant Bake

This dish combines layers of eggplant, tomato sauce, mozzarella, and Parmesan cheese to create a very tasty appetizer.

## NUTRITIONAL INFORMATION

| | | |
|---|---|---|
| Calories .......232 | Sugars .........8g | |
| Protein ........10g | Fat ..........18g | |
| Carbohydrate ....8g | Saturates .......6g | |

  5 MINS  🕐 45 MINS

### SERVES 4

## INGREDIENTS

3–4 tbsp olive oil

2 garlic cloves, crushed

2 large eggplant

3½ oz/100 g mozzarella cheese, sliced thinly

7 oz/200 g crushed tomatoes

½ oz freshly grated Parmesan cheese

1 Heat 2 tablespoons of the olive oil in a large skillet. Add the garlic and sauté for 30 seconds.

2 Slice the eggplant lengthwise. Add the slices to the skillet and cook in the oil for 3–4 minutes on each side, or until tender. (You will probably have to cook them in batches, so add the remaining oil as necessary.)

3 Remove the eggplant with a perforated spoon and drain on absorbent paper towels.

4 Place a layer of eggplant slices in a shallow ovenproof dish. Cover the eggplant with a layer of mozzarella and then pour over a third of the crushed tomatoes. Continue layering in the same order, finishing with a layer of crushed tomatoes on top.

5 Generously sprinkle the grated Parmesan cheese over the top and bake in a preheated oven at 400°F/200°C for 25–30 minutes.

6 Transfer to serving plates and serve warm or chilled.

# Bell Pepper Salad

Colorful marinated Mediterranean vegetables make a tasty appetizer. Serve with fresh bread or Tomato Toasts (see below).

## NUTRITIONAL INFORMATION

| | |
|---|---|
| Calories . . . . . . .234 | Sugars . . . . . . . . .4g |
| Protein . . . . . . . . .6g | Fat . . . . . . . . . .17g |
| Carbohydrate . . .15g | Saturates . . . . . . .2g |

 5–10 MINS  35 MINS

### SERVES 4

## I N G R E D I E N T S

1 onion

2 red bell peppers

2 yellow bell peppers

3 tbsp olive oil

2 large zucchini, sliced

2 garlic cloves, sliced

1 tbsp balsamic vinegar

1¾ oz/50 g anchovy fillets, chopped

¼ cup black olives, halved and pitted

1 tbsp chopped fresh basil

salt and pepper

### T O M A T O   T O A S T S

small stick of French bread

1 garlic clove, crushed

1 tomato, peeled and chopped

2 tbsp olive oil

1 Cut the onion into wedges. Core and seed the bell peppers and cut into thick slices.

2 Heat the oil in a large heavy-based skillet. Add the onion, bell peppers, zucchini, and garlic and cook gently for 20 minutes, stirring occasionally.

3 Add the vinegar, anchovies, olives, and seasoning to taste, then mix thoroughly and leave to cool.

4 Spoon on to individual plates and sprinkle with the basil.

5 To make the tomato toasts, cut the French bread diagonally into ½-inch/1-cm slices.

6 Mix the garlic, tomato, 1 tablespoon oil, and seasoning together, and spread thinly over each slice of bread.

7 Place the bread on a cookie sheet, then drizzle with the remaining olive oil and bake in a preheated oven, 425°F/220°C, for 5–10 minutes, or until crisp. Serve the Tomato Toasts with the Bell Pepper Salad.

# Black Olive Pâté

This pâté is delicious served as an appetizer on Tomato Toasts (see page 63). It can also be served as a cocktail snack on rounds of fried bread.

(see page 63)

## NUTRITIONAL INFORMATION

Calories ........149    Sugars .........1g
Protein .........2g    Fat ..........14g
Carbohydrate ....4g    Saturates .......6g

5 MINS          5 MINS

### SERVES 4

## INGREDIENTS

1⅓ cups pitted juicy black olives

1 garlic clove, crushed

finely grated rind of 1 lemon

4 tbsp lemon juice

½ cup fresh bread crumbs

¼ cup full fat soft cheese

salt and pepper

lemon wedges, to garnish

### TO SERVE

thick slices of bread

mixture of olive oil and butter

1 Coarsely chop the olives and mix with the garlic, lemon rind and juice, bread crumbs and soft cheese. Pound the mixture until smooth, or place in a food processor and work until fully blended. Season to taste with salt and freshly ground black pepper.

2 Store the pâté in a screw-top jar and chill for several hours before using—this lets the flavors develop.

3 For a delicious cocktail snack, use a pastry cutter to cut out small rounds from a thickly sliced loaf.

4 Fry the bread rounds in a mixture of olive oil and butter until they are a light golden brown color. Drain thoroughly on paper towels.

5 Top each round with a little of the pâté. Garnish with lemon wedges and serve immediately. This pâté will keep chilled in an airtight jar for up to 2 weeks.

# Stuffed Globe Artichokes

This specific recipe has been designed for microwave cooking. Use conventional cooking methods if you prefer.

## NUTRITIONAL INFORMATION

| | | |
|---|---|---|
| Calories .......189 | Sugars .........5g | |
| Protein .........5g | Fat ...........11g | |
| Carbohydrate ...17g | Saturates .......1g | |

15 MINUTES      1 HOUR

### SERVES 4

## I N G R E D I E N T S

4 globe artichokes

8 tbsp water

4 tbsp lemon juice

1 onion, chopped

1 garlic clove, crushed

2 tbsp olive oil

4 cups chopped white mushrooms

⅓ cup sliced, pitted black olives

¼ cup sun-dried tomatoes in oil, drained and chopped (reserve the oil for drizzling)

1 tbsp chopped fresh basil

1 cup fresh white bread crumbs

⅓ cup pine nuts, toasted

salt and pepper

1 Cut the stems and lower leaves off the artichokes. Snip off the leaf tips using scissors. Place 2 artichokes in a large bowl with half the water and half the lemon juice. Cover and cook on High power for 10 minutes, turning the artichokes over halfway through, until a leaf pulls away easily from the base. Leave to stand, covered, for 3 minutes before draining. Turn the artichokes upside down and leave to cool. Repeat the process with the remaining artichokes.

2 Place the onion, garlic, and oil in a bowl. Cover and cook on High power for 2 minutes, stirring once. Add the mushrooms, olives, and sun-dried tomatoes. Cover and cook on High power for 2 minutes.

3 Stir in the basil, bread crumbs, and pine nuts. Season to taste.

4 Turn the artichokes the right way up and carefully pull the leaves apart. Remove the purple-tipped central leaves. Using a teaspoon, scrape out the hairy heart and discard.

5 Divide the stuffing into 4 and spoon into the center of each artichoke. Push the leaves back around the stuffing.

6 Arrange in a shallow dish and drizzle over a little oil from the jar of sun-dried tomatoes. Cook on High power for 7–8 minutes to reheat, turning the artichokes around halfway through. Serve.

# Zucchini Fritters

These tasty little fritters are great with the sauce on page 59 as a relish for a drinks party.

## NUTRITIONAL INFORMATION

| | | | |
|---|---|---|---|
| Calories | .......162 | Sugars | .........2g |
| Protein | .........7g | Fat | ...........6g |
| Carbohydrate | ...20g | Saturates | .......2g |

5-10 MINS   20 MINS

### MAKES 16-30

## INGREDIENTS

⅔ cup self–rising flour

2 eggs, beaten

scant ¼ cup milk

10 ½ oz/300 g zucchini

2 tbsp fresh thyme

1 tbsp oil

salt and pepper

1 Sift the self-rising flour into a large bowl and make a well in the center. Add the eggs to the well, and using a wooden spoon, gradually draw in the flour.

2 Slowly add the milk to the mixture, stirring constantly to form a thick batter.

3 Meanwhile, wash the zucchini. Grate the zucchini over a sheet of paper

towels placed in a bowl to absorb some of the juices.

4 Add the zucchini and thyme to the batter, then season to taste and mix thoroughly.

5 Heat the oil in a large, heavy-based skillet. Taking a tablespoon of the batter for a medium-size fritter or half a tablespoon of batter for a smaller-size

fritter, spoon the mixture into the hot oil and cook, in batches, for 3–4 minutes on each side.

6 Remove the fritters with a perforated spoon and drain thoroughly on absorbent paper towels. Keep each batch of fritters warm in the oven while making the rest. Transfer to serving plates and serve hot.

## VARIATION

Try adding ½ teaspoon of crushed dried chiles to the batter in step 4 for spicier tasting fritters.

# Spinach & Ricotta Patties

*Nudo,* or "naked," is the word used to describe this mixture, which can also be made into thin crêpes or used as a filling for tortelloni.

## NUTRITIONAL INFORMATION

| | | | |
|---|---|---|---|
| Calories | .......374 | Sugars | .........4g |
| Protein | ........16g | Fat | ..........31g |
| Carbohydrate | ....9g | Saturates | ......19g |

 5 MINS      30 MINS

### SERVES 4

## INGREDIENTS

1 lb/450 g fresh spinach

9 oz/250 g ricotta cheese

1 egg, beaten

2 tsp fennel seeds, lightly crushed

½ cup finely grated Romano or Parmesan
  cheese, plus extra to garnish

2 tbsp all-purpose flour, mixed with
  1 tsp dried thyme

5 tbsp butter

2 garlic cloves, crushed

salt and pepper

tomato wedges, to serve

1 Wash the spinach and trim off any long stems. Place in a pan, then cover and cook for 4–5 minutes until wilted. This will probably have to be done in batches as the volume of spinach is quite large. Place in a colander and leave to drain and cool.

2 Mash the ricotta and beat in the egg and the fennel seeds. Season with plenty of salt and pepper, then stir in the Romano or Parmesan cheese.

3 Squeeze as much excess water as possible from the spinach and finely chop the leaves. Stir the spinach into the cheese mixture.

4 Taking about 1 tablespoon of the spinach and cheese mixture, shape it into a ball and flatten it slightly to form a patty. Gently roll in the seasoned flour. Continue this process until all of the mixture has been used up.

5 Half-fill a large skillet with water and bring to the boil. Carefully add the patties and cook for 3–4 minutes, or until they rise to the surface. Remove with a perforated spoon.

6 Melt the butter in a pan. Add the garlic and cook for 2–3 minutes. Pour the garlic butter over the patties, then season with freshly ground black pepper and serve at once with tomato wedges.

# Avocado Margherita

The colors of the tomatoes, basil, and mozzarella represent the colors of the Italian flag. This recipe is adapted for the microwave.

## NUTRITIONAL INFORMATION

| | | |
|---|---|---|
| Calories ....... 249 | Sugars ........ .2g | |
| Protein ........ .4g | Fat ......... .24g | |
| Carbohydrate ....4g | Saturates ...... .6g | |

  5–10 MINS     10–15 MINS

### SERVES 4

I N G R E D I E N T S

1 small red onion, sliced

1 garlic clove, crushed

1 tbsp olive oil

2 small tomatoes

2 avocados, halved and pitted

4 fresh basil leaves, torn into shreds

2 oz/55 g mozzarella cheese, sliced thinly

salt and pepper

fresh basil leaves, to garnish

mixed salad greens, to serve

1 Place the onion, garlic and the olive oil in a bowl. Cover and cook on High power for 2 minutes.

2 Meanwhile, skin the tomatoes by cutting a cross in the base of the tomatoes and placing them in a small bowl. Pour on boiling water and leave for about 45 seconds. Drain and then plunge into cold water. The skins will slide off without too much difficulty.

3 Arrange the avocado halves on a plate with the narrow ends pointed toward the center. Spoon the onions into the hollow of each half.

4 Cut and slice the tomatoes in half. Divide the tomatoes, basil, and thin slices of mozzarella between the avocado halves. Season with salt and pepper to taste.

5 Cook on Medium power for 5 minutes, or until the avocados are heated through and the cheese has melted. Transfer the avocados to serving plates, then garnish with basil leaves and serve with mixed salad greens.

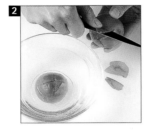

## VARIATION

If you are using a combination microwave oven with broiler—arrange the avocados on the low rack of the broiler, or on the glass turntable. Cook on combination broiler 1 and Low power for 8 minutes until browned and bubbling.

# Deep-Fried Risotto Balls

In Italian this dish is known as *suppli al telefono* or "telephone wires" because of its strings of melted mozzarella cheese.

## NUTRITIONAL INFORMATION

Calories . . . . . . .280   Sugars . . . . . . . . .2g
Protein . . . . . . . . .5g   Fat . . . . . . . . . .13g
Carbohydrate . . .35g   Saturates . . . . . . .3g

5 MINS        35–40 MINS

### SERVES 4

## I N G R E D I E N T S

2 tbsp olive oil

1 medium onion, finely chopped

1 garlic clove, chopped

½ red bell pepper, diced

¾ cup risotto rice, washed

1 tsp dried oregano

1 ¾ cup hot vegetable or chicken stock

scant ½ cup dry white wine

2 ¾ oz/75 g mozzarella cheese

oil, for deep-frying

fresh basil sprig, to garnish

1 Heat the oil in a skillet and cook the onion and garlic for 3–4 minutes, or until just softened.

2 Add the bell pepper, risotto rice, and oregano to the skillet. Cook for 2–3 minutes, stirring to coat the rice in the oil.

3 Mix the stock together with the wine and add to the skillet a ladleful at a time, waiting for the liquid to be absorbed by the rice before adding the next ladleful of liquid.

4 Once all of the liquid has been absorbed and the rice is tender (it should take about 15 minutes in total), remove the pan from the heat and leave until the mixture is cool enough to handle.

5 Cut the cheese into 12 pieces. Taking about 1 tablespoon of risotto, shape the mixture around the cheese pieces to make 12 balls.

6 Heat the oil to 350–375°F/180–190°C, or until a cube of bread browns in 30 seconds. Cook the risotto balls, in batches of 4, for 2 minutes, or until golden.

7 Remove the risotto balls with a perforated spoon and drain thoroughly on absorbent paper towels. Garnish with a sprig of basil and serve the risotto balls hot.

# Mussels in White Wine

This soup of mussels, cooked in white wine with onions and cream, can be served as an appetizer or a main dish with plenty of crusty bread.

## NUTRITIONAL INFORMATION

| | |
|---|---|
| Calories .......396 | Sugars .........2g |
| Protein ........23g | Fat ..........24g |
| Carbohydrate ....8g | Saturates ......15g |

5–10 MINS    25 MINS

### SERVES 4

## INGREDIENTS

12½ cups fresh mussels

¼ cup butter

1 large onion, chopped very finely

2–3 garlic cloves, crushed

1½ cups dry white wine

⅔ cup water

2 tbsp lemon juice

good pinch of finely grated lemon rind

1 bouquet garni sachet

1 tbsp all-purpose flour

4 tbsp light or heavy cream

2–3 tbsp chopped fresh parsley

salt and pepper

warm crusty bread, to serve

1 Scrub the mussels in several changes of cold water to remove all mud, sand, barnacles, etc. Pull off all the "beards." All of the mussels must be tightly closed; if they don't close when given a sharp tap, they must be discarded.

2 Melt half the butter in a large pan. Add the onion and garlic, and cook gently until soft but not colored.

3 Add the wine, water, lemon juice and rind, bouquet garni and plenty of seasoning. Bring to a boil, then cover and simmer for 4–5 minutes.

4 Add the mussels to the pan, then cover tightly and simmer for 5 minutes, shaking the pan frequently, until all the mussels have opened. Discard any mussels that have not opened. Remove the bouquet garni.

5 Remove the empty half shell from each mussel. Blend the remaining butter with the flour and whisk into the soup, a little at a time. Simmer gently for 2–3 minute, or until slightly thickened.

6 Add the cream and half the parsley to the soup and reheat gently. Adjust the seasoning. Ladle the mussels and soup into warmed large soup bowls. Sprinkle with the remaining parsley and serve with plenty of warm crusty bread.

# Deep-Fried Seafood

Deep-fried seafood is popular all around the Mediterranean, where fish of all kinds is fresh and abundant.

## NUTRITIONAL INFORMATION

Calories .......393    Sugars .......0.2g
Protein ........27g    Fat ..........26g
Carbohydrate ...12g    Saturates .......3g

5 MINS          15 MINS

### SERVES 4

## I N G R E D I E N T S

7 oz/200 g prepared squid

7 oz/200 g raw tiger shrimp, shelled

5 ½ oz/150 g whitebait

oil, for deep-frying

⅓ cup all-purpose flour

1 tsp dried basil

salt and pepper

## T O   S E R V E

garlic mayonnaise (see page 30)

lemon wedges

1 Carefully rinse the squid, shrimp, and whitebait under cold running water, completely removing any dirt or grit.

2 Using a sharp knife, slice the squid into rings, leaving the tentacles whole.

3 Heat the oil in a large pan to 350–375°F/180–190°C, or until a cube of bread browns in 30 seconds.

4 Place the flour in a bowl, add the basil and season with salt and pepper to taste. Mix together well.

5 Roll the squid, shrimp, and whitebait in the seasoned flour until coated all over. Carefully shake off any excess flour.

6 Cook the seafood in the heated oil, in batches, for 2–3 minutes, or until crispy and golden all over. Remove all of the seafood with a perforated spoon and leave to drain thoroughly on paper towels.

7 Transfer the deep-fried seafood to serving plates and serve with garlic mayonnaise (see page 30) and a few lemon wedges.

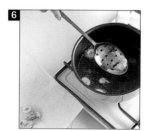

# Pasta & Cheese Pots

A layered pasta, cheese, and prosciutto delight, complemented by a tomato and basil sauce. This recipe is adapted for the microwave.

  15 MINS       35 MINS

### SERVES 4

## INGREDIENTS

1 small onion, chopped

1 garlic clove, chopped

1 tbsp olive oil

4 tomatoes, skinned (see page 68) and chopped

1 tbsp tomato paste

4 fresh basil leaves, chopped

2 tbsp butter

2 tbsp dried brown bread crumbs

2 tbsp chopped hazelnuts, lightly toasted

3 oz/85 g dried cappellini pasta

2 tbsp all-purpose flour

⅔ cup milk

½ oz/15 g Roquefort (blue) cheese

about 2¾ oz/75 g prosciutto, chopped

4 pitted black olives, chopped

salt and pepper

sprigs of fresh basil, to garnish

1 Place the onion, garlic, and oil in a bowl. Cover and cook on High power for 3 minutes. Add the tomatoes and tomato paste and cook on High power for 4 minutes, stirring halfway through. Add the basil and seasoning. Leave to stand, covered.

2 Place half of the butter in a small bowl and cook on High power for 30 seconds, or until melted. Brush the insides of 4 ramekin dishes with the melted butter. Mix the bread crumbs and hazelnuts together and coat the insides of the ramekins. Set aside.

3 Break the pasta into 3 short lengths and place in a large bowl. Pour over enough boiling water to cover the pasta by 1 inch/2.5 cm, and season lightly with salt. Cover and cook on High power for 4 minutes, stirring halfway through. Leave to stand, covered, for 1 minute, then drain thoroughly.

4 Place the remaining butter, the flour, and milk in a small bowl. Cook on High power for 2–2½ minutes, or until thickened, stirring well every 30 seconds. Crumble the cheese into the sauce and stir until melted. Season to taste.

5 Add the pasta to the sauce and mix well. Divide half the pasta mixture between the ramekins and top with the ham and olives. Spoon the remaining pasta mixture on top. Cook on Medium power for 6 minutes. Leave to stand, uncovered, for 2 minutes before carefully turning out on to serving plates with the tomato sauce. Garnish with sprigs of basil.

# Crostini alla Fiorentina

Crostini are small pieces of crusty fried bread,
here topped with a tasty liver and anchovy mix.

## NUTRITIONAL INFORMATION

| | | |
|---|---|---|
| Calories .......393 | Sugars .........2g | |
| Protein ........17g | Fat ..........25g | |
| Carbohydrate ...19g | Saturates .......9g | |

 🥐 🥐 🥐

🥘 10 MINS   ⏱ 40–45 MINS

### SERVES 4

## I N G R E D I E N T S

3 tbsp olive oil

1 onion, chopped

1 celery stalk, chopped

1 carrot, chopped

1–2 garlic cloves, crushed

4½ oz/125 g chicken livers

4½ oz/125 g calf's, lamb's, or pig's liver

⅔ cup red wine

1 tbsp tomato paste

2 tbsp chopped fresh parsley

3–4 canned anchovy fillets, chopped finely

2 tbsp stock or water

2–3 tbsp butter

1 tbsp capers

salt and pepper

small pieces of fried crusty bread, to serve

chopped parsley, to garnish

1 Heat the oil in a skillet, add the onion, celery, carrot and garlic, and cook gently for 4–5 minutes, or until the onion is soft, but not colored.

2 Meanwhile, rinse and dry the chicken livers. Dry the calf's or other liver, and slice into strips. Add the liver to the skillet and fry gently for a few minutes until the strips are well sealed on all sides.

3 Add half of the wine and cook until it has mostly evaporated. Then add the rest of the wine, tomato paste, half of the parsley, the anchovy fillets, stock, and a little salt and plenty of black pepper.

4 Cover the skillet and leave to simmer, stirring occasionally, for 15–20 minutes, or until tender and most of the liquid has been absorbed.

5 Leave the mixture to cool a little, then either coarsely grind or put into a food processor and process to a chunky purée.

6 Return to the skillet and add the butter, capers, and remaining parsley. Heat through gently until the butter melts. Adjust the seasoning and turn out into a bowl. Serve warm or cold spread on the slices of crusty bread and sprinkled with chopped parsley.

# Figs & Prosciutto

This colorful fresh salad is delicious at any time of the year.
Prosciutto di Parma is thought to be the best ham in the world.

## NUTRITIONAL INFORMATION

| | | | |
|---|---|---|---|
| Calories | ........121 | Sugars | .........6g |
| Protein | .........1g | Fat | ...........11g |
| Carbohydrate | ....6g | Saturates | .......2g |

 15 MINS    5 MINS

### SERVES 4

### INGREDIENTS

1½ oz /40 g arugula

4 fresh figs

4 slices prosciutto

4 tbsp olive oil

1 tbsp fresh orange juice

1 tbsp clear honey

1 small red chile

1 Tear the arugula into more manageable pieces and arrange on 4 serving plates.

2 Using a sharp knife, cut each of the figs into fourths and place them on top of the arugula leaves.

3 Using a sharp knife, cut the prosciutto into strips and scatter over the arugula and figs.

4 Place the oil, orange juice, and honey in a screw-top jar. Shake the jar until the mixture emulsifies and forms a thick dressing. Transfer to a bowl.

5 Using a sharp knife, dice the chile, remembering not to touch your face before you have washed your hands (see Cook's Tip, below). Add the chopped chile to the dressing and mix well.

6 Drizzle the dressing over the prosciutto, arugula, and figs, tossing to mix well. Serve at once.

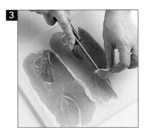

## COOK'S TIP

Chiles can burn the skin for several hours after chopping, so it is advisable to wear gloves when you are handling the very hot varieties.

# Preserved Meats

Mix an attractive selection of these preserved meats with olives and marinated vegetables for extra color and variety.

### NUTRITIONAL INFORMATION

| | | | |
|---|---|---|---|
| Calories | .......227 | Sugars | .........5g |
| Protein | ........10g | Fat | ..........19g |
| Carbohydrate | ....5g | Saturates | .......1g |

 10 MINS    5-10 MINS

### SERVES 4

## I N G R E D I E N T S

3 ripe tomatoes

3 ripe figs

1 small melon

2 oz/55 g Italian salami, sliced thinly

4 thin slices mortadella

6 slices prosciutto

6 slices bresaola

4 fresh basil leaves, chopped

olive oil

½ cup marinated olives, pitted

freshly ground black pepper, to serve

1 Slice the tomatoes thinly and cut the figs into fourths.

2 Halve the melon and scoop out the seeds, then cut the flesh into wedges.

3 Arrange the meats on one half of a serving platter. Arrange the tomato slices in the center and sprinkle with the basil leaves and oil.

4 Cover the rest of the platter with the figs and melon and scatter the olives over the meats.

5 Serve with a little extra olive oil to drizzle over the bresaola, and sprinkle with coarsely ground black pepper.

# Snacks & Light Meals

Recipes for snacks and light meals offer something for every taste, including vegetables, meat, and fish dishes. These recipes are suitable for when you are not too hungry,

but still a bit peckish or if you are in a hurry and want to eat something quick, but still nutritious and tasty. Try the mouthwatering Italian flavors of Tomato & Mozzarella Bruschetta or an Italian-style omelet—these are sure to satisfy even the most discerning taste buds. All of the recipes in this chapter are quick to prepare and easy to cook, and are sure to become staples in your Italian culinary repertoire.

# Tomato & Mozzarella Bruschetta

These simple toasts are filled with color and flavor. They are great as a speedy appetizer or delicious as a light meal or snack.

## NUTRITIONAL INFORMATION

Calories . . . . . . .232  Sugars . . . . . . . . .4g
Protein . . . . . . . . .4g  Fat . . . . . . . . . .15g
Carbohydrate . . .20g  Saturates . . . . . . .8g

5–10 MINS       10 MINS

### SERVES 4

## I N G R E D I E N T S

4 English muffins

4 garlic cloves, crushed

2 tbsp butter

1 tbsp chopped basil

4 large, ripe tomatoes

1 tbsp tomato paste

8 pitted black olives, halved

½ cup sliced mozzarella cheese

salt and pepper

fresh basil leaves, to garnish

### D R E S S I N G

1 tbsp olive oil

2 tsp lemon juice

1 tsp clear honey

## VARIATION

Use balsamic vinegar instead of the lemon juice for an authentic Italian flavor.

  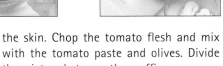

1 Cut the muffins in half to give eight thick pieces. Toast the muffin halves under a hot broiler for 2–3 minute, or until golden.

2 Mix the garlic, butter, and basil together and spread on to each muffin half.

3 Cut a cross shape at the base of each tomato. Plunge the tomatoes in a bowl of boiling water—this will make the skin easier to peel. After a few minutes, pick each tomato up with a fork and peel away the skin. Chop the tomato flesh and mix with the tomato paste and olives. Divide the mixture between the muffins.

4 Mix the dressing ingredients and drizzle over each muffin. Arrange the mozzarella cheese on top and season.

5 Return the muffins to the broiler for 1–2 minutes, or until the cheese melts.

6 Garnish with fresh basil leaves and serve at once.

# Eggplant Sandwiches

Serve these sandwiches as a vegetarian main course for two or as a side dish to accompany other grilled foods.

## NUTRITIONAL INFORMATION

| | | | |
|---|---|---|---|
| Calories | .270 | Sugars | .4g |
| Protein | .10g | Fat | .15g |
| Carbohydrate | .25g | Saturates | .7g |

 5 MINS    10–15 MINS

### SERVES 2

## I N G R E D I E N T S

1 large eggplant

1 tbsp lemon juice

3 tbsp olive oil

1 cup grated mozzarella cheese

2 sun-dried tomatoes, chopped

salt and pepper

### T O   S E R V E

Italian bread, such as focaccia or ciabatta

mixed salad greens

slices of tomato

1 Slice the eggplant into thin rounds.

2 Combine the lemon juice and olive oil in a small bowl and season the mixture with salt and pepper to taste.

3 Brush the eggplant slices with the oil and lemon juice mixture and grill over medium hot coals for 2–3 minutes, without turning, until they are golden on the under side.

4 Turn half of the eggplant slices over and sprinkle with cheese and chopped sun-dried tomatoes.

5 Place the remaining eggplant slices on top of the cheese and tomatoes, turning them so that the pale side is uppermost.

6 Grill for 1–2 minutes, then carefully turn the whole sandwich over and grill for 1–2 minutes. Baste with the oil mixture.

7 Serve the eggplant sandwiches with Italian bread, mixed salad greens, and a few slices of tomato.

## VARIATION

Try feta cheese instead of mozzarella, but omit the salt from the basting oil because feta is quite salty. A creamy goat cheese would be equally delicious.

# Italian Omelet

A baked omelet of substantial proportions with potatoes, onions, artichokes, and sun-dried tomatoes.

## NUTRITIONAL INFORMATION

Calories . . . . . . . .481     Sugars . . . . . . . . .4g
Protein . . . . . . . .22g     Fat . . . . . . . . . .26g
Carbohydrate . . .42g     Saturates . . . . . .10g

10 MINS          45 MINS

### SERVES 4

## INGREDIENTS

2 lb/900 g potatoes

1 tbsp oil

1 large onion, sliced

2 garlic cloves, chopped

6 sun-dried tomatoes, cut into strips

14 oz/400 g canned artichoke hearts,
    drained and halved

scant 1¼ cups ricotta cheese

4 large eggs, beaten

2 tbsp milk

freshly grated Parmesan cheese

3 tbsp chopped thyme

salt and pepper

1 Peel the potatoes and place them in a bowl of cold water (see Cook's Tip). Cut the potatoes into thin slices.

2 Bring a large pan of water to the boil and add the potato slices. Leave the potatoes to simmer for 5–6 minutes, or until just tender.

3 Heat the oil in a large skillet. Add the onions and garlic to the skillet and cook, stirring occasionally, for about 3–4 minutes.

4 Add the sun-dried tomatoes and continue cooking for an additional 2 minutes.

5 Place a layer of potatoes at the bottom of a deep, ovenproof dish. Top with a layer of the onion mixture, artichokes, and ricotta cheese. Repeat the layers in the same order, finishing with a layer of potatoes on top.

6 Mix together the eggs, milk, half of the Parmesan, thyme, and salt and pepper to taste, then pour over the potatoes.

7 Top with the remaining Parmesan cheese and bake in a preheated oven, at 375°F/190°C, for 20–25 minutes, or until golden brown. Cut the omelet into slices and serve.

## COOK'S TIP

Placing the potatoes in a bowl of cold water will prevent them from turning brown while you cut the rest into slices.

# Bean & Tomato Casserole

This quick and easy casserole can be eaten as a healthy supper dish or as a side dish to accompany sausages or grilled fish.

## NUTRITIONAL INFORMATION

| | | |
|---|---|---|
| Calories .......273 | Sugars .........8g | |
| Protein ........15g | Fat ...........7g | |
| Carbohydrate ...40g | Saturates .......1g | |

 10 MINS   15 MINS

### SERVES 4

## I N G R E D I E N T S

14 oz/400g canned cannellini beans

14 oz/400g canned borlotti beans

2 tbsp olive oil

1 celery stalk

2 garlic cloves, chopped

6 oz/175 g baby onions, halved

1 lb/450 g tomatoes

2¾ oz/75 g arugula

1 Drain both cans of beans and reserve 6 tbsp of the liquid.

2 Heat the oil in a large pan. Add the celery, garlic, and onions and sauté for 5 minutes, or until the onions are golden.

3 Cut a cross in the base of each tomato and plunge them into a bowl of boiling water for 30 seconds, or until the skins split. Remove the tomatoes with a perforated spoon and leave until cool enough to handle. Peel off the skin and chop the flesh.

4 Add the tomato flesh and the reserved bean liquid to the pan and cook for 5 minutes.

  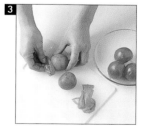

5 Add the beans to the pan and cook for an additional 3–4 minutes, or until the beans are hot.

6 Stir in the arugula and let it wilt slightly before serving. Serve hot.

## VARIATION

For a spicier tasting dish, add 1–2 teaspoons of hot pepper sauce with the cannellini and borlotti beans in step 5.

# Omelet in Tomato Sauce

These omelet strips are delicious smothered in a tomato and rosemary flavored sauce.

## NUTRITIONAL INFORMATION

| | | | |
|---|---|---|---|
| Calories | ....... 198 | Sugars | ......... 6g |
| Protein | ........ 10g | Fat | .......... 15g |
| Carbohydrate | .... 6g | Saturates | ....... 8g |

10 MINS    35 MINS

### SERVES 4

## INGREDIENTS

2 tbsp butter

1 onion, finely chopped

2 garlic cloves, chopped

4 eggs, beaten

⅔ cup milk

¾ cup diced Gruyère cheese

14 oz/400 g canned tomatoes, chopped

1 tbsp rosemary, stems removed

⅔ cup vegetable stock

freshly grated Parmesan cheese,
    for sprinkling

fresh, crusty bread, to serve

1 Melt the butter in a large skillet. Add the onion and garlic and cook for 4–5 minutes, or until softened.

2 Beat together the eggs and milk and add the mixture to the skillet.

3 Using a spatula, raise the edges of the omelet and tip any uncooked egg around the edge of the skillet.

4 Scatter over the cheese. Cook for 5 minutes, turning once, until golden on both sides. Remove the omelet from the skillet and roll up.

5 Add the tomatoes, rosemary, and vegetable stock to the skillet, stirring, and bring to a boil.

6 Leave the tomato sauce to simmer for about 10 minutes, or until reduced and thickened.

7 Slice the omelet into strips and add to the tomato sauce in the skillet. Cook for 3–4 minutes, or until piping hot.

8 Sprinkle the freshly grated Parmesan cheese over the omelet strips and serve with fresh, crusty bread.

## VARIATION

Try adding 3½ oz/100 g diced pancetta or unsmoked bacon in step 1 and cooking the meat with the onions.

# Baked Fennel

Fennel is used extensively in northern Italy. It is a very versatile vegetable, which is good cooked or used raw in salads.

### NUTRITIONAL INFORMATION

| | | |
|---|---|---|
| Calories ........111 | Sugars .........6g | |
| Protein .........7g | Fat ..........7g | |
| Carbohydrate ....7g | Saturates .......3g | |

10 MINS     35 MINS

### SERVES 4

## I N G R E D I E N T S

2 fennel bulbs

2 celery stalks, cut into 3-inch/7.5-cm sticks

6 sun-dried tomatoes, halved

7 oz/200 g crushed tomatoes

2 tsp dried oregano

½ cup grated Parmesan cheese

1 Using a sharp knife, trim the fennel, discarding any tough outer leaves, and cut the bulb into fourths.

2 Bring a large pan of water to a boil, then add the fennel and celery and cook for 8–10 minutes, or until just tender. Remove with a perforated spoon and drain.

3 Place the fennel pieces, celery, and sun-dried tomatoes in a large ovenproof dish.

4 Mix the crushed tomatoes and oregano and pour the mixture over the fennel.

5 Sprinkle with the Parmesan cheese and bake in a preheated oven at 375°F/190°C for 20 minutes, or until hot. Serve as an appetizer with bread or as a vegetable side dish.

# Spinach & Ricotta Shells

This is a classic combination in which the smooth, creamy cheese balances the sharper taste of the spinach.

## NUTRITIONAL INFORMATION

| | | | |
|---|---|---|---|
| Calories | .......672 | Sugars | ........10g |
| Protein | ........23g | Fat | ..........26g |
| Carbohydrate | ...93g | Saturates | .......8g |

 5 MINS     40 MINS

### SERVES 4

### I N G R E D I E N T S

14 oz/400 g dried lumache rigate grande

5 tbsp olive oil

1 cup fresh white bread crumbs

½ cup milk

10½ oz/300 g frozen spinach, thawed
and drained

1 cup ricotta cheese

pinch of freshly grated nutmeg

4 oz/400 g canned chopped tomatoes,
drained

1 garlic clove, crushed

salt and pepper

1 Bring a large pan of lightly salted water to a boil. Add the lumache and 1 tablespoon of the olive oil and cook for 8–10 minutes, or until just tender but still firm to the bite. Drain the pasta, then refresh under cold water and set aside until required.

2 Put the bread crumbs, milk, and 3 tablespoons of the remaining olive oil in a food processor and work to combine.

3 Add the spinach and ricotta cheese to the food processor and work to a smooth mixture. Transfer to a bowl, then stir in the nutmeg and season with salt and pepper to taste.

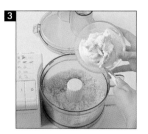

4 Mix together the tomatoes, garlic, and remaining oil and spoon the mixture into the base of a large ovenproof dish.

5 Using a teaspoon, fill the lumache with the spinach and ricotta mixture and arrange on top of the tomato mixture in the dish. Cover and bake in a preheated oven at 350°F/180°C for 20 minutes. Serve hot.

## COOK'S TIP

Ricotta is a creamy Italian cheese traditionally made from ewes' milk whey. It is soft and white, with a smooth texture and a slightly sweet flavor. It should be used within 2–3 days of purchase.

# Rotelle with Spicy Sauce

Prepare the sauce well in advance—it is a good idea to freeze batches of the sauce so that you always have some to hand.

## NUTRITIONAL INFORMATION

| | | |
|---|---|---|
| Calories . . . . . . .530 | Sugars . . . . . . . . .4g | |
| Protein . . . . . . . .13g | Fat . . . . . . . . . .18g | |
| Carbohydrate . . .78g | Saturates . . . . . . .3g | |

8¼ HOURS    40 MINS

### SERVES 4

## I N G R E D I E N T S

scant 1 cup Italian Red Wine Sauce
(see page 29)

5 tbsp olive oil

3 garlic cloves, crushed

2 fresh red chiles, chopped

1 green chile, chopped

3½ cups dried rotelle

salt and pepper

warm Italian bread, to serve

1 Make the Italian Red Wine Sauce (see page 29).

2 Heat 4 tablespoons of the oil in a pan. Add the garlic and chiles and cook for 3 minutes.

3 Stir in the Italian Red Wine Sauce and season with salt and pepper to taste, then simmer gently over low heat for 20 minutes.

4 Bring a large pan of lightly salted water to a boil. Add the rotelle and the remaining oil and cook for 8 minutes, or until just tender but still firm to the bite. Drain the pasta.

5 Pour the Italian Red Wine Sauce over the rotelle and toss to mix.

6 Transfer to a warm serving dish and serve with warm Italian bread.

### COOK'S TIP

Remove chile seeds before chopping the chiles, as they are the hottest part, and do not let them slip into the food.

# Tagliarini with Gorgonzola

This simple, creamy pasta sauce is a classic Italian recipe. You could use Danish blue cheese instead of the Gorgonzola, if you prefer.

## NUTRITIONAL INFORMATION

| | |
|---|---|
| Calories . . . . . . .904 | Sugars . . . . . . . . .4g |
| Protein . . . . . . . .27g | Fat . . . . . . . . . .53g |
| Carbohydrate . . .83g | Saturates . . . . . .36g |

 5 MINS     20 MINS

### SERVES 4

## I N G R E D I E N T S

2 tbsp butter

2 cups Gorgonzola cheese, coarsely crumbled

⅔ cup heavy cream

2 tbsp dry white wine

1 tsp cornstarch

4 fresh sage sprigs, finely chopped

14 oz/400 g dried tagliarini

2 tbsp olive oil

salt and white pepper

1 Melt the butter in a heavy-based pan. Stir in 6 oz/175 g of the cheese and melt, over low heat, for about 2 minutes.

2 Add the cream, wine, and cornstarch and beat with a whisk until fully incorporated.

## COOK'S TIP

Gorgonzola is one of the world's oldest veined cheeses and, arguably, its finest. When buying, always check that it is creamy yellow with delicate green veining. Avoid hard or discolored cheese. It should have a rich, piquant aroma, not a bitter smell.

3 Stir in the sage and season to taste with salt and white pepper. Bring to a boil over low heat, whisking constantly, until the sauce thickens. Remove from the heat and set aside while you cook the pasta.

4 Bring a large pan of lightly salted water to a boil. Add the tagliarini and 1 tablespoon of the olive oil. Cook the pasta for 8–10 minutes, or until just

tender, then drain thoroughly and toss in the remaining olive oil. Transfer the pasta to a serving dish and keep warm.

5 Reheat the sauce over a low heat, whisking constantly. Spoon the Gorgonzola sauce over the tagliarini, then generously sprinkle over the remaining cheese and serve immediately.

# Spaghetti with Ricotta

This light pasta dish has a delicate flavor ideally suited for a summer lunch.

## NUTRITIONAL INFORMATION

| | | |
|---|---|---|
| Calories . . . . . . . . .701 | Sugars . . . . . . . .12g | |
| Protein . . . . . . . .17g | Fat . . . . . . . . . .40g | |
| Carbohydrate . . .73g | Saturates . . . . . .15g | |

  5 MINS     25 MINS

### SERVES 4

## I N G R E D I E N T S

12 oz/350 g dried spaghetti

3 tbsp olive oil

3 tbsp butter

2 tbsp chopped fresh flat-leaf parsley

1⅓ cups freshly ground almonds

generous ½ cup ricotta cheese

pinch of grated nutmeg

pinch of ground cinnamon

⅔ cup sour cream or unsweetened yogurt

½ cup hot chicken stock

1 tbsp pine nuts

salt and pepper

fresh flat-leaf parsley sprigs, to garnish

1 Bring a pan of lightly salted water to a boil. Add the spaghetti and 1 tablespoon of the oil and cook for 8–10 minutes, or until tender but still firm to the bite.

2 Drain the pasta, return to the pan and toss with the butter and chopped parsley. Set aside and keep warm.

3 To make the sauce, mix together the ground almonds, ricotta cheese, nutmeg, cinnamon, and sour cream over low heat to form a thick paste. Gradually stir in the remaining oil. When the oil has been fully incorporated, gradually stir in the hot chicken stock, until smooth. Season to taste with black pepper.

4 Transfer the spaghetti to a warm serving dish, then pour over the sauce and toss together well (see Cook's Tip, right). Sprinkle over the pine nuts, then garnish with the sprigs of flat-leaf parsley and serve warm.

### COOK'S TIP

Use two large forks to toss spaghetti or other long pasta, so that it is thoroughly coated with the sauce. Special spaghetti forks are available from some cookware departments and kitchen shops.

# Three Cheese Bake

Serve this dish while the cheese is still hot and melted, because cooked cheese turns very rubbery if it is left to cool down.

## NUTRITIONAL INFORMATION

| | | | |
|---|---|---|---|
| Calories | .......710 | Sugars | .........6g |
| Protein | ........34g | Fat | ..........30g |
| Carbohydrate | ...80g | Saturates | ......16g |

   5 MINS    1 HOUR

### SERVES 4

## INGREDIENTS

butter, for greasing

14 oz/400 g dried penne

1 tbsp olive oil

2 eggs, beaten

1½ cups ricotta cheese

4 fresh basil sprigs

1 cup grated mozzarella or provolone cheese

4 tbsp freshly grated Parmesan cheese

salt and pepper

fresh basil leaves (optional), to garnish

1 Lightly grease a large ovenproof dish with butter.

2 Bring a large pan of lightly salted water to a boil. Add the penne and olive oil and cook for 8–10 minutes, or until just tender but still firm to the bite. Drain the pasta, then set aside and keep warm.

3 Beat the eggs into the ricotta cheese and season to taste.

4 Spoon half of the penne into the base of the dish and cover with half of the basil leaves.

5 Spoon over half of the ricotta cheese mixture. Sprinkle over the mozzarella or provolone cheese and top with the remaining basil leaves. Cover with the remaining penne and then spoon over the remaining ricotta cheese mixture. Lightly sprinkle over the freshly grated Parmesan cheese.

6 Bake in a preheated oven at 375°F/190°C for 30–40 minutes, or until golden brown and the cheese topping is hot and bubbling. Garnish with fresh basil leaves, if liked, and serve hot.

## VARIATION

Try substituting smoked Bavarian cheese for the mozzarella or provolone and grated Cheddar cheese for the Parmesan, for a slightly different but just as delicious flavor.

# Eggplant & Pasta

Prepare the marinated eggplants well in advance so that all you have to do is cook the pasta.

## NUTRITIONAL INFORMATION

| | | | |
|---|---|---|---|
| Calories | .......378 | Sugars | .........3g |
| Protein | ........12g | Fat | ..........30g |
| Carbohydrate | ...16g | Saturates | .......3g |

12¼ HOURS      15 MINS

### SERVES 4

## I N G R E D I E N T S

⅔ cup vegetable stock

⅔ cup white wine vinegar

2 tsp balsamic vinegar

3 tbsp olive oil

fresh oregano sprig

1 lb/450 g eggplant, peeled and thinly sliced

14 oz/400 g dried linguine

### M A R I N A D E

2 tbsp extra virgin oil

2 garlic cloves, crushed

2 tbsp chopped fresh oregano

2 tbsp finely chopped roasted almonds

2 tbsp diced red bell pepper

2 tbsp lime juice

grated rind and juice of 1 orange

salt and pepper

1 Put the vegetable stock, wine vinegar and balsamic vinegar into a pan and bring to a boil over low heat. Add 2 teaspoon of the olive oil and the sprig of oregano and simmer gently for about 1 minute.

2 Add the eggplant slices to the pan, then remove from the heat and set aside for 10 minutes.

3 Meanwhile make the marinade. Combine the oil, garlic, fresh oregano, almonds, bell pepper, lime juice, orange rind and juice together in a large bowl and season to taste.

4 Carefully remove the eggplant from the pan with a slotted spoon, then drain well. Add the eggplant slices to the marinade, mixing well, and set aside in the refrigerator for about 12 hours.

5 Bring a large pan of lightly salted water to a boil. Add half of the remaining oil and the linguine and cook for 8–10 minutes, or until just tender. Drain the pasta thoroughly and toss with the remaining oil while still warm. Arrange the pasta on a serving plate with the eggplant slices and the marinade and serve immediately.

# Tricolor Timballini

An unusual way of serving pasta, these cheese molds are excellent with a crunchy salad for a light lunch.

## NUTRITIONAL INFORMATION

| | | | |
|---|---|---|---|
| Calories | .......529 | Sugars | .........7g |
| Protein | ........18g | Fat | ..........29g |
| Carbohydrate | ...46g | Saturates | ......12g |

30 MINS     1 HOUR

### SERVES 4

## I N G R E D I E N T S

1 tbsp butter, softened

scant ½ cup dried white bread crumbs

6 oz/175 g dried tricolor spaghetti, broken
  into 2-inch/5-cm lengths

3 tbsp olive oil

1 egg yolk

1 cup grated Gruyère cheese

1¼ cups Béchamel Sauce (see page 28)

1 onion, finely chopped

1 bay leaf

⅔ cup dry white wine

⅔ cup crushed tomatoes

1 tbsp tomato paste

salt and pepper

fresh basil leaves, to garnish

1 Grease four ¾-cup molds or ramekins with the butter. Evenly coat the insides with half of the bread crumbs.

2 Bring a pan of lightly salted water to a boil. Add the spaghetti and 1 tablespoon oil and cook for 8–10 minutes, or until just tender. Drain and transfer to a mixing bowl. Add the egg yolk and cheese to the pasta and season.

3 Pour the Béchamel Sauce into the bowl containing the pasta and mix. Spoon the mixture into the ramekins and sprinkle over the remaining bread crumbs.

4 Stand the ramekins on a cookie sheet and bake in a preheated oven at 425°F/220°C for 20 minutes. Set aside for 10 minutes.

5 Meanwhile, make the sauce. Heat the remaining oil in a pan and gently cook the onion and bay leaf for 2-3 minutes.

6 Stir in the wine, crushed tomatoes, and tomato paste and season with salt and pepper to taste. Simmer for 20 minutes, or until thickened. Remove and discard the bay leaf.

7 Turn the timballini out onto serving plates, then garnish with the basil leaves and serve with the tomato sauce.

# Baked Tuna & Ricotta Rigatoni

Ribbed tubes of pasta are filled with tuna and ricotta cheese
and then baked in a creamy sauce.

## NUTRITIONAL INFORMATION

| | | | |
|---|---|---|---|
| Calories | . . . . . . .949 | Sugars | . . . . . . . . .5g |
| Protein | . . . . . . . .51g | Fat | . . . . . . . . . .48g |
| Carbohydrate | . . .85g | Saturates | . . . . . .26g |

10 MINS          45 MINS

### SERVES 4

## I N G R E D I E N T S

butter, for greasing

1 lb/450 g dried rigatoni

1 tbsp olive oil

7 oz/200 g  canned flaked tuna, drained

1 cup ricotta cheese

½ cup heavy cream

2 cups freshly grated Parmesan cheese

4 oz/125 g sun-dried tomatoes, drained
    and sliced

salt and pepper

1 Lightly grease a large ovenproof dish with butter.

2 Bring a large pan of lightly salted water to a boil. Add the rigatoni and olive oil and cook for 8–10 minutes, or until just tender but still firm to the bite. Drain the pasta and set aside until cool enough to handle.

3 Meanwhile, in a bowl, mix together the tuna and ricotta cheese to form a soft paste. Spoon the mixture into a pastry bag and use to fill the rigatoni. Arrange the filled pasta tubes side by side in the prepared ovenproof dish.

4 To make the sauce, mix the cream and Parmesan cheese and season with salt and pepper to taste. Spoon the sauce over the rigatoni and top with the sun-dried tomatoes, arranged in a crisscross pattern. Bake in a preheated oven at 400°F/200°C for 20 minutes. Serve hot straight from the dish.

## VARIATION

For a vegetarian alternative
of this recipe, simply substitute
a mixture of pitted and chopped
black olives and chopped walnuts
for the tuna. Follow exactly the same
cooking method.

# Crêpes with Smoked Fish

These are delicious as an appetizer or light supper dish
and you can vary the filling with whichever fish you prefer.

## NUTRITIONAL INFORMATION

| | |
|---|---|
| Calories . . . . . . . .399 | Sugars . . . . . . . . .6g |
| Protein . . . . . . . .36g | Fat . . . . . . . . . .18g |
| Carbohydrate . . .25g | Saturates . . . . . .10g |

15 MINS     1 HR 20 MINS

**Makes 12 crêpes**

## I N G R E D I E N T S

### C R E P E S

⅔ cup all-purpose flour

½ tsp salt

1 egg, beaten

1 ¼ cups milk

1 tbsp oil, for frying

### S A U C E

1 lb/450 g smoked haddock, skinned

1 ¼ cups milk

3 tbsp butter or margarine

⅓ cup all-purpose flour

1 ¼ cups fish stock

¾ cup grated Parmesan cheese

scant 1 cup frozen peas, defrosted

1 cup shrimp, cooked and shelled

½ cup grated Gruyère cheese

salt and pepper

1 To make the crêpe batter, sift the flour and salt into a large bowl and make a well in the center. Add the egg and, using a wooden spoon, begin to draw in the flour. Slowly add the milk and beat together to form a smooth batter. Set aside until required.

2 Place the fish in a large skillet and add the milk. Bring to a boil, then simmer for 10 minutes, or until the fish begins to flake. Drain thoroughly, reserving the milk.

3 Melt the butter in a pan. Add the flour, mix to a paste and cook for 2–3 minutes. Remove the pan from the heat and add the reserved milk a little at a time, stirring to make a smooth sauce. Repeat with the fish stock. Return to the heat and bring to a boil, stirring. Stir in the Parmesan and season with salt and pepper to taste.

4 Grease a skillet with oil. Add 2 tablespoons of the crêpe batter, swirling it around the pan and cook for 2–3 minutes. Loosen the sides with a spatula and flip over the crêpe. Cook for 2–3 minute, or until golden; repeat. Stack the crêpes with sheets of baking parchment between them and keep warm in the oven.

5 Stir the flaked fish, peas and shrimp into half of the sauce and use to fill each crêpe. Pour over the remaining sauce, then top with the Gruyère cheese and bake for 20 minutes, or until golden.

# Pasta & Anchovy Sauce

This is an ideal dish for cooks in a hurry, as it is prepared in minutes from store-cupboard ingredients.

## NUTRITIONAL INFORMATION

| | | | |
|---|---|---|---|
| Calories | .......712 | Sugars | .........4g |
| Protein | ........25g | Fat | ..........34g |
| Carbohydrate | ...81g | Saturates | .......8g |

 10 MINS   25 MINS

### SERVES 4

## INGREDIENTS

⅓ cup olive oil

2 garlic cloves, crushed

2 oz/60 g canned anchovy fillets, drained

1 lb/450 g dried spaghetti

2 oz/60 g Pesto Sauce (see page 39)

2 tbsp finely chopped fresh oregano

1 cup grated Parmesan cheese, plus extra
   for serving (optional)

salt and pepper

2 fresh oregano sprigs, to garnish

1 Reserve 1 tablespoon of the oil and heat the remainder in a small pan. Add the garlic and fry for 3 minutes.

2 Lower the heat, stir in the anchovies and cook, stirring occasionally, until the anchovies have disintegrated.

3 Bring a large pan of lightly salted water to a boil. Add the spaghetti and the remaining olive oil and cook for 8–10 minutes or until just tender but still firm to the bite.

4 Add the Pesto Sauce (see page 39) and chopped fresh oregano to the anchovy mixture and then season with pepper to taste.

5 Drain the spaghetti, using a slotted spoon, and transfer to a warm serving dish. Pour the Pesto Sauce over the spaghetti and then sprinkle over the grated Parmesan cheese.

6 Garnish with oregano sprigs and serve with extra cheese, if using.

## COOK'S TIP

If you find canned anchovies rather too salty, soak them in a saucer of cold milk for 5 minutes, then drain and pat dry with paper towels before using. The milk absorbs the salt.

# Potatoes, Olives & Anchovies

This side dish makes a delicious accompaniment for broiled fish or for lamb chops. The fennel adds a subtle anise flavor.

## NUTRITIONAL INFORMATION

| | | |
|---|---|---|
| Calories .......202 | Sugars .........2g |
| Protein .........7g | Fat ..........12g |
| Carbohydrate ...19g | Saturates .......1g |

 10 MINS    30 MINS

### SERVES 4

## I N G R E D I E N T S

1 lb/450 g baby new potatoes, scrubbed

scant ½ cup mixed olives

8 canned anchovy fillets, drained and
    chopped

2 tbsp olive oil

2 fennel bulbs, trimmed and sliced

2 sprigs rosemary, stems removed

1 Bring a large pan of water to a boil and cook the potatoes for 8–10 minutes, or until tender. Remove the potatoes from the pan using a perforated spoon and set aside to cool slightly.

2 Once the potatoes are just cool enough to handle, cut them into wedges, using a sharp knife.

## COOK'S TIP

Fresh rosemary is a particular favorite with Italians, but you can experiment with your favorite herbs in this recipe, if you prefer.

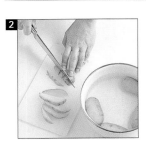

3 Pit the mixed olives and cut them in half, using a sharp knife.

4 Using a sharp knife, chop the anchovy fillets into smaller strips.

5 Heat the oil in a large skillet. Add the potato wedges, sliced fennel, and rosemary. Cook for 7–8 minutes, or until the potatoes are golden.

6 Stir in the olives and anchovies and cook for 1 minute, or until completely warmed through.

7 Transfer to serving plates and serve immediately.

# Mozzarella Snack

These deep-fried mozzarella sandwiches are a tasty snack at any time of the day. Serve smaller triangles as an antipasto with drinks.

## NUTRITIONAL INFORMATION

Calories .......379  Sugars .........4g
Protein ........20g  Fat ..........22g
Carbohydrate ...28g  Saturates .......5g

 20 MINS     5–10 MINS

### SERVES 4

## INGREDIENTS

8 slices bread, preferably slightly stale, crusts removed

1 cup thickly sliced mozzarella cheese

½ cup chopped black olives

8 canned anchovy fillets, drained and chopped

16 fresh basil leaves

4 eggs, beaten

⅔ cup milk

oil, for deep-frying

salt and pepper

1 Cut each slice of bread into 2 triangles. Top 8 of the bread triangles with the mozzarella slices, olives, and chopped anchovies.

2 Place the basil leaves on top and season with salt and pepper to taste.

3 Lay the other 8 triangles of bread over the top and press down round the edges to seal.

4 Mix the eggs and milk and pour into an ovenproof dish. Add the sandwiches and leave to soak for about 5 minutes.

5 Heat the oil in a large pan to 350°–375°F/180°–190°C, or until a cube of bread browns in 30 seconds.

6 Before cooking the sandwiches, squeeze the edges together again.

7 Carefully place the sandwiches in the oil and deep-fry for 2 minutes, or until golden, turning once. Remove the sandwiches with a perforated spoon and drain on absorbent paper towels. Serve immediately while still hot.

# Spinach & Anchovy Pasta

This colorful light meal can be made with a variety of different pasta, including spaghetti and linguine.

## NUTRITIONAL INFORMATION

| Calories | . . . . . . . .619 | Sugars | . . . . . . . . .5g |
| Protein | . . . . . . . .21g | Fat | . . . . . . . . . .31g |
| Carbohydrate | . . .67g | Saturates | . . . . . . .3g |

 10 MINS   25 MINS

### SERVES 4

## I N G R E D I E N T S

2 lb/900 g fresh, young spinach leaves

14 oz/400 g dried fettuccine

6 tbsp olive oil

3 tbsp pine nuts

3 garlic cloves, crushed

8 canned anchovy fillets, drained and
   chopped

salt

1 Trim off any tough spinach stems. Rinse the spinach leaves and place them in a large pan with only the water that is clinging to them after washing. Cover and cook over a high heat, shaking the pan from time, until the spinach has wilted, but retains its color. Drain well, set aside and keep warm.

**COOK'S TIP**

If you are in a hurry, you can use frozen spinach. Thaw and drain it thoroughly, pressing out as much moisture as possible. Cut the leaves into strips and add to the dish with the anchovies in step 4.

2 Bring a large pan of lightly salted water to a boil. Add the fettuccine and 1 tablespoon of the oil and cook for 8–10 minutes until it is just tender but still firm to the bite.

3 Heat 4 tablespoons of the remaining oil in a pan. Add the pine nuts and cook until golden. Remove the pine nuts from the pan and set aside until required.

4 Add the garlic to the pan and cook until golden. Add the anchovies and stir in the spinach. Cook, stirring, for 2-3 minutes, or until heated through. Return the pine nuts to the pan.

5 Drain the fettuccine and toss in the remaining olive oil, then transfer to a warm serving dish. Spoon the anchovy and spinach sauce over the fettuccine and toss lightly. Serve immediately.

# Ciabatta Rolls

Sandwiches are always a welcome snack, but can be mundane. These crisp rolls filled with broiled bell peppers and cheese are irresistible.

## NUTRITIONAL INFORMATION

| | | | |
|---|---|---|---|
| Calories | .......328 | Sugars | .........6g |
| Protein | .........8g | Fat | ..........19g |
| Carbohydrate | ...34g | Saturates | .......9g |

15 MINS     10 MINS

## SERVES 4

## I N G R E D I E N T S

4 ciabatta rolls

2 tbsp olive oil

1 garlic clove, crushed

### F I L L I N G

1 red bell pepper

1 green bell pepper

1 yellow bell pepper

4 radishes, sliced

1 bunch watercress or arugula

scant ½ cup cream cheese

1 Slice the ciabatta rolls in half. Heat the olive oil and crushed garlic in a pan. Pour the garlic and oil mixture over the cut surfaces of the rolls and leave to stand.

2 Halve the bell peppers and place, skin side uppermost, on a broiler rack. Cook under a hot broiler for 8–10 minutes, or until just beginning to char. Remove the bell peppers from the broiler, then peel and slice thinly.

3 Arrange the radish slices on one half of each roll with a few watercress or arugula leaves. Spoon the cream cheese on top. Pile the bell peppers on top of the cream cheese and top with the other half of the roll. Serve immediately.

# Baked Eggplants

This delicious recipe is from Parma. Ensure that you simmer the tomato sauce gently to reduce it slightly before using.

## NUTRITIONAL INFORMATION

| | | | |
|---|---|---|---|
| Calories | .......578 | Sugars | ........22g |
| Protein | ........17g | Fat | ..........43g |
| Carbohydrate | ...25g | Saturates | ......13g |

🍳 15 MINS     🕐 1¼ HOURS

SERVES 4

## I N G R E D I E N T S

4 eggplants, trimmed

3 tbsp olive oil

10½ oz/300 g mozzarella, thinly sliced

4 slices prosciutto, shredded

1 tbsp chopped fresh marjoram

1 tbsp chopped fresh basil

½ quantity Béchamel Sauce (see page 28)

¼ cup freshly grated Parmesan

salt and pepper

### TOMATO SAUCE

4 tbsp olive oil

1 large onion, sliced

4 garlic cloves, crushed

14 oz/400 g canned chopped tomatoes

1 lb/450 g fresh tomatoes, peeled and chopped

4 tbsp chopped fresh parsley

2½ cups hot vegetable stock

1 tbsp sugar

2 tbsp lemon juice

⅔ cup dry white wine

salt and pepper

1 To make the Tomato Sauce, heat the oil in a large pan. Cook the onion and garlic until beginning to soften. Add the canned and fresh tomatoes, parsley, stock, sugar, and lemon juice. Cover and simmer for 15 minutes. Stir in the wine and season.

2 Slice the eggplant thinly lengthwise. Bring a large pan of water to a boil and cook the eggplant slices for 5 minutes. Drain the eggplant slices on paper towels and pat dry.

3 Pour half of the fresh tomato sauce into a large, greased ovenproof dish. Cover with half of the cooked eggplants and drizzle with a little oil. Cover with half of the mozzarella, prosciutto, and herbs. Season with salt and pepper to taste.

4 Repeat the layers and cover with the Béchamel Sauce. Sprinkle with the Parmesan. Bake in a preheated oven, 375°F/190°C, for 35–40 minutes, or until golden on top. Serve.

# Chorizo & Mushroom Pasta

Simple and quick to make, this spicy dish is sure to set the taste buds tingling.

## NUTRITIONAL INFORMATION

| | | | |
|---|---|---|---|
| Calories | .......495 | Sugars | .........1g |
| Protein | ........15g | Fat | ..........35g |
| Carbohydrate | ...33g | Saturates | .......5g |

5 MINS     20 MINS

### SERVES 6

## I N G R E D I E N T S

1 lb 8 oz/680 g dried vermicelli

½ cup olive oil

2 garlic cloves

4½ oz/125 g chorizo, sliced

8 oz/225 g exotic mushrooms

3 fresh red chiles, chopped

2 tbsp freshly grated Parmesan cheese

salt and pepper

10 anchovy fillets, to garnish

1 Bring a large pan of lightly salted water to a boil. Add the vermicelli and 1 tablespoon of the oil and cook for 8–10 minutes, or until just tender but still firm to the bite.

2 Drain the pasta thoroughly, then place on a large, warm serving plate and keep warm.

3 Meanwhile, heat the remaining oil in a large skillet. Add the garlic and cook for 1 minute.

4 Add the chorizo and exotic mushrooms and cook for 4 minutes.

5 Add the chopped chiles and cook for an additional 1 minute.

6 Pour the chorizo and exotic mushroom mixture over the vermicelli and season with a little salt and pepper.

7 Sprinkle with freshly grated Parmesan cheese and garnish with a lattice of anchovy fillets. Serve immediately.

### COOK'S TIP

Many varieties of mushrooms are now cultivated and most are indistinguishable from the wild varieties. Mixed color oyster mushrooms have been used here, but you could also use chanterelles. Remember that chanterelles shrink during cooking, so you may need more.

# Pan Bagna

This is a deliciously moist picnic dish, lunch dish, or snack.
It was originally designed for workers to take to the fields in a box.

## NUTRITIONAL INFORMATION

| | | |
|---|---|---|
| Calories .......377 | Sugars .........3g | |
| Protein ........20g | Fat ..........25g | |
| Carbohydrate ...19g | Saturates .......6g | |

2½ HOURS    30 MINS

### SERVES 4

## INGREDIENTS

1 red bell pepper, halved, cored, and seeded

8 oz/225 g sirloin steak, 1 inch/2.5 cm thick

1 small white bloomer loaf or French stick

4 tbsp olive oil

2 extra-large tomatoes, sliced

10 black olives, halved

½ cucumber, peeled and sliced

6 anchovies, chopped

salt and pepper

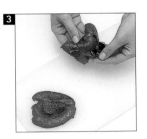
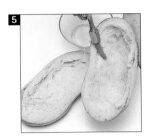

1 Cook the bell pepper over a hot grill for 15 minutes, turning once. Put the bell pepper into a plastic bag and seal.

2 Meanwhile, sear both sides of the steak first and then broil for 8 minutes, turning once.

3 When the bell pepper is cool enough to handle, peel and slice it.

4 Using a sharp knife, cut the steak into thin strips.

5 Cut the loaf of bread lengthwise and hollow out each half, leaving a 1-inch/2.5-cm crust. Brush both halves very liberally with olive oil.

6 Lay the tomatoes, olives, cucumber, steak strips, anchovies, and red bell pepper strips on the bottom half. Season with salt and pepper to taste and cover with the top half.

7 Put the Pan Bagna on top of a piece of waxed paper. Squash the whole loaf and its filling down well and wrap tightly in plastic wrap. Secure with adhesive tape if necessary. Chill for at least 2 hours. If made in the morning, it will be ready to eat by lunchtime and all the flavors will have combined.

## VARIATION

Different fillings, such as pâtés, sausages, and other salad items, can be used according to appetite and taste. Mozzarella cheese is good, as it is so moist. Onions give a bit of a zing to the other ingredients.

# Pasta with Bacon & Tomatoes

As this dish cooks, the mouth-watering aroma of bacon, sweet tomatoes, and oregano is a feast in itself.

## NUTRITIONAL INFORMATION

Calories . . . . . . . .431   Sugars . . . . . . . . .8g
Protein . . . . . . . .10g   Fat . . . . . . . . . .29g
Carbohydrate . . .34g   Saturates . . . . . .14g

 10 MINS   35 MINS

### SERVES 4

## INGREDIENTS

2 lb/900 g small, sweet tomatoes

6 slices rindless smoked bacon

4 tbsp butter

1 onion, chopped

1 garlic clove, crushed

4 fresh oregano sprigs, finely chopped

4 cups dried orecchiette

1 tbsp olive oil

salt and pepper

freshly grated Romano cheese, to serve

1 Blanch the tomatoes in boiling water. Drain, skin, and seed the tomatoes, then coarsely chop the flesh.

2 Using a sharp knife, chop the bacon into small dice.

3 Melt the butter in a skillet. Add the bacon and cook until it is golden.

4 Add the onion and garlic and cook over medium heat for 5-7 minutes, or until just softened.

5 Add the tomatoes and oregano to the pan and then season to taste with salt and pepper. Lower the heat and simmer for 10-12 minutes.

6 Bring a large pan of lightly salted water to a boil. Add the orecchiette and oil and cook for 12 minutes, or until just tender but still firm to the bite. Drain the pasta and transfer to a warm serving dish or bowl.

7 Spoon the bacon and tomato sauce over the pasta, toss to coat and serve with the cheese.

## COOK'S TIP

For an authentic Italian flavor use pancetta, rather than ordinary bacon. This kind of bacon is streaked with fat and adds rich undertones of flavor to many traditional dishes. It is available both smoked and unsmoked from large supermarkets and Italian delicatessens.

# Mozzarella & Ham Snack

A delicious way of serving mozzarella—the cheese stretches out into melted strings as you cut into the bread.

## NUTRITIONAL INFORMATION

| Calories | . . . . . . . .461 | Sugars | . . . . . . . .10g |
| Protein | . . . . . . . .19g | Fat | . . . . . . . . . .2.8g |
| Carbohydrate | . . .37g | Saturates | . . . . . . .7g |

15 MINS     40 MINS

### SERVES 4

## I N G R E D I E N T S

7 oz/200 g mozzarella

4 slices prosciutto, about 3 oz/85 g

butter, for spreading

8 two-day old slices white bread,
   crusts removed

2–3 eggs

3 tbsp milk

vegetable oil, for deep-frying

salt and pepper

### T O M A T O  &  B E L L   P E P P E R   S A U C E

1 onion, chopped

2 garlic cloves, crushed

3 tbsp olive oil

1 red bell pepper, cored, seeded,
   and chopped

14 oz/400 g canned peeled tomatoes

2 tbsp tomato paste

3 tbsp water

1 tbsp lemon juice

salt and pepper

flat-leaf parsley, to garnish (optional)

1 To make the sauce, cook the onion and garlic in the oil until soft. Add the bell pepper and continue to cook for a few minutes. Add the tomatoes, tomato paste, water, lemon juice, and seasoning. Bring to a boil, then cover and simmer for 10–15 minutes, or until tender. Cool the sauce a little, then purée or blend until smooth and return to a clean pan.

2 Cut the mozzarella into 4 slices as large as possible; if the cheese is a square piece cut into 8 slices. Trim the prosciutto slices to the same size as the cheese.

3 Lightly butter the bread and use the cheese and ham to make 4 sandwiches, pressing the edges firmly together. If liked, they may be cut in half at this stage. Cover with plastic wrap and chill.

4 Lightly beat the eggs with the milk and seasoning in a shallow dish. Dip the sandwiches in the egg mixture until well coated, and leave to soak for a few minutes.

5 Heat the oil to 350°–375°F/180°–190°C, or until a cube of bread browns in 30 seconds. Fry the sandwiches in batches until golden on both sides. Drain and keep warm. Serve with the reheated tomato and bell pepper sauce, and garnish with parsley.

# Smoked Ham Linguine

Served with freshly made Italian bread or tossed with pesto, this makes a mouth-watering light lunch.

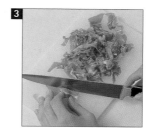

## NUTRITIONAL INFORMATION

| | |
|---|---|
| Calories .......537 | Sugars .........4g |
| Protein ........22g | Fat ..........29g |
| Carbohydrate ....71g | Saturates .......8g |

 25 MINS  15 MINS

### SERVES 4

## INGREDIENTS

1 lb/450 g dried linguine

1 lb/450 g green broccoli florets

8 oz/225 g Italian smoked ham

⅔ cup Italian Cheese Sauce (see page 30)

salt and pepper

Italian bread, such as ciabatta or focaccia,
   to serve

1 Bring a large pan pan of lightly salted water to a boil. Add the linguine and broccoli florets and cook for about 10 minutes, or until the linguine is tender but still firm to the bite.

2 Drain the linguine and broccoli thoroughly, set aside and keep warm until required.

3 Cut the Italian smoked ham into thin strips.

4 Toss the linguine, broccoli and ham into the Italian Cheese Sauce and gently warm through over very low heat.

5 Transfer the pasta mixture to a warm serving dish. Sprinkle with pepper and serve with Italian bread.

### COOK'S TIP

There are many types of Italian bread that would be suitable to serve with this dish. Ciabatta is made with olive oil and is available plain and with different ingredients, such as olives or sun-dried tomatoes.

# Fish & Seafood

Italians eat everything that comes out of the sea, from the smallest whitebait to the massive tuna fish. Fish markets in Italy are fascinating, with a huge variety of fish on

display, but as most of the fish comes from the Mediterranean it is not always easy to find an equivalent elsewhere. However, fresh or frozen imported fish of all kinds is increasingly appearing in fishmongers and supermarkets. After pasta, fish is probably the most important source of food in Italy, and in many recipes fish or seafood are served with one type of pasta or another—a winning combination!

# Orange Mackerel

Mackerel can be quite rich, but when it is stuffed with oranges and toasted ground almonds it is tangy and light.

## NUTRITIONAL INFORMATION

| | | | |
|---|---|---|---|
| Calories | .......623 | Sugars | .........7g |
| Protein | ........42g | Fat | ..........47g |
| Carbohydrate | ....8g | Saturates | .......8g |

🥘 🥘 🥘

15 MINS     35 MINS

### SERVES 4

## INGREDIENTS

2 tbsp oil

4 scallions, chopped

2 oranges

generous ½ cup ground almonds

1 tbsp oats

scant ½ cup chopped mixed green
    and black olives, pitted

8 mackerel fillets

salt and pepper

crisp salad, to serve

1 Heat the oil in a skillet. Add the scallions and cook for 2 minutes.

2 Finely grate the rind of the oranges, then, using a sharp knife, cut away the remaining skin and white pith.

3 Using a sharp knife, segment the oranges by cutting down either side of the lines of pith to loosen each segment. Do this over a plate so that you can reserve any juices. Cut each orange segment in half.

4 Lightly toast the almonds, under a preheated broiler, for 2–3 minutes, or until golden; watch them carefully as they brown very quickly.

5 Mix the scallions, oranges, ground almonds, oats, and olives together in a bowl and season to taste with salt and pepper.

6 Spoon the orange mixture along the center of each fillet. Roll up each fillet, securing it in place with a toothpick or skewer.

7 Bake in a preheated oven at 375°F/190°C, for 25 minutes, or until the fish is tender.

8 Transfer to serving plates and serve warm with a salad.

# Marinated Fish

Marinating fish, for even a short period, adds a subtle flavor to the flesh and makes even simply broiled or fried fish delicious.

## NUTRITIONAL INFORMATION

Calories . . . . . . . .361    Sugars . . . . . . . . .0g
Protein . . . . . . . .26g    Fat . . . . . . . . . .29g
Carbohydrate . . . .0g    Saturates . . . . . . .5g

45 MINS        15 MINS

### SERVES 4

## INGREDIENTS

4 whole mackerel

4 tbsp chopped marjoram

2 tbsp extra virgin olive oil

finely grated rind and juice of 1 lime

2 garlic cloves, crushed

salt and pepper

1 Under gently running water, scrape the mackerel with the blunt side of a knife to remove any scales.

2 Using a sharp knife, make a slit in the stomach of the fish and cut horizontally along until the knife will go no further very easily. Gut the fish and rinse under water. You may prefer to remove the heads before cooking, but it is not necessary.

3 Using a sharp knife, cut 4–5 diagonal slashes on each side of the fish. Place the fish in a shallow, nonmetallic dish.

4 To make the marinade, mix together the marjoram, olive oil, lime rind and juice, garlic, and salt and pepper in a bowl.

5 Pour the mixture over the fish. Leave to marinate in the refrigerator for about 30 minutes.

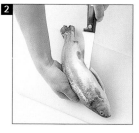  

6 Cook the mackerel, under a preheated broiler, for 5–6 minutes on each side, brushing occasionally with the reserved marinade, until golden.

7 Transfer the fish to serving plates. Pour over any remaining marinade before serving.

## COOK'S TIP

If the lime is too hard to squeeze, microwave on high power for 30 seconds to release the juice. This dish is also excellent cooked on the grill.

# Salt Cod Fritters

These tasty little fried fish cakes make an excellent snack or entrée. Prepare in advance as the salt cod needs to be soaked overnight.

## NUTRITIONAL INFORMATION

| | | | |
|---|---|---|---|
| Calories | .......142 | Sugars | .........2g |
| Protein | ........10g | Fat | ...........5g |
| Carbohydrate | ...14g | Saturates | .......1g |

  30 MINS    45 MINS

### SERVES 6

### INGREDIENTS

⅔ cup self-rising flour

1 egg, beaten

⅔ cup milk

9 oz/250 g salt cod, soaked overnight

1 small red onion, finely chopped

1 small fennel bulb, finely chopped

1 red chile, finely chopped

2 tbsp oil

### TO SERVE

crisp salad and chile relish, or cooked rice
and fresh vegetables

1 Sift the flour into a large bowl. Make a well in the center of the flour and add the egg.

2 Using a wooden spoon, gradually draw in the flour, slowly adding the milk, and mix to form a smooth batter. Leave to stand for 10 minutes.

3 Drain the salt cod and rinse it under cold running water. Drain again thoroughly.

4 Remove and discard the skin and any bones from the fish, then mash the flesh with a fork.

5 Place the fish in a large bowl and combine with the onion, fennel, and chile. Add the mixture to the batter and blend together.

6 Heat the oil in a large skillet and, taking about 1 tablespoon of the mixture at a time, spoon it into the hot oil. Cook the fritters, in batches, for 3–4 minutes on each side, or until golden and slightly puffed. Keep warm while cooking the remaining mixture.

7 Serve with salad and a chile relish for a light meal or with vegetables and rice.

## COOK'S TIP

If you prefer larger fritters, use 2 tablespoons per fritter and cook for slightly longer.

# Celery & Salt Cod Casserole

Salt cod has been dried and salted in order to preserve it. It has an unusual flavor, which goes particularly well with celery in this dish.

## NUTRITIONAL INFORMATION

Calories . . . . . . .173   Sugars . . . . . . . . .3g
Protein . . . . . . . .14g   Fat . . . . . . . . . .12g
Carbohydrate . . . .3g   Saturates . . . . . . .1g

25 MINS          25 MINS

### SERVES 4

## I N G R E D I E N T S

9 oz/250 g salt cod, soaked overnight

1 tbsp oil

4 shallots, finely chopped

2 garlic cloves, chopped

3 celery stalks, chopped

14 oz/400 g canned tomatoes, chopped

⅔ cup fish stock

⅓ cup pine nuts

2 tbsp roughly chopped tarragon

2 tbsp capers

crusty bread or mashed potato, to serve

1 Drain the salt cod, then rinse it under plenty of running water and drain again thoroughly. Remove and discard any skin and bones. Pat the fish dry with paper towels and cut it into chunks.

2 Heat the oil in a large skillet. Add the shallots and garlic and cook for 2–3 minutes. Add the celery and cook for an additional 2 minutes, then add the tomatoes and stock.

3 Bring the mixture to a boil, then reduce the heat and leave to simmer for about 5 minutes.

4 Add the fish and cook for 10 minutes, or until tender.

5 Meanwhile, place the pine nuts on a cookie sheet. Place under a preheated broiler and toast for 2–3 minutes. or until golden.

6 Stir the tarragon, capers, and pine nuts into the fish casserole and heat gently to warm through.

7 Transfer to serving plates and serve with lots of fresh crusty bread or mashed potato.

### COOK'S TIP

Salt cod is a useful ingredient to keep in the pantry and, once soaked, can be used in the same way as any other fish. It does, however, have a stronger, saltier flavor than normal. It can be found in specialty stores, larger supermarkets, and delicatessens.

# Spaghetti alla Bucaniera

In Europe, brill was once known as poor man's turbot, an unfair description as it is a delicately flavored and delicious fish.

## NUTRITIONAL INFORMATION

| | |
|---|---|
| Calories . . . . . . .588 | Sugars . . . . . . . . .5g |
| Protein . . . . . . . .36g | Fat . . . . . . . . . .18g |
| Carbohydrate . . .68g | Saturates . . . . . . .9g |

     25 MINS        50 MINS

### SERVES 4

## INGREDIENTS

¾ cup all-purpose flour

1 lb/450 g brill or sole fillets,
    skinned and chopped

1 lb/450 g hake fillets,
    skinned and chopped

6 tbsp butter

4 shallots, finely chopped

2 garlic cloves, crushed

1 carrot, diced

1 leek, finely chopped

1¼ cups hard cider

1¼ cups medium sweet cider

2 tsp anchovy extract

1 tbsp tarragon vinegar

1 lb/450 g dried spaghetti

1 tbsp olive oil

salt and pepper

chopped fresh parsley, to garnish

crusty brown bread, to serve

1 Season the flour with salt and pepper. Sprinkle ¼ cup of the seasoned flour onto a shallow plate. Press the fish pieces into the seasoned flour to coat thoroughly.

2 Melt the butter in a flameproof casserole. Add the fish fillets, shallots, garlic, carrot, and leek and cook over low heat, stirring frequently, for about 10 minutes.

3 Sprinkle over the remaining seasoned flour and cook, stirring constantly, for 2 minutes. Gradually stir in the cider, anchovy extract and tarragon vinegar. Bring to a boil and simmer over low heat for 35 minutes. Alternatively, bake in a preheated oven at 350°F/180°C for 30 minutes.

4 About 15 minutes before the end of the cooking time, bring a large pan of lightly salted water to a boil. Add the spaghetti and olive oil and cook for 12 minutes, or until tender but still firm to the bite. Drain the pasta thoroughly and transfer to a large serving dish.

5 Arrange the fish on top of the spaghetti and pour over the sauce. Garnish with chopped parsley and serve immediately with warm, crusty brown bread.

# Broiled Stuffed Sole

A delicious mixture of sun-dried tomatoes and fresh lemon thyme is used to stuff whole sole.

## NUTRITIONAL INFORMATION

Calories . . . . . . . .207   Sugars . . . . . . . .0.2g
Protein . . . . . . . .24g   Fat . . . . . . . . . .10g
Carbohydrate . . . .8g   Saturates . . . . . . .4g

25 MINS     20 MINS

### SERVES 4

## I N G R E D I E N T S

1 tbsp olive oil

2 tbsp butter

1 small onion, finely chopped

1 garlic clove, chopped

3 sun-dried tomatoes, chopped

2 tbsp lemon thyme

1 cup fresh bread crumbs

1 tbsp lemon juice

4 small whole sole, gutted and cleaned

salt and pepper

lemon wedges, to garnish

fresh green salad greens, to serve

1 Heat the oil and butter in a skillet until it just begins to froth.

2 Add the onion and garlic to the skillet and cook, stirring, for 5 minutes, or until just softened.

3 To make the stuffing, mix the tomatoes, thyme, bread crumbs, and lemon juice in a bowl, and season.

4 Add the stuffing mixture to the pan, and stir to mix.

5 Using a sharp knife, pare the skin from the bone inside the gut hole of the fish to make a pocket. Spoon the tomato and herb stuffing into the pocket.

6 Cook the fish, under a preheated broiler, for 6 minutes on each side, or until golden brown.

7 Transfer the stuffed fish to serving plates and garnish with lemon wedges. Serve immediately with fresh green salad greens.

## COOK'S TIP

Lemon thyme (*Thymus x citriodorus*) has a delicate lemon scent and flavor. Ordinary thyme can be used instead, but mix it with 1 teaspoon of lemon rind to add extra flavor.

# Lemon Sole & Haddock Ravioli

This delicate-tasting dish is surprisingly satisfying for even the hungriest appetites. Prepare the Italian Red Wine Sauce well in advance.

## NUTRITIONAL INFORMATION

| | | |
|---|---|---|
| Calories ........977 | Sugars .........7g | |
| Protein ........67g | Fat ..........40g | |
| Carbohydrate ...93g | Saturates ......17g | |

  9¾ HOURS 🕐 25 MINS

### SERVES 4

## INGREDIENTS

1 lb/450 g lemon sole fillets, skinned

1 lb/450 g haddock fillets, skinned

3 eggs beaten

1 lb/450 g cooked potato gnocchi
(see page 308)

3 cups fresh bread crumbs

¼ cup heavy cream

1 lb/450 g Basic Pasta Dough
(see page 24)

1¼ cups Italian Red Wine Sauce
(see page 29)

½ cup freshly grated Parmesan cheese

salt and pepper

1 Flake the lemon sole and haddock fillets with a fork and transfer the flesh to a large mixing bowl.

2 Mix the eggs, cooked potato gnocchi, bread crumbs, and cream in a bowl until thoroughly combined. Add the fish to the bowl containing the gnocchi and season the mixture with salt and pepper to taste.

3 Roll out the pasta dough on to a lightly floured surface and cut out 3-inch/7.5-cm rounds using a plain cutter.

4 Place a spoonful of the fish stuffing on each round. Dampen the edges slightly and fold the pasta rounds over, pressing together to seal.

5 Bring a large pan of lightly salted water to a boil. Add the ravioli and cook for 15 minutes.

6 Drain the ravioli, using a slotted spoon, and transfer to a large serving dish. Pour over the Italian Red Wine Sauce, then sprinkle over the Parmesan cheese and serve immediately.

## VARIATION

For square ravioli, divide the dough in two. Roll out one half and cover. Roll out the other half, and pipe on the filling at regular intervals, then brush the spaces in between with water or beaten egg. Uncover the first sheet of dough and lift into position with a rolling pin. Press between the filling to seal. Cut with a ravioli cutter or a knife.

# Trout in Red Wine

This recipe from Trentino is best when the fish are freshly caught, but it is a good way to cook any trout, giving it an interesting flavor.

## NUTRITIONAL INFORMATION

Calories ........489   Sugars .......0.6g
Protein ........48g   Fat ..........27g
Carbohydrate ...0.6g   Saturates ......14g

20 MINS     45 MINS

### SERVES 4

## INGREDIENTS

4 fresh trout, about 10½ oz/300 g each

1 cup red or white wine vinegar

1¼ cups red or dry white wine

⅔ cup water

1 carrot, sliced

2–4 bay leaves

thinly pared rind of 1 lemon

1 small onion, sliced very thinly

4 sprigs fresh parsley

4 sprigs fresh thyme

1 tsp black peppercorns

6–8 whole cloves

6 tbsp butter

1 tbsp chopped fresh mixed herbs

salt and pepper

### TO GARNISH

sprigs of herbs

lemon slices

1 Gut the trout but leave their heads on. Dry on paper towels and lay the fish head to tail in a shallow container or baking pan large enough to hold them.

2 Bring the wine vinegar to a boil and pour slowly all over the fish. Leave the fish to marinate in the refrigerator for about 20 minutes.

3 Meanwhile, put the wine, water, carrot, bay leaves, lemon rind, onion, herbs, peppercorns, and cloves into a pan with a good pinch of sea salt and heat gently.

4 Drain the fish thoroughly, discarding the vinegar. Place the fish in a fish kettle or large skillet so they touch. When the wine mixture boils, strain gently over the fish so they are about half covered. Cover the pan and simmer very gently for 15 minutes.

5 Carefully remove the fish from the pan, draining off as much of the liquid as possible, and arrange on a serving dish. Keep warm.

6 Boil the cooking liquid until reduced to about 4–6 tablespoons. Melt the butter in a pan and strain in the cooking liquor. Add the herbs and season to taste, then spoon the sauce over the fish. Garnish and serve.

# Trout with Smoked Bacon

Most trout available nowadays is farmed rainbow trout—
however, if you can, buy wild brown trout for this recipe.

## NUTRITIONAL INFORMATION

| Calories | .......802 | Sugars | .........8g |
|---|---|---|---|
| Protein | ........68g | Fat | ..........36g |
| Carbohydrate | ...54g | Saturates | ......10g |

    35 MINS        25 MINS

### SERVES 4

## I N G R E D I E N T S

butter, for greasing

4 x 9½ oz/275 g trout, gutted and cleaned

12 anchovies in oil, drained and chopped

2 apples, peeled, cored, and sliced

4 fresh mint sprigs

juice of 1 lemon

12 slices rindless smoked fatty bacon

1 lb/450 g dried tagliatelle

1 tbsp olive oil

salt and pepper

### TO GARNISH

2 apples, cored and sliced

4 fresh mint sprigs

1 Grease a deep cookie sheet with butter.

2 Open up the cavities of each trout and rinse with warm salt water.

3 Season each cavity with salt and pepper. Divide the anchovies, sliced apples, and mint sprigs between each of the cavities. Squeeze some of the lemon juice into each cavity.

4 Carefully cover the whole of each trout, except the head and tail, with three slices of smoked bacon in a spiral.

5 Arrange the trout on the cookie sheet with the loose ends of bacon tucked underneath. Season with pepper and bake in a preheated oven at 400°F/200°C for 20 minutes, turning the trout over after 10 minutes.

6 Meanwhile, bring a large pan of lightly salted water to a boil. Add the tagliatelle and olive oil and cook for 12 minutes, or until tender but still firm to the bite. Drain the pasta and transfer to a large, warm serving dish.

7 Remove the trout from the oven and arrange on the tagliatelle. Garnish with sliced apples and fresh mint sprigs and serve immediately.

# Fillets of Red Mullet & Pasta

This simple recipe perfectly complements the sweet flavor and delicate texture of the fish.

## NUTRITIONAL INFORMATION

| | | |
|---|---|---|
| Calories . . . . . . . .457 | Sugars . . . . . . . . .3g | |
| Protein . . . . . . . .39g | Fat . . . . . . . . . .12g | |
| Carbohydrate . . .44g | Saturates . . . . . . .5g | |

15 MINS     1 HOUR

### SERVES 4

## I N G R E D I E N T S

2 lb 4 oz/1 kg red mullet fillets

1¼ cups dry white wine

4 shallots, finely chopped

1 garlic clove, crushed

3 tbsp finely chopped mixed fresh herbs

finely grated rind and juice of 1 lemon

pinch of freshly grated nutmeg

3 anchovy fillets, roughly chopped

2 tbsp heavy cream

1 tsp cornstarch

1 lb/450 g dried vermicelli

1 tbsp olive oil

salt and pepper

### T O   G A R N I S H

1 fresh mint sprig

lemon slices

lemon rind

1 Put the red mullet fillets in a large casserole. Pour over the wine and add the shallots, garlic, herbs, lemon rind and juice, nutmeg and anchovies. Season. Cover and bake in a preheated oven at 350°F/180°C for 35 minutes.

2 Transfer the mullet to a warm dish. Set aside and keep warm.

3 Pour the cooking liquid into a pan and bring to a boil. Simmer for 25 minutes, or until reduced by half. Mix the cream and cornstarch and stir into the sauce to thicken.

4 Meanwhile, bring a pan of lightly salted water to a boil. Add the vermicelli and oil and cook for 8–10 minutes, or until tender but still firm to the bite. Drain the pasta and transfer to a warm serving dish.

5 Arrange the red mullet fillets on top of the vermicelli and pour over the sauce. Garnish with a fresh mint sprig, slices of lemon, and strips of lemon rind. Serve immediately.

# Italian Cod

Cod roasted with herbs and topped with a lemon and rosemary crust is a delicious main course.

## NUTRITIONAL INFORMATION

| | | | |
|---|---|---|---|
| Calories . . . . . . . .313 | Sugars . . . . . . .0.4g |
| Protein . . . . . . . .29g | Fat . . . . . . . . . .20g |
| Carbohydrate . . . .6g | Saturates . . . . . . .5g |

10 MINS     35 MINS

### SERVES 4

## INGREDIENTS

2 tbsp butter

1 cup fresh whole-wheat bread crumbs

scant ¼ cup chopped walnuts

grated rind and juice of 2 lemons

2 sprigs rosemary, stems removed

2 tbsp chopped parsley

4 cod fillets, each about 5½ oz/150 g

1 garlic clove, crushed

1 small red chile, diced

3 tbsp walnut oil

salad greens, to serve

## VARIATION

If preferred, the walnuts may be omitted from the crust. In addition, extra virgin olive oil can be used instead of walnut oil, if you prefer.

1 Melt the butter in a large pan, stirring.

2 Remove the pan from the heat and add the bread crumbs, walnuts, the rind and juice of 1 lemon, half of the rosemary, and half of the parsley.

3 Press the bread crumb mixture over the top of the cod fillets. Place the cod fillets in a shallow, foil-lined roasting tin.

4 Bake in a preheated oven at 400°F/200°C for 25–30 minutes.

5 Mix the garlic, the remaining lemon rind and juice, rosemary, parsley, and chile in a bowl. Beat in the walnut oil and mix to combine. Drizzle the dressing over the cod steaks as soon as they are cooked.

6 Transfer to serving plates and serve immediately.

# Smoked Fish Lasagna

Use smoked cod or haddock in this delicious lasagna.
It's a great way to make a little go a long way.

## NUTRITIONAL INFORMATION

| | | |
|---|---|---|
| Calories .......483 | Sugars .........8g | |
| Protein ........36g | Fat ..........24g | |
| Carbohydrate ...32g | Saturates ......12g | |

 20 MINS     1¼ HOURS

### SERVES 4

## I N G R E D I E N T S

2 tsp olive or vegetable oil

1 garlic clove, crushed

1 small onion, chopped finely

generous 2 cups sliced mushrooms

14 oz/400 g canned chopped tomatoes

1 small zucchini, sliced

⅔ cup vegetable stock or water

2 tbsp butter or margarine

1¼ cups skim milk

scant ¼ cup all-purpose flour

1 cup grated sharp Cheddar cheese

1 tbsp chopped fresh parsley

4½ oz/125 g (6 sheets) precooked lasagna

12 oz/350 g skinned and boned smoked
   cod or haddock, cut into chunks

salt and pepper

fresh parsley sprigs to garnish

1 Heat the oil in a pan and cook the garlic and onion for 5 minutes. Add the mushrooms and cook for 3 minutes, stirring.

2 Add the tomatoes, zucchini, and stock, then simmer, uncovered, for 15–20 minutes, or until the vegetables are soft. Season.

3 Put the butter, milk, and flour into a small pan and heat, whisking constantly, until the sauce boils and thickens. Remove from the heat and add half of the cheese and all of the parsley. Stir gently to melt the cheese and season to taste.

4 Spoon the tomato sauce mixture into a large, shallow ovenproof dish and top with half of the lasagna sheets. Scatter the chunks of fish evenly over the top, then pour over half of the cheese sauce. Top with the remaining lasagna sheets and then spread the rest of the cheese sauce on top. Sprinkle with the remaining cheese.

5 Bake in a preheated oven at 375°F/190°C for 40 minutes, or until the top is golden brown and bubbling. Garnish with parsley sprigs and serve hot.

# Mediterranean Fish Stew

Popular in fishing ports around Europe, gentle stewing is an excellent way to maintain the flavor and succulent texture of fish and shellfish.

## NUTRITIONAL INFORMATION

| | | | |
|---|---|---|---|
| Calories .......533 | Sugars ........11g |
| Protein ........71g | Fat ..........10g |
| Carbohydrate ...30g | Saturates ......2g |

 1¼ HOURS    25 MINS

### SERVES 4

## I N G R E D I E N T S

2 tsp olive oil

2 red onions, sliced

2 garlic cloves, crushed

2 tbsp red wine vinegar

2 tsp superfine sugar

1¼ cups Fresh Fish Stock (see page 30)

1¼ cups dry red wine

1 lb 12 oz/800 g canned chopped tomatoes

8 oz/225 g baby eggplants, cut into fourths

8 oz/225 g yellow zucchini, cut into fourths or sliced

1 green bell pepper, sliced

1 tbsp chopped fresh rosemary

1 lb 2 oz/500 g halibut fillet, skinned and cut into 1-inch/2.5-cm cubes

1 lb 10 oz/750 g fresh mussels, prepared

8 oz/225 g baby squid, cleaned, trimmed, and sliced into rings

8 oz/225 g fresh jumbo shrimp, peeled and deveined

salt and pepper

4 slices toasted French bread rubbed with a cut garlic clove

lemon wedges, to serve

1 Heat the oil in a large nonstick pan and cook the onions and garlic gently for 3 minutes.

2 Stir in the vinegar and sugar and cook for an additional 2 minutes.

3 Stir in the stock, wine, canned tomatoes, eggplants, zucchini, bell pepper, and rosemary. Bring to a boil and simmer, uncovered, for 10 minutes.

4 Add the halibut, mussels, and squid. Mix well and simmer, covered, for 5 minutes until the fish is opaque.

5 Stir in the shrimp and continue to simmer, covered, for an additional 2–3 minutes, or until the shrimp are pink and cooked through.

6 Discard any mussels that haven't opened and season to taste.

7 To serve, put a slice of the prepared garlic bread in the base of each warmed serving bowl and ladle the stew over the top. Serve with lemon wedges.

# Seafood Pizza

Make a change from the standard pizza toppings—this dish is piled high with seafood baked with a red bell pepper and tomato sauce.

## NUTRITIONAL INFORMATION

| | | | |
|---|---|---|---|
| Calories | .......248 | Sugars | .........7g |
| Protein | ........27g | Fat | ...........6g |
| Carbohydrate | ...22g | Saturates | ......2g |

25 MINS     55 MINS

### SERVES 4

## INGREDIENTS

5 oz/140 g standard pizza base mix

4 tbsp chopped fresh dill or 2 tbsp dried dill

fresh dill, to garnish

### SAUCE

1 large red bell pepper

14 oz/400 g canned chopped tomatoes with onion and herbs

3 tbsp tomato paste

salt and pepper

### TOPPING

12 oz/350 g assorted cooked seafood, thawed if frozen

1 tbsp capers in brine, drained

9–10 pitted black olives in brine, drained

¼ cup grated mozzarella cheese

1 tbsp freshly grated Parmesan cheese

1 Preheat the oven to 400°F/200°C. Place the pizza base mix in a bowl and stir in the dill. Make the dough according to the instructions on the package.

2 Press the dough into a round measuring 10 inches/25 cm across on a cookie sheet lined with baking parchment. Set aside to rise.

3 Preheat the broiler to hot. To make the sauce, halve and seed the bell pepper and arrange on a broiler rack. Cook for 8–10 minutes, or until softened and charred. Leave to cool slightly, then peel off the skin and chop the flesh.

4 Place the tomatoes and bell pepper in a pan. Bring to a boil and simmer for 10 minutes. Stir in the tomato paste and season to taste.

5 Spread the sauce over the pizza base and top with the seafood. Sprinkle over the capers and olives, top with the cheeses and bake for 25–30 minutes.

6 Garnish with sprigs of dill and serve piping hot.

# Spaghetti al Tonno

The classic Italian combination of pasta and tuna is enhanced in this recipe with a delicious parsley sauce.

## NUTRITIONAL INFORMATION

| | | | |
|---|---|---|---|
| Calories | .......1065 | Sugars | .........3g |
| Protein | ........27g | Fat | ..........85g |
| Carbohydrate | ...52g | Saturates | ......18g |

🍲 10 MINS   🕐 15 MINS

### SERVES 4

## I N G R E D I E N T S

7 oz/200 g canned tuna, drained

2 oz/55 g canned anchovies, drained

generous 1 cup olive oil

1 cup roughly chopped flat-leaf parsley

²/₃ cup sour cream

1 lb/450 g dried spaghetti

2 tbsp butter

salt and pepper

black olives, to garnish

crusty bread, to serve

1 Remove any bones from the tuna. Put the tuna into a food processor or blender, together with the anchovies, scant 1 cup of the olive oil and the flat-leaf parsley. Process until the sauce is very smooth.

## VARIATION

If liked, you could add 1–2 garlic cloves to the sauce, substitute ½ cup chopped fresh basil for half the parsley and garnish with capers instead of black olives.

2 Spoon the sour cream into the food processor or blender and process again for a few seconds to blend thoroughly. Season with salt and pepper to taste.

3 Bring a large pan of lightly salted water to a boil. Add the spaghetti and the remaining olive oil and cook for 8–10 minutes, or until tender but still firm to the bite.

4 Drain the spaghetti, then return to the pan and place over medium heat. Add the butter and toss well to coat. Spoon in the sauce and quickly toss into the spaghetti, using 2 forks.

5 Remove the pan from the heat and divide the spaghetti between 4 warm individual serving plates. Garnish with the olives and serve immediately with warm, crusty bread.

# Tuna with Roast Bell Peppers

Fresh tuna will be either a small bonito fish or steaks from a skipjack. The more delicately flavored fish have a paler flesh.

## NUTRITIONAL INFORMATION

| | | |
|---|---|---|
| Calories .......428 | Sugars .........5g | |
| Protein ........60g | Fat ..........19g | |
| Carbohydrate ....5g | Saturates .......3g | |

 20 MINS    30 MINS

### SERVES 4

## INGREDIENTS

4 tuna steaks, about 9 oz/250 g each

3 tbsp lemon juice

4 cups water

6 tbsp olive oil

2 orange bell peppers

2 red bell peppers

12 black olives

1 tsp balsamic vinegar

salt and pepper

1 Put the tuna steaks into a bowl with the lemon juice and water. Leave for 15 minutes.

2 Drain and brush the steaks all over with olive oil and season well with salt and pepper.

3 Halve, core, and seed the bell peppers. Put them over a hot grill and cook for 12 minutes, or until they are charred all over. Put them into a plastic bag and seal it. Set aside.

4 Meanwhile, cook the tuna over a hot grill for 12–15 minutes, turning once.

5 When the bell peppers are cool enough to handle, peel them and cut each piece into 4 strips. Toss them with the remaining olive oil, olives, and balsamic vinegar.

6 Serve the tuna steaks piping hot, with the roasted bell pepper salad.

### COOK'S TIP

Red, orange, and yellow bell peppers can also be peeled by cooking them in a hot oven for 30 minutes, turning them frequently, or roasting them straight over a naked gas flame, again turning them frequently. In both methods, seed the bell peppers after peeling.

# Salmon with Caper Sauce

The richness of salmon is beautifully balanced by the tangy capers in this creamy herb sauce.

## NUTRITIONAL INFORMATION

Calories . . . . . . .302   Sugars . . . . . . . . .0g
Protein . . . . . . . .21g   Fat . . . . . . . . . .24g
Carbohydrate . . . .1g   Saturates . . . . . .9g

5 MINS        25 MINS

### SERVES 4

## I N G R E D I E N T S

4 salmon fillets, skinned

1 fresh bay leaf

few black peppercorns

1 tsp white wine vinegar

⅔ cup fish stock

3 tbsp heavy cream

1 tbsp capers

1 tbsp chopped fresh dill

1 tbsp chopped fresh chives

1 tsp cornstarch

2 tbsp skim milk

salt and pepper

new potatoes, to serve

### T O   G A R N I S H

fresh dill sprigs

chive flowers

1 Lay the salmon fillets in a shallow ovenproof dish. Add the bay leaf, peppercorns, vinegar, and stock.

2 Cover with foil and bake in a preheated oven at 350°F/180°C for 15–20 minutes, or until the flesh is opaque and flakes easily when tested with a fork.

3 Transfer the fish to warmed serving plates, then cover and keep warm.

4 Strain the cooking liquid into a pan. Stir in the cream, capers, dill, and chives and seasoning to taste.

5 Blend the cornstarch with the milk. Add to the pan and heat, stirring, until thickened slightly. Boil for 1 minute.

6 Spoon the sauce over the salmon, then garnish with dill sprigs and chive flowers.

7 Serve with new potatoes.

## COOK'S TIP

The cooking time for the salmon will depend on the thickness of the fish: the thin tail end of the salmon takes the least time to cook.

# Baked Red Snapper

You can substitute other whole fish for the snapper,
or use cutlets of cod or halibut.

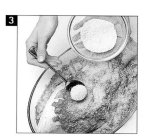

## NUTRITIONAL INFORMATION

| | | | |
|---|---|---|---|
| Calories | .519 | Sugars | .12g |
| Protein | .61g | Fat | .23g |
| Carbohydrate | .18g | Saturates | .3g |

20 MINS        50 MINS

### SERVES 4

## I N G R E D I E N T S

1 red snapper, about 2 lb 12 oz/1.25 kg,
   cleaned

juice of 2 limes, or 1 lemon

4–5 sprigs of thyme or parsley

3 tbsp olive oil

1 large onion, chopped

2 garlic cloves, finely chopped

14 oz/400 g canned chopped tomatoes

2 tbsp tomato paste

2 tbsp red wine vinegar

5 tbsp lowfat yogurt

2 tbsp chopped parsley

2 tsp dried oregano

6 tbsp dry bread crumbs

¼ cup feta cheese, crumbled

salt and pepper

### S A L A D

1 small lettuce, thickly sliced

10–12 young spinach leaves, torn

½ small cucumber, sliced and cut
   into fourths

4 scallions, thickly sliced

3 tbsp chopped parsley

2 tbsp olive oil

2 tbsp plain lowfat yogurt

1 tbsp red wine vinegar

1 Sprinkle the lime or lemon juice inside and over the fish and season. Place the herbs inside the fish.

2 Heat the oil in a pan and cook the onion until translucent. Stir in the garlic and cook for 1 minute, then add the chopped tomatoes, tomato paste, and vinegar. Simmer, uncovered, for 5 minutes. Leave the sauce to cool, then stir in the yogurt, parsley, and oregano.

3 Pour half of the sauce into an ovenproof dish just large enough for the fish. Add the fish and then pour the remainder of the sauce over it, and sprinkle with bread crumbs. Bake uncovered for 30–35 minutes. Sprinkle the cheese over the fish and serve with lime wedges and dill sprigs.

4 Arrange the salad ingredients in a bowl. Whisk the oil, yogurt, and vinegar and pour over the salad.

# Smoky Fish Pie

This flavorsome and colorful fish pie is perfect for a light supper.
The addition of smoked salmon gives it a touch of luxury.

## NUTRITIONAL INFORMATION

Calories . . . . . . .523   Sugars . . . . . . . .15g
Protein . . . . . . . .58g   Fat . . . . . . . . . . .6g
Carbohydrate . . .63g   Saturates . . . . . .2g

15 MINS        1 HOUR

### SERVES 4

## INGREDIENTS

2 lb/900 g smoked haddock or
  cod fillets

2½ cups skim milk

2 bay leaves

4 oz/115 g white mushrooms, cut into
  fourths

1 cup frozen peas

¾ cup frozen corn kernels

1½ lb/675 g potatoes, diced

5 tbsp lowfat plain yogurt

4 tbsp chopped fresh parsley

2 oz/55 g smoked salmon, sliced into
  thin strips

3 tbsp cornstarch

¼ cup grated smoked cheese

salt and pepper

1 Preheat the oven to 400°F/200°C. Place the fish in a pan and add the milk and bay leaves. Bring to a boil, then cover and simmer for 5 minutes.

2 Add the mushrooms, peas, and corn, bring back to a simmer, cover and cook for 5–7 minutes. Leave to cool.

3 Place the potatoes in a pan and cover with water. Bring to a boil and cook for 8 minutes. Drain well and mash with a fork or a potato masher. Stir in the yogurt, parsley, and seasoning. Set aside.

4 Using a slotted spoon, remove the fish from the pan. Flake the cooked fish away from the skin and place in an ovenproof gratin dish. Reserve the cooking liquid.

5 Drain the vegetables, reserving the cooking liquid, and gently stir into the fish with the salmon strips.

6 Blend a little cooking liquid into the cornstarch to make a paste. Transfer the rest of the liquid to a pan and add the paste. Heat through, stirring, until thickened. Discard the bay leaves and season to taste. Pour the sauce over the fish and vegetables and mix. Spoon over the mashed potato so that the fish is covered, then sprinkle with cheese and bake for 25–30 minutes.

## COOK'S TIP

If possible, use smoked haddock or cod that has not been dyed bright yellow or artificially flavored to give the illusion of having been smoked.

# Salmon Fillet with Herbs

This is a great party dish, as the salmon on the barbecue.
The combination of the herbs and the grill gives a great flavor.

## NUTRITIONAL INFORMATION

| | | |
|---|---|---|
| Calories . . . . . . . .507 | Sugars . . . . . . .0.4g |
| Protein . . . . . . . .46g | Fat . . . . . . . . . .35g |
| Carbohydrate . . .0.5g | Saturates . . . . . .6g |

5 MINS    30 MINS

### SERVES 4

### I N G R E D I E N T S

½ large bunch dried thyme

5 fresh rosemary branches, 6–8 inches/
15–20 cm long

8 bay leaves

2 lb 4 oz/1 kg salmon fillet

1 bulb fennel, cut into 8 pieces

2 tbsp lemon juice

2 tbsp olive oil

### T O   S E R V E

crusty bread

green salad

1 Make a base on a hot grill with the dried thyme, rosemary branches, and bay leaves, overlapping them so that they cover a slightly bigger area than the salmon.

2 Carefully place the salmon on top of the herbs.

3 Arrange the fennel around the edge of the fish.

4 Combine the lemon juice and oil and brush the salmon with it.

5 Cover the salmon loosely with a piece of foil, to keep it moist.

6 Cook for about 20–30 minutes, basting frequently with the lemon juice mixture.

7 Remove the salmon from the barbecue, then cut it into slices and serve with the fennel.

8 Serve with slices of crusty bread and a green salad.

### VARIATION

Use whatever combination of herbs you may have to hand—but avoid the stronger tasting herbs, such as sage and marjoram, which are unsuitable for fish.

# Salmon Lasagna Rolls

Sheets of green lasagna are filled with a mixture of fresh salmon and oyster mushrooms. This recipe has been adapted for the microwave.

## NUTRITIONAL INFORMATION

| | | |
|---|---|---|
| Calories | .......352 | Sugars .........5g |
| Protein | ........19g | Fat ..........19g |
| Carbohydrate | ...25g | Saturates .......9g |

20 MINS     35 MINS

**SERVES 4**

## INGREDIENTS

8 sheets green lasagna

1 onion, sliced

1 tbsp butter

½ red bell pepper, chopped

1 zucchini, diced

1 tsp chopped fresh gingerroot

4½ oz/125 g oyster mushrooms, preferably yellow, chopped coarsely

8 oz/225 g fresh salmon fillet, skinned, and cut into chunks

2 tbsp dry sherry

2 tsp cornstarch

3 tbsp all-purpose flour

scant 1 tbsp butter

1¼ cups milk

¼ cup grated Cheddar cheese

¼ cup fresh white bread crumbs

salt and pepper

salad greens, to serve

1 Place the lasagna sheets in a large shallow dish. Cover with plenty of boiling water. Cook on High power for 5 minutes. Leave to stand, covered, for a few minutes before draining. Rinse in cold water and lay the sheets out on a clean counter.

2 Put the onion and butter into a bowl. Cover and cook on High power for 2 minutes. Add the bell pepper, zucchini, and gingerroot. Cover and cook on High power for 3 minutes.

3 Add the mushrooms and salmon to the bowl. Mix the sherry into the cornstarch, then stir into the bowl. Cover and cook on High power for 4 minutes, or until the fish flakes when tested with a fork. Season to taste.

4 Whisk the flour, butter, and milk in a bowl. Cook on High power for 3–4 minutes, whisking every minute, to give a sauce of coating consistency. Stir in half the cheese and season with salt and pepper to taste.

5 Spoon the salmon filling in equal quantities along the shorter side of each lasagna sheet. Roll up to enclose the filling. Arrange in a lightly oiled large rectangular dish. Pour over the sauce and sprinkle over the remaining cheese and the bread crumbs.

6 Cook on High power for 3 minutes, or until heated through. If possible, lightly brown under a preheated broiler before serving. Serve with salad.

# Spaghetti & Smoked Salmon

Made in moments, this is a luxurious dish to astonish and delight unexpected guests.

## NUTRITIONAL INFORMATION

| | | | |
|---|---|---|---|
| Calories | .......803 | Sugars | .........3g |
| Protein | ........21g | Fat | ..........49g |
| Carbohydrate | ...52g | Saturates | ......27g |

10 MINS    20 MINS

### SERVES 4

## I N G R E D I E N T S

1 lb/450 g dried buckwheat spaghetti

2 tbsp olive oil

½ cup crumbled feta cheese

salt

fresh cilantro or parsley leaves, to garnish

### S A U C E

1¼ cups heavy cream

⅔ cup whiskey or brandy

4½ oz/125 g smoked salmon

pinch of cayenne pepper

pepper

2 tbsp chopped fresh cilantro or parsley

1 Bring a large pan of lightly salted water to a boil. Add the spaghetti and 1 tablespoon of the olive oil and cook for 8–10 minutes, or until tender but still firm to the bite. Drain the spaghetti, then return to the pan and sprinkle over the remaining olive oil. Cover and shake the pan, then set aside and keep warm.

2 Pour the cream into a small pan and bring to simmering point, but do not let it boil. Pour the whiskey into another small pan and bring to simmering point, but do not let it boil. Remove both pans from the heat and mix the cream and whisky together.

3 Cut the smoked salmon into thin strips and add to the cream mixture. Season to taste with cayenne and pepper. Just before serving, stir in the fresh cilantro or parsley.

4 Transfer the spaghetti to a warm serving dish, pour over the sauce and toss thoroughly with 2 large forks. Scatter over the crumbled feta cheese, then garnish with the cilantro and serve immediately.

# Squid & Macaroni Stew

This delicious seafood dish is quick and easy to make,
yet delightfully satisfying to eat.

## NUTRITIONAL INFORMATION

| Calories | .......292 | Sugars | ........3g |
| Protein | ........13g | Fat | ..........14g |
| Carbohydrate | ...24g | Saturates | .......2g |

15 MINS       35 MINS

### SERVES 6

## I N G R E D I E N T S

2 cups dried short-cut macaroni or other
  small pasta shapes

7 tbsp olive oil

2 onions, sliced

12 oz/350 g prepared squid, cut into
  1½-inch/4-cm strips

scant 1 cup fish stock

⅔ cup red wine

12 oz/350 g tomatoes, skinned and
  thinly sliced

2 tbsp tomato paste

1 tsp dried oregano

2 bay leaves

2 tbsp chopped fresh parsley

salt and pepper

crusty bread, to serve

## COOK'S TIP

To prepare squid, peel off the
skin, then cut off the head and
tentacles. Discard the transparent
flat oval bone from the body.
Remove the sac of black ink, then
turn the body sac inside out. Wash in
cold water. Cut up the tentacles; slice
the body into rings; discard the rest.

1 Bring a large pan of lightly salted water to a boil. Add the
pasta and 1 tablespoon of the olive oil and cook for
3 minutes. Drain and return to the pan. Cover and keep warm.

2 Heat the remaining oil in a pan over medium heat. Add
the onions and cook until they are translucent. Add the
squid and stock and simmer for 5 minutes. Pour in the wine
and add the tomatoes, tomato paste, oregano, and bay
leaves. Bring the sauce to a boil, then season to taste and
cook for 5 minutes.

3 Stir the pasta into the pan, then cover and simmer for
10 minutes, or until the squid and macaroni are tender
and the sauce has thickened. If the sauce remains too
liquid, uncover the pan and continue cooking for a few
minutes longer.

4 Remove and discard the bay leaves. Reserve a little
parsley and stir the remainder into the pan. Transfer to
a warm serving dish and sprinkle over the remaining
parsley. Serve with crusty bread to soak up the sauce.

# Stuffed Squid

Whole squid are stuffed with a mixture of fresh herbs and sun-dried tomatoes and then cooked in a wine sauce.

## NUTRITIONAL INFORMATION

| | | | |
|---|---|---|---|
| Calories | ......276 | Sugars | .........1g |
| Protein | ........23g | Fat | ...........8g |
| Carbohydrate | ...20g | Saturates | .......1g |

 25 MINS   35 MINS

### SERVES 4

## I N G R E D I E N T S

8 squid, cleaned and gutted but left whole (ask your fishmonger to do this)

6 canned anchovies, chopped

2 garlic cloves, chopped

2 tbsp rosemary, stems removed and leaves chopped

2 sun-dried tomatoes, chopped

3 cups fresh bread crumbs

1 tbsp olive oil

1 onion, finely chopped

generous ¾ cup white wine

generous ¾ cup fish stock

cooked rice, to serve

1 Remove the tentacles from the body of the squid and chop the flesh finely.

2 Grind the anchovies, garlic, rosemary, and tomatoes to a paste in a mortar and pestle.

3 Add the bread crumbs and the chopped squid tentacles and mix. If the mixture is too dry to form a thick paste at this point, add 1 teaspoon of water.

4 Spoon the paste into the body sacs of the squid, then tie a length of cotton around the end of each sac to fasten them. Do not overfill the sacs, because they will expand during cooking.

5 Heat the oil in a skillet. Add the onion and cook, stirring, for 3–4 minutes, or until golden.

6 Add the stuffed squid to the pan and cook for 3–4 minutes, or until brown all over.

7 Add the wine and stock and bring to a boil. Reduce the heat, then cover and leave to simmer for 15 minutes.

8 Remove the lid and cook for an additional 5 minutes, or until the squid is tender and the juices reduced. Serve with plenty of cooked rice.

# Squid Casserole

Squid is often served fried in Italy, but here it is casseroled with tomatoes and bell peppers to give a rich sauce.

## NUTRITIONAL INFORMATION

Calories . . . . . . . .281   Sugars . . . . . . . . .8g
Protein . . . . . . . .31g   Fat . . . . . . . . . .10g
Carbohydrate . . . .9g   Saturates . . . . . . .1g

25 MINS     1½ HOURS

### SERVES 4

## INGREDIENTS

2 lb 4 oz/1 kg whole squid, cleaned or
   1 lb 10 oz/750 g squid rings, defrosted if
   frozen

3 tbsp olive oil

1 large onion, sliced thinly

2 garlic cloves, crushed

1 red bell pepper, cored,
   seeded, and sliced

1–2 sprigs fresh rosemary

⅔ cup dry white wine and 1 cup water,
   or 1½ cups water or fish stock

14 oz/400 g canned chopped tomatoes

2 tbsp tomato paste

1 tsp paprika

salt and pepper

fresh sprigs of rosemary or parsley,
to garnish

1 Cut the squid pouch into ½-inch/1-cm slices; cut the tentacles into lengths of about 2 inches/5 cm. If using frozen squid rings, make sure they are fully defrosted and well drained.

2 Heat the oil in a flameproof casserole and cook the onion and garlic gently until soft. Add the squid, then increase the heat and continue to cook for 10 minutes, or until sealed and beginning to color lightly. Add the red bell pepper, rosemary, and wine and water, then bring up to a boil. Cover and simmer gently for 45 minutes.

3 Discard the sprigs of rosemary (but don't take out any leaves that have come off). Add the tomatoes, tomato paste, seasonings, and paprika. Continue to simmer gently for 45–60 minutes, or cover the casserole tightly and cook in a moderate oven, 350°F/180°C, for 45–60 minutes, or until tender.

# Pasta & Shrimp Pockets

This is the ideal dish when you have unexpected guests because the pockets can be prepared in advance, then put in the oven when you are ready to eat.

## NUTRITIONAL INFORMATION

| | | |
|---|---|---|
| Calories | ....... | 640 | Sugars ......... 1g |
| Protein | ........ | 50g | Fat .......... 29g |
| Carbohydrate | ... | 42g | Saturates ....... 4g |

15 MINS    30 MINS

### SERVES 4

## I N G R E D I E N T S

1 lb/450 g dried fettuccine

⅔ cup Pesto Sauce (see page 39)

4 tsp extra virgin olive oil

1 lb 10 oz/750 g large raw shrimp,

peeled and deveined

2 garlic cloves, crushed

½ cup dry white wine

salt and pepper

1 Cut out 4 x 12-inch/30-cm squares of waxed paper.

2 Bring a large pan of lightly salted water to a boil. Add the fettuccine and cook for 2–3 minutes, or until just softened. Drain and set aside.

3 Mix together the fettuccine and half of the Pesto Sauce. Spread out the paper squares and put 1 teaspoon olive oil in the middle of each. Divide the fettuccine between the the squares, then divide the shrimp and place on top of the fettuccine.

4 Mix together the remaining Pesto Sauce and the garlic and spoon it over the shrimp. Season each parcel with salt and black pepper and sprinkle with the white wine.

5 Dampen the edges of the waxed paper and wrap the parcels loosely, twisting the edges to seal.

6 Place the parcels on a cookie sheet and bake in a preheated oven at 400°F/200°C for 10–15 minutes. Transfer the parcels to 4 individual serving plates and serve.

### COOK'S TIP
Traditionally, these parcels are designed to look like money bags. The resemblance is more effective with waxed paper but foil may be used.

# Pasta Shells with Mussels

Serve this aromatic seafood dish to family and friends
who admit to a love of garlic.

## NUTRITIONAL INFORMATION

| | | | |
|---|---|---|---|
| Calories | .......686 | Sugars | .........2g |
| Protein | ........30g | Fat | .........45g |
| Carbohydrate | ...36g | Saturates | ......27g |

 15 MINS     25 MINS

### SERVES 6

### I N G R E D I E N T S

2 lb 12 oz/1.25 kg mussels

scant 1 cup dry white wine

2 large onions, chopped

½ cup unsalted butter

6 large garlic cloves, finely chopped

5 tbsp chopped fresh parsley

1¼ cups heavy cream

3½ cups dried pasta shells

1 tbsp olive oil

salt and pepper

crusty bread, to serve

1 Scrub and debeard the mussels under cold running water. Discard any mussels that do not close immediately when sharply tapped. Put the mussels into a large pan, together with the wine and half of the onions. Cover and cook over medium heat, shaking the pan frequently, for 2–3 minutes, or until the shells open.

2 Remove the pan from the heat. Drain the mussels and reserve the cooking liquid. Discard any mussels that have not opened. Strain the cooking liquid through a clean cloth into a glass pitcher or bowl and reserve.

3 Melt the butter in a pan over medium heat. Add the remaining onion and cook until translucent. Stir in the garlic and cook for 1 minute. Gradually stir in the reserved cooking liquid. Stir in the parsley and cream and season to taste with salt and pepper. Bring to simmering point over low heat.

4 Meanwhile, bring a large pan of lightly salted water to a boil. Add the pasta and oil and cook for 8–10 minutes, or until just tender but still firm to the bite. Drain the pasta and return to the pan, then cover and keep warm.

5 Reserve a few mussels for the garnish and remove the remainder from their shells. Stir the shelled mussels into the cream sauce and warm briefly.

6 Transfer the pasta to a serving dish. Pour over the sauce and toss to coat. Garnish with the reserved mussels.

# Mussels with Tomato Sauce

This recipe for Mediterranean-style baked mussels, topped with a fresh tomato sauce and bread crumbs, has been adapted for the microwave.

## NUTRITIONAL INFORMATION

| | | | |
|---|---|---|---|
| Calories | .......254 | Sugars | .........1g |
| Protein | ........37g | Fat | ..........10g |
| Carbohydrate | ....4g | Saturates | .......3g |

20 MINS    15 MINS

### SERVES 4

## I N G R E D I E N T S

½ small onion, chopped

1 garlic clove, crushed

1 tbsp olive oil

3 tomatoes

1 tbsp chopped fresh parsley

2 lb/900 g live mussels

1 tbsp freshly grated Parmesan cheese

1 tbsp fresh white bread crumbs

salt and pepper

chopped fresh parsley, to garnish

1 Place the onion, garlic, and oil in a bowl. Cover and cook on High power for 3 minutes.

2 Cut a cross in the base of each tomato and place them in a small bowl. Pour on boiling water and leave for about 45 seconds. Drain and then plunge into cold water. The skins will slide off easily. Chop the tomatoes, removing any hard cores.

3 Add the tomatoes to the onion mixture, then cover and cook on High power for 3 minutes. Stir in the parsley and season to taste.

4 Scrub the mussels well in several changes of cold water. Remove the beards and discard any open mussels and those which do not close when tapped sharply with the back of a knife.

5 Place the mussels in a large bowl. Add enough boiling water to cover them. Cover and cook on High power for 2 minutes, stirring halfway through, until the mussels open. Drain well and remove the empty half of each shell. Arrange the mussels in 1 layer on a plate.

6 Spoon the tomato sauce over each mussel. Mix the Parmesan cheese with the bread crumbs and sprinkle on top.

Cook, uncovered, on High power for 2 minutes. Garnish with parsley and serve.

## COOK'S TIP

Dry out the bread crumbs in the microwave for an extra crunchy topping. Spread them on a plate and cook on High power for 2 minutes, stirring once. Leave to stand, uncovered.

# Vermicelli with Clams

A quickly cooked recipe that transforms pantry ingredients into a dish with style.

## NUTRITIONAL INFORMATION

| | | | |
|---|---|---|---|
| Calories | .......520 | Sugars | .........2g |
| Protein | ........26g | Fat | ..........13g |
| Carbohydrate | ....71g | Saturates | .......4g |

  10 MINS    25 MINS

### SERVES 4

## INGREDIENTS

14 oz/400 g dried vermicelli, spaghetti, or
other long pasta

2 tbsp olive oil

2 tbsp butter

2 onions, chopped

2 garlic cloves, chopped

2 x 7oz/200 g jars clams in brine

½ cup white wine

4 tbsp chopped fresh parsley

½ tsp dried oregano

pinch of freshly grated nutmeg

salt and pepper

### TO GARNISH

2 tbsp Parmesan cheese shavings

fresh basil sprigs

1 Bring a large pan of lightly salted water to a boil. Add the pasta and half of the olive oil and cook for 8–10 minutes, or until tender but still firm to the bite. Drain, then return to the pan and add the butter. Cover the pan and shake well, then keep warm.

2 Heat the remaining oil in a pan over medium heat. Add the onions and cook until they are translucent. Stir in the garlic and cook for 1 minute.

3 Strain the liquid from 1 jar of clams and add the liquid to the pan, with the wine. Stir and bring to simmering point, then simmer for 3 minutes. Drain the second jar of clams and discard the liquid.

4 Add the clams, parsley, and oregano to the pan and season with pepper and nutmeg. Lower the heat and cook until the sauce is heated through.

5 Transfer the pasta to a warm serving dish and pour over the sauce. Sprinkle with the Parmesan cheese, then garnish with the basil and serve immediately.

## COOK'S TIP

There are many different types of clams found along almost every coast in the world. Those traditionally used in this dish are the tiny ones—only 1-2 inches/2.5-5 cm across— known in Italy as vongole.

# Farfallini Buttered Lobster

This is one of those dishes that looks almost too lovely to eat— but you should!

## NUTRITIONAL INFORMATION

| | | | |
|---|---|---|---|
| Calories | .......686 | Sugars | .........1g |
| Protein | ........45g | Fat | ..........36g |
| Carbohydrate | ...44g | Saturates | ......19g |

 30 MINS    25 MINS

### SERVES 4

## I N G R E D I E N T S

1 lb 9 oz/2 x 700 g lobsters, split into halves

juice and grated rind of 1 lemon

½ cup butter

4 tbsp fresh white bread crumbs

2 tbsp brandy

5 tbsp heavy cream or sour cream

1 lb/450 g dried farfallini

1 tbsp olive oil

½ cup freshly grated Parmesan cheese

salt and pepper

### T O   G A R N I S H

1 kiwifruit, sliced

4 unpeeled, cooked jumbo shrimp

fresh dill sprigs

1 Carefully discard the stomach sac, vein, and gills from each lobster. Remove all the meat from the tail and chop. Crack the claws and legs, then remove the meat and chop. Transfer the meat to a bowl and add the lemon juice and grated lemon rind.

2 Clean the shells thoroughly and place in a warm oven at 325°F/170°C to dry out.

3 Melt 2 tbsp of the butter in a skillet. Add the bread crumbs and cook for about 3 minutes, or until crisp and golden brown.

4 Melt the remaining butter in a pan. Add the lobster meat and heat through gently. Add the brandy and cook for an additional 3 minutes, then add the cream and season to taste with salt and pepper.

5 Meanwhile, bring a large pan of lightly salted water to a boil. Add the farfallini and olive oil and cook for 8–10 minutes, or until tender but still firm to the bite. Drain and spoon the pasta into the clean lobster shells.

6 Top with the buttered lobster and sprinkle with a little grated Parmesan cheese and the bread crumbs. Broil for 2–3 minutes, or until golden brown.

7 Transfer the lobster shells to a warm serving dish, garnish with the lemon slices, kiwifruit, jumbo shrimp, and dill sprigs and serve immediately.

# Baked Scallops & Pasta

This is another tempting seafood dish where the eye
is delighted as much as the taste-buds.

## NUTRITIONAL INFORMATION

| | | |
|---|---|---|
| Calories .......725 | Sugars .........2g | |
| Protein ........38g | Fat ..........48g | |
| Carbohydrate ...38g | Saturates ......25g | |

20 MINS     30 MINS

### SERVES 4

## I N G R E D I E N T S

12 scallops

3 tbsp olive oil

3 cups small, dried whole-wheat
   pasta shells

⅔ cup fish stock

juice and finely grated rind of 2 lemons

1 onion, chopped

⅔ cup heavy cream

2 cups grated Cheddar cheese

salt and pepper

crusty brown bread, to serve

1 Remove the scallops from their shells.
Scrape off the skirt and the black
intestinal thread. Reserve the white part
(the flesh) and the orange part (the coral,
or roe). Very carefully ease the flesh and
coral from the shell with a short, but very
strong knife.

2 Wash the shells thoroughly and dry
them well. Put the shells on a cookie
sheet, then sprinkle lightly with two
thirds of the olive oil and set aside.

3 Meanwhile, bring a large pan of
lightly salted water to a boil. Add the
pasta shells and remaining olive oil and
cook for 8–10 minutes, or until tender but
still firm to the bite. Drain well and spoon
about 1 oz/25 g of pasta into each scallop
shell.

4 Put the scallops, fish stock, lemon
rind, and onion in an ovenproof dish
and season to taste with pepper. Cover
with foil and bake in a preheated oven at
350°F/180°C for 8 minutes.

5 Remove the dish from the oven.
Remove the foil and, using a slotted
spoon, transfer the scallops to the shells.

Add 1 tablespoon of the cooking liquid to
each shell, together with a drizzle of
lemon juice and a little cream, and top
with the grated cheese.

6 Increase the oven temperature to
450°F/230°C and return the scallops
to the oven for an additional
4 minutes.

7 Serve the scallops in their shells with
crusty brown bread and butter.

# Seafood Lasagna

You can use any fish and any sauce you like in this recipe:
try smoked finnan haddock and whisky sauce or cod with cheese sauce.

## NUTRITIONAL INFORMATION

Calories . . . . . . .790   Sugars . . . . . . . .23g
Protein . . . . . . . .55g   Fat . . . . . . . . . .32g
Carbohydrate . . .74g   Saturates . . . . . .19g

30 MINS       45 MINS

### SERVES 4

## I N G R E D I E N T S

1 lb/450 g finnan haddock, filleted, skin
   removed, and flesh flaked

4 oz/115 g shrimp

4 oz/115 g sole fillet, skin removed and
   flesh sliced

juice of 1 lemon

4 tbsp butter

3 leeks, very thinly sliced

scant ⅓ cup all-purpose flour

about 2½ cups milk

2 tbsp clear honey

1¾ cups grated mozzarella cheese

1 lb/450 g precooked lasagna

½ cup freshly grated Parmesan cheese

pepper

1 Put the haddock fillet, shrimp, and sole fillet into a large bowl and season with pepper and lemon juice according to taste. Set aside while you make the sauce.

2 Melt the butter in a large pan. Add the leeks and cook, stirring occasionally, for 8 minutes. Add the flour and cook, stirring constantly, for 1 minute. Gradually stir in enough milk to make a thick, creamy sauce.

3 Blend in the honey and mozzarella cheese and cook for an additional 3 minutes. Remove the pan from the heat and mix in the fish and shrimp.

4 Make alternate layers of fish sauce and lasagna in an ovenproof dish, finishing with a layer of fish sauce on top. Generously sprinkle over the grated Parmesan cheese and bake in a preheated oven at 350°F/180°C for 30 minutes. Serve immediately.

## VARIATION

For a cider sauce, substitute 1 finely chopped shallot for the leeks, 1¼ cups cider and 1¼ cups heavy cream for the milk and 1 tsp mustard for the honey. For a Tuscan sauce, substitute 1 chopped fennel bulb for the leeks; omit the honey.

# Meat

Italians have their very own special way of butchering meat, producing very different cuts. Most meat is sold ready-boned and often cut straight across the grain. Veal is a great favorite and widely available. Pork is also popular, with roast pig being the traditional dish of Umbria. Suckling pig is roasted with lots of fresh herbs,

especially rosemary, until the skin is crisp and brown. Lamb is often served for special occasions, cooked on a spit or roasted in the oven with wine, garlic, and herbs; and the very small cutlets from young lambs feature widely, especially in Rome. Variety meats play an important role, too, with liver, brains, sweetbreads, tongue, heart, tripe, and kidneys always available. Whatever your favorite Italian meat dish is, it's sure to be included in this chapter.

# Layered Meat Loaf

The cheese-flavored pasta layer comes as a pleasant surprise inside this lightly spiced meat loaf.

## NUTRITIONAL INFORMATION

| | | | |
|---|---|---|---|
| Calories | .......412 | Sugars | .........3g |
| Protein | .......21g | Fat | ..........30g |
| Carbohydrate | ...15g | Saturates | ......13g |

35 MINS   1¹/₂ HOURS

### SERVES 6

### I N G R E D I E N T S

2 tbsp butter, plus extra for greasing

1 small onion, finely chopped

1 small red bell pepper, cored, seeded, and chopped

1 garlic clove, chopped

1 lb/450 g ground beef

½ cup fresh white bread crumbs

½ tsp cayenne pepper

1 tbsp lemon juice

½ tsp grated lemon rind

2 tbsp chopped fresh parsley

¾ cup dried short pasta, such as fusilli

1 tbsp olive oil

1 cup Italian Cheese Sauce (see page 30)

4 bay leaves

6 oz/175 g fatty bacon, rinds removed

salt and pepper

salad greens, to serve

  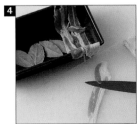

1 Melt the butter in a pan over a medium heat and cook the onion and bell pepper for about 3 minutes. Stir in the garlic and cook for 1 minute.

2 Put the meat into a bowl and mash with a wooden spoon until sticky. Add the onion mixture, bread crumbs, cayenne pepper, lemon juice, lemon rind, and parsley. Season and set aside.

3 Bring a pan of salted water to a boil. Add the pasta and oil and cook for 8–10 minutes, until almost tender. Drain and stir into the Italian Cheese Sauce.

4 Grease a 2 lb 4 oz/1 kg loaf pan and arrange the bay leaves in the base. Stretch the bacon slices with the back of a knife and line the base and sides of the pan with them. Spoon in half the meat mixture and smooth the surface. Cover with the pasta mixed with Italian Cheese Sauce, then spoon in the remaining meat mixture. Level the top and cover with foil.

5 Bake the meat loaf in a preheated oven, at 350°F/180°C, for 1 hour, or until the juices run clear when a skewer is inserted into the center and the loaf has shrunk away from the sides. Pour off any fat and turn out the loaf on to a serving dish. Serve with salad greens.

# Rich Beef Stew

This slow-cooked beef stew is flavored with oranges, red wine, and porcini mushrooms.

## NUTRITIONAL INFORMATION

Calories .......388  Sugars ........15g
Protein ........30g  Fat ..........21g
Carbohydrate ...16g  Saturates .......9g

45 MINS      1³/₄ HOURS

### SERVES 4

## INGREDIENTS

1 tbsp oil

1 tbsp butter

8 oz/225 g pearl onions, peeled and halved

1 lb 5 oz/600 g stewing steak, diced into
    1½-inch/4-cm chunks

1¼ cup beef stock

⅔ cup red wine

4 tbsp chopped oregano

1 tbsp sugar

1 orange

1 oz/25 g porcini or other dried mushrooms

8 oz/225 g fresh plum tomatoes

cooked rice or potatoes, to serve

1 Heat the oil and butter in a large skillet. Add the onions and sauté for 5 minutes or until golden. Remove the onions with a perforated spoon, set aside and keep warm.

2 Add the beef to the pan and cook, stirring, for 5 minutes or until browned all over.

3 Return the onions to the skillet and add the stock, wine, oregano, and sugar, stirring to mix well. Transfer the mixture to an ovenproof casserole dish.

4 Pare the rind from the orange and cut it into strips. Slice the orange flesh into rings. Add the orange rings and the rind to the casserole. Cook in a preheated oven, at 350°F/180°C, for 1¼ hours.

5 Soak the porcini mushrooms for 30 minutes in a small bowl containing 4 tablespoons of warm water.

6 Peel and halve the tomatoes. Add the tomatoes and the porcini mushrooms and their soaking liquid to the casserole. Cook for an additional 20 minutes, or until the beef is tender and the juices thickened. Serve with cooked rice or potatoes.

# Creamed Strips of Sirloin

This quick and easy dish tastes superb and would make a delicious treat for a special occasion.

## NUTRITIONAL INFORMATION

| | | |
|---|---|---|
| Calories .......796 | Sugars .........2g | |
| Protein ........29g | Fat ..........63g | |
| Carbohydrate ...26g | Saturates ......39g | |

🕐 15 MINS        ⏱ 30 MINS

### SERVES 4

## INGREDIENTS

6 tbsp butter

1 lb/450 g sirloin steak, trimmed
   and cut into thin strips

6 oz/175 g white mushrooms, sliced

1 tsp mustard

pinch of grated fresh ginger

2 tbsp dry sherry

⅔ cup heavy cream

salt and pepper

4 slices hot toast, cut into triangles,
   to serve

### PASTA

1 lb/450 g dried rigatoni

2 tbsp olive oil

2 fresh basil sprigs

½ cup butter

1 Melt the butter in a large skillet and gently cook the steak over a low heat, stirring frequently, for 6 minutes. Using a slotted spoon, transfer the steak to an ovenproof dish and keep warm.

2 Add the sliced mushrooms to the skillet and cook for 2–3 minutes in the juices remaining in the pan. Add the mustard, ginger, and salt and pepper. Cook for 2 minutes, then add the sherry and cream. Cook for an additional 3 minutes, then pour the cream sauce over the steak.

3 Bake the steak and cream mixture in a preheated oven, at 375°F/190°C, for 10 minutes.

4 Meanwhile, cook the pasta. Bring a large pan of lightly salted water to a boil. Add the rigatoni, olive oil and 1 of the basil sprigs and boil rapidly for 10 minutes, or until tender but still firm to the bite. Drain the pasta and transfer to a warm serving plate. Toss the pasta with the butter and garnish with a sprig of basil.

5 Serve the creamed steak strips with the pasta and triangles of warm toast.

## COOK'S TIP

Dried pasta will keep for up to 6 months. Keep it in the package and reseal it once you have opened it, or transfer the pasta to an airtight jar.

# Pizzaiola Steak

This has a Neapolitan sauce, using the delicious red tomatoes so abundant in that area, but canned ones make an excellent alternative.

## NUTRITIONAL INFORMATION

Calories . . . . . . . .371   Sugars . . . . . . . . .7g
Protein . . . . . . . .43g   Fat . . . . . . . . . .19g
Carbohydrate . . . .7g   Saturates . . . . . . .5g

25 MINS        30 MINS

### SERVES 4

## I N G R E D I E N T S

1 lb 12 oz/800 g canned peeled tomatoes
or 1 lb 10 oz/750 g fresh tomatoes

4 tbsp olive oil

2–3 garlic cloves, crushed

1 onion, chopped finely

1 tbsp tomato paste

1½ tsp chopped fresh marjoram or oregano
or ¾ tsp dried marjoram or oregano

4 thin sirloin or rump steaks

2 tbsp chopped fresh parsley

1 tsp sugar

salt and pepper

fresh herbs, to garnish (optional)

sauté potatoes, to serve

1 If using canned tomatoes, purée them in a food processor, then strain to remove the seeds. If using fresh tomatoes, peel, remove the seeds and chop finely.

2 Heat half of the oil in a pan and cook the garlic and onions very gently for about 5 minutes, or until softened.

3 Add the tomatoes, seasoning, tomato paste, and chopped herbs to the pan. If using fresh tomatoes, add 4 tablespoons water too, and then simmer very gently for 8–10 minutes, giving an occasional stir.

4 Meanwhile, trim the steaks if necessary and season. Heat the remaining oil in a skillet and cook the steaks quickly on both sides to seal, then continue until cooked to your liking— 2 minutes for rare, 3–4 minutes for medium, or 5 minutes for well done. Alternatively, cook the steaks under a hot broiler after brushing lightly with oil.

5 When the sauce has thickened a little, adjust the seasoning and stir in the chopped parsley and sugar.

6 Pour off the excess fat from the pan containing the steaks and add the tomato sauce. Reheat gently and serve at once, with the sauce spooned over and around the steaks. Garnish with sprigs of fresh herbs, if liked. Sauté potatoes and a green vegetable make very good accompaniments.

# Fresh Spaghetti & Meatballs

This well-loved Italian dish is famous across the world.
Make the most of it by using high-quality steak for the meatballs.

## NUTRITIONAL INFORMATION

| | | |
|---|---|---|
| Calories . . . . . . .665 | Sugars . . . . . . . . .9g | |
| Protein . . . . . . . .39g | Fat . . . . . . . . . .24g | |
| Carbohydrate . . .77g | Saturates . . . . . . .8g | |

45 MINS     1¼ HOURS

### SERVES 4

## INGREDIENTS

scant 3 cups fresh brown bread crumbs

⅔ cup milk

2 tbsp butter

¼ cup whole-wheat flour

scant 1 cup beef stock

14 oz/400 g canned chopped tomatoes

2 tbsp tomato paste

1 tsp sugar

1 tbsp finely chopped fresh tarragon

1 large onion, chopped

1 lb/450 g ground steak

1 tsp paprika

4 tbsp olive oil

1 lb/450 g fresh spaghetti

salt and pepper

fresh tarragon sprigs, to garnish

1 Place the bread crumbs in a bowl, add the milk and set aside to soak for about 30 minutes.

2 Melt half of the butter in a pan. Add the flour and cook, stirring constantly, for 2 minutes. Gradually stir in the beef stock and cook, stirring constantly, for an additional 5 minutes. Add the tomatoes, tomato paste, sugar, and tarragon. Season well and simmer for 25 minutes.

3 Mix the onion, steak, and paprika into the bread crumbs and season to taste. Shape the mixture into 14 meatballs.

4 Heat the oil and remaining butter in a skillet and cook the meatballs, turning, until brown all over. Place in a deep casserole, then pour over the tomato sauce. Cover and bake in a preheated oven, at 350°F/180°C, for 25 minutes.

5 Bring a large pan of lightly salted water to a boil. Add the fresh spaghetti, then bring back to a boil and cook for about 2–3 minutes, or until tender but still firm to the bite.

6 Meanwhile, remove the meatballs from the oven and leave them to cool for 3 minutes. Serve the meatballs and their sauce with the spaghetti, garnished with tarragon sprigs.

# Beef & Potato Ravioli

In this recipe the "pasta" dough is made with potatoes instead of flour. The small round ravioli are filled with a rich bolognese sauce.

## NUTRITIONAL INFORMATION

Calories . . . . . . . .618   Sugars . . . . . . . . .4g
Protein . . . . . . . .16g   Fat . . . . . . . . . .31g
Carbohydrate . . .74g   Saturates . . . . . .12g

30 MINS       50 MINS

### SERVES 4

## I N G R E D I E N T S

### FILLING

1 tbsp vegetable oil

½ cup ground beef

1 shallot, diced

1 garlic clove, crushed

1 tbsp all-purpose flour

1 tbsp tomato paste

⅔ cup beef stock

1 celery stalk, chopped

2 tomatoes, peeled and diced

2 tsp chopped fresh basil

salt and pepper

### RAVIOLI

1 lb/450 g mealy potatoes, diced

3 small egg yolks

3 tbsp olive oil

scant 1¼ cups all-purpose flour

¼ cup butter, for frying

shredded basil leaves, to garnish

1 To make the filling, heat the vegetable oil in a pan and cook the beef for 3-4 minutes, breaking it up with a spoon.

2 Add the shallots and garlic to the pan and cook for 2-3 minutes, or until the shallots have softened.

3 Stir in the flour and tomato paste and cook for 1 minute. Stir in the beef stock, celery, tomatoes, and chopped fresh basil. Season to taste with salt and pepper.

4 Cook the mixture over low heat for 20 minutes. Remove from the heat and leave to cool.

5 To make the ravioli, cook the potatoes in a pan of boiling water for 10 minutes until cooked.

6 Mash the potatoes and place them in a mixing bowl. Blend in the egg yolks and oil. Season with salt and pepper, then stir in the flour and mix to form a dough.

7 On a lightly floured surface, divide the dough into 24 pieces and shape into flat rounds. Spoon the filling onto one half of each round and fold the dough over to encase the filling, pressing down to seal the edges.

8 Melt the butter in a skillet and cook the ravioli for 6-8 minutes, turning once, until golden. Serve hot, garnished with shredded basil leaves.

# Beef Olives in Rich Gravy

Wafer-thin slices of tender beef with a rich garlic and bacon stuffing, flavored with the tang of orange.

## NUTRITIONAL INFORMATION

| | | |
|---|---|---|
| Calories | .......379 | Sugars .........4g |
| Protein | ........26g | Fat ..........24g |
| Carbohydrate | ....4g | Saturates .......8g |

20 MINS      20 MINS

### SERVES 4

### INGREDIENTS

8 ready prepared beef olives

4 tbsp chopped fresh parsley

4 garlic cloves, chopped finely

4½ oz/125 g smoked streaky bacon, rinded and chopped finely

grated rind of ½ small orange

2 tbsp olive oil

1¼ cups dry red wine

1 bay leaf

1 tsp sugar

⅓ cup pitted black olives, drained

salt and pepper

### TO GARNISH

orange slices

chopped fresh parsley

1 Unroll the beef olives and flatten out as thinly as possible using a meat tenderizer or mallet. Trim the edges to neaten them.

2 Mix together the parsley, garlic, bacon, orange rind, and salt and pepper to taste. Spread this mixture evenly over each beef olive.

3 Roll up each beef olive tightly, then secure with a toothpick. Heat the oil in

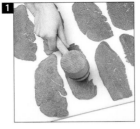

a skillet and cook the beef on all sides for 10 minutes.

4 Drain the beef olives, reserving the pan juices, and keep warm. Pour the wine into the juices, then add the bay leaf, sugar, and seasoning. Bring to a boil and boil rapidly for 5 minutes to reduce slightly, stirring.

5 Return the cooked beef to the pan along with the black olives and heat through for an additional 2 minutes. Discard the bay leaf and toothpicks.

6 Transfer the beef olives and gravy to a serving dish, and serve garnished with orange slices and parsley.

# Meatballs in Red Wine Sauce

A different twist is given to this traditional pasta dish with a rich, but subtle sauce.

## NUTRITIONAL INFORMATION

| | | | |
|---|---|---|---|
| Calories | . . . . . . . .811 | Sugars | . . . . . . . . .7g |
| Protein | . . . . . . . .30g | Fat | . . . . . . . . . .43g |
| Carbohydrate | . . .76g | Saturates | . . . . . .12g |

45 MINS     1¹/₂ HOURS

### SERVES 4

## I N G R E D I E N T S

⅔ cup milk

3 cups fresh white bread crumbs

2 tbsp butter

9 tbsp olive oil

4 cups sliced oyster mushrooms

¼ cup whole-wheat flour

scant 1 cup beef stock

⅔ cup red wine

4 tomatoes, skinned and chopped

1 tbsp tomato paste

1 tsp brown sugar

1 tbsp finely chopped fresh basil

12 shallots, chopped

1 lb/450 g ground steak

1 tsp paprika

1 lb/450 g dried egg tagliarini

salt and pepper

fresh basil sprigs, to garnish

1 Pour the milk into a bowl and soak the bread crumbs in the milk for 30 minutes.

2 Heat half of the butter and 4 tablespoon of the oil in a pan. Cook the mushrooms for 4 minutes, then stir in the flour and cook for 2 minutes. Add the stock and wine and simmer for 15 minutes. Add the tomatoes, tomato paste, sugar, and basil. Season and simmer for 30 minutes.

3 Mix the shallots, steak, and paprika with the bread crumbs and season to taste. Shape the mixture into 14 meatballs.

4 Heat 4 tablespoon of the remaining oil and the remaining butter in a large skillet. Cook the meatballs, turning frequently, until brown all over. Transfer to a deep casserole, then pour over the red wine and the mushroom sauce. Cover and bake in a preheated oven, at 350°F/180°C, for 30 minutes.

5 Bring a pan of salted water to a boil. Add the pasta and the remaining oil and cook for 8–10 minutes, or until tender. Drain and transfer to a serving dish. Remove the casserole from the oven and cool for 3 minutes. Pour the meatballs and sauce on to the pasta, garnish and serve.

# Neapolitan Pork Steaks

An Italian version of grilled pork steaks, this dish is easy to make and delicious to eat.

## NUTRITIONAL INFORMATION

| | | | |
|---|---|---|---|
| Calories | .......353 | Sugars | .........3g |
| Protein | ........39g | Fat | ..........20g |
| Carbohydrate | ....4g | Saturates | .......5g |

 10 MINS     25 MINS

### SERVES 4

## I N G R E D I E N T S

2 tbsp olive oil

1 large onion, sliced

1 garlic clove, chopped

14 oz/400 g canned tomatoes

2 tsp yeast extract

4 pork loin steaks, each about 4½ oz/125 g

scant ½ cup black olives, pitted

2 tbsp fresh basil, shredded

freshly grated Parmesan cheese, to serve

1 Heat the oil in a large skillet. Add the onions and garlic and cook, stirring, for 3–4 minutes, or until they just begin to soften.

2 Add the tomatoes and yeast extract to the skillet and leave to simmer for about 5 minutes, or until the sauce starts to thicken.

## COOK'S TIP

Parmesan is a mature and exceptionally hard cheese produced in Italy. You only need to add a little as it has a very strong flavor.

3 Cook the pork steaks, under a preheated broiler, for 5 minutes on both sides, or until the the meat is cooked through. Set the pork aside and keep warm.

4 Add the olives and fresh shredded basil to the sauce in the skillet and stir quickly to combine.

5 Transfer the steaks to warm serving plates. Top the steaks with the sauce, then sprinkle with freshly grated Parmesan cheese. Serve immediately.

# Pork Chops with Sage

The fresh taste of sage is the perfect ingredient to counteract the richness of pork.

## NUTRITIONAL INFORMATION

Calories .......364  Sugars .........5g
Protein ........34g  Fat ..........19g
Carbohydrate ...14g  Saturates .......7g

10 MINS    15 MINS

### SERVES 4

INGREDIENTS

2 tbsp flour

1 tbsp chopped fresh sage or 1 tsp dried

4 lean boneless pork chops, trimmed of excess fat

2 tbsp olive oil

1 tbsp butter

2 red onions, sliced into rings

1 tbsp lemon juice

2 tsp superfine sugar

4 plum tomatoes, cut into fourths

salt and pepper

1 Mix the flour, sage, and salt and pepper to taste on a plate. Lightly dust the pork chops on both sides with the seasoned flour.

2 Heat the oil and butter in a skillet, then add the chops and cook them for 6–7 minutes on each side, or until cooked through. Drain the chops, reserving the pan juices, and keep warm.

3 Toss the onion in the lemon juice and cook along with the sugar and tomatoes for 5 minutes, or until tender.

4 Serve the pork with the tomato and onion mixture and a green salad.

# Pork with Fennel & Juniper

The addition of juniper and fennel to the pork chops gives an unusual and delicate flavor to this dish.

## NUTRITIONAL INFORMATION

| | | | |
|---|---|---|---|
| Calories | .......277 | Sugars | .......0.4g |
| Protein | ........32g | Fat | ..........16g |
| Carbohydrate | ...0.4g | Saturates | .......5g |

2¼ HOURS      15 MINS

### SERVES 4

## INGREDIENTS

½ fennel bulb

1 tbsp juniper berries

about 2 tbsp olive oil

finely grated rind and juice of 1 orange

4 pork chops, each about 5½ oz/150 g

fresh bread and a crisp salad, to serve

1 Finely chop the fennel bulb, discarding the green parts.

2 Grind the juniper berries in a pestle and mortar. Mix the crushed juniper berries with the fennel flesh, olive oil, and orange rind.

3 Using a sharp knife, score a few cuts all over each chop.

## COOK'S TIP

Juniper berries are most commonly associated with gin, but they are often added to meat dishes in Italy for a delicate citrus flavor. They can be bought dried from most health food stores and some larger supermarkets.

4 Place the pork chops in a roasting pan or an ovenproof dish. Spoon the fennel and juniper mixture over the chops.

5 Pour the orange juice over the top of each chop, then cover and marinate in the refrigerator for about 2 hours.

6 Cook the pork chops, under a preheated broiler, for 10–15 minutes, depending on the thickness of the meat, or until the meat is tender and cooked through, turning occasionally.

7 Transfer the pork chops to serving plates and serve with a crisp, fresh salad and plenty of fresh bread to mop up the cooking juices.

# Pasta & Pork in Cream Sauce

This unusual and attractive dish is extremely delicious. Make the Italian Red Wine Sauce well in advance to reduce the preparation time.

## NUTRITIONAL INFORMATION

| | | |
|---|---|---|
| Calories ...... .735 | Sugars ......... .4g |
| Protein ........31g | Fat ......... .52g |
| Carbohydrate ...37g | Saturates ......19g |

8³/₄ HOURS    35 MINS

### SERVES 4

## INGREDIENTS

1 lb/450 g pork tenderloin, thinly sliced

4 tbsp olive oil

8 oz/225 g white mushrooms, sliced

scant 1 cup Italian Red Wine Sauce
  (see page 29)

1 tbsp lemon juice

pinch of saffron

3 cups dried orecchioni

4 tbsp heavy cream

12 quail eggs (see Cook's Tip)

salt

1 Pound the slices of pork between 2 sheets of plastic wrap until wafer thin, then cut into strips.

2 Heat the olive oil in a large skillet, then add the pork and stir-fry for 5 minutes. Add the mushrooms to the pan and stir-fry for an additional 2 minutes.

3 Pour over the Italian Red Wine Sauce, lower the heat and simmer gently for 20 minutes.

4 Meanwhile, bring a large pan of lightly salted water to a boil. Add the lemon juice, saffron, and orecchioni and cook for 8–10 minutes, or until tender but still firm to the bite. Drain the pasta and keep warm.

5 Stir the cream into the pan with the pork and heat gently for a few minutes.

6 Boil the quail eggs for 3 minutes, then cool them in cold water and remove the shells.

7 Transfer the pasta to a large, warm serving plate, then top with the pork and the sauce and garnish with the eggs. Serve immediately.

### COOK'S TIP

In this recipe, the quail eggs are soft-cooked. As they are extremely difficult to shell when warm, it is important that they are thoroughly cooled first. Otherwise, they will break up unattractively.

# Stuffed Cannelloni

Cannelloni, the thick, round pasta tubes, make perfect containers for close-textured sauces of all kinds.

## NUTRITIONAL INFORMATION

| | | | |
|---|---|---|---|
| Calories | .......520 | Sugars | .........5g |
| Protein | ........21g | Fat | ..........39g |
| Carbohydrate | ...23g | Saturates | ......18g |

30 MINS        1¼ HOURS

### SERVES 4

## I N G R E D I E N T S

8 dried cannelloni tubes

1 tbsp olive oil

¼ cup freshly grated Parmesan cheese

fresh herb sprigs, to garnish

### FILLING

2 tbsp butter

10½ oz/300 g frozen spinach, thawed
    and chopped

½ cup ricotta cheese

¼ cup freshly grated Parmesan cheese

scant ¼ cup chopped ham

pinch of freshly grated nutmeg

2 tbsp heavy cream

2 eggs, lightly beaten

salt and pepper

### SAUCE

2 tbsp butter

scant ¼ cup all-purpose flour

1¼ cups milk

2 bay leaves

pinch of freshly grated nutmeg

1 To make the filling, melt the butter in a pan and stir-fry the spinach for 2–3 minutes. Remove from the heat and stir in the ricotta and Parmesan cheeses and the ham. Season to taste with nutmeg and salt and pepper. Beat in the cream and eggs to make a thick paste.

2 Bring a pan of lightly salted water to a boil. Add the pasta and the oil and cook for 10–12 minutes, or until almost tender. Drain and set aside to cool.

3 To make the sauce, melt the butter in a pan. Stir in the flour and cook, stirring, for 1 minute. Gradually stir in the milk. Add the bay leaves and simmer, whisking, for 5 minutes. Add the nutmeg and salt and pepper to taste. Remove from the heat and discard the bay leaves.

4 Spoon the filling into a pastry bag and fill the cannelloni.

5 Spoon a little sauce into the base of an ovenproof dish. Arrange the cannelloni in the dish in a single layer and pour over the remaining sauce. Sprinkle over the Parmesan cheese and bake in a preheated oven at 375°F/190°C for 40–45 minutes. Garnish with fresh herb sprigs and serve.

# Pork Stuffed with Prosciutto

This sophisticated roast with Mediterranean flavors is ideal
served with a pungent olive paste.

## NUTRITIONAL INFORMATION

Calories .......427   Sugars .........0g
Protein ........31g   Fat ..........34g
Carbohydrate ...0.2g   Saturates .......7g

### SERVES 4

## INGREDIENTS

1 lb 2 oz/500 g piece of lean pork tenderloin

small bunch fresh of basil leaves, washed

2 tbsp freshly grated Parmesan cheese

2 tbsp sun-dried tomato paste

6 thin slices prosciutto

1 tbsp olive oil

salt and pepper

### OLIVE PASTE

scant scant ¾ cup pitted black olives

4 tbsp olive oil

2 garlic cloves, peeled

1 Trim away excess fat and membrane from the pork tenderloin. Slice the pork lengthwise down the middle, taking care not to cut all the way through.

2 Open out the pork and season the inside. Lay the basil leaves down the center. Mix the cheese and sun-dried tomato paste and spread over the basil.

3 Press the pork back together. Wrap the ham around the pork, overlapping, to cover. Place on a rack in a roasting pan, seamside down, and brush with oil. Bake in a preheated oven, 375°F/190°C, for 30–40 minutes depending on thickness until cooked through. Leave to stand for 10 minutes.

4 For the olive paste, place all the ingredients in a blender or food processor and blend until smooth. Alternatively, for a coarser paste, finely chop the olives and garlic and mix with the olive oil.

5 Drain the cooked pork and slice thinly. Serve with the olive paste and a salad.

# Pot Roasted Leg of Lamb

This dish from the Abruzzi uses a slow cooking method, which ensures that the meat absorbs the flavorings and becomes very tender.

## NUTRITIONAL INFORMATION

| | | |
|---|---|---|
| Calories .......734 | Sugars ........6g | |
| Protein ........71g | Fat ..........42g | |
| Carbohydrate ....7g | Saturates ......15g | |

35 MINS    3 HOURS

### SERVES 4

## INGREDIENTS

3 lb 8 oz/1.75 kg leg of lamb

3–4 sprigs fresh rosemary

4½ oz/125 g streaky bacon slices

4 tbsp olive oil

2–3 garlic cloves, crushed

2 onions, sliced

2 carrots, sliced

2 celery stalks, sliced

1¼ cups dry white wine

1 tbsp tomato paste

1¼ cups stock

12 oz/350 g tomatoes, peeled, cut
    into fourths, and seeded

1 tbsp chopped fresh parsley

1 tbsp chopped fresh oregano or marjoram

salt and pepper

fresh rosemary sprigs, to garnish

1 Wipe the joint of lamb all over, trimming off any excess fat, then season well with salt and pepper, rubbing well in. Lay the sprigs of rosemary over the lamb, cover evenly with the bacon slices and tie in place with string.

2 Heat the oil in a skillet and cook the lamb for 10 minutes, or until browned all over, turning several times. Remove from the pan.

3 Transfer the oil from the skillet to a large fireproof casserole and cook the garlic and onion together for 3–4 minutes until beginning to soften. Add the carrots and celery and continue to cook for a few minutes longer.

4 Lay the lamb on top of the vegetables and press down to partly submerge. Pour the wine over the lamb, then add the tomato paste and simmer for 3–4 minutes. Add the stock, tomatoes, herbs, and seasoning, then bring back to a boil for an additional 3–4 minutes.

5 Cover the casserole tightly and cook in a moderate oven, 350°F/180°C, for 2–2½ hours, or until very tender.

6 Remove the lamb from the casserole and if preferred, take off the bacon and herbs along with the string. Keep warm. Strain the juices, skimming off any excess fat, and serve in a jug. The vegetables may be put around the joint or in a serving dish. Garnish with fresh sprigs of rosemary.

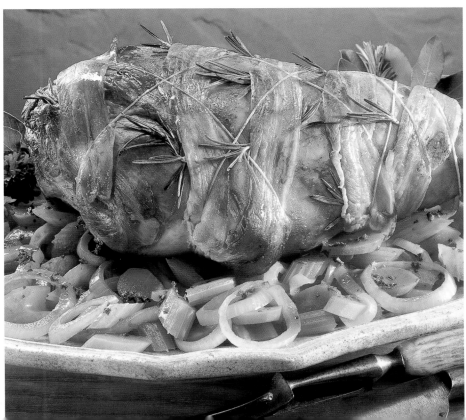

# Roman Pan-Fried Lamb

Chunks of tender lamb, pan-fried with garlic and stewed in red wine, are a real Roman dish.

## NUTRITIONAL INFORMATION

Calories .......299  Sugars .........1g
Protein ........31g  Fat ..........16g
Carbohydrate ....1g  Saturates .......7g

15 MINS    50 MINS

### SERVES 4

## I N G R E D I E N T S

1 tbsp oil

1 tbsp butter

1 lb 5 oz/600 g lamb (shoulder or leg),
    cut into 1-inch/2.5-cm chunks

4 garlic cloves, peeled

3 sprigs thyme, stems removed

6 canned anchovy fillets

⅔ cup red wine

⅔ cup lamb or vegetable stock

1 tsp sugar

⅓ cup black olives, pitted and halved

2 tbsp chopped parsley, to garnish

mashed potato, to serve

1 Heat the oil and butter in a large skillet. Add the lamb and cook for 4–5 minutes, stirring, until the meat is browned all over.

2 Using a pestle and mortar, grind together the garlic, thyme, and anchovies to make a smooth paste.

3 Add the wine and lamb stock to the skillet. Stir in the garlic and anchovy paste together with the sugar.

4 Bring the mixture to a boil. Reduce the heat, then cover and simmer for 30–40 minutes, or until the lamb is tender. For the last 10 minutes of the cooking time, remove the lid to let the sauce reduce slightly.

5 Stir the olives into the sauce and mix to combine.

6 Transfer the lamb and the sauce to a serving bowl and garnish. Serve with creamy mashed potatoes.

## COOK'S TIP

Rome is the capital of both the region of Lazio and Italy and thus has become a focal point for specialties from all over Italy. Food from this region tends to be fairly simple and quick to prepare, all with plenty of herbs and seasonings giving really robust flavors.

# Pasta & Lamb Loaf

Any dried pasta shape can be used for this delicious recipe.
It has been adapted for microwave cooking for convenience.

## NUTRITIONAL INFORMATION

| | | |
|---|---|---|
| Calories . . . . . . .245 | Sugars . . . . . . . . .2g | |
| Protein . . . . . . . .15g | Fat . . . . . . . . . .18g | |
| Carbohydrate . . . .6g | Saturates . . . . . . .7g | |

35 MINS     35 MINS

### SERVES 4

## INGREDIENTS

1 tbsp butter

½ small eggplant, diced

½ cup multicolored fusilli

2 tsp olive oil

8 oz/225 g cup ground lamb

½ small onion, chopped

½ red bell pepper, chopped

1 garlic clove, crushed

1 tsp dried mixed herbs

2 eggs, beaten

2 tbsp light cream

salt and pepper

### TO SERVE

salad

pasta sauce of your choice

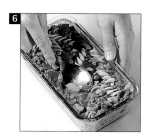

1 Place the butter in a 1 lb 2 oz/500 g loaf dish. Cook on High power for 30 seconds, or until melted. Brush over the base and sides of the dish.

2 Sprinkle the eggplant with salt, then put in a colander and leave for 20 minutes. Rinse the eggplant well and pat dry with paper towels.

3 Place the pasta in a bowl, then add a little salt and enough boiling water to cover by 1 inch/2.5 cm. Cover and cook on High power for 8 minutes, stirring halfway through. Leave to stand, covered, for a few minutes.

4 Place the oil, lamb, and onion in a bowl. Cover and cook on High power for 2 minutes.

5 Break up any lumps of meat using a fork. Add the bell pepper, garlic, herbs, and eggplant. Cover and cook on High power for 5 minutes, stirring halfway through.

6 Drain the pasta and add to the lamb with the eggs and cream. Season well. Turn into the loaf dish and pat down using the back of a spoon.

7 Cook on Medium power for 10 minutes until firm to the touch. Leave to stand for 5 minutes before turning out. Serve in slices with a salad and a pasta sauce.

# Lamb Chops with Rosemary

A classic combination of flavors, this grill would make a perfect Sunday lunch. Serve with tomato and onion salad and baked potatoes.

## NUTRITIONAL INFORMATION

Calories .......560    Sugars .........1g
Protein ........48g    Fat ..........40g
Carbohydrate ....1g    Saturates ......13g

1¼ HOURS      15 MINS

### SERVES 4

## INGREDIENTS

8 lamb chops

5 tbsp olive oil

2 tbsp lemon juice

1 clove garlic, crushed

½ tsp lemon pepper

salt

8 sprigs rosemary

baked potatoes in their skins, to serve

### SALAD

4 tomatoes, sliced

4 scallions, sliced diagonally

### DRESSING

2 tbsp olive oil

1 tbsp lemon juice

1 clove garlic, chopped

¼ tsp fresh rosemary, chopped finely

1 Trim the lamb chops by cutting away the flesh with a sharp knife to expose the tips of the bones.

2 Place the oil, lemon juice, garlic, lemon pepper, and salt in a shallow, nonmetallic dish and whisk with a fork to combine.

3 Lay the sprigs of rosemary in the dish and place the lamb on top. Leave to marinate for at least 1 hour, turning the lamb chops once. Meanwhile, light the barbecue.

4 Remove the chops from the marinade and wrap a little kitchen foil around the bones to stop them from burning.

5 Place the rosemary sprigs on the rack and place the lamb on top. Grill for 10–15 minutes, turning once.

6 Meanwhile make the salad and dressing. Arrange the tomatoes on a serving dish and scatter the scallions on top. Place all the ingredients for the dressing in a screw-top jar and shake well, then pour over the salad. Serve with the lamb chops and jacket potatoes.

## COOK'S TIP

Choose medium to small baking potatoes if you want to cook jacket potatoes on the barbecue. Scrub them well, prick with a fork and wrap in buttered kitchen foil. Bury them in the hot coals and grill for 50–60 minutes.

# Eggplant Cake

Layers of toasty-brown eggplant, meat sauce and cheese-flavored pasta make this a popular family supper dish.

## NUTRITIONAL INFORMATION

| | | |
|---|---|---|
| Calories . . . . . . .859 | Sugars . . . . . . . .39g | |
| Protein . . . . . . . .36g | Fat . . . . . . . . . .58g | |
| Carbohydrate . . .51g | Saturates . . . . . .19g | |

1¹/₂ HOURS     1¹/₂ HOURS

### SERVES 4

## I N G R E D I E N T S

1 eggplant, thinly sliced

5 tbsp olive oil

2 cups dried fusilli

2½ cups Béchamel Sauce (see page 28)

¾ cup grated Cheddar cheese

butter, for greasing

¼ cup freshly grated Parmesan cheese

salt and pepper

### L A M B   S A U C E

2 tbsp olive oil

1 large onion, sliced

2 celery stalks, thinly sliced

1 lb/450 g ground lamb

3 tbsp tomato paste

5½ oz/150 g bottled sun-dried tomatoes, drained and chopped

1 tsp dried oregano

1 tbsp red wine vinegar

⅔ cup chicken stock

salt and pepper

2 To make the lamb sauce, heat the oil in a pan. Cook the onion and celery for 3–4 minutes. Add the lamb and cook, stirring frequently, until browned. Stir in the remaining sauce ingredients, then bring to a boil and cook for 20 minutes.

3 Rinse the eggplant slices, then drain and pat dry. Heat 4 tablespoons of the oil in a skillet. Cook the eggplant slices for about 4 minutes on each side. Remove from the pan and drain well.

4 Bring a large pan of lightly salted water to a boil. Add the fusilli and the remaining oil and cook for 8–10 minutes,

or until almost tender but still firm to the bite. Drain well.

5 Gently heat the Béchamel Sauce, stirring constantly. Stir in the Cheddar cheese. Stir half of the cheese sauce into the fusilli.

6 Make layers of fusilli, lamb sauce, and eggplant slices in a greased dish. Spread the remaining cheese sauce over the top. Sprinkle over the Parmesan and bake in a preheated oven, at 375°F/190°C, for 25 minutes. Serve hot or cold.

1 Put the eggplant slices in a colander, then sprinkle with salt and set aside for 45 minutes.

# Grilled Butterfly Lamb

The appearance of the lamb as it is opened out to cook on the barbecue gives this dish its name. Marinate the lamb in advance if possible.

## NUTRITIONAL INFORMATION

Calories .......733   Sugars .........6g
Protein ........69g   Fat ..........48g
Carbohydrate ....6g   Saturates ......13g

 6¼ HOURS   1 HOUR

### SERVES 4

## INGREDIENTS

boned leg of lamb, about 4 lb/1.8 kg

8 tbsp balsamic vinegar

grated rind and juice of 1 lemon

⅔ cup corn oil

4 tbsp chopped, fresh mint

2 cloves garlic, crushed

2 tbsp light muscovado sugar

salt and pepper

### TO SERVE

broiled vegetables

green salad greens

1 Open out the boned leg of lamb so that its shape resembles a butterfly. Thread 2–3 skewers through the meat in order to make it easier to turn on the grill.

2 Combine the balsamic vinegar, lemon rind and juice, oil, mint, garlic, sugar, and salt and pepper to taste in a non-metallic dish that is large enough to hold the lamb.

3 Place the lamb in the dish and turn it over a few times so that the meat is coated on both sides with the marinade. Leave to marinate for at least 6 hours or preferably overnight, turning occasionally.

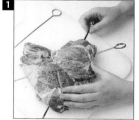

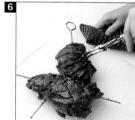

4 Remove the lamb from the marinade and reserve the liquid. Prepare the barbecue. for basting.

5 Place the rack about 6 inches/15 cm above the coals and grill the lamb for 30 minutes on each side, turning once and basting frequently with the marinade.

6 Transfer the lamb to a cutting board and remove the skewers. Cut the lamb into slices across the grain and serve.

### COOK'S TIP
If you prefer, cook the lamb for half the cooking time in a preheated oven at 350°F/180°C, then finish off on the grill.

# Saltimbocca

The Italian name for this dish means "jump into the mouth."
The stuffed rolls are quick and easy to make and taste delicious.

## NUTRITIONAL INFORMATION

Calories .......303  Sugars .......0.3g
Protein ........29g  Fat ..........17g
Carbohydrate ....1g  Saturates .......1g

15 MINS    20 MINS

### SERVES 4

## INGREDIENTS

4 veal scallops or 4 turkey fillets, about
    1 lb/450 g in total

3½ oz/100 g prosciutto

8 sage leaves

1 tbsp olive oil

1 onion, finely chopped

generous ¾ cup white wine

generous ¾ cup chicken stock

1 Place the fillets between sheets of waxed paper. Pound the meat with a meat mallet or the end of a rolling pin to flatten it slightly. Cut each scallop in half.

2 Trim the prosciutto to fit each piece of fillet and place over the meat. Lay a sage leaf on top. Roll up the scallops and secure with a toothpick.

3 Heat the oil in a skillet and cook the onion for 3–4 minutes. Add the veal or turkey rolls to the pan and cook for 5 minutes, or until browned all over.

4 Pour the white wine and chicken stock into the pan and leave to simmer for 15 minutes if using turkey, and 20 minutes if using veal, or until tender. Serve immediately.

## VARIATION

Try a similar recipe called *bocconcini*, meaning "little mouthfuls." Follow the same method as given here, but replace the sage leaf with a piece of Gruyère cheese.

# Veal in a Rose Petal Sauce

This truly spectacular dish is equally delicious whether you use veal or pork fillet. Make sure the roses are free of blemishes and pesticides.

## NUTRITIONAL INFORMATION

| | | |
|---|---|---|
| Calories . . . . . . . .810 | Sugars . . . . . . . . .2g |
| Protein . . . . . . . .31g | Fat . . . . . . . . . .56g |
| Carbohydrate . . .49g | Saturates . . . . . .28g |

 10 MINS    35 MINS

### SERVES 4

## INGREDIENTS

4 cups dried fettuccine

scant ½ cup olive oil

1 tsp chopped fresh oregano

1 tsp chopped fresh marjoram

¾ cup butter

1 lb/450 g veal fillet, thinly sliced

⅔ cup rose petal vinegar (see Cook's Tip)

⅔ cup fish stock

¼ cup grapefruit juice

¼ cup heavy cream

salt

### TO GARNISH

12 pink grapefruit segments

12 pink peppercorns

rose petals, washed

fresh herb leaves

1 Bring a large pan of lightly salted water to a boil. Add the fettuccine and 1 tablespoon of the oil and cook for 8–10 minutes, or until tender but still firm to the bite. Drain and transfer to a warm serving dish, then sprinkle over 2 tablespoons of the olive oil, the oregano and marjoram.

2 Heat 4 tbsp of the butter with the remaining oil in a large skillet. Add the veal and cook over low heat for 6 minutes. Remove the veal from the skillet and place on top of the pasta.

3 Add the vinegar and fish stock to the skillet and bring to a boil. Boil vigorously until reduced by two-thirds. Add the grapefruit juice and cream and simmer over low heat for 4 minutes. Dice the remaining butter and add to the skillet, one piece at a time, whisking constantly until it has been incorporated.

4 Pour the sauce around the veal, then garnish with grapefruit segments, pink peppercorns, the rose petals, and your favorite herb leaves.

### COOK'S TIP

To make rose petal vinegar, infuse the petals of 8 pesticide-free roses in ⅔ cup white wine vinegar for 48 hours. Prepare well in advance to reduce the preparation time.

# Veal Italienne

This dish is really superb if made with tender veal. However, if veal is unavailable, use pork or turkey scallops instead.

## NUTRITIONAL INFORMATION

| Calories | .......592 | Sugars | .........5g |
|---|---|---|---|
| Protein | ........44g | Fat | ..........23g |
| Carbohydrate | ...48g | Saturates | .......9g |

 25 MINS   1 HR 20 MINS

### SERVES 4

### I N G R E D I E N T S

¼ cup butter

1 tbsp olive oil

1 lb 8 oz/675 g potatoes, cubed

4 veal scallops, weighing 6 oz/175 g each

1 onion, cut into 8 wedges

2 garlic cloves, crushed

2 tbsp all-purpose flour

2 tbsp tomato paste

⅔ cup red wine

1¼ cups chicken stock

8 ripe tomatoes, peeled, seeded and diced

9–10 pitted black olives, halved

2 tbsp chopped fresh basil

salt and pepper

fresh basil leaves, to garnish

1 Heat the butter and oil in a large skillet. Add the potato cubes and cook for 5-7 minutes, stirring frequently, until they begin to brown.

2 Remove the potatoes from the skillet with a perforated spoon and set aside.

3 Place the veal in the skillet and cook for 2-3 minutes on each side until sealed. Remove from the skillet and set aside.

4 Stir the onion and garlic into the skillet and cook for 2-3 minutes.

5 Add the flour and tomato paste and cook for 1 minute, stirring. Gradually blend in the red wine and chicken stock, stirring to make a smooth sauce.

6 Return the potatoes and veal to the skillet. Stir in the tomatoes, olives, and chopped basil and season with salt and pepper.

7 Transfer to a casserole dish and cook in a preheated oven, 350°F/180°C, for 1 hour, or until the potatoes and veal are cooked through. Garnish with basil leaves and serve immediately.

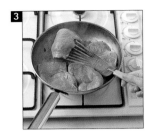

## COOK'S TIP

For a quicker cooking time and really tender meat, pound the meat with a meat mallet to flatten it slightly before cooking.

# Scallops & Italian Sausage

Anchovies are often used to enhance flavor, particularly in meat dishes. Either veal or turkey scallops can be used for this pan-fried dish.

## NUTRITIONAL INFORMATION

Calories . . . . . . .233    Sugars . . . . . . . . .1g
Protein . . . . . . . .28g    Fat . . . . . . . . . .13g
Carbohydrate . . . .1g    Saturates . . . . . . .1g

10 MINS          20 MINS

### SERVES 4

## I N G R E D I E N T S

1 tbsp olive oil

6 canned anchovy fillets, drained

1 tbsp capers, drained

1 tbsp fresh rosemary, stems removed

finely grated rind and juice of 1 orange

2¾ oz/75 g Italian sausage, diced

3 tomatoes, skinned and chopped

4 turkey or veal scallops, each about
   4½ oz/125 g

salt and pepper

crusty bread or cooked polenta, to serve

1 Heat the oil in a large skillet. Add the anchovies, capers, fresh rosemary, orange rind and juice, Italian sausage, and tomatoes to the pan and cook for 5–6 minutes, stirring occasionally.

2 Meanwhile, place the meat scallops between sheets of waxed paper. Pound the meat with a meat mallet or the end of a rolling pin to flatten it.

3 Add the meat to the mixture in the skillet. Season to taste with salt and pepper, then cover and cook for 3–5 minutes on each side, slightly longer if the meat is thicker.

4 Transfer to serving plates and serve with fresh crusty bread or cooked polenta, if you prefer.

### VARIATION
Try using 4 minute steaks, slightly flattened, instead of the turkey or veal. Cook them for 4–5 minutes on top of the sauce in the pan.

# Sausage & Bean Casserole

In this traditional Tuscan dish, Italian sausages are cooked with cannellini beans and tomatoes.

## NUTRITIONAL INFORMATION

Calories .......609    Sugars .........7g
Protein ........27g    Fat ..........47g
Carbohydrate ...20g    Saturates ......16g

 15 MINS     35 MINS

### SERVES 4

## I N G R E D I E N T S

1 green bell pepper

8 Italian sausages

1 tbsp olive oil

1 large onion, chopped

2 garlic cloves, chopped

8 oz/225g fresh tomatoes, skinned and chopped or 14 oz/400 g canned tomatoes, chopped

2 tbsp sun-dried tomato paste

14 oz/400 g canned cannellini beans

mashed potato or rice, to serve

1 Using a sharp knife, seed the bell pepper and cut it into thin strips.

2 Prick the Italian sausages all over with a fork. Cook the sausages, under a preheated broiler, for 10–12 minutes, turning occasionally, until brown all over. Set aside and keep warm.

3 Heat the oil in a large skillet. Add the onion, garlic, and bell pepper to the skillet and cook for 5 minutes, stirring occasionally, or until softened.

4 Add the tomatoes to the skillet and leave the mixture to simmer for about 5 minutes, stirring occasionally, or until slightly reduced and thickened.

5 Stir the sun-dried tomato paste, cannellini beans, and Italian sausages into the mixture in the skillet. Cook for 4–5 minutes, or until the mixture is piping hot. Add 4–5 tablespoons of water, if the mixture becomes too dry during cooking.

6 Transfer the Italian sausage and bean casserole to serving plates and serve with mashed potato or cooked rice.

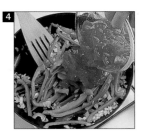

## COOK'S TIP

Italian sausages are coarse in texture and have quite a strong flavor. They can be bought in specialist sausage shops, Italian delicatessens, and some larger supermarkets. They are replaceable in this recipe only by game sausages.

# Liver with Wine Sauce

Liver is popular in Italy and is served in many ways. Tender calf's liver is the best type to use for this recipe, but you could use lamb's liver.

## NUTRITIONAL INFORMATION

Calories . . . . . . .435    Sugars . . . . . . . . .2g
Protein . . . . . . . .30g    Fat . . . . . . . . . .31g
Carbohydrate . . . .4g    Saturates . . . . . .12g

25 MINS    20 MINS

### SERVES 4

## I N G R E D I E N T S

4 slices calf's liver or 8 slices lamb's liver,
　about 1 lb 2 oz/500 g

flour, for coating

1 tbsp olive oil

2 tbsp butter

4½ oz/125 g lean bacon slices, rinded and
　cut into narrow strips

1 garlic clove, crushed

1 onion, chopped

1 celery stalk, sliced thinly

⅔ cup red wine

⅔ cup beef stock

good pinch of ground allspice

1 tsp Worcestershire sauce

1 tsp chopped fresh sage or
　½ tsp dried sage

3–4 tomatoes, peeled, cut into fourths,
　and seeded

salt and pepper

fresh sage leaves, to garnish

new potatoes or sauté potatoes, to serve

1 Wipe the liver with paper towels, then season with salt and pepper to taste. Coat lightly in flour, shaking off any excess.

2 Heat the oil and butter in a skillet and cook the liver until well sealed on both sides and just cooked through—take care not to overcook. Remove the liver from the skillet, then cover and keep warm, but do not let dry out.

3 Add the bacon to the fat left in the skillet, with the garlic, onion, and celery. Cook gently until soft.

4 Add the red wine, beef stock, allspice, Worcestershire sauce, sage, and salt and pepper to taste. Bring to a boil and simmer for 3–4 minutes.

5 Cut each tomato segment in half. Add to the sauce and continue to cook for 2–3 minutes.

6 Serve the liver on a little of the sauce, with the remainder spooned over. Garnish with fresh sage leaves and serve with tiny new potatoes or sauté potatoes.

# Poultry & Game

Poultry dishes provide some of Italy's finest food. Every part of the chicken is used, including the feet and innards for making soup. Spit-roasted chicken, flavored strongly with aromatic rosemary, has become almost a national dish. Turkey, capon, duck, goose, and guinea fowl are also popular, as is game. Wild rabbit, hare, wild boar, and deer are available, especially in Sardinia. This chapter contains a superb collection of mouthwatering recipes. You will be astonished at how quickly and easily you can prepare some of these gourmet dishes.

# Italian Chicken Spirals

These little foil parcels retain all the natural juices of the chicken while cooking conveniently over the pasta while it boils.

## NUTRITIONAL INFORMATION

| | | | |
|---|---|---|---|
| Calories | ......367 | Sugars | .........1g |
| Protein | ........33g | Fat | ..........12g |
| Carbohydrate | ...35g | Saturates | .......2g |

🍲 20 MINS    🕐 20 MINS

### SERVES 4

## INGREDIENTS

4 skinless, boneless chicken breasts

1 cup fresh basil leaves

2 tbsp hazelnuts

1 garlic clove, crushed

2 cups whole-wheat pasta spirals

2 sun-dried tomatoes or fresh tomatoes

1 tbsp lemon juice

1 tbsp olive oil

1 tbsp capers

scant ½ cup black olives

1 Beat the chicken breasts with a rolling pin to flatten evenly.

2 Place the basil and hazelnuts in a food processor and process until finely chopped. Mix with the garlic and salt and pepper to taste.

3 Spread the basil mixture over the chicken breasts and roll up from one short end to enclose the filling. Wrap the chicken roll tightly in foil so that they hold their shape, then seal the ends well.

4 Bring a pan of lightly salted water to a boil. Cook the pasta for 8–10 minutes, or until tender but still firm to the bite. Meanwhile, place the chicken parcels in a steamer or colander set over the pan, then cover tightly and steam for 10 minutes.

5 Using a sharp knife, dice the tomatoes.

6 Drain the pasta, then return to the pan with the lemon juice, olive oil, tomatoes, capers, and olives. Heat through.

7 Pierce the chicken with a skewer to make sure that the juices run clear and not pink (this shows that the chicken is cooked through). Slice the chicken, arrange over the pasta and serve.

## COOK'S TIP

Sun-dried tomatoes have a wonderful, rich flavor, but if they're unavailable, use fresh tomatoes instead.

# Chicken Marengo

Napoleon's chef was ordered to cook a sumptuous meal on the eve of the battle of Marengo—this feast of flavors was the result.

## NUTRITIONAL INFORMATION

| | | | |
|---|---|---|---|
| Calories | .521 | Sugars | .6g |
| Protein | .47g | Fat | .19g |
| Carbohydrate | .34g | Saturates | .8g |

🕐 20 MINS    🕐 50 MINS

### SERVES 4

## INGREDIENTS

8 chicken pieces

2 tbsp olive oil

10½ oz/300 g crushed tomatoes

generous ¾ cup white wine

2 tsp dried mixed herbs

3 tbsp butter, melted

2 garlic cloves, crushed

8 slices white bread

3½ oz/100 g mixed mushrooms
   (such as white, oyster, and cèpes)

generous ¼ cup chopped black olives

1 tsp sugar

fresh basil, to garnish

1 Using a sharp knife, remove the bone from each of the chicken pieces.

2 Heat 1 tablespoon of oil in a large skillet. Add the chicken pieces and cook for about 4–5 minutes, turning occasionally, or until browned all over.

3 Add the crushed tomatoes, wine, and mixed herbs to the skillet. Bring to a boil and then leave to simmer for 30 minutes, or until the chicken is tender and the juices run clear when a skewer is inserted into the thickest part of the meat.

4 Mix the melted butter and crushed garlic together. Lightly toast the slices of bread and brush with the garlic butter.

5 Add the remaining oil to a separate skillet and cook the mushrooms for 2–3 minutes, or until just browned.

6 Add the olives and sugar to the chicken mixture and warm through.

7 Transfer the chicken and sauce to serving plates. Serve with the bruschetta (toasted bread) and fried mushrooms.

# Mustard Baked Chicken

Chicken pieces are cooked in a succulent, mild mustard sauce, then coated in poppy seeds and served on a bed of fresh pasta shells.

## NUTRITIONAL INFORMATION

| | | |
|---|---|---|
| Calories . . . . . . .652 | Sugars . . . . . . . . .5g | |
| Protein . . . . . . . .51g | Fat . . . . . . . . . .31g | |
| Carbohydrate . . .46g | Saturates . . . . . .12g | |

10 MINS     35 MINS

### SERVES 4

## I N G R E D I E N T S

8 chicken pieces (about 4 oz/115 g each)

4 tbsp butter, melted

4 tbsp mild mustard (see Cook's Tip)

2 tbsp lemon juice

1 tbsp brown sugar

1 tsp paprika

3 tbsp poppy seeds

3½ cups fresh pasta shells

1 tbsp olive oil

salt and pepper

1 Arrange the chicken pieces in a single layer in a large ovenproof dish.

2 Mix together the butter, mustard, lemon juice, sugar, and paprika in a bowl and season with salt and pepper to taste. Brush the mixture over the upper

 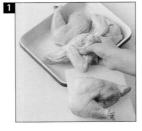 

surfaces of the chicken pieces and bake in a preheated oven at 400°F/200°C for 15 minutes.

3 Remove the dish from the oven and carefully turn over the chicken pieces. Coat the upper surfaces of the chicken with the remaining mustard mixture, then sprinkle the chicken pieces with poppy seeds and return to the oven for an additional 15 minutes.

4 Meanwhile, bring a large pan of lightly salted water to a boil. Add the pasta shells and olive oil and cook for 8–10 minutes, or until tender but still firm to the bite.

5 Drain the pasta thoroughly and arrange on a warmed serving dish. Top the pasta with the chicken, then pour over the sauce and serve immediately.

## COOK'S TIP

Dijon is the type of mustard most often used in European cooking, as it has a clean and only mildly spicy flavor. German mustard has a sweet-sour taste, with Bavarian mustard being slightly sweeter.

# Pan-Cooked Chicken

Artichokes are a familiar ingredient in Italian cookery. In this dish, they are used to delicately flavor chicken.

## NUTRITIONAL INFORMATION

Calories . . . . . . .296    Sugars . . . . . . . . .2g
Protein . . . . . . . .27g    Fat . . . . . . . . . .15g
Carbohydrate . . . .7g    Saturates . . . . . . .6g

🥘 15 MINS        🕐 55 MINS

### SERVES 4

## INGREDIENTS

4 chicken breasts, part boned

2 tbsp olive oil

2 tbsp butter

2 red onions, cut into wedges

2 tbsp lemon juice

⅔ cup dry white wine

⅔ cup chicken stock

2 tsp all-purpose flour

14 oz/400 g canned artichoke halves,
    drained and halved

salt and pepper

chopped fresh parsley, to garnish

1 Season the chicken with salt and pepper to taste. Heat the oil and 1 tablespoon of the butter in a large skillet. Add the chicken and cook for 4–5 minutes on each side, or until lightly golden. Remove from the pan using a slotted spoon.

2 Toss the onion in the lemon juice, then add to the skillet. Gently cook, stirring, for 3–4 minutes, or until just beginning to soften.

3 Return the chicken to the pan. Pour in the wine and stock, and bring to a boil. Cover and simmer gently for 30 minutes.

4 Remove the chicken from the pan, reserving the cooking juices, and keep warm. Bring the juices to a boil, and boil rapidly for 5 minutes.

5 Blend the remaining butter with the flour to form a paste. Reduce the juices to a simmer and spoon the paste into the skillet, stirring until thickened.

6 Adjust the seasoning according to taste, then stir in the artichoke hearts and cook for an additional 2 minutes. Pour the mixture over the chicken and garnish with chopped parsley.

# Boned Chicken & Parmesan

It's really very easy to bone a whole chicken, but if you prefer, you can ask your butcher to do this for you.

## NUTRITIONAL INFORMATION

| | | | |
|---|---|---|---|
| Calories | .......578 | Sugars | .......0.4g |
| Protein | ........42g | Fat | ..........42g |
| Carbohydrate | ....9g | Saturates | ......15g |

🍲 35 MINS    🕐 1½ HOURS

### SERVES 6

## INGREDIENTS

1 chicken, weighing about 5 lb/2.25 kg

8 slices mortadella or salami

generous 2 cups fresh white or
  brown bread crumbs

generous 1 cup freshly grated
  Parmesan cheese

2 garlic cloves, crushed

6 tbsp chopped fresh basil or parsley

1 egg, beaten

pepper

fresh spring vegetables, to serve

1 Bone the chicken, keeping the skin intact. Dislocate each leg by breaking it at the thigh joint. Cut down each side of the backbone, taking care not to pierce the breast skin.

2 Pull the backbone clear of the flesh and discard. Remove the ribs, severing any attached flesh with a sharp knife.

3 Scrape the flesh from each leg and cut away the bone at the joint with a knife or shears.

4 Use the bones for stock. Lay out the boned chicken on a board, skin side down. Arrange the mortadella slices over the chicken, overlapping slightly.

5 Put the bread crumbs, Parmesan, garlic and basil or parsley in a bowl.

Season with pepper to taste and mix together well. Stir in the beaten egg to bind the mixture together. Spoon the mixture down the middle of the boned chicken, roll the meat around it and then tie securely with string.

6 Place in a roasting dish and brush lightly with olive oil. Roast in a preheated oven, 400°F/200°C, for 1½ hours, or until the juices run clear when pierced.

7 Serve hot or cold, in slices, with fresh spring vegetables.

## VARIATION

Replace the mortadella with slices of lean bacon, if preferred.

# Chicken Cacciatora

This is a popular Italian classic in which browned chicken pieces are cooked in a tomato and bell pepper sauce.

## NUTRITIONAL INFORMATION

| | | | |
|---|---|---|---|
| Calories | .......397 | Sugars | .........4g |
| Protein | ........37g | Fat | ..........17g |
| Carbohydrate | ...22g | Saturates | .......4g |

20 MINS    1 HOUR

### SERVES 4

## INGREDIENTS

1 roasting chicken, about 3 lb 5 oz/1.5 kg, cut into 6 or 8 serving pieces

scant 1 cup all-purpose flour

3 tbsp olive oil

⅔ cup dry white wine

1 green bell pepper, seeded and sliced

1 red bell pepper, seeded and sliced

1 carrot, chopped finely

1 celery stalk, chopped finely

1 garlic clove, crushed

7 oz/200 g canned chopped tomatoes

salt and pepper

1 Rinse and pat dry the chicken pieces with paper towels. Lightly dust them with seasoned flour.

2 Heat the oil in a large skillet. Add the chicken and cook over medium heat until browned all over. Remove from the pan and set aside.

3 Drain off all but 2 tablespoons of the fat in the pan. Add the wine and stir for a few minutes. Then add the bell peppers, carrot, celery, and garlic, then season with salt and pepper to taste and simmer together for 15 minutes.

4 Add the chopped tomatoes to the pan. Cover and simmer for 30 minutes, stirring often, until the chicken is completely cooked through.

5 Check the seasoning before serving piping hot.

# Chicken Lasagna

You can use your favorite mushrooms, such as chanterelles or oyster mushrooms, for this delicately flavored dish.

## NUTRITIONAL INFORMATION

| | | | |
|---|---|---|---|
| Calories | .708 | Sugars | .17g |
| Protein | .35g | Fat | .35g |
| Carbohydrate | .57g | Saturates | .14g |

40 MINS    1¾ HOURS

### SERVES 4

### INGREDIENTS

butter, for greasing

14 sheets precooked lasagna

3¾ cups Béchamel Sauce (see page 28)

¾ cup freshly grated Parmesan cheese

#### EXOTIC MUSHROOM SAUCE

2 tbsp olive oil

2 garlic cloves, crushed

1 large onion, finely chopped

8 oz/225 g exotic mushrooms, sliced

10½ oz/300 g ground chicken

3 oz/85 g chicken livers, finely chopped

½ cup diced prosciutto

⅔ cup Marsala

10 oz/280g canned chopped tomatoes

1 tbsp chopped fresh basil leaves

2 tbsp tomato paste

salt and pepper

1 To make the exotic mushroom sauce, heat the olive oil in a large pan. Add the garlic, onion and mushrooms and cook, stirring frequently, for 6 minutes.

2 Add the ground chicken, chicken livers, and prosciutto, then cook over low heat for 12 minutes, or until the meat has browned.

3 Stir the Marsala, tomatoes, basil, and tomato paste into the mixture in the pan and cook for 4 minutes. Season with salt and pepper to taste, then cover and leave to simmer for 30 minutes. Uncover the pan and stir, then leave to simmer for an additional 15 minutes.

4 Lightly grease an ovenproof dish with butter. Arrange sheets of lasagna over the base of the dish, spoon over a layer of exotic mushroom sauce, then spoon over a layer of Béchamel Sauce. Place another layer of lasagna on top and repeat the process twice, finishing with a layer of Béchamel Sauce. Sprinkle over the grated cheese and bake in a preheated oven at 375°F/190°C for 35 minutes, or until golden brown and bubbling. Serve immediately.

# Grilled Chicken

You need a bit of brute force to prepare the chicken, but once marinated it's an easy and tasty candidate for the grill.

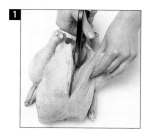

### NUTRITIONAL INFORMATION

| | | |
|---|---|---|
| Calories | .......129 | Sugars .........0g |
| Protein | ........22g | Fat ...........5g |
| Carbohydrate | ....0g | Saturates .......1g |

 2¹/₂ HOURS    30 MINS

### SERVES 4

## I N G R E D I E N T S

3 lb 5 oz/1.5 kg chicken

grated rind of 1 lemon

4 tbsp lemon juice

2 sprigs rosemary

1 small red chile, chopped finely

²/₃ cup olive oil

1 Split the chicken down the breast bone and open it out. Trim off excess fat, and remove the parson's nose, wing, and leg tips. Break the leg and wing joints to enable you to pound it flat. This ensures that it cooks evenly. Cover the split chicken with plastic wrap and pound it as flat as possible with a rolling pin.

2 Mix the lemon rind and juice, rosemary sprigs, chile, and olive oil together in a small bowl. Place the chicken in a large dish and pour over the marinade, turning the chicken to coat it evenly. Cover the dish and leave the chicken to marinate for at least 2 hours.

3 Cook the chicken over a hot grill (the coals should be white, and red when fanned) for about 30 minutes, turning it regularly until the skin is golden and crisp. To test if it is cooked, pierce one of the chicken thighs; the juices will run clear, not pink, when it is ready. Serve.

# Chicken & Lobster on Penne

While this is certainly a treat to get the taste buds tingling,
it is not as extravagant as it sounds.

## NUTRITIONAL INFORMATION

| | | | |
|---|---|---|---|
| Calories | .......696 | Sugars | ........4g |
| Protein | ........59g | Fat | ..........32g |
| Carbohydrate | ...45g | Saturates | .......9g |

  20 MINS   30 MINS

### SERVES 6

### INGREDIENTS

butter, for greasing

6 chicken suprêmes

4 cups dried penne rigate

6 tbsp extra virgin olive oil

¾ cup freshly grated Parmesan cheese

salt

#### FILLING

4 oz/115 g lobster meat, chopped

2 shallots, very finely chopped

2 figs, chopped

1 tbsp Marsala

2 tbsp fresh bread crumbs

1 large egg, beaten

salt and pepper

### COOK'S TIP

The cut of chicken known as
suprême consists of the breast
and wing. It is always skinned.

  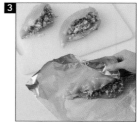

1 Grease 6 pieces of foil large enough to enclose each chicken suprême and lightly grease a cookie sheet.

2 Place all of the filling ingredients into a mixing bowl and blend together thoroughly with a spoon.

3 Cut a pocket in each chicken suprême with a sharp knife and fill with the lobster mixture. Wrap each chicken suprême in foil, place the parcels on the greased cookie sheet and bake in a preheated oven at 400°F/200°C for 30 minutes.

4 Meanwhile, bring a large pan of lightly salted water to a boil. Add the pasta and 1 tablespoon of the olive oil and cook for 10 minutes, or until tender but still firm to the bite. Drain the pasta thoroughly and transfer to a large serving plate. Sprinkle over the remaining olive oil and the grated Parmesan cheese, then set aside and keep warm.

5 Carefully remove the foil from around the chicken suprêmes. Slice the suprêmes very thinly and arrange over the pasta. Serve immediately.

# Skewered Chicken Spirals

These unusual chicken kabobs have a wonderful Italian flavor, and the bacon helps keep them moist during cooking.

## NUTRITIONAL INFORMATION

Calories . . . . . . . .231   Sugars . . . . . . . . .1g

Protein . . . . . . . .29g   Fat . . . . . . . . . .13g

Carbohydrate . . . .1g   Saturates . . . . . . .5g

 15 MINS     10 MINS

### SERVES 4

## INGREDIENTS

4 skinless, boneless chicken breasts

1 garlic clove, crushed

2 tbsp tomato paste

4 slices smoked Canadian bacon

large handful of fresh basil leaves

oil for brushing

salt and pepper

1 Spread out a piece of chicken between two sheets of plastic wrap and beat firmly with a rolling pin to flatten the chicken to an even thickness. Repeat with the remaining chicken breasts.

2 Mix the garlic and tomato paste and spread over the chicken. Lay a bacon slice over each, then scatter with the basil. Season with salt and pepper.

3 Roll up each piece of chicken firmly, then cut into thick slices.

4 Thread the slices onto 4 skewers, making sure the skewer holds the chicken in a spiral shape.

5 Brush lightly with oil and cook on a preheated hot grill or broiler for 10 minutes, turning once. Serve hot with a green salad.

# Chicken with Orange Sauce

The refreshing combination of chicken and orange sauce makes this a perfect dish for a warm summer evening.

## NUTRITIONAL INFORMATION

| | | | |
|---|---|---|---|
| Calories | .......797 | Sugars | ........28g |
| Protein | ........59g | Fat | ..........25g |
| Carbohydrate | ...77g | Saturates | .......6g |

 15 MINS   25 MINS

### SERVES 4

### INGREDIENTS

2 tbsp canola oil

3 tbsp olive oil

4 x 8 oz/225 g chicken suprêmes

⅔ cup orange brandy

2 tbsp all-purpose flour

⅔ cup freshly squeezed orange juice

3 tbsp zucchini, cut into short thin sticks

3 tbsp red bell pepper, cut into short
   thin sticks

6 tbsp leek, finely shredded

14 oz/400 g dried whole-wheat spaghetti

3 large oranges, peeled and cut into
   segments

rind of 1 orange, cut into very fine strips

2 tbsp chopped fresh tarragon

⅔ cup ricotta cheese

salt and pepper

fresh tarragon leaves, to garnish

1 Heat the canola oil and 1 tablespoon of the olive oil in a skillet. Add the chicken and cook quickly until golden brown. Add the orange brandy and cook for 3 minutes. Sprinkle over the flour and cook for 2 minutes.

2 Lower the heat and add the orange juice, zucchini, bell pepper, and leek and season. Simmer for 5 minutes, or until the sauce has thickened.

3 Meanwhile, bring a pan of salted water to a boil. Add the spaghetti and 1 tablespoon of the olive oil and cook for 10 minutes. Drain the spaghetti, then transfer to a serving dish and drizzle over the remaining oil.

4 Add half of the orange segments, half of the orange rind, the tarragon, and ricotta cheese to the sauce in the pan and cook for 3 minutes.

5 Place the chicken on top of the pasta, then pour over a little sauce and garnish with orange segments, rind, and tarragon. Serve immediately.

# Chicken Pepperonata

All the sunshine colors and flavors of Italy are combined in this easy dish.

## NUTRITIONAL INFORMATION

Calories .......328   Sugars .........7g
Protein ........35g   Fat ..........15g
Carbohydrate ...13g   Saturates .......4g

 15 MINS     40 MINS

### SERVES 4

## I N G R E D I E N T S

8 skinless chicken thighs

2 tbsp whole-wheat flour

2 tbsp olive oil

1 small onion, sliced thinly

1 garlic clove, crushed

1 each large red, yellow, and green bell
    peppers, sliced thinly

14 oz/400 g canned chopped tomatoes

1 tbsp chopped oregano

salt and pepper

fresh oregano, to garnish

crusty whole-wheat bread, to serve

1 Remove the skin from the chicken thighs and toss in the flour.

2 Heat the oil in a wide skillet and cook the chicken thighs quickly until sealed and lightly browned. Then remove from the skillet.

3 Add the onion to the skillet and gently cook until soft. Add the garlic, bell peppers, tomatoes, and oregano, then bring to a boil, stirring.

4 Arrange the chicken thighs over the vegetables in the skillet and season well with salt and pepper. Then cover the skillet tightly and simmer for 20–25 minutes, or until the chicken is completely cooked and tender.

5 Season with salt and pepper to taste, garnish with oregano and serve with crusty whole-wheat bread.

### COOK'S TIP

For extra flavor, halve the bell peppers and broil under a preheated broiler until the skins are charred. Leave to cool, then remove the skins and seeds. Slice the bell peppers thinly and use in the recipe.

# Prosciutto-Wrapped Chicken

Stuffed with ricotta, nutmeg, and spinach, then wrapped with wafer-thin slices of prosciutto and gently cooked in white wine.

## NUTRITIONAL INFORMATION

Calories .......426  Sugars .........4g
Protein ........44g  Fat ..........21g
Carbohydrate ....9g  Saturates .......8g

30 MINS    45 MINS

### SERVES 4

## INGREDIENTS

½ cup frozen spinach, defrosted

½ cup ricotta cheese

pinch of freshly grated nutmeg

4 skinless, boneless chicken breasts, each weighing 6 oz/175 g

4 prosciutto slices

2 tbsp butter

1 tbsp olive oil

12 small onions or shallots

2½ cups sliced white mushrooms

1 tbsp all-purpose flour

⅔ cup dry white or red wine

1¼ cups chicken stock

salt and pepper

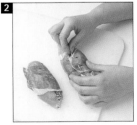

1 Put the spinach into a strainer and press out the water with a spoon. Mix with the ricotta and nutmeg and season with salt and pepper to taste.

2 Using a sharp knife, slit each chicken breast through the side and enlarge each cut to form a pocket. Fill with the spinach mixture, then reshape the chicken breasts. Wrap each breast tightly in a slice of ham and secure with toothpicks. Cover and chill in the refrigerator.

3 Heat the butter and oil in a skillet and brown the chicken breasts for 2 minutes on each side. Transfer the chicken to a large, shallow ovenproof dish and keep warm until required.

4 Cook the onions and mushrooms for 2–3 minutes, or until lightly browned. Stir in the all-purpose flour, then gradually add the wine and stock. Bring to a boil, stirring constantly. Season with salt and pepper and spoon the mixture around the chicken.

5 Cook the chicken uncovered in a preheated oven, 400°F/200°C, for 20 minutes. Turn the breasts over and cook for an additional 10 minutes. Remove the toothpicks and serve with the sauce, together with carrot purée and green beans, if wished.

# Chicken Tortellini

Tortellini were said to have been created in the image of the goddess Venus's navel. Whatever the story, they are a delicious blend of Italian flavors.

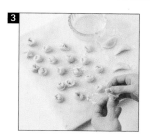

## NUTRITIONAL INFORMATION

| | | | |
|---|---|---|---|
| Calories | .......635 | Sugars | .........4g |
| Protein | ........31g | Fat | ..........36g |
| Carbohydrate | ...50g | Saturates | ......16g |

🍴 1 HOUR    🕐 35 MINS

### SERVES 4

## I N G R E D I E N T S

4 oz/115 g boned chicken breast, skinned

2 oz/55 g prosciutto

¼ cup cooked spinach, well drained

1 tbsp finely chopped onion

2 tbsp freshly grated Parmesan cheese

pinch of ground allspice

1 egg, beaten

1 lb/450 g Basic Pasta Dough (see page 24)

salt and pepper

2 tbsp chopped fresh parsley, to garnish

### S A U C E

1¼ cups light cream

2 garlic cloves, crushed

2 cups thinly sliced white mushrooms

4 tbsp freshly grated Parmesan cheese

1 Bring a pan of seasoned water to a boil. Add the chicken and poach for about 10 minutes. Leave to cool slightly, then put in a food processor with the prosciutto, spinach, and onion and process until finely chopped. Stir in the Parmesan cheese, allspice, and egg and season with salt and pepper to taste.

2 Thinly roll out the pasta dough and cut into 1½–2 inch/4–5 cm rounds.

3 Place ½ tsp of the filling in the center of each round. Fold the pieces in half and press the edges to seal. Wrap each piece around your index finger, then cross over the ends and curl the rest of the dough backward to make a navel shape. Re-roll the trimmings and repeat until all of the dough is used up.

4 Bring a pan of salted water to a boil. Add the tortellini, in batches, then bring back to a boil and cook for 5 minutes. Drain well and transfer to a serving dish.

5 To make the sauce, bring the cream and garlic to a boil in a small pan, then simmer for 3 minutes. Add the mushrooms and half of the cheese, then season with salt and pepper to taste and simmer for 2–3 minutes. Pour the sauce over the chicken tortellini. Sprinkle over the remaining Parmesan cheese and garnish with the parsley, then serve.

# Rich Chicken Casserole

This casserole is packed with the sunshine flavors of Italy. Sun-dried tomatoes add a wonderful richness.

## NUTRITIONAL INFORMATION

Calories . . . . . . .320   Sugars . . . . . . . . .8g
Protein . . . . . . . .34g   Fat . . . . . . . . . .17g
Carbohydrate . . . .8g   Saturates . . . . . . .4g

 🥘🥘🥘

 15 MINS     🕐 1¼ HOURS

### SERVES 4

## INGREDIENTS

8 chicken thighs

2 tbsp olive oil

1 medium red onion, sliced

2 garlic cloves, crushed

1 large red bell pepper, sliced thickly

thinly pared rind and juice of 1 small orange

½ cup chicken stock

14 oz/400 g canned chopped tomatoes

½ cup sun-dried tomatoes, thinly sliced

1 tbsp chopped fresh thyme

⅓ cup pitted black olives

salt and pepper

orange rind and thyme sprigs, to garnish

crusty fresh bread, to serve

1 In a heavy or nonstick large skillet, cook the chicken without fat over a fairly high heat, turning occasionally until golden brown. Using a slotted spoon, drain off any excess fat from the chicken and transfer to a flameproof casserole.

2 Add the oil to the pan and cook the onion, garlic, and bell pepper over moderate heat for 3–4 minutes. Transfer the vegetables to the casserole.

3 Add the orange rind and juice, chicken stock, canned tomatoes, and sun-dried tomatoes to the casserole and stir to combine.

4 Bring to a boil, then cover the casserole with a lid and simmer very gently over low heat for about 1 hour, stirring occasionally. Add the chopped fresh thyme and pitted black olives, then adjust the seasoning with salt and pepper to taste.

5 Scatter orange rind and thyme over the casserole to garnish, and serve with crusty bread.

## COOK'S TIP

Sun-dried tomatoes have a dense texture and concentrated taste, and add intense flavor to slow-cooking casseroles.

# Chicken with Vegetables

This dish combines succulent chicken with tasty vegetables, flavored with wine and olives.

## NUTRITIONAL INFORMATION

| | | | |
|---|---|---|---|
| Calories | .470 | Sugars | .7g |
| Protein | .29g | Fat | .34g |
| Carbohydrate | .7g | Saturates | .16g |

20 MINS  1¹/₂ HOURS

### SERVES 4

## INGREDIENTS

4 chicken breasts, part boned

2 tbsp olive oil

2 tbsp butter

1 large onion, chopped finely

2 garlic cloves, crushed

2 bell peppers, red, yellow, or green, cored, seeded, and cut into large pieces

8 oz/225 g large closed-cup mushrooms, sliced or cut into fourths

6 oz/175 g tomatoes, peeled and halved

²/₃ cup dry white wine

²/₃–1 cup green olives, pitted

4–6 tbsp heavy cream

salt and pepper

chopped flat-leaf parsley, to garnish

1 Season the chicken with salt and pepper to taste. Heat the oil and butter in a skillet, add the chicken and cook until browned all over. Remove the chicken from the skillet.

2 Add the onion and garlic to the skillet and cook gently until they are just beginning to soften. Add the bell peppers to the skillet with the mushrooms and continue to cook for a few minutes longer, stirring occasionally.

3 Add the tomatoes and plenty of seasoning to the skillet and then transfer the vegetable mixture to an ovenproof casserole. Place the chicken on the bed of vegetables.

4 Add the wine to the skillet and bring to a boil. Pour the wine over the chicken and cover the casserole tightly. Cook in a preheated oven, 350°F/180°C, for 50 minutes.

5 Add the olives to the chicken and mix lightly, then pour on the cream. Re-cover the casserole and return to the oven for 10–20 minutes, or until the chicken is very tender.

6 Adjust the seasoning and serve the pieces of chicken, surrounded by the vegetables and sauce, with pasta or tiny new potatoes. Sprinkle with chopped parsley to garnish.

# Chicken & Seafood Pockets

These mouth-watering mini-pockets of chicken and shrimp
on a bed of pasta will delight your guests.

## NUTRITIONAL INFORMATION

| | | | |
|---|---|---|---|
| Calories | .......799 | Sugars | .........5g |
| Protein | ........50g | Fat | ..........45g |
| Carbohydrate | ...51g | Saturates | ......13g |

🍲 45 MINS     🕐 25 MINS

### SERVES 4

## I N G R E D I E N T S

4 tbsp butter, plus extra for greasing

4 x 7 oz/200 g chicken suprêmes, trimmed

4 oz/115 g large spinach leaves, trimmed
and blanched in hot salted water

4 slices of prosciutto

12–16 raw jumbo shrimp, shelled and
deveined

1 lb/450 g dried tagliatelle

1 tbsp olive oil

3 leeks, shredded

1 large carrot, grated

⅔ cup thick mayonnaise

2 large cooked beets

salt

1 Grease 4 large pieces of foil and set
aside. Place each suprême between
2 pieces of baking parchment and pound
with a rolling pin to flatten.

2 Divide half of the spinach between
the suprêmes, then add a slice of ham
to each and top with more spinach. Place
3–4 shrimp on top of the spinach. Fold the
pointed end of the suprême over the
shrimp, then fold over again to form a
pocket. Wrap in foil, then place on a

cookie sheet and bake in a preheated oven
at 400°F/200°C for 20 minutes.

3 Meanwhile, bring a pan of salted
water to a boil. Add the pasta and oil
and cook for 8–10 minutes, or until tender.
Drain and transfer to a serving dish.

4 Melt the butter in a skillet. Cook the
leeks and carrot for 3 minutes.
Transfer the vegetables to the center of
the pasta.

5 Work the mayonnaise and 1 beet in a
food processor or blender until
smooth. Rub through a strainer and pour
around the pasta and vegetables.

6 Cut the remaining beet into diamond
shapes and place them neatly around
the mayonnaise. Remove the foil from the
chicken and, using a sharp knife, cut the
suprêmes into thin slices. Arrange the
chicken and shrimp slices on top of the
vegetables and pasta, and serve.

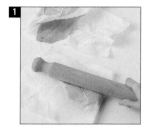
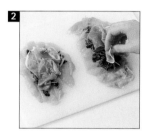
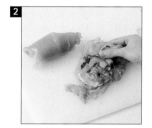

# Garlic & Herb Chicken

There is a delicious surprise of creamy herb and garlic soft cheese hidden inside these chicken pockets!

## NUTRITIONAL INFORMATION

Calories ........272   Sugars .........4g
Protein ........29g   Fat ..........13g
Carbohydrate ....4g   Saturates .......6g

  20 MINS    25 MINS

**SERVES 4**

## I N G R E D I E N T S

4 chicken breasts, skin removed

3½ oz/100 g full-fat soft cheese, flavored
  with herbs and garlic

8 slices prosciutto

⅔ cup red wine

⅔ cup chicken stock

1 tbsp brown sugar

1 Using a sharp knife, make a horizontal slit along the length of each chicken breast to form a pocket.

2 Beat the cheese with a wooden spoon to soften it. Spoon the cheese into the pocket of the chicken breasts.

3 Wrap 2 slices of prosciutto around each chicken breast and secure firmly in place with a length of string.

4 Pour the wine and chicken stock into a large skillet and bring to a boil. When the mixture is just starting to boil, add the sugar and stir well to dissolve.

5 Add the chicken to the mixture in the skillet. Leave to simmer for 12–15 minutes, or until the chicken is tender and the juices run clear when a skewer is inserted into the thickest part of the meat.

6 Remove the chicken from the pan, then set aside and keep warm.

7 Reheat the sauce and boil until reduced and thickened. Remove the string from the chicken and cut into slices. Pour the sauce over the chicken to serve.

## VARIATION

Try adding 2 finely chopped sun-dried tomatoes to the soft cheese in step 2, if you prefer.

# Italian-Style Sunday Roast

A mixture of cheese, rosemary, and sun-dried tomatoes is stuffed under the chicken skin, then roasted with garlic, potatoes, and vegetables.

## NUTRITIONAL INFORMATION

| | | | |
|---|---|---|---|
| Calories | .......488 | Sugars | .........6g |
| Protein | ........37g | Fat | ..........23g |
| Carbohydrate | ...34g | Saturates | ......11g |

35 MINS    1½ HOURS

### SERVES 6

## INGREDIENTS

5 lb 8 oz/2.5 kg chicken

sprigs of fresh rosemary

6 oz/175 g feta cheese, coarsely grated

2 tbsp sun-dried tomato paste

4 tbsp butter, softened

1 bulb garlic

2 lb 4 oz/1 kg new potatoes, halved if large

1 each red, green, and yellow bell pepper,
  cut into chunks

3 zucchini, sliced thinly

2 tbsp olive oil

2 tbsp all-purpose flour

2½ cups chicken stock

salt and pepper

1 Rinse the chicken inside and out with cold water and drain well. Carefully cut between the skin and the top of the breast meat using a small pointed knife. Slide a finger into the slit and carefully enlarge it to form a pocket. Continue until the skin is completely lifted away from both breasts and the top of the legs.

2 Chop the leaves from 3 rosemary stems. Mix with the feta cheese, sun-dried tomato paste, butter, and pepper to taste, then spoon under the skin. Put the chicken in a large roasting pan, then cover with foil and cook in a preheated oven, 375°F/190°C, for 20 minutes per 1 lb 2 oz/ 500 g, plus 20 minutes.

3 Break the garlic bulb into cloves, but do not peel. Add the vegetables to the chicken after 40 minutes.

4 Drizzle with oil, then tuck in a few stems of rosemary and season with salt and pepper. Cook for the remaining calculated time, removing the foil for the last 40 minutes to brown the chicken.

5 Transfer the chicken to a serving platter. Place some of the vegetables around the chicken and transfer the remainder to a warmed serving dish. Pour the fat out of the roasting pan and stir the flour into the remaining pan juices. Cook for 2 minutes, then gradually stir in the stock. Bring to a boil, stirring until thickened. Strain into a sauce boat and serve with the chicken.

# Slices of Duckling with Pasta

A raspberry and honey sauce superbly counterbalances the richness of the duckling.

## NUTRITIONAL INFORMATION

| | | | |
|---|---|---|---|
| Calories | .......686 | Sugars | ........15g |
| Protein | ........62g | Fat | ..........20g |
| Carbohydrate | ...70g | Saturates | .......7g |

🍳 🍳 🍳

🥘 15 MINS    🕐 25 MINS

### SERVES 4

## INGREDIENTS

4 x 9 oz/275 g boned breasts of duckling

2 tbsp butter

⅓ cup finely chopped carrots

⅓ cups tbsp finely chopped shallots

1 tbsp lemon juice

⅔ cup meat stock

4 tbsp clear honey

¾ cup fresh or thawed frozen raspberries

2 tbsp all-purpose flour

1 tbsp Worcestershire sauce

14 oz/400 g fresh linguine

1 tbsp olive oil

salt and pepper

### TO GARNISH

fresh raspberries

fresh sprigs of flat-leaf parsley

1 Trim and score the duck breasts with a sharp knife and season well all over. Melt the butter in a skillet, then add the duck breasts and cook all over until lightly colored.

2 Add the carrots, shallots, lemon juice, and half the meat stock, then simmer over low heat for 1 minute. Stir in half of the honey and half of the raspberries.

Sprinkle over half of the flour and cook, stirring constantly for 3 minutes. Season with pepper to taste and add the Worcestershire sauce.

3 Stir in the remaining stock and cook for 1 minute. Stir in the remaining honey and remaining raspberries and sprinkle over the remaining flour. Cook for an additional 3 minutes.

4 Remove the duck breasts from the skillet, but leave the sauce to continue simmering over very low heat.

5 Meanwhile, bring a large pan of lightly salted water to a boil. Add the linguine and olive oil and cook for 8–10 minutes or until tender but still firm to the bite. Drain and divide between 4 individual plates.

6 Slice the duck breast into ¼ inch/ 5 mm thick pieces. Pour a little sauce over the pasta and arrange the sliced duck in a fan shape on top of it. Garnish with raspberries and flat-leaf parsley and serve immediately.

# Pheasant Lasagna

This scrumptious and unusual baked lasagna is virtually a meal in itself. It is served with pearl onions and green peas.

## NUTRITIONAL INFORMATION

| | | | |
|---|---|---|---|
| Calories . . . . . . .1038 | Sugars . . . . . . . .13g |
| Protein . . . . . . . .65g | Fat . . . . . . . . . .64g |
| Carbohydrate . . .54g | Saturates . . . . . .27g |

🧀 🧀 🧀 🧀

40 MINS          1¼ HOURS

### SERVES 4

## INGREDIENTS

butter, for greasing

14 sheets precooked lasagna

3¾ cups Béchamel Sauce (see page 28)

¾ cup grated mozzarella cheese

### FILLING

8 oz/225 g pork fat, diced

2 tbsp butter

16 small onions

8 large pheasant breasts, thinly sliced

2 tbsp all-purpose flour

2½ cups chicken stock

bouquet garni

1 lb/450 g fresh peas, shelled

salt and pepper

1 To make the filling, put the pork fat into a pan of boiling, salted water and simmer for 3 minutes, then drain and pat dry with paper towels.

2 Melt the butter in a large skillet. Add the pork fat and onions to the skillet and cook for about 3 minutes, or until lightly browned.

3 Remove the pork fat and onions from the skillet and set aside. Add the slices of pheasant and cook over low heat for 12 minutes, or until browned all over. Transfer to an ovenproof dish.

4 Stir the flour into the skillet and cook until just brown, then blend in the stock. Pour the mixture over the pheasant, add the bouquet garni and cook in a preheated oven, at 400°F/200°C, for 5 minutes. Remove the bouquet garni. Add the onions, pork fat, and peas and return to the oven for 10 minutes.

5 Put the pheasant and pork fat in a food processor and grind finely.

6 Lower the oven temperature to 375°F/190°C. Grease an ovenproof dish with butter. Make layers of lasagne, pheasant sauce, and Béchamel Sauce in the dish, ending with Béchamel Sauce. Sprinkle over the cheese and bake for 30 minutes.

# Pesto Baked Partridge

Partridge has a more delicate flavor than many game birds and this subtle sauce perfectly complements it.

## NUTRITIONAL INFORMATION

| | | | |
|---|---|---|---|
| Calories | .......895 | Sugars | .........5g |
| Protein | ........79g | Fat | ..........45g |
| Carbohydrate | ...45g | Saturates | ......18g |

15 MINS      40 MINS

### SERVES 4

## INGREDIENTS

8 partridge pieces (about 4 oz/115 g each)

4 tbsp butter, melted

4 tbsp Dijon mustard

2 tbsp lime juice

1 tbsp brown sugar

6 tbsp Pesto Sauce (see page 39)

1 lb/450 g dried rigatoni

1 tbsp olive oil

1 cup freshly grated Parmesan cheese

salt and pepper

1 Arrange the partridge pieces, smooth side down, in a single layer in a large, ovenproof dish.

2 Mix together the butter, Dijon mustard, lime juice, and brown sugar in a bowl. Season to taste. Brush this mixture over the partridge pieces and bake in a preheated oven at 400°F/200°C for 15 minutes.

3 Remove the dish from the oven. Coat the partridge pieces with 3 tablespoons of the Pesto Sauce. Return to the oven and bake for an additional 12 minutes.

4 Remove the dish from the oven and carefully turn over the partridge pieces. Coat the top of the partridges with the remaining mustard mixture and return to the oven for an additional 10 minutes.

5 Meanwhile, bring a large pan of lightly salted water to a boil. Add the rigatoni and olive oil and cook for 8–10 minutes, or until tender but still firm to the bite. Drain and transfer to a serving dish. Toss the pasta with the remaining Pesto Sauce and the Parmesan cheese.

6 Serve the partridge with the pasta, pouring over the cooking juices.

### VARIATION

You could also prepare young pheasant in the same way.

# Vegetables

Vegetables are a staple ingredient in Italian cooking. The different areas supply a prolific amount of fresh and succulent vegetables, including globe artichokes that grow wild on Sicily, and sweet bell peppers that are sun-ripened in Italy, as are the universally popular sun-ripened tomatoes. Vegetables work well with a variety of different

ingredients, including pasta, rice, grains, and pulses, to make a selection of delicious dishes. However, vegetables can make a tasty meal in themselves. Try vegetables grilled on rosemary skewers—the aromatic flavor of this wonderful herb is imparted during the cooking process to make a very Italian dish. Vegetables have so much potential—experiment and enjoy!

# Vegetable Ravioli

It is important not to overcook the vegetable filling, or it will become sloppy and unexciting, instead of firm to the bite and delicious.

## NUTRITIONAL INFORMATION

| | | |
|---|---|---|
| Calories . . . . . . .622 | Sugars . . . . . . . .10g | |
| Protein . . . . . . . .12g | Fat . . . . . . . . . .40g | |
| Carbohydrate . . .58g | Saturates . . . . . . .6g | |

🕒 1½ HOURS   ⏲ 55 MINS

### SERVES 4

## INGREDIENTS

1 lb/450 g Basic Pasta Dough (see page 24)

1 tbsp olive oil

⅓ cup butter

⅔ cup light cream

¾ cup freshly grated Parmesan cheese

fresh basil sprigs, to garnish

### STUFFING

2 large eggplant

3 large zucchini

6 large tomatoes

1 large green bell pepper

1 large red bell pepper

3 garlic cloves

1 large onion

½ cup olive oil

¼ cup tomato paste

½ tsp chopped fresh basil

salt and pepper

1 To make the stuffing, cut the eggplant and zucchini into 1-inch/2.5-cm chunks. Put the eggplant pieces in a colander, then sprinkle with salt and set aside for 20 minutes. Rinse and drain.

2 Blanch the tomatoes in boiling water for 2 minutes. Drain, skin, and chop the flesh. Core and seed the bell peppers and cut into 1-inch/2.5-cm dice. Chop the garlic and onion.

3 Heat the oil in a pan. Add the garlic cloves and onion and cook for 3 minutes.

4 Stir in the eggplant, zucchini, tomatoes, bell peppers, tomato paste, and basil. Season with salt and pepper to taste, then cover and simmer for 20 minutes, stirring frequently.

5 Roll out the pasta dough and cut out 3-inch/7.5-cm rounds with a plain cutter. Put a spoonful of the vegetable stuffing on each round. Dampen the edges slightly and fold the pasta rounds over, pressing together to seal.

6 Bring a pan of salted water to a boil. Add the ravioli and the oil and cook for 3–4 minutes. Drain and transfer to a greased ovenproof dish, dotting each layer with butter. Pour over the cream and sprinkle over the Parmesan cheese. Bake in a preheated oven at 400°F/200°C for 20 minutes. Serve hot.

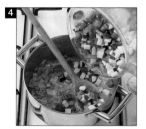

# Braised Fennel & Linguine

This anise-flavored vegetable gives that extra punch to this delicious creamy pasta dish.

## NUTRITIONAL INFORMATION

| | | | |
|---|---|---|---|
| Calories | .......650 | Sugars | .........6g |
| Protein | ........14g | Fat | ..........39g |
| Carbohydrate | ...62g | Saturates | ......22g |

20 MINS    50 MINS

### SERVES 4

## INGREDIENTS

6 fennel bulbs

⅔ cup vegetable stock

2 tbsp butter

6 slices rindless smoked bacon, diced

6 shallots, cut into fourths

2 tbsp all-purpose flour

⅓ cup heavy cream

1 tbsp Madeira

1 lb/450 g dried linguine

1 tbsp olive oil

salt and pepper

1 Trim the fennel bulbs, then gently peel off and reserve the first layer of the bulbs. Cut the bulbs into fourths and put them in a large pan, together with the vegetable stock and the reserved outer layers. Bring to a boil, then lower the heat and simmer for 5 minutes.

2 Using a slotted spoon, transfer the fennel to a large dish. Discard the outer layers of the fennel bulb. Bring the vegetable stock to a boil and leave to reduce by half. Set aside.

3 Melt the butter in a skillet. Add the bacon and shallots and cook for 4 minutes. Add the flour, reduced stock, cream, and Madeira and cook, stirring constantly, for 3 minutes, or until the sauce is smooth. Season to taste and pour over the fennel.

4 Bring a large pan of lightly salted water to a boil. Add the linguine and olive oil and cook for 8–10 minutes, or until tender but still firm to the bite. Drain and transfer to a deep ovenproof dish.

5 Add the fennel and sauce and braise in a preheated oven at 350°F/180°C for 20 minutes. Serve immediately.

## COOK'S TIP

Fennel will keep in the salad drawer of the refrigerator for 2–3 days, but it is best eaten as fresh as possible. Cut surfaces turn brown quickly, so do not prepare it too much in advance of cooking.

# Spinach & Mushroom Lasagna

Always check the seasoning of vegetables—you can always add a little more to a recipe, but you cannot take it out once it has been added.

## NUTRITIONAL INFORMATION

| | | | |
|---|---|---|---|
| Calories | . . . . . . .720 | Sugars | . . . . . . . . .9g |
| Protein | . . . . . . . .31g | Fat | . . . . . . . . . .52g |
| Carbohydrate | . . .36g | Saturates | . . . . . .32g |

20 MINS     40 MINS

### SERVES 4

## INGREDIENTS

½ cup butter, plus extra for greasing

2 garlic cloves, finely chopped

4 oz/115 g shallots

8 oz/225 g exotic mushrooms,
    such as chanterelles

1 lb/450 g spinach, cooked, drained and
    finely chopped

2 cups grated Cheddar cheese

¼ tsp freshly grated nutmeg

1 tsp chopped fresh basil

⅓ cup all-purpose flour

2½ cups hot milk

½ cup grated Cheshire cheese

salt and pepper

8 sheets precooked lasagna

1 Lightly grease a large ovenproof dish with a little butter.

2 Melt 4 tablespoons of the butter in a skillet. Add the garlic, shallots, and exotic mushrooms and cook over low heat for 3 minutes. Stir in the spinach, Cheddar cheese, nutmeg, and basil. Season with salt and pepper to taste and set aside.

3 Melt the remaining butter in a pan over low heat. Add the flour and cook, stirring constantly, for 1 minute. Gradually stir in the hot milk, whisking constantly until smooth. Stir in ¼ cup of the Cheshire cheese and season to taste with salt and pepper.

4 Spread half of the mushroom and spinach mixture over the base of the prepared dish. Cover with a layer of lasagna and then with half of the cheese sauce. Repeat the process and sprinkle over the remaining Cheshire cheese.

5 Bake in a preheated oven, at 400°F/200°C, for 30 minutes, or until golden brown. Serve hot.

## VARIATION

You could substitute 4 bell peppers for the spinach. Roast in a preheated oven, at 400°F/200°C, for 20 minutes. Rub off the skins under cold water, seed and chop before using.

# Twice Baked Potatoes

The potatoes are baked until fluffy, then the flesh is scooped out and mixed with pesto before being returned to the potato shells and baked again.

## NUTRITIONAL INFORMATION

| | | | |
|---|---|---|---|
| Calories | .......424 | Sugars | .........3g |
| Protein | .........9g | Fat | ..........27g |
| Carbohydrate | ...40g | Saturates | ......13g |

 10 MINS     1¹/₂ HOURS

### SERVES 4

## I N G R E D I E N T S

4 baking potatoes, about 8 oz/225 g each

⅔ cup heavy cream

⅓ cup vegetable stock

1 tbsp lemon juice

2 garlic cloves, crushed

3 tbsp chopped fresh basil

2 tbsp pine nuts

2 tbsp freshly grated Parmesan cheese

salt and pepper

1 Scrub the potatoes and prick the skins all over with a fork. Rub a little salt into the skins and place the potatoes onto a cookie sheet.

2 Cook in a preheated oven, 375°F/ 190°C, for 1 hour, or until the potatoes are cooked through and the skins are crisp.

3 Remove the potatoes from the oven and cut them in half lengthwise. Using a spoon, scoop the potato flesh into a mixing bowl, leaving a thin shell of potato inside the skins. Mash the potato flesh with a fork.

4 Meanwhile, mix the cream and stock in a pan and simmer for 8–10 minutes, or until reduced by half.

5 Stir in the lemon juice, garlic, and chopped basil and season to taste with salt and pepper. Stir the mixture into the potato flesh with the pine nuts.

6 Spoon the mixture back into the potato shells and sprinkle the Parmesan cheese on top. Return the potatoes to the oven for 10 minutes, or until the cheese has browned. Serve with salad.

## VARIATION

Add full-fat soft cheese or thinly sliced mushrooms to the mashed potato flesh in step 5, if you prefer.

# Pepperonata

A delicious mixture of bell peppers and onions, cooked with tomatoes and herbs for a rich side dish.

## NUTRITIONAL INFORMATION

| | | | |
|---|---|---|---|
| Calories | .......180 | Sugars | ........14g |
| Protein | .........3g | Fat | ..........12g |
| Carbohydrate | ...15g | Saturates | .......2g |

 15 MINS    40 MINS

### SERVES 4

## INGREDIENTS

4 tbsp olive oil

1 onion, halved and finely sliced

2 red bell peppers, cut into strips

2 green bell peppers, cut into strips

2 yellow bell peppers, cut into strips

2 garlic cloves, crushed

1 lb 12 oz/800 g canned chopped
  tomatoes, drained

2 tbsp chopped cilantro

2 tbsp chopped pitted black olives

salt and pepper

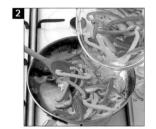

## VARIATION

If you don't like the distinctive flavor of fresh cilantro, you can replace it with 2 tbsp chopped fresh flat-leaf parsley. Use green olives instead of black ones, if you prefer.

1 Heat the oil in a large skillet. Add the onion and sauté for 5 minutes, stirring until just beginning to color.

2 Add the bell peppers and garlic to the skillet and cook for an additional 3–4 minutes.

3 Stir in the tomatoes and cilantro and season with salt and pepper. Cover the skillet and cook the vegetables gently for 30 minutes, or until the mixture is dry.

4 Stir in the pitted black olives and serve the pepperonata immediately.

# Ricotta & Spinach Pockets

Ricotta and spinach make a great flavor combination, especially when encased in light puff-pastry parcels.

## NUTRITIONAL INFORMATION

| | | | |
|---|---|---|---|
| Calories | .......639 | Sugars | .........4g |
| Protein | ........13g | Fat | .........48g |
| Carbohydrate | ...41g | Saturates | ......21g |

25 MINS    30 MINS

### SERVES 4

## INGREDIENTS

12 oz/350 g spinach, trimmed and
  washed thoroughly

2 tbsp butter

1 small onion, chopped finely

1 tsp green peppercorns

1 lb 2 oz/500 g puff pastry

1 cup ricotta

1 egg, beaten

salt

sprigs of fresh herbs, to garnish

fresh vegetables, to serve

1 Pack the spinach into a large pan. Add a little salt and a very small amount of water and cook until wilted. Drain well and leave to cool, then squeeze out any excess moisture with the back of a spoon. Chop roughly.

2 Melt the butter in a small pan and cook the onion gently for 2 minutes or until softened, but not browned. Add the green peppercorns and cook for 2 minutes. Remove from the heat, then add the spinach and mix together.

3 Roll out the puff pastry thinly on a lightly floured counter and cut into 4 squares, each 7 inches/18 cm across. Place one fourth of the spinach mixture in the center of each square and top with one fourth of the cheese.

4 Brush a little beaten egg around the edges of the pastry squares and bring the corners together to form parcels. Press the edges together firmly to seal. Lift the parcels onto a greased cookie sheet, brush with beaten egg and bake in a preheated oven, at 400°F/200°C, for 20–25 minutes, or until risen and golden brown.

5 Serve hot, garnished with sprigs of fresh herbs and accompanied by fresh vegetables.

# Garlic Potato Wedges

This is a great recipe for the grill. Serve this tasty potato dish with broiled meat or fish.

## NUTRITIONAL INFORMATION

| | | | |
|---|---|---|---|
| Calories | .......259 | Sugars | .........1g |
| Protein | .........3g | Fat | ..........17g |
| Carbohydrate | ...26g | Saturates | .......5g |

 10 MINS    35 MINS

### SERVES 4

## I N G R E D I E N T S

3 large baking potatoes, scrubbed

4 tbsp olive oil

2 tbsp butter

2 garlic cloves, chopped

1 tbsp chopped, fresh rosemary

1 tbsp chopped, fresh parsley

1 tbsp chopped, fresh thyme

salt and pepper

1 Bring a large pan of water to a boil, then add the potatoes and par-boil them for 10 minutes. Drain the potatoes and refresh under cold water, then drain them again thoroughly.

2 Transfer the potatoes to a cutting board. When the potatoes are cold enough to handle, cut them into thick wedges, but do not remove the skins.

### COOK'S TIP

You may find it easier to grill these potatoes in a hinged rack or in a specially designed grill roasting pan.

3 Heat the oil and butter in a small pan together with the garlic. Cook gently until the garlic begins to brown, then remove the pan from the heat.

4 Stir the herbs and salt and pepper to taste into the mixture in the pan.

5 Brush the herb mixture all over the potatoes.

6 Grill the potatoes over hot coals for 10–15 minutes, brushing liberally with any of the remaining herb and butter mixture, or until the potatoes are just tender.

7 Transfer the grilled garlic potatoes to a warm serving plate and serve as an appetizer or as a side dish.

# Spinach Frittata

This Italian dish may be made with many flavorings. Spinach is used as the main ingredient in this recipe for colour and flavor.

## NUTRITIONAL INFORMATION

Calories . . . . . . . .307    Sugars . . . . . . . . .4g
Protein . . . . . . . .15g    Fat . . . . . . . . . .25g
Carbohydrate . . . .6g    Saturates . . . . . . .8g

 20 MINS    20 MINS

### SERVES 4

## INGREDIENTS

1 lb/450 g spinach

2 tsp water

4 eggs, beaten

2 tbsp light cream

2 garlic cloves, crushed

generous ½ cup canned corn, drained

1 celery stalk, chopped

1 red chile, chopped

2 tomatoes, seeded and diced

2 tbsp olive oil

2 tbsp butter

¼ cup pecan nut halves

2 tbsp grated Romano cheese

1 oz/25 g fontina cheese, cubed

a pinch of paprika

1 Cook the spinach in 2 teaspoons of water in a covered pan for 5 minutes. Drain thoroughly and pat dry on absorbent paper towels.

2 Beat the eggs in a bowl and stir in the spinach, light cream, garlic, corn, celery, chile, and tomatoes until the ingredients are well mixed.

3 Heat the oil and butter in a 8-inch/20-cm heavy-based skillet.

4 Spoon the egg mixture into the skillet and sprinkle with the pecan nut halves, romano and fontina cheeses, and paprika. Cook, without stirring, over medium heat for 5–7 minute,s or until the underside of the frittata is brown.

5 Put a large plate over the pan and invert to turn out the frittata. Slide it back into the skillet and cook the other side for an additional 2–3 minutes. Serve the frittata straight from the skillet or transfer to a serving plate.

### COOK'S TIP

Be careful not to burn the underside of the frittata during the initial cooking stage—this is why it is important to use a heavy-based skillet. Add a little extra oil to the pan when you turn the frittata over, if required.

# Bell Peppers & Rosemary

The flavor of broiled or roasted bell peppers is very different from when they are eaten raw, so do try them cooked in this way.

## NUTRITIONAL INFORMATION

| | | | |
|---|---|---|---|
| Calories . . . . . . . .201 | Sugars . . . . . . . . .6g |
| Protein . . . . . . . . .2g | Fat . . . . . . . . . .19g |
| Carbohydrate . . . .6g | Saturates . . . . . . .2g |

 20 MINS    10 MINS

### SERVES 4

## I N G R E D I E N T S

4 tbsp olive oil

finely grated rind of 1 lemon

4 tbsp lemon juice

1 tbsp balsamic vinegar

1 tbsp crushed fresh rosemary, or
  1 tsp dried rosemary

2 garlic cloves, crushed

2 red and 2 yellow bell peppers, halved,
  cored, and seeded

2 tbsp pine nuts

salt and pepper

sprigs of fresh rosemary, to garnish

1 Mix together the olive oil, lemon rind, lemon juice, balsamic vinegar, rosemary, and garlic. Season with salt and pepper to taste.

2 Place the bell peppers, skin-side uppermost, on the rack of a broiler pan, lined with foil. Brush the olive oil mixture over them.

3 Broil the bell peppers for 3–4 minutes or until the skin begins to char, basting frequently with the lemon juice mixture. Remove from the heat, then cover with foil to trap the steam and leave for 5 minutes.

4 Meanwhile, scatter the pine nuts onto the broiler rack and toast them lightly for 2–3 minutes. Keep a close eye on the pine nuts as they tend to burn very quickly.

5 Peel the bell peppers, slice them into strips and place them in a warmed serving dish. Sprinkle with the pine nuts and drizzle any remaining lemon juice mixture over them. Garnish with sprigs of fresh rosemary and serve at once.

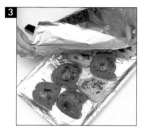

# Pasta-Stuffed Tomatoes

This unusual and inexpensive dish would make a good starter for eight people or a delicious lunch for four.

## NUTRITIONAL INFORMATION

| | |
|---|---|
| Calories .......298 | Sugars .........4g |
| Protein ........10g | Fat ..........20g |
| Carbohydrate ...20g | Saturates .......5g |

15 MINS       35 MINS

### SERVES 4

### I N G R E D I E N T S

5 tbsp extra virgin olive oil, plus extra
   for greasing

8 beef tomatoes or large round tomatoes

1 cup dried ditalini or other very small
   pasta shapes

8 black olives, pitted and finely chopped

2 tbsp finely chopped fresh basil

1 tbsp finely chopped fresh parsley

½ cup freshly grated Parmesan cheese

salt and pepper

fresh basil sprigs, to garnish

1 Brush a cookie sheet with olive oil.

2 Slice the tops off the tomatoes and reserve to make "lids." If the tomatoes will not stand up, cut a thin slice off the bottom of each tomato.

3 Using a teaspoon, scoop out the tomato pulp into a strainer, but do not pierce the tomato shells. Invert the tomato shells on to kitchen paper, pat dry and then set aside to drain.

4 Bring a large pan of lightly salted water to a boil. Add the ditalini or other pasta and 1 tablespoon of the remaining olive oil and cook for 8–10 minutes, or until tender but still firm to the bite. Drain the pasta and set aside.

5 Put the olives, basil, parsley, and Parmesan cheese into a large mixing bowl and stir in the drained tomato pulp. Add the pasta to the bowl. Stir in the remaining olive oil and mix together well, then season to taste with salt and pepper.

6 Spoon the pasta mixture into the tomato shells and replace the lids.

Arrange the tomatoes on the cookie sheet and bake in a preheated oven, at 375°F/ 190°C, for 15–20 minutes.

7 Remove the tomatoes from the oven and leave to cool until just warm.

8 Arrange the pasta-stuffed tomatoes on a serving dish, then garnish with the basil sprigs and serve.

# Vegetable Lasagna

This rich baked pasta dish is packed full of vegetables, tomatoes, and Italian mozzarella cheese.

## NUTRITIONAL INFORMATION

| | | | |
|---|---|---|---|
| Calories | .........510 | Sugars | .........14g |
| Protein | .........17g | Fat | ..........38g |
| Carbohydrate | ...28g | Saturates | ......14g |

🍲 50 MINS     🕐 50 MINS

### SERVES 6

## I N G R E D I E N T S

2 lb 4 oz/1 kg eggplants

8 tbsp olive oil

2 tbsp garlic and herb butter

1 lb/450 g zucchini, sliced

2 cups grated mozzarella cheese

2½ cups crushed tomatoes

6 sheets precooked green lasagna

2½ cups Béchamel Sauce (see page 28)

½ cup freshly grated Parmesan cheese

1 tsp dried oregano

salt and pepper

1 Thinly slice the eggplant and place in a colander. Sprinkle with salt and set aside for 20 minutes. Rinse and pat dry with paper towels.

2 Heat 4 tablespoons of the oil in a large skillet. Cook half of the eggplant slices over low heat for 6–7 minutes, or until golden. Drain thoroughly on paper towels. Repeat with the remaining oil and eggplant slices.

3 Melt the garlic and herb butter in the skillet. Add the zucchini and cook for 5–6 minutes, or until golden brown all over. Drain thoroughly on paper towels.

4 Place half of the eggplant and zucchini slices in a large ovenproof dish. Season with pepper and sprinkle over half of the mozzarella cheese. Spoon over half of the crushed tomatoes and top with 3 sheets of lasagna. Repeat the process, ending with a layer of lasagna.

5 Spoon over the Béchamel Sauce and sprinkle over the Parmesan cheese and oregano. Put the dish on a cookie sheet and bake in a preheated oven, at 425°F/220°C, for 30–35 minutes, or until golden brown. Serve immediately.

# Macaroni Bake

This satisfying dish would make an excellent supper for a mid-week family meal.

## NUTRITIONAL INFORMATION

| | | | |
|---|---|---|---|
| Calories | .......728 | Sugars | ........11g |
| Protein | ........17g | Fat | ..........42g |
| Carbohydrate | ...75g | Saturates | ......23g |

15 MINS     45 MINS

### SERVES 4

## INGREDIENTS

4 cups dried short-cut macaroni

1 tbsp olive oil

4 tbsp beef drippings

1 lb/450 g potatoes, thinly sliced

1 lb/450 g onions, sliced

2 cups grated mozzarella cheese

⅔ cup heavy cream

salt and pepper

crusty brown bread and butter, to serve

1 Bring a large pan of lightly salted water to a boil. Add the macaroni and olive oil and cook for about 12 minutes, or until tender but still firm to the bite. Drain the macaroni thoroughly and set aside.

2 Melt the drippings in a large flame-proof casserole, then remove from the heat.

3 Make alternate layers of potatoes, onions, macaroni, and grated cheese in the casserole, seasoning well with salt and pepper between each layer and finishing with a layer of cheese on top. Finally, pour the cream over the top layer of cheese.

4 Bake in a preheated oven at 400°F/ 200°C for 25 minutes. Remove the casserole from the oven and gently brown the top of the bake under a hot broiler.

5 Serve the bake straight from the dish with crusty brown bread and butter as a main course. Alternatively, serve as a vegetable accompaniment with your favorite main course.

### VARIATION

For a stronger flavor, use mozzarella affumicata, a smoked version of this cheese, or Gruyère cheese instead of the mozzarella.

# Filled Eggplant

Combined with tomatoes and mozzarella cheese, pasta makes a tasty filling for baked eggplant shells.

## NUTRITIONAL INFORMATION

Calories . . . . . . . .342    Sugars . . . . . . . . .6g
Protein . . . . . . . .11g    Fat . . . . . . . . . .16g
Carbohydrate . . .40g    Saturates . . . . . . .4g

25 MINS          55 MINS

### SERVES 4

## I N G R E D I E N T S

2¼ cups dried penne or other short
    pasta shapes

4 tbsp olive oil, plus extra for brushing

2 eggplants

1 large onion, chopped

2 garlic cloves, crushed

14 oz/400 g canned chopped tomatoes

2 tsp dried oregano

½ cup thinly sliced mozzarella cheese

¼ cup freshly grated Parmesan cheese

2 tbsp dry bread crumbs

salt and pepper

salad greens, to serve

1 Bring a pan of lightly salted water to a boil. Add the pasta and 1 tablespoon of the olive oil and cook for 8–10 minutes, or until tender but still firm to the bite. Drain, return to the pan, cover and keep warm.

2 Cut the eggplant in half lengthwise and score around the inside with a sharp knife, being careful not to pierce the shells. Scoop out the flesh with a spoon. Brush the insides of the shells with olive oil. Chop the flesh and set aside.

3 Heat the remaining oil in a skillet. Cook the onion until translucent. Add the garlic and cook for 1 minute. Add the chopped eggplant and cook, stirring frequently, for 5 minutes. Add the tomatoes and oregano and season to taste with salt and pepper. Bring to a boil and simmer for 10 minutes, or until thickened. Remove the skillet from the heat and stir in the pasta.

4 Brush a cookie sheet with oil and arrange the eggplant shells in a single layer. Divide half of the tomato and pasta mixture between them. Sprinkle over the mozzarella, then pile the remaining tomato and pasta mixture on top. Mix the Parmesan cheese and bread crumbs and sprinkle over the top, patting it lightly into the mixture.

5 Bake in a preheated oven, at 400°F/ 200°C for 25 minutes, or until the topping is golden brown. Serve hot with a selection of salad greens.

# Spinach & Ricotta Tart

Frozen phyllo pastry is used to line a flan pan, which is then filled with spinach, red bell peppers, cream, eggs, and ricotta cheese.

## NUTRITIONAL INFORMATION

| | |
|---|---|
| Calories .......375 | Sugars .........3g |
| Protein .........8g | Fat ..........32g |
| Carbohydrate ...14g | Saturates ......18g |

 30 MINS      30 MINS

### SERVES 8

## I N G R E D I E N T S

8 oz/225 g frozen phyllo pastry, thawed

½ cup butter, melted

12 oz/350 g frozen spinach, thawed

2 eggs

⅔ cup light cream

1 cup ricotta cheese

1 red bell pepper, seeded and sliced
  into strips

scant ½ cup pine kernels

salt and pepper

1 Use the sheets of phyllo pastry to line an 8-inch/20-cm flan pan, brushing each layer with melted butter.

2 Put the spinach into a strainer or colander and squeeze out the excess moisture with the back of a spoon or your hand. Form into small balls and arrange in the prepared flan pan.

3 Beat the eggs, cream, and ricotta cheese together until thoroughly blended. Season with salt and pepper to taste and pour over the spinach.

4 Put the remaining butter into a skillet and sauté the red bell pepper strips until softened, about 4–5 minutes. Arrange the strips in the filling.

5 Scatter the pine kernels over the surface and bake in a preheated oven, at 375°F/190°C, for 20–25 minutes, or until the filling has set and the pastry is golden brown. Serve.

## VARIATION

If you're not fond of bell peppers, substitute mushrooms instead. Add a few sliced sun-dried tomatoes for extra color and flavor. This recipe makes an ideal dish for vegetarians, although everyone else is sure to enjoy it too.

# Patriotic Pasta

The ingredients of this dish have the same bright colors as the Italian flag—hence its name.

## NUTRITIONAL INFORMATION

| | | | |
|---|---|---|---|
| Calories | .......325 | Sugars | .........5g |
| Protein | .........8g | Fat | ..........13g |
| Carbohydrate | ...48g | Saturates | .......2g |

 5 MINS   15 MINS

### SERVES 4

### INGREDIENTS

4 cups dried farfalle

4 tbsp olive oil

1 lb/450 g cherry tomatoes

3 oz/85 g arugula

salt and pepper

Romano cheese, to garnish

1 Bring a large pan of lightly salted water to a boil. Add the farfalle and 1 tablespoon of the olive oil and cook for 8–10 minute,s or until tender but still firm to the bite. Drain the farfalle thoroughly and return to the pan.

2 Cut the cherry tomatoes in half and trim the arugula.

## COOK'S TIP

Romano cheese is a hard sheep's milk cheese that resembles Parmesan and is often used for grating over a variety of dishes. It has a sharp flavor and is used only in small quantities.

3 Heat the remaining olive oil in a skillet. Add the tomatoes to the skillet and cook for 1 minute. Add the farfalle and the arugula to the pan and stir gently to mix. Heat through and then season to taste with salt and pepper.

4 Meanwhile, using a vegetable peeler, shave thin slices of Romano cheese.

5 Transfer the farfalle and vegetables to a warm serving dish. Garnish with the Romano cheese shavings and serve immediately.

# Potatoes in Italian Dressing

The warm potatoes quickly absorb the wonderful flavors of olives, tomatoes, and olive oil. This salad is good warm, and cold.

## NUTRITIONAL INFORMATION

| | | | |
|---|---|---|---|
| Calories | .......239 | Sugars | .........2g |
| Protein | .........4g | Fat | ..........10g |
| Carbohydrate | ...36g | Saturates | .......1g |

 15 MINS  15 MINS

### SERVES 4

## I N G R E D I E N T S

1 lb 10 oz/750 g waxy potatoes

1 shallot

2 tomatoes

1 tbsp chopped fresh basil

salt

### I T A L I A N   D R E S S I N G

1 tomato, skinned and chopped finely

4 black olives, pitted and chopped finely

4 tbsp olive oil

1 tbsp wine vinegar

1 garlic clove, crushed

salt and pepper

1 Cook the potatoes in a pan of boiling salted water for 15 minutes, or until they are tender.

2 Drain the potatoes well, then chop coarsely and put into a bowl.

3 Chop the shallot. Cut the tomatoes into wedges and add the shallot and tomatoes to the potatoes.

4 To make the dressing, put all the ingredients into a screw-top jar and mix together thoroughly.

5 Pour the dressing over the potato mixture and toss thoroughly.

6 Transfer the salad to a serving dish and sprinkle with the basil.

### COOK'S TIP

This recipe works well with mealy potatoes. It doesn't look so attractive, as the potatoes break up when they are cooked, but they absorb the dressing wonderfully. Be sure to use an extra virgin olive oil for the dressing to give a really fruity flavor to the potatoes.

# Green Tagliatelle with Garlic

A rich pasta dish for garlic lovers everywhere. It is quick and easy to prepare and full of flavor.

## NUTRITIONAL INFORMATION

| | | | |
|---|---|---|---|
| Calories | .......474 | Sugars | .........3g |
| Protein | ........16g | Fat | ..........24g |
| Carbohydrate | ...52g | Saturates | .......9g |

 20 MINS  15 MINS

### SERVES 4

## INGREDIENTS

2 tbsp walnut oil

1 bunch scallions, sliced

2 garlic cloves, thinly sliced

4 cups sliced mushrooms

1 lb/450 g fresh green and white tagliatelle

1 tbsp olive oil

8 oz/225 g frozen spinach, thawed
    and drained

½ cup full-fat soft cheese with garlic
    and herbs

4 tbsp light cream

scant ½ cup chopped, unsalted
    pistachio nuts

2 tbsp shredded fresh basil

salt and pepper

Italian bread, to serve

### TO GARNISH

fresh basil sprigs

1 Heat the walnut oil in a large skillet. Add the scallions and garlic and cook for 1 minute, or until just softened.

2 Add the mushrooms to the skillet and stir well, then cover and cook over low heat for 5 minutes, or until softened.

3 Meanwhile, bring a large pan of lightly salted water to a boil. Add the tagliatelle and olive oil and cook for 3–5 minutes, or until tender but still firm to the bite. Drain the tagliatelle thoroughly and return to the pan.

4 Add the spinach to the skillet and heat through for 1–2 minutes. Add the cheese to the skillet and let melt slightly. Stir in the cream and cook, without letting the mixture to come to a boil, until warmed through.

5 Pour the sauce over the pasta, then season to taste with salt and pepper and mix well. Heat through gently, stirring constantly, for 2–3 minutes.

6 Transfer the pasta to a serving dish and sprinkle with the pistachio nuts and shredded basil. Garnish with the basil sprigs and serve immediately with the Italian bread of your choice.

# Roasted Bell Pepper Terrine

This delicious terrine is ideal for Sunday lunch. It goes particularly well with Italian bread and a green salad.

## NUTRITIONAL INFORMATION

| | | | |
|---|---|---|---|
| Calories | .......196 | Sugars | .........6g |
| Protein | .........6g | Fat | ..........14g |
| Carbohydrate | ...13g | Saturates | .......3g |

30 MINS     30 MINS

### SERVES 8

## INGREDIENTS

1 lb 2 oz/500 g fava beans

6 red bell peppers, halved and seeded

3 small zucchini, sliced lengthwise

1 eggplant, sliced lengthwise

3 leeks, halved lengthwise

6 tbsp olive oil, plus extra for greasing

6 tbsp light cream

2 tbsp chopped fresh basil

salt and pepper

1 Grease a 5-cup terrine. Blanch the fava beans in boiling water for 1–2 minutes and pop them out of their skins. It is not essential to do this, but the effort is worthwhile as the beans taste a lot sweeter.

2 Roast the red bell peppers over a hot grill until the skin is black – about 10–15 minutes. Remove and put into a plastic bag. Seal and set aside.

3 Brush the zucchini, eggplant, and leeks with 5 tablespoons of the olive oil, and season with salt and pepper to taste. Cook over the hot grill until tender, about 8–10 minutes, turning once.

4 Meanwhile, purée the fava beans in a blender or food processor with 1 tablespoon of the olive oil, the cream, and seasoning. Alternatively, chop and then press through a strainer.

5 Remove the red bell peppers from the bag and peel.

6 Put a layer of red bell pepper along the bottom and up the sides of the terrine.

7 Spread a third of the bean purée over the bell pepper. Cover with the eggplant slices and spread over half of the remaining bean purée.

8 Sprinkle over the basil. Top with zucchini and the remaining bean purée. Lay the leeks on top. Add any remaining pieces of red bell pepper. Put a piece of foil, folded 4 times, on the top and weigh down with cans.

9 Chill until required. Turn out on to a serving platter, then slice and serve with Italian bread and a green salad.

# Roast Leeks

Use a good-quality Italian olive oil for this deliciously simple yet sophisticated vegetable accompaniment.

## NUTRITIONAL INFORMATION

| | | |
|---|---|---|
| Calories ........52 | Sugars .......0.4g | |
| Protein ........0.3g | Fat ...........5g | |
| Carbohydrate ....1g | Saturates .......1g | |

5 MINS  7 MINS

### SERVES 6

## I N G R E D I E N T S

4 leeks

3 tbsp olive oil

2 tsp balsamic vinegar

sea salt and pepper

1 Halve the leeks lengthwise, making sure that your knife goes straight, so that the leek is held together by the root.

2 Brush each leek liberally with the olive oil.

3 Cook over a hot grill for 6–7 minutes, turning once.

4 Remove the leeks from the grill and brush with balsamic vinegar.

5 Sprinkle with salt and pepper and serve hot or warm.

## VARIATION

If in season, 8 baby leeks may be used instead of 4 standard-sized ones. Sherry vinegar makes a good substitute for the expensive balsamic vinegar and would work as well in this recipe.

# Pesto Potatoes

Pesto sauce is more commonly used as a pasta sauce, but is delicious served over potatoes as well.

## NUTRITIONAL INFORMATION

| | | | |
|---|---|---|---|
| Calories | . . . . . . . .531 | Sugars | . . . . . . . . .3g |
| Protein | . . . . . . . .13g | Fat | . . . . . . . . . .38g |
| Carbohydrate | . . .36g | Saturates | . . . . . . .8g |

 15 MINS     🕐 15 MINS

### SERVES 4

## I N G R E D I E N T S

2 lb/900 g small new potatoes

2¾ oz/75 g fresh basil

2 tbsp pine nuts

3 garlic cloves, crushed

scant ½ cup olive oil

¾ cup freshly grated Parmesan cheese
  and Romano cheese, mixed

salt and pepper

fresh basil sprigs, to garnish

1 Cook the potatoes in a pan of boiling salted water for 15 minutes, or until tender. Drain well, transfer to a warm serving dish and keep warm until required.

2 Meanwhile, put the basil, pine nuts, garlic, and a little salt and pepper to taste in a food processor. Blend for 30 seconds, adding the oil gradually, until smooth.

3 Remove the mixture from the food processor and place in a mixing bowl. Stir in the grated Parmesan and romano cheeses.

4 Spoon the pesto sauce over the potatoes and mix well. Garnish with fresh basil sprigs and serve immediately.

# Parmesan Potatoes

This is a very simple way to jazz up roast potatoes. Serve them in the same way as ordinary roast potatoes with roasted meats or fish.

## NUTRITIONAL INFORMATION

| | | |
|---|---|---|
| Calories . . . . . . . .307 | Sugars . . . . . . . . .2g | |
| Protein . . . . . . . .11g | Fat . . . . . . . . . .14g | |
| Carbohydrate . . .37g | Saturates . . . . . . .6g | |

15 MINS        1 HR 5 MINS

### SERVES 4

## INGREDIENTS

6 potatoes

¹/₂ cup freshly grated Parmesan cheese

pinch of grated nutmeg

1 tbsp chopped fresh parsley

4 smoked bacon slices, cut into strips

oil, for roasting

salt

1 Cut the potatoes in half lengthwise and cook them in a pan of boiling salted water for 10 minutes. Drain thoroughly.

2 Mix the grated Parmesan cheese, nutmeg, and parsley together in a shallow bowl.

3 Roll the potato pieces in the cheese mixture to coat them completely. Shake off any excess.

## VARIATION

If you prefer, use slices of salami or prosciutto instead of the bacon, adding it to the dish 5 minutes before the end of the cooking time.

4 Pour a little oil into a roasting pan and heat it in a preheated oven, 400°F/200°C, for 10 minutes. Remove from the oven and place the potatoes into the pan. Return the pan to the oven and cook for 30 minutes, turning once.

5 Remove from the oven and sprinkle the bacon on top of the potatoes. Return to the oven for 15 minutes, or until the potatoes and bacon are cooked. Drain off any excess fat and serve.

# Pesto Potatoes

Pesto sauce is more commonly used as a pasta sauce, but is delicious served over potatoes as well.

## NUTRITIONAL INFORMATION

| | | | |
|---|---|---|---|
| Calories | .......531 | Sugars | .........3g |
| Protein | ........13g | Fat | ..........38g |
| Carbohydrate | ...36g | Saturates | .......8g |

 15 MINS     15 MINS

### SERVES 4

## I N G R E D I E N T S

2 lb/900 g small new potatoes

2¾ oz/75 g fresh basil

2 tbsp pine nuts

3 garlic cloves, crushed

scant ½ cup olive oil

¾ cup freshly grated Parmesan cheese
   and Romano cheese, mixed

salt and pepper

fresh basil sprigs, to garnish

1 Cook the potatoes in a pan of boiling salted water for 15 minutes, or until tender. Drain well, transfer to a warm serving dish and keep warm until required.

2 Meanwhile, put the basil, pine nuts, garlic, and a little salt and pepper to taste in a food processor. Blend for 30 seconds, adding the oil gradually, until smooth.

3 Remove the mixture from the food processor and place in a mixing bowl. Stir in the grated Parmesan and romano cheeses.

4 Spoon the pesto sauce over the potatoes and mix well. Garnish with fresh basil sprigs and serve immediately.

# Italian Vegetable Tart

A rich tomato pastry base topped with a mouthwatering selection of vegetables and cheese makes a tart that's tasty as well as attractive.

## NUTRITIONAL INFORMATION

Calories . . . . . . .438    Sugars . . . . . . . . .8g
Protein . . . . . . . . .9g   Fat . . . . . . . . . .28g
Carbohydrate . . .40g   Saturates . . . . . .15g

1³/₄ HOURS          40 MINS

## SERVES 6

## INGREDIENTS

1 eggplant, sliced

2 tbsp salt

4 tbsp olive oil

1 garlic clove, crushed

1 large yellow bell pepper, seeded
    and sliced

1¼ cups ready-made tomato pasta sauce

⅔ cup sun-dried tomatoes in oil, drained
    and halved if necessary

6 oz/175 g mozzarella cheese,
    drained and sliced thinly

### PASTRY

1½ cups all-purpose flour

pinch of celery salt

½ cup butter or margarine

2 tbsp tomato paste

2–3 tbsp milk

1 To make the pastry, sift the flour and celery salt into a bowl and rub in the butter until the mixture resembles fine bread crumbs.

2 Mix together the tomato paste and milk and stir into the mixture to form a firm dough. Knead gently on a lightly floured counter until smooth. Wrap and chill for 30 minutes.

3 Grease an 11-inch/28-cm loose-bottomed flan tin. Roll out the pastry on a lightly floured counter and use to line the tin. Trim and prick all over with a fork. Chill for 30 minutes.

4 Meanwhile, layer the eggplant in a dish, sprinkling with the salt. Leave for 30 minutes.

5 Bake the pastry case in a preheated oven, 400°F/200°C, for 20–25 minutes, or until cooked and lightly golden. Set aside. Increase the oven temperature to 450°F/230°C.

6 Rinse the eggplant and pat dry. Heat 3 tablespoons of oil in a skillet and cook the garlic, eggplant and bell pepper for 5–6 minutes, or until just softened. Drain on paper towels.

7 Spread the pastry case with pasta sauce and arrange the cooked vegetables, sun-dried tomatoes and mozzarella on top. Brush with the remaining oil and bake for 5 minutes, until the cheese is just melting.

# Spinach & Ricotta Pie

This puff pastry pie looks impressive and is actually fairly easy to make. Serve it hot or cold.

## NUTRITIONAL INFORMATION

| | | | |
|---|---|---|---|
| Calories | .......545 | Sugars | .........3g |
| Protein | ........19g | Fat | ..........42g |
| Carbohydrate | ...25g | Saturates | ......13g |

🍲 25 MINS   🕐 50 MINS

### SERVES 4

## INGREDIENTS

8 oz/225 g spinach

⅛ cup pine nuts

scant ½ cup ricotta cheese

2 large eggs, beaten

½ cup ground almonds

½ cup freshly grated Parmesan cheese

9 oz/250 g puff pastry, defrosted if frozen

1 small egg, beaten

1 Rinse the spinach, then place in a large pan and cook for 4-5 minutes until wilted. Drain thoroughly. When the spinach is cool enough to handle, squeeze out the excess liquid.

2 Place the pine nuts on a cookie sheet and lightly toast under a preheated broiler for 2–3 minutes, or until golden.

3 Place the ricotta, spinach, and eggs in a bowl and mix together. Add the pine nuts, beat well, then stir in the ground almonds and Parmesan cheese.

4 Roll out the puff pastry and make 2 x 8-inch/20-cm squares. Trim the edges, reserving the pastry trimmings.

5 Place 1 pastry square on a cookie sheet. Spoon over the spinach mixture, keeping within ½ inch/12 mm of

 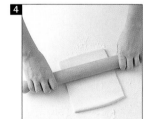 

the edge of the pastry. Brush the edges with beaten egg and place the second square over the top.

6 Using a round-bladed knife, press the pastry edges together by tapping along the sealed edge. Use the pastry trimmings to make a few leaves to decorate the pie.

7 Brush the pie with the beaten egg and bake in a preheated oven, at 425°F/220°C, for 10 minutes. Reduce the oven temperature to 375°F/190°C and bake for an additional 25–30 minutes. Serve hot.

## COOK'S TIP

Spinach is very nutritious as it is full of iron—this is particularly important for women and elderly people who may need more of this mineral in their diet.

# Parmesan Potatoes

This is a very simple way to jazz up roast potatoes. Serve them in the same way as ordinary roast potatoes with roasted meats or fish.

## NUTRITIONAL INFORMATION

| | | | |
|---|---|---|---|
| Calories | 307 | Sugars | 2g |
| Protein | 11g | Fat | 14g |
| Carbohydrate | 37g | Saturates | 6g |

15 MINS    1 HR 5 MINS

### SERVES 4

### I N G R E D I E N T S

6 potatoes

¹/₂ cup freshly grated Parmesan cheese

pinch of grated nutmeg

1 tbsp chopped fresh parsley

4 smoked bacon slices, cut into strips

oil, for roasting

salt

1 Cut the potatoes in half lengthwise and cook them in a pan of boiling salted water for 10 minutes. Drain thoroughly.

2 Mix the grated Parmesan cheese, nutmeg, and parsley together in a shallow bowl.

3 Roll the potato pieces in the cheese mixture to coat them completely. Shake off any excess.

## VARIATION

If you prefer, use slices of salami or prosciutto instead of the bacon, adding it to the dish 5 minutes before the end of the cooking time.

4 Pour a little oil into a roasting pan and heat it in a preheated oven, 400°F/200°C, for 10 minutes. Remove from the oven and place the potatoes into the pan. Return the pan to the oven and cook for 30 minutes, turning once.

5 Remove from the oven and sprinkle the bacon on top of the potatoes. Return to the oven for 15 minutes, or until the potatoes and bacon are cooked. Drain off any excess fat and serve.

# Spaghetti & Mushroom Sauce

This easy vegetarian dish is ideal for busy people with little time but good taste!

## NUTRITIONAL INFORMATION

Calories ......604    Sugars .........5g
Protein ........11g    Fat ..........39g
Carbohydrate ...54g    Saturates ......21g

 20 MINS     35 MINS

### SERVES 4

## INGREDIENTS

4 tbsp butter

2 tbsp olive oil

6 shallots, sliced

1 lb/450 g white mushrooms, sliced

1 tsp all-purpose flour

⅔ cup heavy cream

2 tbsp port

4 oz/115 g sun-dried tomatoes, chopped

freshly grated nutmeg

1 lb/450 g dried spaghetti

1 tbsp freshly chopped parsley

salt and pepper

6 triangles of fried white bread, to serve

  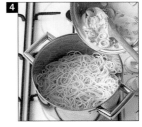

1 Heat the butter and 1 tablespoon of the oil in a large pan. Add the shallots and cook over medium heat for 3 minutes. Add the mushrooms and cook over low heat for 2 minutes. Season with salt and pepper, then sprinkle over the flour and cook, stirring constantly, for 1 minute.

2 Gradually stir in the cream and port, then add the sun-dried tomatoes and a pinch of grated nutmeg and cook over low heat for 8 minutes.

3 Meanwhile, bring a large pan of lightly salted water to a boil. Add the spaghetti and remaining olive oil and cook for 12–14 minutes, or until tender but still firm to the bite.

4 Drain the spaghetti and return to the pan. Pour over the mushroom sauce and cook for 3 minutes. Transfer the spaghetti and mushroom sauce to a large serving plate and sprinkle over the chopped parsley. Serve with crispy triangles of fried bread.

## VARIATION

Non-vegetarians could add 4 oz/115 g prosciutto, cut into thin strips and heated gently in 2 tbsp butter, to the pasta along with the mushroom sauce.

# Fettuccine all'Alfredo

This simple, traditional dish can be made with any long pasta, but is especially good with flat noodles, such as fettuccine or tagliatelle.

## NUTRITIONAL INFORMATION

Calories . . . . . . . .627    Sugars . . . . . . . . .2g
Protein . . . . . . . .18g    Fat . . . . . . . . . .41g
Carbohydrate . . .51g    Saturates . . . . . .23g

5 MINS          10 MINS

### SERVES 4

### INGREDIENTS

2 tbsp butter

generous ¾ cup heavy cream

1 lb/450 g fresh fettuccine

1 tbsp olive oil

¾ cup freshly grated Parmesan cheese,
    plus extra to serve

pinch of freshly grated nutmeg

salt and pepper

fresh parsley sprigs, to garnish

1 Put the butter and ⅔ cup of the cream in a large pan and bring the mixture to a boil over a medium heat. Reduce the heat and then simmer gently for 1½ minutes, or until slightly thickened.

2 Meanwhile, bring a large pan of lightly salted water to a boil. Add the fettuccine and olive oil and cook for

## VARIATION

This classic Roman dish is often served with the addition of strips of ham and fresh peas. Add 2 cups shelled cooked peas and 6 oz/175 g ham strips with the Parmesan cheese in step 4.

2–3 minutes, or until tender but still firm to the bite. Drain the fettuccine thoroughly and then pour over the cream sauce.

3 Toss the fettuccine in the sauce over low heat until thoroughly coated.

4 Add the remaining cream, the Parmesan cheese, and nutmeg to the fettuccine mixture and season to taste

with salt and pepper. Toss thoroughly to coat while gently heating through.

5 Transfer the fettuccine mixture to a warm serving plate and garnish with sprigs of fresh parsley. Serve immediately, handing extra grated Parmesan cheese separately.

# Italian Spaghetti

Delicious vegetables, cooked in a rich tomato sauce, make an ideal topping for nutty whole-wheat pasta.

## NUTRITIONAL INFORMATION

| | | |
|---|---|---|
| Calories . . . . . . . .381 | Sugars . . . . . . . . .9g | |
| Protein . . . . . . . .11g | Fat . . . . . . . . . .16g | |
| Carbohydrate . . .53g | Saturates . . . . . . .5g | |

20 MINS     35 MINS

### SERVES 4

### I N G R E D I E N T S

2 tbsp olive oil

1 large red onion, chopped

2 garlic cloves, crushed

1 tbsp lemon juice

4 baby eggplants, cut into fourths

2½ cups crushed tomatoes

2 tsp superfine sugar

2 tbsp tomato paste

14 oz/400 g canned artichoke hearts,
    drained and halved

⅔ cup pitted black olives

12 oz/350 g dried spaghetti

2 tbsp butter

salt and pepper

fresh basil sprigs, to garnish

olive bread, to serve

1 Heat 1 tablespoon of the olive oil in a large skillet. Add the onion, garlic, lemon juice, and eggplant and cook over low heat for 4–5 minutes, or until the onion and eggplants are lightly golden brown.

2 Pour in the crushed tomatoes, then season to taste with salt and pepper and stir in the superfine sugar and tomato paste. Bring to a boil, then lower the heat and simmer, stirring occasionally, for 20 minutes.

3 Gently stir in the artichoke hearts and black olives and cook for 5 minutes.

4 Meanwhile, bring a large pan of lightly salted water to a boil. Add the spaghetti and the remaining oil and cook for 7–8 minutes, or until tender but still firm to the bite.

5 Drain the spaghetti thoroughly and toss with the butter. Transfer the spaghetti to a large serving dish.

6 Pour the vegetable sauce over the spaghetti, garnish with the sprigs of fresh basil and serve immediately with olive bread.

# Pasta & Green Vegetables

The different shapes and textures of the vegetables make a mouthwatering presentation in this light and summery dish.

### NUTRITIONAL INFORMATION

| | |
|---|---|
| Calories . . . . . . . .389 | Sugars . . . . . . . . . .4g |
| Protein . . . . . . . .16g | Fat . . . . . . . . . .20g |
| Carbohydrate . . .38g | Saturates . . . . . .11g |

10 MINS     30 MINS

### SERVES 4

## I N G R E D I E N T S

2 cups dried gemelli or other pasta shapes

1 tbsp olive oil

1 head green broccoli, cut into florets

2 zucchini, sliced

8 oz/225 g asparagus spears

generous 1 cup snow peas

1 cup frozen peas

2 tbsp butter

3 tbsp vegetable stock

4 tbsp heavy cream

freshly grated nutmeg

2 tbsp chopped fresh parsley

2 tbsp freshly grated Parmesan cheese

salt and pepper

1 Bring a large pan of lightly salted water to a boil. Add the pasta and olive oil and cook for 8–10 minutes, or until tender but still firm to the bite. Drain the pasta and return to the pan, then cover and keep warm.

2 Steam the broccoli, zucchini, asparagus spears, and snow peas over a pan of boiling salted water until they are just beginning to soften. Remove from the heat and refresh in cold water. Drain and set aside.

3 Bring a small pan of lightly salted water to a boil. Add the frozen peas and cook for 3 minutes. Drain the peas and refresh in cold water, then drain again. Set aside with the other vegetables.

4 Put the butter and vegetable stock in a skillet over a medium heat. Add all of the vegetables, reserving a few of the asparagus spears, and toss carefully with a wooden spoon until they have heated through, taking care not to break them up.

5 Stir in the cream and heat through without bringing to a boil. Season to taste with salt, pepper, and nutmeg.

6 Transfer the pasta to a warmed serving dish and stir in the chopped parsley. Spoon over the vegetable sauce and sprinkle over the Parmesan cheese. Arrange the reserved asparagus spears in a pattern on top and serve.

# Paglia e Fieno

The name of this dish—"straw and hay"—refers to the colors of the pasta when mixed together.

## NUTRITIONAL INFORMATION

| | | | |
|---|---|---|---|
| Calories | .......699 | Sugars | .........7g |
| Protein | ........26g | Fat | ..........39g |
| Carbohydrate | ...65g | Saturates | ......23g |

 10 MINS       10 MINS

### SERVES 4

## I N G R E D I E N T S

4 tbsp butter

1 lb/450 g fresh peas, shelled

generous ¾ cup heavy cream

1 lb/450 g mixed fresh green and white
    spaghetti or tagliatelle

1 tbsp olive oil

½ cup freshly grated Parmesan
    cheese, plus extra to serve

pinch of freshly grated nutmeg

salt and pepper

1 Melt the butter in a large pan. Add the peas and cook, over low heat, for 2–3 minutes.

2 Using a measuring pitcher, pour ⅔ cup of the cream into the pan, then bring to a boil and simmer for 1–1½ minutes, or until slightly thickened. Remove the pan from the heat.

3 Meanwhile, bring a large pan of lightly salted water to a boil. Add the spaghetti or tagliatelle and olive oil and cook for 2–3 minutes, or until just tender but still firm to the bite. Remove the pan from the heat, drain the pasta thoroughly and return to the pan.

4 Add the peas and cream sauce to the pasta. Return the pan to the heat and add the remaining cream and the Parmesan cheese, then season to taste with salt, pepper, and grated nutmeg.

5 Using 2 forks, gently toss the pasta to coat with the peas and cream sauce, while heating through.

6 Transfer the pasta to a serving dish and serve immediately, with extra Parmesan cheese.

### VARIATION

Cook 2½ cups sliced white or oyster mushrooms in 4 tablespoons butter over low heat for 4–5 minutes. Stir into the peas and cream sauce just before adding to the pasta in step 4.

# Spaghetti Olio e Aglio

This easy and satisfying Roman dish originated as a cheap meal for poor people, but has now become a favorite in restaurants and trattorias.

## NUTRITIONAL INFORMATION

| | | | |
|---|---|---|---|
| Calories | . . . . . . . .515 | Sugars | . . . . . . . . .1g |
| Protein | . . . . . . . . .8g | Fat | . . . . . . . . . .33g |
| Carbohydrate | . . .50g | Saturates | . . . . . . .5g |

5 MINS      5 MINS

### SERVES 4

## I N G R E D I E N T S

½ cup olive oil

3 garlic cloves, crushed

1 lb/450 g fresh spaghetti

3 tbsp roughly chopped fresh parsley

salt and pepper

1 Reserve 1 tablespoon of the olive oil and heat the remainder in a medium pan. Add the garlic and a pinch of salt and cook over low heat, stirring constantly, until golden brown, then remove the pan from the heat. Do not let the garlic burn as it will taint its flavor. (If it does burn, you will have to start all over again!)

2 Meanwhile, bring a large pan of lightly salted water to a boil. Add the spaghetti and remaining olive oil to the pan and cook for 2–3 minutes, or until tender but still firm to the bite. Drain the spaghetti thoroughly and return to the pan.

3 Add the oil and garlic mixture to the spaghetti and toss to coat thoroughly. Season with pepper, then add the chopped fresh parsley and toss to coat again.

4 Transfer the spaghetti to a warm serving dish and serve immediately.

## COOK'S TIP

Oils produced by different countries, mainly Italy, Spain, and Greece, have their own characteristic flavors. Some produce an oil which has a hot, peppery taste while others have a "green" flavor.

# Vegetables & Bean Curd

This is a simple, clean-tasting dish of green vegetables, bean curd, and pasta, lightly tossed in olive oil.

## NUTRITIONAL INFORMATION

Calories .......400  Sugars .........5g
Protein ........19g  Fat ..........17g
Carbohydrate ...46g  Saturates .......5g

25 MINS          20 MINS

### SERVES 4

## INGREDIENTS

8 oz/225 g asparagus

1⅓ cups snow peas

2 cups green beans

1 leek

8 oz/225 g shelled small fava beans

2⅔ cups dried fusilli

2 tbsp olive oil

2 tbsp butter or margarine

1 garlic clove, crushed

8 oz/225 g bean curd, cut into
    1-inch/2.5-cm cubes

⅓ cup pitted green olives in brine, drained

salt and pepper

freshly grated Parmesan, to serve

1 Cut the asparagus into 2-inch/5-cm lengths. Finely slice the snow peas diagonally and slice the green beans into 1-inch/2.5-cm pieces. Finely slice the leek.

2 Bring a large pan of water to a boil and add the asparagus, green beans and fava beans. Bring back to a boil and cook for 4 minutes, or until just tender. Drain well and rinse in cold water. Set aside until needed.

3 Bring a large pan of salted water to a boil and cook the fusilli for 8–9 minutes, until just tender. Drain well. Toss in 1 tablespoon of the oil and season well.

4 Meanwhile, in a wok or large skillet, heat the remaining oil and the butter and gently cook the leek, garlic, and bean curd for 1–2 minutes, or until the vegetables have just softened.

5 Stir in the snow peas and cook for 1 minute.

6 Add the boiled vegetables and olives to the pan and heat through for 1 minute. Carefully stir in the pasta and seasoning. Cook for 1 minute and pile into a warmed serving dish. Serve sprinkled with Parmesan.

# Salads

If you need inspiration for salads to accompany your main courses, look no further than this chapter. All of the salads complement a wide variety of dishes, and many make ideal appetizers. You could even serve a proportion of these salads as main meals as they are often quite filling. Use plenty of colorful, fresh ingredients in your salad—

including vegetables such as bell peppers, snow peas, and baby corn cobs, which are all readily available. If possible, use Italian staple ingredients, such as extra-virgin olive oil and balsamic vinegar, for salad dressings, and sprinkle over some Italian cheeses, such as Parmesan and romano, for extra taste. All of the salads in this chapter are refreshing and full of flavor and are sure to get the tastebuds tingling.

# Yellow Bell Pepper Salad

A colorful combination of yellow bell peppers, red radishes, and celery combine to give a wonderfully crunchy texture and fresh taste.

## NUTRITIONAL INFORMATION

| | |
|---|---|
| Calories . . . . . . .176 | Sugars . . . . . . . . .4g |
| Protein . . . . . . . . .4g | Fat . . . . . . . . . .16g |
| Carbohydrate . . . .4g | Saturates . . . . . . .4g |

25 MINS      5 MINS

### SERVES 4

## I N G R E D I E N T S

4 slices lean bacon, chopped

2 yellow bell peppers

8 radishes, washed and trimmed

1 celery stalk, finely chopped

3 plum tomatoes, cut into wedges

3 tbsp olive oil

1 tbsp fresh thyme

1 Dry fry the chopped bacon in a skillet for 4–5 minutes, or until crispy. Remove the bacon from the skillet, then set aside and leave to cool until required.

2 Using a sharp knife, halve and seed the bell peppers. Slice the bell peppers into long strips.

3 Using a sharp knife, halve the radishes and cut them into wedges.

## COOK'S TIP

Tomatoes are actually berries and are related to potatoes. There are many different shapes and sizes of this versatile fruit. The one most used in Italian cooking is the plum tomato, which is very flavorsome.

4 Mix together the bell peppers, radishes, celery, and tomatoes and toss the mixture in the olive oil and fresh thyme. Season to taste with a little salt and pepper.

5 Transfer the salad to serving plates and garnish with the reserved crispy bacon pieces.

# Pasta & Garlic Mayo Salad

This crisp salad would make an excellent accompaniment to broiled meat and is ideal for summer grills.

## NUTRITIONAL INFORMATION

| | | | |
|---|---|---|---|
| Calories | .......858 | Sugars | ........35g |
| Protein | ........11g | Fat | ..........64g |
| Carbohydrate | ...64g | Saturates | .......8g |

 1½ HOURS   10 MINS

### SERVES 4

## I N G R E D I E N T S

2 large lettuces

2¾ cups dried penne

1 tbsp olive oil

8 red eating apples

juice of 4 lemons

1 head of celery, sliced

1 cup shelled, halved walnuts

1 cup fresh garlic mayonnaise
(see Cook's Tip)

salt

1 Wash and drain, then pat dry the lettuce leaves with paper towels. Transfer them to the refrigerator for 1 hour, or until crisp.

2 Meanwhile, bring a large pan of lightly salted water to the boil. Add the pasta and olive oil and cook for 8–10 minutes, or until tender but still firm to the bite. Drain the pasta and refresh under cold running water. Drain thoroughly again and set aside.

3 Core and dice the apples, then place them in a small bowl and sprinkle with the lemon juice.

 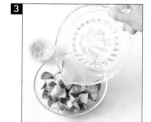 

4 Mix together the pasta, celery, apples, and walnuts and toss the mixture in the garlic mayonnaise. Add more mayonnaise, if liked.

5 Line a salad bowl with the lettuce leaves and spoon the pasta salad into the lined bowl. Serve when required.

### COOK'S TIP

To make garlic mayo, beat 2 egg yolks with a pinch of salt and 6 crushed garlic cloves. Start beating in 1½ cups oil, 1–2 teaspoons at a time. When ¼ of the oil has been incorporated, beat in 1–2 tablespoons white wine vinegar. Continue beating in the oil. Stir in 1 teaspoon Dijon mustard and season.

# Eggplant Salad

An appetizer with a difference from Sicily. It has a real bite, both from the sweet-sour sauce, and from the texture of the celery.

## NUTRITIONAL INFORMATION

| | | | |
|---|---|---|---|
| Calories | .......390 | Sugars | ........15g |
| Protein | .........8g | Fat | .........33g |
| Carbohydrate | ...16g | Saturates | .......5g |

1½ HOURS    25 MINS

### SERVES 4

## INGREDIENTS

2 large eggplants, about 2 lb 4 oz/1 kg

6 tbsp olive oil

1 small onion, chopped finely

2 garlic cloves, crushed

6–8 celery stalks,
    cut into ½-inch/1-cm slices

2 tbsp capers

12–16 green olives, pitted and sliced

2 tbsp pine nuts

1 oz/25 g bitter or dark
    chocolate, grated

4 tbsp wine vinegar

1 tbsp brown sugar

salt and pepper

2 hard-cooked eggs, sliced, to serve

celery leaves or curly endive,
    to garnish

1 Cut the eggplants into 1-inch/2.5-cm cubes and sprinkle liberally with 2–3 tablespoons of salt. Leave to stand for 1 hour to extract the bitter juices, then rinse off the salt thoroughly under cold water. Drain, then dry on paper towels.

2 Heat most of the oil in a skillet and cook the eggplant cubes until golden brown all over. Drain on paper towels, then put in a large bowl.

3 Add the onion and garlic to the pan with the remaining oil and cook very gently until just soft. Add the celery to the pan and cook for a few minutes, stirring frequently, until lightly colored but still crisp.

4 Add the celery to the eggplants with the capers, olives, and pine nuts and mix lightly.

5 Add the chocolate, vinegar, and sugar to the residue in the pan. Heat gently until melted, then bring to a boil. Season with salt and pepper to taste. Pour over the salad and mix lightly. Cover and leave until cold, then chill thoroughly.

6 Serve with sliced hard-cooked eggs and garnish with celery leaves or curly endive.

# Green Salad

Herb-flavored croûtons are topped with peppery arugula, red Swiss chard, green olives, and pistachios to make an elegant combination.

## NUTRITIONAL INFORMATION

Calories ........256    Sugars .........3g
Protein .........4g    Fat ..........17g
Carbohydrate ...23g    Saturates .......3g

  25 MINS     10 MINS

### SERVES 4

## INGREDIENTS

½ cup pistachio nuts

5 tbsp extra virgin olive oil

1 tbsp rosemary, chopped

2 garlic cloves, chopped

4 slices rustic bread

1 tbsp red wine vinegar

1 tsp whole-grain mustard

1 tsp sugar

1 oz/25 g arugula

1 oz/25 g red Swiss chard

⅓ cup green olives, pitted

2 tbsp fresh basil, shredded

1 Shell the pistachios and coarsely chop them, using a sharp knife.

2 Place 2 tablespoons of the extra virgin olive oil in a skillet. Add the rosemary and garlic and cook for 2 minutes.

3 Add the slices of bread to the skillet and cook for 2–3 minutes on both sides until golden. Remove the bread from the pan and drain on absorbent paper towels.

4 To make the dressing, whisk together the remaining olive oil with the red wine vinegar, mustard, and sugar.

5 Place a slice of bread onto a serving plate and top with the arugula and red Swiss chard. Sprinkle with the olives.

6 Drizzle the dressing over the top of the salad leaves. Sprinkle with the chopped pistachios and shredded basil leaves and serve the salad immediately.

## COOK'S TIP

If you cannot find red chard, try slicing a tomato into very thin wedges to add a splash of vibrant red color to the salad.

# Niçoise with Pasta Shells

This is an Italian variation of the traditional Niçoise salad from southern France.

## NUTRITIONAL INFORMATION

| | | | |
|---|---|---|---|
| Calories | .......484 | Sugars | .........5g |
| Protein | ........28g | Fat | ..........26g |
| Carbohydrate | ...35g | Saturates | .......4g |

 45 MINS    30 MINS

### SERVES 4

## I N G R E D I E N T S

3 cups dried small pasta shells

1 tbsp olive oil

¾ cup green beans

1¾ oz/50 g can anchovies, drained

⅛ cup milk

2 small crisp lettuces

1 lb/450 g or 3 large beef tomatoes

4 hard-cooked eggs

8 oz/225 g canned tuna, drained

⅔ cup pitted black olives

salt and pepper

### V I N A I G R E T T E   D R E S S I N G

¼ cup extra virgin olive oil

⅛ cup white wine vinegar

1 tsp whole-grain mustard

salt and pepper

## COOK'S TIP

It is very convenient to make salad dressings in a screw-top jar. Put all the ingredients in the jar and cover securely, then shake well to mix and emulsify the oil.

1 Bring a large pan of lightly salted water to a boil. Add the pasta and the olive oil and cook for 8–10 minutes, or until tender but still firm to the bite. Drain and refresh in cold water.

2 Bring a small pan of lightly salted water to a boil. Add the beans and cook for 10–12 minutes, until tender but still firm to the bite. Drain and refresh in cold water, then drain thoroughly once more and set aside.

3 Put the anchovies in a shallow bowl, then pour over the milk and set aside for 10 minutes. Meanwhile, tear the lettuces into large pieces. Blanch the tomatoes in boiling water for 1–2 minutes, then drain, skin, and roughly chop the flesh. Shell the eggs and cut into fourths. Cut the tuna into large chunks.

4 Drain the anchovies and the pasta. Put all of the salad ingredients, the beans, and the olives into a large bowl and gently mix together.

5 To make the vinaigrette dressing, beat together all of the dressing ingredients and keep in the refrigerator until required. Just before serving, pour the vinaigrette dressing over the salad.

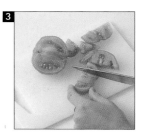

# Tuscan Bean & Tuna Salad

The combination of beans and tuna is a favorite in Tuscany. The hint of honey and lemon in the dressing makes this salad very refreshing.

## NUTRITIONAL INFORMATION

Calories .......224  Sugars .........4g
Protein ........19g  Fat ..........10g
Carbohydrate ...16g  Saturates .......2g

30 MINS          0 MINS

### SERVES 4

## INGREDIENTS

1 small white onion or 2 scallions,
    finely chopped

1 lb 12 oz/800 g canned lima beans,
    drained

2 medium tomatoes

6½ oz/185 g canned tuna, drained

2 tbsp flat-leaf parsley, chopped

2 tbsp olive oil

1 tbsp lemon juice

2 tsp clear honey

1 garlic clove, crushed

1 Place the chopped onions and lima beans in a bowl and mix well to combine.

2 Using a sharp knife, cut the tomatoes into wedges.

3 Add the tomatoes to the onion and bean mixture.

4 Flake the tuna with a fork and add it to the onion and bean mixture together with the parsley.

5 In a screw-top jar, mix together the olive oil, lemon juice, honey, and garlic. Shake the jar until the dressing emulsifies and thickens.

6 Pour the dressing over the bean salad. Toss the ingredients together using 2 spoons and serve.

## VARIATION

Substitute fresh salmon for the tuna if you wish to create a luxurious version of this recipe for a special occasion.

# Chargrilled Chicken Salad

This is a quick appetizer to serve at a barbecue—if the bread is bent in half, the chicken salad can be put in the middle and eaten as finger food.

## NUTRITIONAL INFORMATION

Calories .......225  Sugars .........5g
Protein ........16g  Fat ..........12g
Carbohydrate ...15g  Saturates ......2g

 10 MINS     15 MINS

### SERVES 4

## INGREDIENTS

2 skinless, boneless chicken breasts

1 red onion

oil for brushing

1 avocado, peeled and pitted

1 tbsp lemon juice

½ cup lowfat mayonnaise

¼ tsp chili powder

½ tsp pepper

¼ tsp salt

4 tomatoes, cut into fourths

½ loaf sun-dried tomato-flavored focaccia bread

green salad, to serve

1 Using a sharp knife, cut the chicken breasts into ½ inch/1 cm strips.

2 Cut the onion into eight pieces, held together at the root. Rinse under cold running water and then brush with oil.

3 Purée or mash the avocado and lemon juice together. Whisk in the mayonnaise. Add the chili powder, pepper, and salt.

4 Put the chicken and onion over a grill and grill for 3–4 minutes on each

side. Combine the chicken, onion, tomatoes, and avocado mixture together.

5 Cut the bread in half twice, so that you have quarter-circle-shaped pieces, then in half horizontally. Toast on the hot grill for 2 minutes on each side.

6 Spoon the chicken mixture onto the toasts and serve with a green salad.

## VARIATION

Instead of focaccia, serve the salad in pita breads that have been warmed through on the grill.

# Roast Bell Pepper Salad

Serve chilled as an antipasto with cold meats, or warm as a side dish. Garlic bread makes a delicious accompaniment.

## NUTRITIONAL INFORMATION

| | | |
|---|---|---|
| Calories . . . . . . . . .141 | Sugars . . . . . . . . .8g | |
| Protein . . . . . . . . .1g | Fat . . . . . . . . . . .11g | |
| Carbohydrate . . . .9g | Saturates . . . . . . .2g | |

 20 MINS    20 MINS

### SERVES

## I N G R E D I E N T S

4 large mixed red, green, and yellow
bell peppers

4 tbsp olive oil

1 large red onion, sliced

2 garlic cloves, crushed

4 tomatoes, peeled and chopped

pinch of sugar

1 tsp lemon juice

salt and pepper

1 Trim and halve the bell peppers and remove the seeds.

2 Place the bell peppers, skin-side up, under a preheated hot broiler. Cook until the skins char. Rinse under cold water and remove the skins.

3 Trim off any thick membranes and slice thinly.

4 Heat the oil in a skillet and cook the onion and garlic until softened. Then add the bell peppers and tomatoes and cook over low heat for 10 minutes.

5 Remove from the heat. Add the sugar and lemon juice, then season to taste. Serve immediately or leave to cool (the flavors will develop as the salad cools).

# Spinach Salad

Fresh baby spinach is tasty and light, and it makes an excellent salad to go with the chicken and creamy dressing.

## NUTRITIONAL INFORMATION

Calories .......145   Sugars .........3g
Protein ........10g   Fat ..........10g
Carbohydrate ....4g   Saturates .......1g

30 MINS     0 MINS

### SERVES 4

## INGREDIENTS

scant ½ cup mushrooms

3½ oz/100 g baby spinach, washed

2¾ oz/75 g radicchio leaves, shredded

3½ oz/100 g cooked chicken,
   preferably breast

1¾ oz/50 g prosciutto

2 tbsp olive oil

finely grated rind of ½ orange and juice
   of 1 orange

1 tbsp plain yogurt

1 Wipe the mushrooms with a damp cloth to remove any excess dirt.

2 Gently mix together the spinach and radicchio in a large salad bowl.

3 Using a sharp knife, thinly slice the wiped mushrooms and add them to the bowl containing the spinach and radicchio.

4 Tear the cooked chicken breast and prosciutto into strips and mix them into the spinach salad.

5 To make the dressing, place the olive oil, orange rind, juice and yogurt into a screw-top jar. Shake the jar until the mixture is well combined. Season to taste with salt and pepper.

6 Drizzle the dressing over the spinach salad and toss to mix well. Serve.

## VARIATION

Spinach is delicious when served raw. Try raw spinach in a salad garnished with bacon or garlicky croûtons. The young leaves have a wonderfully sharp flavor.

# Goat Cheese & Penne Salad

This superb salad is delicious when served with strongly flavored meat dishes, such as venison.

## NUTRITIONAL INFORMATION

| | | | |
|---|---|---|---|
| Calories | .......634 | Sugars | ........13g |
| Protein | ........18g | Fat | ..........51g |
| Carbohydrate | ...27g | Saturates | ......13g |

   1½ HOURS   15 MINS

### SERVES 4

## INGREDIENTS

2¼ cups dried penne

5 tbsp olive oil

1 head radicchio, torn into pieces

1 Webbs lettuce, torn into pieces

7 tbsp chopped walnuts

2 ripe pears, cored and diced

1 fresh basil sprig

1 bunch of watercress, or arugula

2 tbsp lemon juice

3 tbsp garlic vinegar

4 tomatoes, cut into fourths

1 small onion, sliced

1 large carrot, grated

9 oz/250 g goat cheese, diced

salt and pepper

1 Bring a large pan of lightly salted water to a boil. Add the penne and 1 tablespoon of the olive oil and cook for 8–10 minutes, or until tender but still firm to the bite. Drain the pasta and refresh under cold running water, then drain thoroughly again and set aside to cool.

2 Place the radicchio and Webbs lettuce in a large salad bowl and mix together well. Top with the pasta, walnuts, pears, basil, and watercress leaves.

3 Mix together the lemon juice, the remaining olive oil, and the vinegar in a pitcher. Pour the mixture over the salad ingredients and toss to coat the salad leaves well.

4 Add the tomatoes, onion slices, grated carrot, and diced goat cheese and toss together, using 2 forks, until well mixed. Leave the salad to chill in the refrigerator for about 1 hour before serving.

### COOK'S TIP

Radicchio is a variety of endive originating in Italy. It has a slightly bitter flavor.

# Rare Beef Pasta Salad

This salad is a meal in itself and would be perfect for an *al fresco* lunch, perhaps with a bottle of red wine.

## NUTRITIONAL INFORMATION

Calories .......575  Sugars .........4g
Protein ........31g  Fat ..........33g
Carbohydrate ...44g  Saturates .......9g

15 MINS     30 MINS

### SERVES 4

## INGREDIENTS

1 lb/450 g rump or sirloin steak in
   one piece

4 cups dried fusilli

5 tbsp olive oil

2 tbsp lime juice

2 tbsp Thai fish sauce
   (see Cook's Tip)

2 tsp clear honey

4 scallions, sliced

1 cucumber, peeled and cut into
   1-inch/2.5-cm chunks

3 tomatoes, cut into wedges

3 tsp finely chopped fresh mint

salt and pepper

1 Season the steak with salt and pepper. Broil or pan-fry the steak for 4 minutes on each side. Leave to rest for 5 minutes, then slice thinly across the grain.

2 Meanwhile, bring a large pan of lightly salted water to a boil. Add the fusilli and 1 tablespoon of the olive oil and cook for 8–10 minutes, or until tender but still firm to the bite. Drain the fusilli and refresh in cold water, then drain again thoroughly. Toss the fusilli in the remaining olive oil.

3 Combine the lime juice, fish sauce, and honey in a small pan and cook over medium heat for 2 minutes.

4 Add the scallions, cucumber, tomatoes, and mint to the pan, then add the steak and mix well. Season to taste with salt.

5 Transfer the fusilli to a large, warm serving dish and top with the steak and salad mixture. Serve just warm or leave to cool completely.

## COOK'S TIP

Thai fish sauce, also known as nam pla, is made from salted anchovies and has quite a strong flavor, so it should be used with discretion. It is available from some supermarkets and from Southeast Asian food stores.

# Mushroom Salad

Raw mushrooms are a great favourite in Italian dishes—they have a fresh, almost creamy flavor.

## NUTRITIONAL INFORMATION

| | | | |
|---|---|---|---|
| Calories | .......121 | Sugars | .......0.1g |
| Protein | .........2g | Fat | ..........13g |
| Carbohydrate | ...0.1g | Saturates | .......2g |

20 MINS     0 MINS

### SERVES 4

## I N G R E D I E N T S

scant 1½ cups firm white mushrooms

4 tbsp virgin olive oil

1 tbsp lemon juice

5 anchovy fillets, drained and chopped

1 tbsp fresh marjoram

salt and pepper

1 Gently wipe each mushroom with a damp cloth in order to remove any excess dirt.

2 Slice the mushrooms thinly, using a sharp knife.

3 To make the dressing, mix together the olive oil and lemon juice.

4 Pour the dressing mixture over the mushrooms. Toss together so that the mushrooms are completely coated with the lemon juice and oil.

5 Stir the chopped anchovy fillets into the mushrooms.

6 Season the mushroom mixture with pepper to taste and garnish with the fresh marjoram.

7 Leave the mushroom salad to stand for about 5 minutes before serving in order for all the flavors to be absorbed.

8 Season the mushroom salad with a little salt (see Cook's Tip) and then serve.

### COOK'S TIP

Do not season the mushroom salad with salt until the very last minute as it will cause the mushrooms to blacken and the juices to leak. The result will not be as tasty as it should be as the full flavors won't be absorbed and it will also look very unattractive.

# Pasta Salad & Mixed Cabbage

This crunchy, colorful salad would be a good accompaniment for broiled meat or fish.

## NUTRITIONAL INFORMATION

Calories . . . . . . .388  Sugars . . . . . . . .17g
Protein . . . . . . . .18g  Fat . . . . . . . . . .18g
Carbohydrate . . .41g  Saturates . . . . . . .3g

 25 MINS      30 MINS

### SERVES 4

## I N G R E D I E N T S

2¼ cups dried short-cut macaroni

5 tbsp olive oil

1 large red cabbage, shredded

1 large white cabbage, shredded

2 large apples, diced

1 cup diced cooked smoked bacon or ham

8 tbsp wine vinegar

1 tbsp sugar

salt and pepper

1 Bring a pan of lightly salted water to a boil. Add the macaroni and 1 tablespoon of the oil and cook for 8–10 minutes, or until tender but still firm to the bite. Drain the pasta, then refresh in cold water. Drain again and set aside.

## VARIATION

For an alternative dressing to go with this salad mix 4 tablespoons each of olive oil, red wine and red wine vinegar with 1 tablespoon sugar. Or substitute 3 tablespoons olive oil and 1 tablespoon walnut or hazelnut oil for the olive oil.

2 Bring a large pan of lightly salted water to a boil. Add the shredded red cabbage and cook for 5 minutes. Drain the cabbage thoroughly and set aside to cool.

3 Bring a large pan of lightly salted water to a boil. Add the white cabbage and cook for 5 minutes. Drain the cabbage thoroughly and set aside to cool.

4 In a large bowl, mix together the pasta, red cabbage, and apple. In a separate bowl, mix together the white cabbage and bacon.

5 In a small bowl, mix together the remaining oil, the vinegar, and sugar, then season to taste with salt and pepper. Pour the dressing over each of the 2 cabbage mixtures and, finally, mix them all together. Serve immediately.

# Italian Potato Salad

Potato salad is always a favorite, but it is even more delicious with the addition of sun-dried tomatoes and fresh parsley.

## NUTRITIONAL INFORMATION

Calories .......425   Sugars .........6g
Protein .........6g   Fat ..........27g
Carbohydrate ...43g   Saturates .......5g

40 MINS     15 MINS

### SERVES 4

## I N G R E D I E N T S

1 lb/450 g baby potatoes, unpeeled, or
   larger potatoes, halved

8 sun-dried tomatoes

4 tbsp plain yogurt

4 tbsp mayonnaise

2 tbsp flat-leaf parsley, chopped

salt and pepper

1 Rinse and clean the potatoes and place them in a large pan of water. Bring to a boil and cook for 8–12 minutes, or until just tender. (The cooking time will vary according to the size of the potatoes.)

2 Using a sharp knife, cut the sun-dried tomatoes into thin slices.

3 To make the dressing, mix together the yogurt and mayonnaise in a bowl and season to taste with a little salt and pepper. Stir in the sun-dried tomato slices and the chopped flat-leaf parsley.

4 Remove the potatoes with a perforated spoon and drain them thoroughly, then set them aside to cool. If you are using larger potatoes, cut them into 2-inch/5-cm chunks.

5 Pour the dressing over the potatoes and toss to mix.

6 Leave the potato salad to chill in the refrigerator for about 20 minutes, then serve as an appetizer or as an accompaniment.

## COOK'S TIP

It is easier to cut the larger potatoes once they are cooked. Although smaller pieces of potato will cook more quickly, they tend to disintegrate and become mushy.

# Italian Bell Pepper Salad

This salad goes well with all grilled foods, especially meats. Alternatively, serve it with a selection of Italian bread for a simple appetizer.

## NUTRITIONAL INFORMATION

| | |
|---|---|
| Calories . . . . . . .150 | Sugars . . . . . . . . .6g |
| Protein . . . . . . . . .4g | Fat . . . . . . . . . .12g |
| Carbohydrate . . . .7g | Saturates . . . . . . .1g |

  30 MINS  30 MINS

### SERVES 4

## I N G R E D I E N T S

2 red bell peppers, halved and seeded

2 yellow bell peppers, halved and seeded

3 tbsp extra virgin olive oil

1 onion, cut into wedges

2 large zucchini, sliced

2 garlic cloves, sliced

1 tbsp balsamic vinegar

1¾ oz/50 g anchovy fillets, chopped

scant ¼ cup pitted black olives,
  cut into fourths

fresh basil leaves

1 Place the bell pepper halves, cut side down, on a broiler pan and cook until the skin blackens and chars. Leave to cool slightly, then pop them into a plastic bag for about 10 minutes.

2 Peel away the skin from the bell peppers and discard. Cut the flesh into thick strips.

3 Heat the oil in a large skillet, then add the onion and cook gently for 10 minutes, or until softened. Add the zucchini slices, garlic, and bell pepper strips to the skillet and cook, stirring occasionally, for a further 10 minutes.

4 Add the vinegar, anchovies, and olives to the skillet. Season with salt and pepper to taste. Mix well and leave to cool.

5 Reserve a few basil leaves for garnishing, then tear the remainder into small pieces. Stir them into the salad.

6 Transfer the salad to a serving dish and garnish with a few whole basil leaves.

## COOK'S TIP

Balsamic vinegar is made in and around Modena in Italy. Its rich, mellow flavor is perfect for Mediterranean-style salads, but if it is unavailable, use sherry vinegar or white wine vinegar instead.

# Lentil & Tuna Salad

In this recipe, lentils, combined with spices, lemon juice, and tuna, make a wonderfully tasty and filling salad.

## NUTRITIONAL INFORMATION

| | | | |
|---|---|---|---|
| Calories | .......227 | Sugars | .........2g |
| Protein | ........19g | Fat | ..........9g |
| Carbohydrate | ...19g | Saturates | .......1g |

25 MINS          0 MINS

### SERVES 4

## INGREDIENTS

2 ripe tomatoes

1 small red onion

3 tbsp virgin olive oil

1 tbsp lemon juice

1 tsp whole-grain mustard

1 garlic clove, crushed

½ tsp cumin powder

½ tsp ground coriander

14 oz/400 g canned lentils, drained

6 oz/170 g canned tuna, drained

2 tbsp fresh cilantro, chopped

pepper

1 Using a sharp knife, seed the tomatoes and then chop them into fine dice.

2 Using a sharp knife, finely chop the red onion.

3 To make the dressing, whisk together the virgin olive oil, lemon juice, mustard, garlic, cumin powder, and ground coriander in a small bowl. Set aside until required.

4 Mix together the chopped onion, diced tomatoes, and drained lentils in a large bowl.

5 Flake the tuna and stir it into the onion, tomato, and lentil mixture.

6 Stir in the chopped fresh cilantro.

7 Pour the dressing over the lentil and tuna salad and season with pepper to taste. Serve at once.

## COOK'S TIP

Lentils are a good source of protein and contain important vitamins and minerals. Buy them dried for soaking and cooking yourself, or buy canned varieties for speed and convenience.

# Spicy Sausage Salad

A warm sausage and pasta dressing spooned over chilled salad leaves makes a refreshing combination to start a meal.

## NUTRITIONAL INFORMATION

| | | | |
|---|---|---|---|
| Calories | .......383 | Sugars | .........2g |
| Protein | ........11g | Fat | ..........28g |
| Carbohydrate | ...20g | Saturates | .......1g |

 15 MINS    25 MINS

### SERVES 4

## INGREDIENTS

generous 1 cup small pasta shapes,
  such as elbow tubetti

3 tbsp olive oil

1 medium onion, chopped

2 cloves garlic, crushed

1 small yellow bell pepper, cored, seeded,
and cut into short thin sticks

6 oz/175 g spicy pork sausage such as
  chorizo, skinned and sliced

2 tbsp red wine

1 tbsp red wine vinegar

mixed salad leaves, chilled

salt

## VARIATION

Other sausages to use are the Italian pepperoni, flavored with chile peppers, fennel, and spices, and one of the many varieties of salami, usually flavored with garlic and pepper.

1 Cook the pasta in a pan of boiling salted water, adding 1 tablespoon of the oil, for 8–10 minutes, or until tender. Drain in a colander and set aside.

2 Heat the remaining oil in a pan over medium heat. Cook the onion until it is translucent, then stir in the garlic, bell pepper, and sliced sausage and cook for 3-4 minutes, stirring once or twice.

3 Add the wine, wine vinegar, and reserved pasta to the pan, then stir to blend well and bring the mixture just to a boil.

4 Arrange the chilled salad leaves on 4 individual serving plates and spoon on the warm sausage and pasta mixture. Serve at once.

# Capri Salad

This tomato, olive, and mozzarella salad, dressed with balsamic vinegar and olive oil, makes a delicious appetizer on its own.

## NUTRITIONAL INFORMATION

Calories ........95   Sugars .........3g
Protein ........3g   Fat ..........8g
Carbohydrate ....3g   Saturates .......3g

20 MINS    3–5 MINS

### SERVES 4

## I N G R E D I E N T S

2 beef tomatoes

4½ oz/125 g mozzarella cheese

12 black olives

8 basil leaves

1 tbsp balsamic vinegar

1 tbsp olive oil

salt and pepper

basil leaves, to garnish

1 Using a sharp knife, cut the tomatoes into thin slices.

2 Using a sharp knife, cut the mozzarella into slices.

3 Pit the olives and slice them into rings.

4 Layer the tomato, mozzarella cheese olives, and basil leaves in a stack, finishing with a layer of cheese on top.

5 Place each stack under a preheated hot broiler for 2–3 minutes, or just long enough to melt the mozzarella.

6 Drizzle over the vinegar and olive oil, and season to taste with a little salt and pepper.

7 Transfer to serving plates and garnish with basil leaves. Serve immediately.

## COOK'S TIP

Buffalo mozzarella cheese is usually more expensive because of the comparative rarity of buffalo, but it does have a better flavor than the cow's milk variety. It is popular in salads, but also provides a tangy layer in baked dishes.

# Goat Cheese Salad

The black olive vinaigrette and bitter salad leaves give a real tang to this quick snack.

## NUTRITIONAL INFORMATION

Calories .......362  Sugars .........3g
Protein ........14g  Fat ..........22g
Carbohydrate ...29g  Saturates ......10g

30 MINS    5–6 MINS

### SERVES 4

## I N G R E D I E N T S

3 tbsp olive oil

1 tbsp white wine vinegar

1 tsp black olive paste

1 garlic clove, crushed

1 tsp chopped fresh thyme

1 ciabatta loaf

4 small tomatoes, sliced

12 fresh basil leaves

2 x 4½ oz/125 g logs goat cheese

fresh basil sprigs, to garnish

salad greens, to serve

1 Put the oil, vinegar, olive paste, garlic, and thyme in a small bowl and whisk together.

2 Cut the ciabatta in half horizontally then in half vertically to make 4 pieces.

## COOK'S TIP

Goat cheeses range in flavor from fresh and creamy to strong and tangy, developing flavor as they mature. Fresh goat cheese must be eaten within 2 days, but the mature cheeses, which have a firmer, drier texture, will keep for longer.

3 Drizzle some of the dressing over the bread, then arrange the tomatoes and basil leaves on top.

4 Cut each log of goat cheese into 6 slices and lay 3 slices on each piece of ciabatta.

5 Brush the cheese with some of the dressing and place in a preheated oven, at 450°F/230°C, for 5-6 minutes or until just turning brown at the edges.

6 Cut each piece of bread in half. Arrange the salad greens onto serving plates and top with the baked bread. Pour over the remaining dressing, then garnish with the fresh basil sprigs and serve with salad leaves.

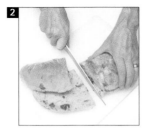  

# Cheese, Nut & Pasta Salad

Use colorful salad greens to provide visual contrast to match the contrasts of taste and texture.

## NUTRITIONAL INFORMATION

| | | | |
|---|---|---|---|
| Calories | .......694 | Sugars | .........1g |
| Protein | ........22g | Fat | ..........57g |
| Carbohydrate | ...24g | Saturates | ......15g |

 15 MINS     15–20 MINS

### SERVES 4

## I N G R E D I E N T S

2 cups dried pasta shells

1 tbsp olive oil

1 cup shelled and halved walnuts

mixed salad greens, such as
    radicchio, escarole, arugula,
    corn salad and frisée

2 cups crumbled Gorgonzola cheese

salt

### D R E S S I N G

2 tbsp walnut oil

4 tbsp extra virgin olive oil

2 tbsp red wine vinegar

salt and pepper

1 Bring a large pan of lightly salted water to a boil. Add the pasta shells and olive oil and cook for 8–10 minutes, or until just tender but still firm to the bite. Drain the pasta and refresh under cold running water, then drain thoroughly again and set aside.

2 Spread out the shelled walnut halves on to a cookie sheet and toast under a preheated broiler for 2–3 minutes. Set aside to cool while you make the dressing.

3 To make the dressing, whisk together the walnut oil, olive oil, and vinegar in a small bowl, and season to taste.

4 Arrange the salad greens in a large serving bowl. Pile the cooled pasta in the middle of the salad greens and sprinkle over the Gorgonzola cheese. Pour the dressing over the pasta salad and scatter over the walnut halves, then toss together to mix. Serve immediately.

## COOK'S TIP

Gorgonzola is a blue-veined cheese from Italy. Its texture is creamy and smooth and the flavor is delicate, but piquant. You could use Roquefort instead. It is essential that whatever cheese you choose, it is of the best quality and in peak condition.

# Artichoke & Ham Salad

This elegant appetizer would make a good first course.
Serve it with a little fresh bread for mopping up the juices.

## NUTRITIONAL INFORMATION

Calories . . . . . . .124    Sugars . . . . . . . . .2g
Protein . . . . . . . . .2g    Fat . . . . . . . . . . .11g
Carbohydrate . . . .4g    Saturates . . . . . . .1g

 25 MINS     0 MINS

### SERVES 4

## I N G R E D I E N T S

9 ½ oz/275 g canned artichoke hearts
  in oil, drained

4 small tomatoes

1 oz/25 g sun-dried tomatoes in oil

1½ oz/40 g prosciutto

9–10 pitted black olives, halved

a few basil leaves

### D R E S S I N G

3 tbsp olive oil

1 tbsp white wine vinegar

1 clove garlic, crushed

½ tsp mild mustard

1 tsp clear honey

salt and pepper

## COOK'S TIP

Use bottled artichokes in oil
if you can find them as they
have a better flavor. If only
canned artichokes are available,
rinse them carefully to remove
the salty liquid.

1 Make sure the artichokes hearts are thoroughly drained, then cut them into fourths and place in a bowl.

2 Cut each fresh tomato into wedges. Slice the sun-dried tomatoes into thin strips. Cut the prosciutto into thin strips and add to the bowl with the tomatoes and olive halves.

3 Keeping a few basil leaves whole for garnishing, tear the remainder of the leaves into small pieces and add to the bowl containing the other salad ingredients.

4 To make the dressing, put the oil, wine vinegar, garlic, mustard, honey, and salt and pepper to taste in a screw-top jar and shake vigorously until the ingredients are well blended.

5 Pour the dressing over the salad and toss together.

6 Serve the salad garnished with a few whole basil leaves.

# Tuna, Bean & Anchovy Salad

Serve as part of a selection of *antipasti*, or for a summer lunch with hot garlic bread.

## NUTRITIONAL INFORMATION

| | | | |
|---|---|---|---|
| Calories | .......397 | Sugars | .........8g |
| Protein | ........23g | Fat | ..........30g |
| Carbohydrate | ...10g | Saturates | .......4g |

35 MINS    0 MINS

### SERVES 4

## INGREDIENTS

1 lb 2 oz/500 g tomatoes

7 oz/200 g canned tuna fish, drained

2 tbsp chopped fresh parsley

½ cucumber

1 small red onion

8 oz/225 g cooked green beans

1 small red bell pepper, cored and seeded

1 small crisp lettuce

6 tbsp Italian-style dressing

3 hard-cooked eggs

2 oz/55 g canned anchovies, drained

12 black olives, pitted

1 Cut the tomatoes into wedges and flake the tuna, then put both into the bowl with the parsley.

2 Cut the cucumber in half lengthwise, then cut into slices. Slice the onion. Add the cucumber and onion to the bowl.

3 Cut the beans in half and chop the bell pepper, then add both to the bowl with the lettuce leaves. Pour over the dressing and toss to mix, then spoon into a salad bowl. Cut the eggs into fourths, then arrange over the top with the anchovies and scatter with the olives.

# Italian Pasta Salad

Tomatoes and mozzarella cheese are a classic Italian combination. Here they are joined with pasta and avocado for an extra touch of luxury.

## NUTRITIONAL INFORMATION

Calories . . . . . . . .541    Sugars . . . . . . . . .5g
Protein . . . . . . . .12g    Fat . . . . . . . . . .43g
Carbohydrate . . .29g    Saturates . . . . . .10g

15 MINS          15 MINS

### SERVES 4

## I N G R E D I E N T S

2 tbsp pine nuts

1½ cups dried fusilli

1 tbsp olive oil

6 tomatoes

8 oz/225 g mozzarella cheese

1 large avocado

2 tbsp lemon juice

3 tbsp chopped fresh basil

salt and pepper

fresh basil sprigs, to garnish

### D R E S S I N G

6 tbsp extra virgin olive oil

2 tbsp white wine vinegar

1 tsp whole-grain mustard

pinch of sugar

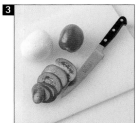

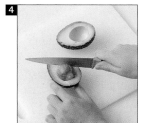

1 Spread the pine nuts out on a cookie sheet and toast them under a preheated broiler for 1–2 minutes. Remove and set aside to cool.

2 Bring a large pan of lightly salted water to a boil. Add the fusilli and olive oil and cook for 8–10 minutes, or until tender but still firm to the bite. Drain the pasta and refresh in cold water. Drain again and set aside to cool.

3 Thinly slice the tomatoes and the mozzarella cheese.

4 Cut the avocado in half, then carefully remove the pit and skin. Cut into thin slices lengthwise and sprinkle with lemon juice to prevent discoloration.

5 To make the dressing, whisk together the oil, vinegar, mustard, and sugar in a small bowl, and season to taste with salt and pepper.

6 Arrange the tomatoes, mozzarella cheese, and avocado alternately in overlapping slices on to a large serving platter.

7 Toss the pasta with half of the dressing and the basil and season to taste with salt and pepper. Spoon the pasta into the center of the platter and pour over the remaining dressing. Sprinkle over the pine nuts and garnish with fresh basil sprigs, then serve immediately.

# Pasta with Pesto Vinaigrette

Sun-dried tomatoes and olives enhance this delicious pesto-inspired salad, which is just as tasty served cold.

## NUTRITIONAL INFORMATION

Calories . . . . . . .275    Sugars . . . . . . . . .2g
Protein . . . . . . . . .9g    Fat . . . . . . . . . .19g
Carbohydrate . . .17g    Saturates . . . . . . .4g

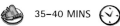

35–40 MINS    15 MINS

### SERVES 6

## I N G R E D I E N T S

2 cups pasta spirals

4 tomatoes, skinned

scant ½ cup black olives

¼ cup sun-dried tomatoes

2 tbsp pine nuts, toasted

2 tbsp freshly grated Parmesan cheese

sprig of fresh basil, to garnish

### P E S T O   V I N A I G R E T T E

4 tbsp chopped fresh basil

1 garlic clove, crushed

2 tbsp freshly grated Parmesan cheese

4 tbsp olive oil

2 tbsp lemon juice

pepper

1 Cook the pasta spirals in a pan of boiling salted water for 8–10 minutes or until al dente. Drain the pasta and rinse well in hot water, then drain again thoroughly.

2 To make the vinaigrette, whisk the basil, garlic, Parmesan, olive oil, lemon juice, and pepper until well blended.

3 Put the pasta into a bowl, then pour over the pesto vinaigrette and toss thoroughly.

4 Cut the tomatoes into wedges. Halve and pit the olives and slice the sun-dried tomatoes.

5 Add the tomatoes, olives, and sun-dried tomatoes to the pasta and mix.

6 Transfer to a salad bowl and scatter the nuts and grated Parmesan over the top. Serve warm, garnished with a sprig of basil.

# Artichoke Salad

Use bottled artichokes rather than canned ones if possible, as they have a better flavor.

## NUTRITIONAL INFORMATION

| | | | |
|---|---|---|---|
| Calories | .......139 | Sugars | .........4g |
| Protein | .........2g | Fat | ..........12g |
| Carbohydrate | ....6g | Saturates | .......1g |

 30 MINS    0 MINS

### SERVES 4

### I N G R E D I E N T S

9 oz/250 g bottled artichokes in oil, drained

4 small tomatoes

¼ cup sun-dried tomatoes, cut into strips

scant ¼ cup black olives, halved and pitted

1 oz/25 g prosciutto, cut into strips

1 tbsp chopped fresh basil

### D R E S S I N G

3 tbsp olive oil

1 tbsp wine vinegar

1 small garlic clove, crushed

½ tsp mustard

1 tsp clear honey

salt and pepper

1 Drain the artichokes thoroughly, then cut them into fourths and place in a serving bowl.

2 Cut each tomato into 6 wedges and place in the bowl with the sun-dried tomatoes, olives, and prosciutto.

3 To make the dressing, put the olive oil, wine vinegar, garlic clove, mustard, honey, and salt and pepper into a screw-top jar and shake vigorously until the ingredients are thoroughly blended.

4 Pour the dressing over the salad and toss well together. Transfer the salad to individual plates and sprinkle with the chopped basil.

# Italian Mozzarella Salad

This colorful salad is packed full of delicious flavors but is easy to make.

## NUTRITIONAL INFORMATION

| | | | |
|---|---|---|---|
| Calories | ........79 | Sugars | .........2g |
| Protein | .........4g | Fat | ...........6g |
| Carbohydrate | ....2g | Saturates | .......2g |

20 MINS     0 MINS

### SERVES 6

## INGREDIENTS

7 oz/200 g baby spinach

4 ½ oz/125 g watercress or arugula

4 ½ oz/125 g mozzarella cheese

8 oz/225 g cherry tomatoes

2 tsp balsamic vinegar

1 ½ tbsp extra virgin olive oil

salt and pepper

1 Wash the spinach and watercress and drain thoroughly on absorbent paper towels. Remove any tough stems. Place the spinach and watercress leaves in a large serving dish.

2 Cut the mozzarella into small pieces and scatter them over the spinach and watercress leaves.

3 Cut the cherry tomatoes in half and scatter them over the salad.

4 Sprinkle over the balsamic vinegar and oil, and season with salt and pepper to taste. Toss the mixture together to coat the leaves. Serve at once or leave to chill in the refrigerator until required.

# Sesame Seed Salad

This salad uses sesame seed paste as a flavoring for the dressing, which complements the eggplant.

## NUTRITIONAL INFORMATION

| | | | |
|---|---|---|---|
| Calories | ........89 | Sugars | .........1g |
| Protein | .........3g | Fat | ...........8g |
| Carbohydrate | ....1g | Saturates | .......1g |

45 MINS          15 MINS

### SERVES 4

## INGREDIENTS

1 large eggplant

3 tbsp sesame seed paste

juice and rind of 1 lemon

1 garlic clove, crushed

pinch of paprika

1 tbsp chopped cilantro

salt and pepper

Boston lettuce leaves

### GARNISH

strips of pimiento

lemon wedges

toasted sesame seeds

1 Cut the eggplant in half, then place in a colander and sprinkle with salt. Leave to stand for 30 minutes, then rinse under cold running water and drain well. Pat dry with paper towels.

2 Place the eggplant halves, skin-side uppermost, on an oiled cookie sheet. Cook in a preheated oven, 450°F/230°C, for 10–15 minutes. Remove from the oven and leave to cool.

3 Cut the eggplant into cubes and set aside until required. Mix together the sesame seed paste, lemon juice and rind, garlic, paprika, and cilantro. Season with salt and pepper to taste and stir in the eggplant.

4 Line a serving dish with lettuce leaves and spoon the eggplant into the center. Garnish the salad with pimiento slices, lemon wedges, and toasted sesame seeds, then serve.

## COOK'S TIP

Sesame seed paste is a nutty-flavored sauce available from most health food stores.

# Pink Grapefruit & Cheese Salad

Fresh pink grapefruit segments, ripe avocados, and sliced Italian Gorgonzola cheese make a deliciously different salad combination.

## NUTRITIONAL INFORMATION

| | | | |
|---|---|---|---|
| Calories | .......390 | Sugars | .........3g |
| Protein | ........13g | Fat | ..........36g |
| Carbohydrate | ....4g | Saturates | ......13g |

  25 MINS   0 MINS

### SERVES 4

## I N G R E D I E N T S

½ romaine lettuce

½ oak leaf lettuce

2 pink grapefruit

2 ripe avocados

6 oz/175 g Gorgonzola cheese, sliced thinly

sprigs of fresh basil, to garnish

### D R E S S I N G

4 tbsp olive oil

1 tbsp white wine vinegar

salt and pepper

1 Arrange the lettuce leaves on 4 serving plates or in a salad bowl.

2 Remove the peel and pith from the grapefruit with a sharp serrated knife, catching the grapefruit juice in a bowl.

3 Segment the grapefruit by cutting down each side of the membrane. Remove all the membrane. Arrange the segments on the serving plates.

4 Peel and pit, then slice the avocados, dipping them in the grapefruit juice to prevent them from going brown. Arrange the slices on the salad with the Gorgonzola cheese.

5 To make the dressing, combine any remaining grapefruit juice with the olive oil and wine vinegar. Season with salt and pepper to taste, mixing well to combine.

6 Drizzle the dressing over the salads. Garnish with fresh basil leaves and serve at once.

### COOK'S TIP

Pink grapefruit segments make a very attractive color combination with the avocados, but ordinary grapefruit will work just as well. To help avocados to ripen, keep them at room temperature in a brown paper bag.

# Pasta

The simplicity and satisfying nature of pasta in all its varieties makes it a universal favorite. Easy to cook and economical, pasta is wonderfully versatile. It can be served with sauces made from meat, fish, or vegetables, or baked in the oven. The classic Spaghetti Bolognese needs no introduction, and yet it is said that there are almost as

many versions of this delicious regional dish as there are lovers of Italian food! Fish and seafood are irresistible combined with pasta and need only the briefest of cooking times. Pasta combined with vegetables provides inspiration for countless dishes that will please vegetarians and meat-eaters alike. The delicious pasta dishes in this chapter range from easy, economic mid-week suppers to sophisticated and elegant meals for special occasions.

# Pasta Carbonara

Lightly cooked eggs and pancetta are combined with cheese to make this rich, classic sauce.

## NUTRITIONAL INFORMATION

| | | | |
|---|---|---|---|
| Calories | .......547 | Sugars | .........1g |
| Protein | ........21g | Fat | ..........31g |
| Carbohydrate | ...49g | Saturates | ......14g |

15 MINS        20 MINS

### SERVES 4

## INGREDIENTS

1 tbsp olive oil

3 tbsp butter

⅓ cup diced pancetta or unsmoked bacon

3 eggs, beaten

2 tbsp milk

1 tbsp thyme, stems removed

1 lb 8 oz/675 g fresh or 12 oz/350 g dried
  conchiglioni rigati

½ cup freshly grated Parmesan cheese

salt and pepper

1 Heat the oil and butter in a skillet until the mixture is just beginning to froth.

2 Add the pancetta or bacon to the skillet and cook for 5 minutes, or until browned all over.

3 Mix together the eggs and milk in a small bowl. Stir in the thyme and season to taste with salt and pepper.

4 Cook the pasta in a pan of boiling water for 8–10 minutes until tender but still firm to the bite. Drain thoroughly.

5 Add the cooked, drained pasta to the skillet with the eggs and cook over high heat for about 30 seconds, or until the eggs just begin to cook and set. Do not overcook the eggs or they will become rubbery.

6 Add half of the grated Parmesan cheese, stirring to combine.

7 Transfer the pasta to a serving plate, then pour over the sauce and toss to mix well.

8 Sprinkle the rest of the grated Parmesan over the top and serve immediately.

## VARIATION

For an extra rich Carbonara sauce, stir in 4 tablespoons of heavy cream with the eggs and milk in step 3. Follow exactly the same cooking method.

# Spaghetti Bolognese

The original recipe takes about four hours to cook and should be left overnight to let the flavors mingle. This version is much quicker.

## NUTRITIONAL INFORMATION

| | | | |
|---|---|---|---|
| Calories | 591 | Sugars | 7g |
| Protein | 29g | Fat | 24g |
| Carbohydrate | 64g | Saturates | 9g |

20 MINS  1 HR 5 MINS

### SERVES 4

## INGREDIENTS

1 tbsp olive oil

1 onion, finely chopped

2 garlic cloves, chopped

1 carrot, scraped and chopped

1 celery stalk, chopped

scant ¼ cup diced pancetta or lean bacon

1½ cups lean ground beef

14 oz/400 g canned chopped tomatoes

2 tsp dried oregano

scant ½ cup red wine

2 tbsp tomato paste

salt and pepper

1 lb 8 oz/675 g fresh spaghetti or
    12 oz/350 g dried spaghetti

1 Heat the oil in a large skillet. Add the onions and cook for 3 minutes.

2 Add the garlic, carrot, celery, and pancetta and sauté for 3–4 minutes, or until just beginning to brown.

3 Add the beef and cook over high heat for another 3 minutes, or until all of the meat is brown.

4 Stir in the tomatoes, oregano, and red wine and bring to a boil. Reduce the heat and leave to simmer for about 45 minutes.

5 Stir in the tomato paste and season with salt and pepper.

6 Cook the spaghetti in a pan of boiling water for 8–10 minutes, or until tender but still firm to the bite. Drain thoroughly.

7 Transfer the spaghetti to a serving plate and pour over the bolognese sauce. Toss to mix well and serve hot.

## VARIATION

Try adding 1 oz/25 g dried porcini, soaked for 10 minutes in 2 tablespoons of warm water, to the Bolognese sauce in step 4, if you wish.

# Chicken & Tomato Lasagna

This variation of the traditional beef dish has layers of pasta and chicken or turkey baked in red wine, tomatoes, and a delicious cheese sauce.

### NUTRITIONAL INFORMATION

| | |
|---|---|
| Calories .......550 | Sugars ........11g |
| Protein ........35g | Fat ..........29g |
| Carbohydrate ...34g | Saturates ......12g |

 20 MINS    1¼ HOURS

### SERVES 4

## I N G R E D I E N T S

12 oz/350 g fresh lasagna (about 9 sheets)
  or 5½ oz/150 g dried lasagna
  (about 9 sheets)

1 tbsp olive oil

1 red onion, finely chopped

1 garlic clove, crushed

1 cup mushrooms, wiped and sliced

12 oz/350 g chicken or turkey breast, cut
  into chunks

⅔ cup red wine, diluted with
  scant ½ cup water

9 oz/250 g crushed tomatoes

1 tsp sugar

### B É C H A M E L   S A U C E

5 tbsp butter

⅓ cup all-purpose flour

2½ cups milk

1 egg, beaten

¾ cup freshly grated Parmesan cheese

salt and pepper

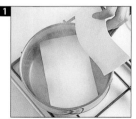  

1 Cook the lasagna in a pan of boiling water according to the instructions on the packet. Lightly grease a deep ovenproof dish.

2 Heat the oil in a large skillet. Add the onion and garlic and cook for 3–4 minutes. Add the mushrooms and chicken and stir-fry for 4 minutes, or until the meat browns.

3 Add the wine and bring to a boil, then simmer for 5 minutes. Stir in the crushed tomatoes and sugar and cook for 3–5 minutes, or until the meat is tender and cooked through. The sauce should have thickened, but still be quite runny.

4 To make the Béchamel Sauce, melt the butter in a pan, then stir in the flour and cook for 2 minutes. Remove the pan from the heat and gradually add the milk, mixing to form a smooth sauce. Return the pan to the heat and bring to a boil, stirring until thickened. Leave to cool slightly, then beat in the egg and half of the cheese. Season to taste.

5 Place 3 sheets of lasagna in the base of the dish and spread with half of the chicken mixture. Repeat the layers. Top with the last 3 sheets of lasagna, pour over the Béchamel Sauce and sprinkle with the Parmesan. Bake in a preheated oven, at 375°F/190°C, for 30 minutes, or until golden and the pasta is cooked.

# Traditional Cannelloni

You can buy ready-made dried pasta tubes. However, if using fresh pasta (see page 24), you must cut out squares and roll them yourself.

## NUTRITIONAL INFORMATION

| | | | |
|---|---|---|---|
| Calories | ......342 | Sugars | .........6g |
| Protein | ........15g | Fat | ..........15g |
| Carbohydrate | ...38g | Saturates | .......8g |

🍲 50 MINS   🕐 30 MINS

### SERVES 4

## I N G R E D I E N T S

20 tubes dried cannelloni (about 7 oz/ 200 g) or 20 square sheets of fresh pasta (about 12 oz/350 g)

1 cup ricotta cheese

5½ oz/150 g frozen spinach, defrosted

½ small red bell pepper, diced

2 scallions, chopped

⅔ cup hot vegetable or chicken stock

1 portion of Basil & Tomato Sauce (see page 276)

¼ cup freshly grated Parmesan or Romano cheese

salt and pepper

1 If you are using dried cannelloni, check the package instructions; many varieties do not need precooking. If necessary, precook your pasta: bring a large pan of water to a boil, then add 1 tablespoon of oil and cook the pasta for 3–4 minutes—it is far easier to do this in batches.

2 In a bowl, mix the ricotta, spinach, bell pepper, and scallions together, then season to taste with salt and pepper.

3 Lightly butter an ovenproof dish, large enough to contain all of the pasta tubes in a single layer. Spoon the ricotta mixture into the pasta tubes and place them into the prepared dish. If you are using fresh sheets of pasta, spread the ricotta mixture along one side of each fresh pasta square and roll up to form a tube.

4 Mix together the stock and Basil and Tomato Sauce and pour over the pasta tubes.

5 Sprinkle the Parmesan cheese over the cannelloni and bake in a preheated oven, 375°F/190°C, for 20–25 minutes. or until the pasta is cooked through. Serve.

## VARIATION

If you would prefer a creamier version, omit the stock and the Basil and Tomato sauce and replace with Béchamel Sauce (see page 256).

# Tagliatelle & Chicken Sauce

Spinach ribbon noodles covered with a rich tomato sauce and topped with creamy chicken make a very appetizing dish.

## NUTRITIONAL INFORMATION

| | | | |
|---|---|---|---|
| Calories | .......853 | Sugars | .........6g |
| Protein | ........32g | Fat | ...........71g |
| Carbohydrate | ...23g | Saturates | ......34g |

30 MINS          25 MINS

**SERVES 4**

## INGREDIENTS

Basic Tomato Sauce (see page 28)

8 oz/225 g fresh green ribbon noodles

1 tbsp olive oil

salt

basil leaves, to garnish

### CHICKEN SAUCE

¼ cup unsalted butter

14 oz/400 g boned, skinned chicken
  breast, thinly sliced

generous ½ cup blanched almonds

1¼ cups heavy cream

salt and pepper

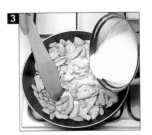

1 Make the tomato sauce, and keep warm.

2 To make the chicken sauce, melt the butter in a skillet over medium heat and cook the chicken strips and almonds for 5–6 minutes, stirring frequently, until the chicken is cooked through.

3 Meanwhile, pour the cream into a small pan over low heat, then bring it to a boil and boil for about 10 minutes, or until reduced by almost half. Pour the cream over the chicken and almonds, then stir well and season with salt and pepper to taste. Set aside and keep warm.

4 Cook the pasta in a pan of boiling salted water, to which you have added the oil, for 8–10 minutes. or until tender. Drain and return to the pan. Cover and keep warm.

5 Turn the pasta into a warmed serving dish and spoon the tomato sauce over it. Spoon the chicken and cream over the center, then scatter over the basil leaves and serve at once.

# Meat & Pasta Loaf

The cheesy pasta layer comes as a pleasant surprise inside this lightly spiced meat loaf.

## NUTRITIONAL INFORMATION

| | | | |
|---|---|---|---|
| Calories | .......497 | Sugars | .........4g |
| Protein | ........26g | Fat | ..........37g |
| Carbohydrate | ...16g | Saturates | ......16g |

45 MINS        1¼ HOURS

### SERVES 6

## I N G R E D I E N T S

2 tbsp butter, plus extra
   for greasing

1 onion, chopped finely

1 small red bell pepper, cored, seeded,
   and chopped

1 garlic clove, chopped

1 lb 2 oz/500 g ground lean beef

½ cup soft white bread crumbs

½ tsp cayenne pepper

1 tbsp lemon juice

½ tsp grated lemon rind

2 tbsp chopped fresh parsley

¾ cup short pasta, such as fusilli

1 tbsp olive oil

Cheese Sauce (see page 29)

4 bay leaves

6 oz/175 g lean bacon slices, rind removed

salt and pepper

salad greens, to garnish

1 Melt the butter in a pan over medium heat and cook the onion and pepper for about 3 minutes, or until the onion is translucent. Stir in the garlic and cook for 1 minute.

2 Put the meat into a large bowl and mash it with a wooden spoon until it becomes a sticky paste. Tip in the fried vegetables and stir in the bread crumbs, cayenne, lemon juice, lemon rind, and parsley. Season the mixture with salt and pepper and set aside.

3 Cook the pasta in a large pan of boiling water, to which you have added salt and the olive oil, for 8–10 minutes, or until tender. Drain the pasta, then stir it into the Cheese Sauce.

4 Grease a 2 lb 4 oz/1 kg loaf pan and arrange the bay leaves in the base. Stretch the bacon slices with the back of a knife blade and arrange them to line the base and the sides of the pan.

5 Spoon in half of the meat mixture, then level the surface and cover it with the pasta. Spoon in the remaining meat mixture and level the top, then cover the pan with foil.

6 Cook the meat loaf in the preheated oven, 350°F/180°C, for 1 hour, or until the juices run clear and the loaf has shrunk away from the sides of the pan. Pour off any excess fat from the pan and turn the loaf out on a warmed serving dish. Garnish with the salad greens and serve hot.

# Tortelloni

These tasty little squares of pasta stuffed with mushrooms and cheese are surprisingly filling. This recipe makes 36 tortelloni.

## NUTRITIONAL INFORMATION

Calories . . . . . . .360  Sugars . . . . . . . . .1g
Protein . . . . . . . . .9g  Fat . . . . . . . . . .21g
Carbohydrate . . .36g  Saturates . . . . . .12g

1¼ HOURS    25 MINS

### SERVES 4

## INGREDIENTS

about 10½ oz/300 g fresh pasta (see page
24), rolled out to thin sheets

5 tbsp butter

⅓ cup finely chopped shallot

3 garlic clove, crushed

scant ½ cup mushrooms, wiped and
finely chopped

½ celery stalk, finely chopped

¼ cup finely grated Romano cheese,
plus extra to garnish

1 tbsp oil

salt and pepper

1 Using a serrated pasta cutter, cut 2-inch/5-cm squares from the sheets of fresh pasta. To make 36 tortelloni, you will need 72 squares. Once the pasta is cut, cover the squares with plastic wrap to stop them drying out.

2 Heat 2 tbsp of the butter in a skillet. Add the shallots, 1 crushed garlic clove, the mushrooms, and celery and cook for 4–5 minutes.

3 Remove the pan from the heat, then stir in the cheese and season with salt and pepper to taste.

4 Spoon ½ teaspoon of the mixture on to the middle of 36 pasta squares. Brush the edges of the squares with water and top with the remaining 36 squares. Press the edges together to seal. Leave to rest for 5 minutes.

5 Bring a large pan of water to a boil, then add the oil and cook the tortelloni, in batches, for 2–3 minutes. The tortelloni will rise to the surface when cooked and the pasta should be tender with a slight bite. Remove from the pan with a perforated spoon and drain thoroughly.

6 Meanwhile, melt the remaining butter in a pan. Add the remaining garlic and plenty of pepper and cook for 1–2 minutes. Transfer the tortelloni to serving plates and pour over the garlic butter. Garnish with grated romano cheese and serve immediately.

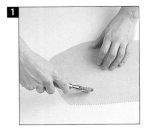

# Tagliatelle with Meatballs

There is an appetizing contrast of textures and flavors in this satisfying family dish.

## NUTRITIONAL INFORMATION

| | | | |
|---|---|---|---|
| Calories | . . . . . . . .910 | Sugars | . . . . . . . .13g |
| Protein | . . . . . . . .40g | Fat | . . . . . . . . . .54g |
| Carbohydrate | . . .65g | Saturates | . . . . . .19g |

45 MINS          1 HR 5 MINS

### SERVES 4

### I N G R E D I E N T S

1 lb 2 oz/500 g ground lean beef

1 cup soft white bread crumbs

1 garlic clove, crushed

2 tbsp chopped fresh parsley

1 tsp dried oregano

large pinch of freshly grated nutmeg

¼ tsp ground coriander

½ cup freshly grated Parmesan cheese

2–3 tbsp milk

flour, for dusting

4 tbsp olive oil

14 oz/400 g tagliatelle

2 tbsp butter, diced

salt and pepper

### S A U C E

3 tbsp olive oil

2 large onions, sliced

2 celery stalks, sliced thinly

2 garlic cloves, chopped

14 oz/400 g canned chopped tomatoes

4½ oz/125 g bottled sun-dried tomatoes, drained and chopped

2 tbsp tomato paste

1 tbsp dark muscovado sugar

⅔ cup white wine, or water

1 To make the sauce, heat the oil in a skillet and cook the onions and celery until translucent. Add the garlic and cook for 1 minute. Stir in the tomatoes, tomato paste, sugar, and wine, then season. Bring to a boil and simmer for 10 minutes.

2 Meanwhile, break up the meat in a bowl with a wooden spoon until it becomes a sticky paste. Stir in the bread crumbs, garlic, herbs, and spices. Stir in the cheese and enough milk to make a firm paste. Flour your hands, take large spoonfuls of the mixture and shape it into 12 balls. Heat 3 tablespoons of the oil in a skillet and cook the meatballs for 5–6 minutes, or until browned.

3 Pour the tomato sauce over the meatballs. Lower the heat, then cover the pan and simmer for 30 minutes, turning once or twice. Add a little extra water if the sauce begins to dry.

4 Cook the pasta in a large pan of boiling salted water, adding the remaining oil, for 8–10 minutes, or until tender. Drain the pasta and turn into a warmed serving dish, then dot with the butter and toss with two forks. Spoon the meatballs and sauce over the pasta and serve.

# Stuffed Cannelloni

Cannelloni, the thick round pasta tubes, make perfect containers for close-textured sauces of all kinds.

## NUTRITIONAL INFORMATION

Calories .......575  Sugars .........6g
Protein ........22g  Fat ..........42g
Carbohydrate ...28g  Saturates ......21g

30 MINS        1¼ HOURS

### SERVES 4

## INGREDIENTS

8 cannelloni tubes

1 tbsp olive oil

fresh herb sprigs, to garnish

### FILLING

2 tbsp butter

10½ oz/300 g frozen spinach, defrosted and chopped

½ cup ricotta

¼ cup freshly grated Parmesan cheese

scant ¼ cup chopped ham

¼ tsp freshly grated nutmeg

2 tbsp heavy cream

2 eggs, lightly beaten

salt and pepper

### SAUCE

2 tbsp butter

2 tbsp all-purpose flour

1¼ cups milk

2 bay leaves

large pinch of grated nutmeg

¼ cup freshly grated Parmesan cheese

1 To prepare the filling, melt the butter in a pan and stir in the spinach. Cook for 2–3 minutes, stirring, to let the moisture to evaporate, then remove the pan from the heat. Stir in the cheeses and the ham. Season with nutmeg, and salt and pepper. Beat in the cream and eggs to make a thick paste. Set aside to cool.

2 Cook the cannelloni in a large pan of boiling salted water, adding the olive oil, for 8–10 minutes, or until tender. Drain the cannelloni in a colander and set aside to cool.

3 To make the sauce, melt the butter in a pan, then stir in the flour and, when it has formed a roux, gradually pour on the milk, stirring all the time. Add the bay leaves, bring to simmering point, and cook for 5 minutes. Season with nutmeg and salt and pepper. Remove the pan from the heat and discard the bay leaves.

4 To assemble the dish, spoon the filling into a pastry bag and pipe it into each of the cannelloni tubes.

5 Spoon a little of the sauce into a shallow baking dish. Arrange the cannelloni in a single layer, then pour over the remaining sauce. Sprinkle on the remaining Parmesan cheese and bake in a preheated oven, 375°F/190°C, for 40–45 minutes, or until the sauce is golden brown and bubbling. Serve garnished with fresh herb sprigs.

# Pasticcio

A recipe that has both Italian and Greek origins, this dish may be served hot or cold, cut into thick, satisfying squares.

## NUTRITIONAL INFORMATION

Calories .......590   Sugars .........8g
Protein ........34g   Fat ..........39g
Carbohydrate ...23g   Saturates ......16g

35 MINS        1¼ HOURS

### SERVES 6

## I N G R E D I E N T S

2 cups fusilli, or other short pasta shapes

1 tbsp olive oil

4 tbsp heavy cream

salt

rosemary sprigs, to garnish

### S A U C E

2 tbsp olive oil, plus extra for brushing

1 onion, sliced thinly

1 red bell pepper, cored, seeded, and chopped

2 garlic cloves, chopped

1 lb 6 oz/625 g ground lean beef

14 oz/400 g canned chopped tomatoes

½ cup dry white wine

2 tbsp chopped fresh parsley

1¾ oz/50 g canned anchovies, drained and chopped

salt and pepper

### T O P P I N G

1¼ cups plain yogurt

3 eggs

pinch of freshly grated nutmeg

⅓ cup freshly grated Parmesan cheese

1 To make the sauce, heat the oil in a large skillet and cook the onion and red bell pepper for 3 minutes. Stir in the garlic and cook for 1 minute more. Stir in the beef and cook, stirring frequently, until no longer pink.

2 Add the tomatoes and wine, then stir well and bring to a boil. Simmer, uncovered, for 20 minutes, or until the sauce is fairly thick. Stir in the parsley and anchovies, and season to taste.

3 Cook the pasta in a large pan of boiling salted water, adding the oil, for 8–10 minutes, or until tender. Drain the pasta in a colander, then transfer to a bowl. Stir in the cream and set aside.

4 To make the topping, beat together the yogurt and eggs and season with nutmeg, and salt and pepper to taste.

5 Brush a shallow baking dish with oil. Spoon in half of the pasta and cover with half of the meat sauce. Repeat these layers, then spread the topping evenly over the final layer. Sprinkle the cheese on top.

6 Bake in a preheated oven, 375°F/190°C, for 25 minutes, or until the topping is golden brown and bubbling. Garnish with sprigs of rosemary and serve with a selection of raw vegetable crudités.

# Lasagna Verde

The sauce in this delicious baked pasta dish can be used as an alternative sauce for Spaghetti Bolognese (see page 255).

## NUTRITIONAL INFORMATION

| | | | |
|---|---|---|---|
| Calories | .619 | Sugars | .7g |
| Protein | .29g | Fat | .45g |
| Carbohydrate | ...21g | Saturates | .19g |

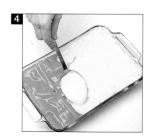

1¾ HOURS    55 MINS

### SERVES 6

## INGREDIENTS

Ragù Sauce (see page 12)

1 tbsp olive oil

8 oz/225 g lasagna verde

Béchamel Sauce (see page 28)

½ cup freshly grated Parmesan cheese

salt and pepper

green salad, tomato salad, or black olives,
   to serve

1 Begin by making the Ragù Sauce as described on page 12, but cook for 10–12 minutes longer than the time given, in an uncovered pan, to let the excess liquid evaporate. To layer the sauce with lasagna, it needs to be reduced to the consistency of a thick paste.

2 Have ready a large pan of boiling, salted water and add the olive oil. Drop the pasta sheets into the boiling water a few at a time, and return the water to a boil before adding further pasta sheets. If you are using fresh lasagna, cook the sheets for a total of 8 minutes. If you are using dried or partly precooked pasta, cook it according to the directions given on the package.

3 Remove the pasta sheets from the pan with a slotted spoon. Spread them in a single layer on damp dish towels.

4 Grease a rectangular ovenproof dish, about 10–11 inches/25–28 cm long. To assemble the dish, spoon a little of the meat sauce into the prepared dish and cover with a layer of lasagna, then spoon over a little Béchamel Sauce and sprinkle with some of the cheese. Continue making layers in this way, covering the final layer of lasagna with the remaining Béchamel Sauce.

5 Sprinkle on the remaining cheese and bake in a preheated oven, 375°F/190°C, for 40 minutes, or until the sauce is golden brown and bubbling. Serve with a green salad, a tomato salad, or a bowl of black olives.

# Vegetable Pasta Nests

These large pasta nests look impressive when presented filled with broiled mixed vegetables, and taste delicious.

## NUTRITIONAL INFORMATION

Calories . . . . . . .392   Sugars . . . . . . . . .1g
Protein . . . . . . . . .6g   Fat . . . . . . . . . .28g
Carbohydrate . . .32g   Saturates . . . . . . .9g

🍲 25 MINS    🕐 40 MINS

### SERVES 4

## INGREDIENTS

6 oz/175 g spaghetti

1 eggplant, halved and sliced

1 zucchini, diced

1 red bell pepper, seeded and chopped
    diagonally

6 tbsp olive oil

2 garlic cloves, crushed

4 tbsp butter or margarine, melted

¼ cup dry white bread crumbs

salt and pepper

fresh parsley sprigs, to garnish

1 Bring a large pan of water to a boil and cook the spaghetti for 8–10 minutes or until *al dente* (see Cook's Tip).Drain the spaghetti in a colander and set aside until required.

2 Place the eggplant, zucchini, and bell pepper on a cookie sheet.

3 Mix the oil and garlic together and pour over the vegetables, tossing to coat all over.

4 Cook under a preheated hot broiler for 10 minutes, turning, until tender and lightly charred. Set aside and keep warm.

5 Divide the spaghetti among 4 lightly greased Yorkshire muffin pans. Using 2 forks, curl the spaghetti to form nests.

6 Brush the pasta nests with melted butter or margarine and sprinkle with the bread crumbs. Bake in a preheated oven, at 400°F/200°C, for 15 minutes, or until lightly golden. Remove the pasta nests from the pans and transfer to serving plates. Divide the broiled vegetables between the pasta nests, then season and garnish.

### COOK'S TIP

*Al dente* means "to the bite" and describes cooked pasta that is not too soft, but still has a "bite" to it.

# Eggplant Layers

Layers of toasty-brown eggplant, meat sauce, and cheese-flavored pasta make this a popular family supper dish.

## NUTRITIONAL INFORMATION

| | | | |
|---|---|---|---|
| Calories | .......900 | Sugars | ........10g |
| Protein | ........43g | Fat | ..........62g |
| Carbohydrate | ...44g | Saturates | ......27g |

🍮 1¹/₂ HOURS  🕐 50 MINS

### SERVES 4

## I N G R E D I E N T S

1 eggplant, sliced thinly

5 tbsp olive oil

2 cups short pasta shapes, such as fusilli

¼ cup butter, plus extra for greasing

scant ⅓ cup all-purpose flour

1¼ cups milk

⅔ cup light cream

⅔ cup chicken stock

large pinch of freshly grated nutmeg

¾ cup grated sharp Cheddar cheese

Lamb Sauce (see page 28)

¼ cup freshly grated Parmesan cheese

salt and pepper

artichoke heart and tomato salad, to serve

1 Put the eggplant slices in a colander, sprinkle with salt and leave for about 45 minutes. Rinse under cold, running water and drain. Pat dry with paper towels.

2 Heat 4 tablespoons of the oil in a skillet over medium heat. Cook the eggplant slices for about 4 minutes on each side, until golden. Remove with a slotted spoon and drain on paper towels.

3 Meanwhile, cook the pasta in a large pan of boiling salted water, adding 1 tablespoon of olive oil, for 8–10 minutes, or until tender. Drain the pasta in a colander and return to the pan. Cover and keep warm.

4 Melt the butter in a small pan, then stir in the flour and cook for 1 minute. Gradually pour in the milk, stirring all the time, then stir in the cream and chicken stock. Season with nutmeg and salt and pepper to taste, then bring to a boil and simmer for 5 minutes. Stir in the Cheddar and remove from the heat. Pour half of the sauce over the pasta and mix well. Reserve the remaining sauce.

5 Grease a shallow ovenproof dish. Spoon in half of the pasta, cover with half of the Lamb Sauce and then with the eggplant in a single layer. Repeat the layers of pasta and Lamb Sauce and spread the remaining cheese sauce over the top. Sprinkle with Parmesan. Bake in the preheated oven, 375°F/190°C, for 25 minutes, or until golden brown. Serve hot or cold, with an artichoke heart and tomato salad.

# Sicilian Spaghetti Cake

Any variety of long pasta could be used for this very tasty dish from Sicily.

## NUTRITIONAL INFORMATION

| | | | |
|---|---|---|---|
| Calories | .......876 | Sugars | ........10g |
| Protein | ........37g | Fat | ..........65g |
| Carbohydrate | ...39g | Saturates | ......18g |

30 MINS     50 MINS

### SERVES 4

## INGREDIENTS

2 eggplants, about 1 lb 7 oz/650 g

⅔ cup olive oil

12 oz/350 g finely ground lean beef

1 onion, chopped

2 garlic cloves, crushed

2 tbsp tomato paste

14 oz/400 g canned chopped tomatoes

1 tsp Worcestershire sauce

1 tsp chopped fresh oregano or marjoram
   or ½ tsp dried oregano or marjoram

scant ⅓ cup pitted black olives, sliced

1 green, red, or yellow bell pepper, cored,
   seeded, and chopped

6 oz/175 g spaghetti

1 cup freshly grated Parmesan cheese

1 Brush a 8-inch/20-cm loose-based round cake pan with olive oil, then place a disk of baking parchment in the base and brush with oil. Trim the eggplants and cut into slanting slices, ¼ inch/5 mm thick. Heat some of the oil in a skillet. Cook a few slices of eggplant at a time until lightly browned, turning once, and adding more oil as necessary. Drain on paper towels.

2 Put the ground beef, onion, and garlic into a pan and cook, stirring frequently, until browned all over. Add the tomato paste, tomatoes, Worcestershire sauce, herbs, and seasoning. Simmer for 10 minutes, stirring occasionally, then add the olives and bell pepper and cook for 10 minutes.

3 Bring a large pan of salted water to a boil. Cook the spaghetti for 8–10 minutes, or until just tender. Drain the spaghetti thoroughly. Turn the spaghetti into a bowl and mix in the meat mixture and Parmesan, tossing together with 2 forks.

4 Lay overlapping slices of eggplant over the base of the cake pan and up the sides. Add the meat mixture, pressing it down, and cover with the remaining eggplant slices.

5 Stand the cake pan in a baking pan and cook in a preheated oven, 400°F/200°C, for 40 minutes. Leave to stand for 5 minutes, then loosen around the edges and invert on to a warmed serving dish, releasing the pan clip. Remove the baking parchment. Serve immediately.

# Pasta Vongole

Fresh clams are readily available, but if you prefer, use canned clams, which are less messy to eat but not as attractive.

## NUTRITIONAL INFORMATION

| | | |
|---|---|---|
| Calories . . . . . . . . .410 | Sugars . . . . . . . . .1g | |
| Protein . . . . . . . .39g | Fat . . . . . . . . . . .9g | |
| Carbohydrate . . .39g | Saturates . . . . . . .1g | |

20 MINS       20 MINS

### SERVES 4

## INGREDIENTS

1 lb 8 oz/675 g fresh clams or 10 oz/280 g

   canned clams, drained

2 tbsp olive oil

2 cloves garlic, finely chopped

14 oz/400 g mixed seafood, such as

shrimp, squid, and mussels, defrosted

if frozen

⅔ cup white wine

⅔ cup fish stock

1 lb 8 oz/675 g fresh pasta or

   12 oz/350 g dried pasta

2 tbsp chopped tarragon

salt and pepper

1   If you are using fresh clams, scrub them clean and discard any that are already open.

2   Heat the oil in a large skillet. Add the garlic and the clams to the skillet and cook for 2 minutes, shaking the skillet to ensure that all of the clams are coated in the oil.

3   Add the remaining seafood mixture to the skillet and cook for an additional 2 minutes.

4   Pour the wine and stock over the mixed seafood and garlic and bring to a boil. Cover, then reduce the heat and leave to simmer for 8–10 minutes, or until the shells open. Discard any clams or mussels that do not open.

5   Meanwhile, cook the pasta in a pan of boiling water for 8–10 minutes or until it is cooked through, but still has "'bite." Drain the pasta thoroughly.

6   Stir the tarragon into the sauce and season with salt and pepper to taste.

7   Transfer the pasta to a serving plate and pour over the sauce. Serve immediately.

## VARIATION

Red clam sauce can be made by adding 8 tablespoons of crushed tomatoes to the sauce along with the stock in step 4. Follow the same cooking method.

# Spaghetti & Shellfish

Frozen shelled shrimp from the freezer can become the star ingredient in this colorful and tasty dish.

## NUTRITIONAL INFORMATION

| | | | |
|---|---|---|---|
| Calories | .......510 | Sugars | ........38g |
| Protein | ........33g | Fat | ..........24g |
| Carbohydrate | ...44g | Saturates | ......11g |

35 MINS     30 MINS

### SERVES 4

## INGREDIENTS

8 oz/225 g short-cut spaghetti, or long
    spaghetti broken into 6-inch/15-cm
    lengths

2 tbsp olive oil

1¼ cups chicken stock

1 tsp lemon juice

1 small cauliflower, cut into florets

2 carrots, sliced thinly

scant 1⅓ cups snow peas, trimmed

¼ cup butter

1 onion, sliced

8 oz/225 g zucchini, sliced thinly

1 garlic clove, chopped

12 oz/350 g frozen shelled shrimp,
    defrosted

2 tbsp chopped fresh parsley

¼ cup freshly grated Parmesan cheese

salt and pepper

½ tsp paprika, to sprinkle

4 unshelled shrimp, to garnish (optional)

1 Cook the spaghetti in a large pan of boiling salted water, with 1 tablespoon oil, for 8–10 minutes, or until tender. Drain,

then return to the pan and stir in the remaining oil. Cover and keep warm.

2 Bring the chicken stock and lemon juice to a boil. Add the cauliflower and carrots and cook for 3–4 minutes, or until they are barely tender. Remove with a slotted spoon and set aside. Add the snow peas and cook for 1–2 minutes, or until they begin to soften. Remove with a slotted spoon and add to the other vegetables. Reserve the chicken stock for future use.

3 Melt half the butter in a skillet over medium heat and cook the onion and

zucchini for 3 minutes. Add the garlic and shrimp and cook for an additional 2–3 minutes, or until thoroughly heated through.

4 Stir in the reserved vegetables and heat through. Season with salt and pepper, then stir in the remaining butter.

5 Transfer the spaghetti to a warmed serving dish. Pour on the sauce and parsley. Toss well using 2 forks, until thoroughly coated. Sprinkle on the grated cheese and paprika, and garnish with unshelled shrimp, if using. Serve immediately.

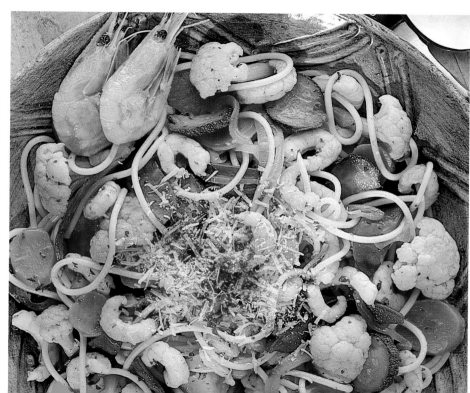

# Pasta Pudding

A tasty mixture of creamy fish and pasta cooked in a bowl, unmolded and drizzled with tomato sauce presents macaroni in a new guise.

## NUTRITIONAL INFORMATION

Calories .......536   Sugars .........4g
Protein ........35g   Fat ..........35g
Carbohydrate ...21g   Saturates ......17g

35 MINS        2 HOURS

### SERVES 4

## INGREDIENTS

generous 1 cup short-cut macaroni,
    or other short pasta shapes

1 tbsp olive oil

1 tbsp butter, plus extra for greasing

1 lb 2 oz/500 g white fish fillets, such as
    cod, haddock, etc

a few parsley stems

6 black peppercorns

½ cup heavy cream

2 eggs, separated

2 tbsp chopped dill, or parsley

pinch of freshly grated nutmeg

½ cup freshly grated Parmesan cheese

Basic Tomato Sauce (see page 28), to serve

pepper

dill or parsley sprigs, to garnish

1 Cook the pasta in a pan of salted boiling water, adding the oil, for 8–10 minutes. Drain, return to the pan, add the butter and cover. Keep warm.

2 Place the fish in a skillet with the parsley stems and peppercorns and pour on just enough water to cover. Bring to a boil, then cover and simmer for 10 minutes. Lift out the fish with a spatula,

reserving the liquor. When the fish is cool enough to handle, skin and remove any bones. Cut into bite-size pieces.

3 Transfer the pasta to a large bowl and stir in the cream, egg yolks, dill, nutmeg and Parmesan. Stir in the fish, taking care not to break it up, and enough liquor to make a moist but firm mixture. It should fall easily from a spoon, but not be too runny. Whisk the egg whites until stiff but not dry, then fold into the mixture.

4 Grease a heatproof bowl or pudding basin and spoon in the mixture to within 1½ inch/4 cm of the rim. Cover the

top with greased waxed paper and a cloth, or with foil, and tie firmly around the rim. Do not use foil if you cook the pudding in a microwave.

5 Stand the pudding on a trivet in a large pan of boiling water to come halfway up the sides. Cover and steam for 1½ hours, topping up the boiling water as needed, or cook in a microwave on maximum power for 7 minutes.

6 Run a knife around the inside of the bowl and invert on to a warm serving dish. Pour some tomato sauce over the top; serve the rest separately. Garnish and serve.

# Macaroni & Shrimp Bake

This adaptation of an 18th-century Italian dish is baked until it is golden brown and sizzling, then cut into wedges, like a cake.

## NUTRITIONAL INFORMATION

Calories . . . . . . .576   Sugars . . . . . . . . .6g
Protein . . . . . . . .25g   Fat . . . . . . . . . .35g
Carbohydrate . . .42g   Saturates . . . . . .19g

20 MINS      1 HR 5 MINS

### SERVES 4

## INGREDIENTS

3 cups short pasta, such as short-cut
   macaroni

1 tbsp olive oil, plus extra for brushing

6 tbsp butter, plus extra for greasing

2 small fennel bulbs, sliced thinly,
   leaves reserved

6 oz/175 g mushrooms, sliced thinly

6 oz/175 g shelled shrimp

Béchamel Sauce (see page 28)

pinch of cayenne

½ cup freshly grated Parmesan cheese

2 large tomatoes, sliced

1 tsp dried oregano

salt and pepper

1 Cook the pasta in a large pan of boiling, salted water, with 1 tablespoon of olive oil, for 8–10 minutes, or until tender. Drain the pasta in a colander, then return to the pan and dot with 2 tablespoons of the butter. Shake the pan well, then cover and keep warm.

2 Melt the remaining butter in a pan over medium heat and cook the fennel for 3–4 minutes, or until it begins to soften. Stir in the mushrooms and cook for 2 minutes. Stir in the shrimp, then remove the pan from the heat and set aside until required.

3 Make the Béchamel Sauce and add the cayenne. Remove the pan from the heat and stir in the reserved vegetables, shrimp, and the pasta.

4 Grease a round, shallow baking dish. Pour in the pasta mixture and spread evenly. Sprinkle with the Parmesan and arrange the tomato slices in a ring around the edge of the dish. Brush the tomato with olive oil and sprinkle with the dried oregano.

5 Bake in a preheated oven, 350°F/ 180°C, for 25 minutes, or until golden brown. Serve hot.

# Spaghetti & Salmon Sauce

The smoked salmon ideally complements the spaghetti to give a very luxurious dish.

## NUTRITIONAL INFORMATION

| | | | |
|---|---|---|---|
| Calories | .......782 | Sugars | .........3g |
| Protein | ........20g | Fat | ..........48g |
| Carbohydrate | ...48g | Saturates | ......27g |

🍲 10 MINS  🕐 15 MINS

### SERVES 4

## I N G R E D I E N T S

1 lb 2 oz/500 g buckwheat spaghetti

2 tbsp olive oil

½ cup crumbled feta cheese

cilantro or parsley, to garnish

### S A U C E

1¼ cups heavy cream

⅔ cup whisky or brandy

4½ oz/125 g smoked salmon

large pinch of cayenne pepper

2 tbsp chopped cilantro or parsley

salt and pepper

1 Cook the spaghetti in a large pan of salted boiling water, adding 1 tablespoon of the olive oil, for 8–10 minutes, or until tender. Drain the pasta in a colander. Return the pasta to the pan and sprinkle over the remaining oil, then cover and shake the pan. Set aside and keep warm until required.

2 In separate small pans, heat the cream and the whisky or brandy to simmering point. Do not let them boil.

3 Combine the cream with the whisky or brandy.

4 Cut the smoked salmon into thin strips and add to the cream mixture. Season with a little black pepper and cayenne pepper to taste, and then stir in the chopped cilantro or parsley.

5 Transfer the spaghetti to a warmed serving dish, then pour on the sauce and toss thoroughly using two large forks. Scatter the crumbled cheese over the pasta and garnish with the cilantro or parsley. Serve at once.

# Seafood Pasta

This attractive seafood salad platter is full of different flavors, textures, and colors.

## NUTRITIONAL INFORMATION

Calories .......188    Sugars .........2g
Protein ........16g    Fat ...........7g
Carbohydrate ...13g    Saturates .......1g

30 MINS          30 MINS

### SERVES 8

## I N G R E D I E N T S

1½ cups dried pasta shapes

1 tbsp oil

4 tbsp Italian dressing

2 garlic cloves, crushed

6 tbsp white wine

1 cup baby white mushrooms, trimmed

3 carrots

2½ cups fresh mussels in shells

4½–6 oz/125–175 g frozen squid or
   octopus rings, thawed

1 cup shelled jumbo shrimp, thawed
   if frozen

6 sun-dried tomatoes, drained and sliced

3 tbsp chives, cut into 1-inch/2.5-cm pieces

salt and pepper

### TO GARNISH

24 snow peas, trimmed

12 baby corn

12 shrimp in shells

1 Cook the pasta in a pan of boiling salted water, with the oil added, for 8–10 minutes, or until just tender. Drain the pasta thoroughly.

2 Combine the dressing, garlic, and 2 tablespoons of wine. Mix in the mushrooms and leave to marinate.

3 Slice the carrots about ½ inch/1 cm thick and, using a cocktail cutter, cut each slice into shapes. Blanch for 3–4 minutes, then drain and add to the mushrooms.

4 Scrub the mussels, discarding any that are open or do not close when sharply tapped. Put into a pan with ⅔ cup water and the remaining wine. Bring to a boil, then cover and simmer for 3–4 minutes, or until they open. Drain, discarding any that are still closed. Reserve 12 mussels for garnish, leaving them on the half shell; remove the other mussels from the shells and add to the mushroom mixture with the squid or octopus rings and shrimp.

5 Add the sun-dried tomatoes, pasta, and chives to the salad. Toss to mix and turn onto a large platter.

6 Blanch the snow peas for 1 minute and baby corn for 3 minutes, then rinse under cold water and drain. Arrange around the edge of the salad, alternating with the mussels on shells and whole shrimp. Cover with plastic wrap and leave to chill until ready to serve.

# Macaroni & Tuna Fish Layer

A layer of tuna fish with garlic, mushroom, and red bell pepper is sandwiched between two layers of macaroni with a crunchy topping.

## NUTRITIONAL INFORMATION

Calories . . . . . . . .691    Sugars . . . . . . . .10g
Protein . . . . . . . .41g    Fat . . . . . . . . . .33g
Carbohydrate . . .62g    Saturates . . . . . .15g

20 MINS          50 MINS

### SERVES 2

## I N G R E D I E N T S

generous 1–scant 1½ cup dried macaroni

2 tbsp oil

1 garlic clove, crushed

1 cup sliced white mushrooms

½ red bell pepper, thinly sliced

7 oz/200 g canned tuna fish in brine,
    drained and flaked

½ tsp dried oregano

2 tomatoes, sliced

2 tbsp dried bread crumbs

¼ cup freshly grated sharp Cheddar or
    Parmesan cheese

salt and pepper

### S A U C E

2 tbsp butter or margarine

1 tbsp all-purpose flour

1 cup milk

## VARIATION

Replace the tuna fish with chopped cooked chicken, beef, pork, or ham or with 3–4 sliced hard-cooked eggs.

1 Cook the macaroni in boiling salted water, with 1 tablespoon of the oil added, for 10–12 minutes, or until tender. Drain, rinse and drain thoroughly.

2 Heat the remaining oil in a pan or skillet and cook the garlic, mushrooms, and bell pepper until soft. Add the tuna fish, oregano, and seasoning, and heat through.

3 Grease an ovenproof dish (about 4-cup capacity), and add half of the cooked macaroni. Cover with the tuna mixture and then add the remaining macaroni.

4 To make the sauce, melt the butter in a pan, then stir in the flour and cook for 1 minute. Add the milk gradually and bring to a boil. Simmer for 1–2 minutes, stirring continuously, until thickened. Season to taste. Pour the sauce over the macaroni.

5 Lay the sliced tomatoes over the sauce and sprinkle with the bread crumbs and cheese.

6 Place the dish in a preheated oven, at 400°F/200°C, for about 25 minutes, or until piping hot and the top is well browned.

# Pasta with Nuts & Cheese

Simple and inexpensive, this tasty pasta dish can be prepared fairly quickly.

## NUTRITIONAL INFORMATION

| | | |
|---|---|---|
| Calories . . . . . . . . .531 | Sugars . . . . . . . . .4g | |
| Protein . . . . . . . .20g | Fat . . . . . . . . . .35g | |
| Carbohydrate . . .35g | Saturates . . . . . .16g | |

10 MINS        30 MINS

### SERVES 4

## INGREDIENTS

generous ⅓ cup pine nuts

3 cups dried pasta shapes

2 zucchini, sliced

4½ oz/125 g broccoli, broken into florets

scant 1 cup full-fat soft cheese

⅔ cup milk

1 tbsp chopped fresh basil

generous 2 cups sliced white mushrooms

½ cup crumbled blue cheese

salt and pepper

sprigs of fresh basil, to garnish

green salad, to serve

1 Scatter the pine nuts onto a cookie sheet and broil, turning occasionally, until lightly browned all over. Set aside.

2 Cook the pasta in plenty of boiling salted water for 8–10 minutes, or until just tender.

3 Meanwhile, cook the zucchini and broccoli in a small amount of boiling, lightly salted water for about 5 minutes, or until just tender.

4 Put the soft cheese into a pan and heat gently, stirring constantly. Add the milk and stir to mix. Add the basil and mushrooms and cook gently for 2–3 minutes. Stir in the blue cheese and season to taste.

5 Drain the pasta and the vegetables and mix together. Pour over the cheese and mushroom sauce and add the pine nuts. Toss gently to mix. Garnish with basil sprigs and serve with a green salad.

# Basil & Tomato Pasta

Roasting the tomatoes gives a sweeter flavor to this sauce. Buy Italian tomatoes, such as plum or flavia, as these have a better flavor and color.

## NUTRITIONAL INFORMATION

| | | |
|---|---|---|
| Calories .......177 | Sugars .........4g | |
| Protein .........5g | Fat ...........4g | |
| Carbohydrate ...31g | Saturates .......1g | |

15 MINS     35 MINS

### SERVES 4

## I N G R E D I E N T S

1 tbsp olive oil

2 sprigs rosemary

2 cloves garlic

1 lb/450 g tomatoes, halved

1 tbsp sun-dried tomato paste

12 fresh basil leaves, plus extra to garnish

salt and pepper

1 lb 8 oz/675 g fresh farfalle or
    12 oz/350 g dried farfalle

1 Place the oil, rosemary, garlic, and tomatoes, skin side up, in a shallow roasting pan.

2 Drizzle with a little oil and cook under a preheated broiler for 20 minutes, or until the tomato skins are slightly charred.

3 Peel the skin from the tomatoes. Coarsely chop the tomato flesh and place in a pan.

4 Squeeze the pulp from the garlic cloves and mix with the tomato flesh and sun-dried tomato paste.

5 Roughly tear the fresh basil leaves into smaller pieces and then stir them into the sauce. Season with a little salt and pepper to taste. Set aside.

6 Cook the farfalle in a pan of rapidly boiling water for 8–10 minutes, or until it is cooked through, but still has "bite." Drain well.

7 Gently re-heat the tomato and basil sauce, stirring.

8 Transfer the farfalle to serving plates and pour over the basil and tomato sauce. Serve at once.

## COOK'S TIP

This sauce tastes just as good when served cold in a pasta salad.

# Tagliatelle & Garlic Sauce

This pasta dish can be prepared in a moment—the intense flavors are sure to make this a popular recipe.

## NUTRITIONAL INFORMATION

| | | |
|---|---|---|
| Calories . . . . . . . .501 | Sugars . . . . . . . . .3g | |
| Protein . . . . . . . .15g | Fat . . . . . . . . . .31g | |
| Carbohydrate . . .43g | Saturates . . . . . .11g | |

 15 MINS  20 MINS

### SERVES 4

### INGREDIENTS

2 tbsp walnut oil

1 bunch scallions, sliced

2 garlic cloves, sliced thinly

4 cups sliced mushrooms

1 lb 2 oz/500 g fresh green and white
   tagliatelle

8 oz/225 g frozen chopped leaf spinach,
   thawed and drained

½ cup full-fat soft cheese with garlic
   and herbs

4 tbsp light cream

scant ½ cup chopped, unsalted
   pistachio nuts

2 tbsp shredded fresh basil

salt and pepper

sprigs of fresh basil, to garnish

Italian bread, to serve

1 Gently heat the oil in a wok or skillet and cook the scallions and garlic for 1 minute, or until just softened. Add the mushrooms and stir well, then cover and cook gently for 5 minutes, or until softened.

2 Meanwhile, bring a large pan of lightly salted water to a boil and cook the pasta for 3–5 minutes, or until just tender. Drain the pasta thoroughly and return to the pan.

3 Add the spinach to the mushrooms and heat through for 1–2 minutes. Add the cheese and let it melt slightly. Stir in the cream and continue to heat without letting it boil.

4 Pour the mixture over the pasta, then season to taste and mix well. Heat gently, stirring, for 2–3 minutes.

5 Pile into a warmed serving bowl and sprinkle over the pistachio nuts and shredded basil. Garnish with basil sprigs and serve with Italian bread.

# Chile & Bell Pepper Pasta

This roasted bell pepper and chile sauce is sweet and spicy—the perfect combination!

## NUTRITIONAL INFORMATION

| | | | |
|---|---|---|---|
| Calories | .......423 | Sugars | .........5g |
| Protein | .........9g | Fat | ..........27g |
| Carbohydrate | ...38g | Saturates | .......4g |

25 MINS        30 MINS

### SERVES 4

## INGREDIENTS

2 red bell peppers, halved and seeded

1 small red chile

4 tomatoes, halved

2 garlic cloves

½ cup ground almonds

scant ½ cup olive oil

1 lb 8 oz/675 g fresh pasta or
    12 oz/350 g dried pasta

fresh oregano leaves, to garnish

1 Place the bell peppers, skin-side up, on a cookie sheet with the chile and tomatoes. Cook under a preheated broiler for 15 minutes, or until charred. After 10 minutes, turn the tomatoes skin-side up. Place the bell peppers and chiles in a plastic bag and leave to sweat for 10 minutes.

## VARIATION

Add 2 tablespoons of red wine vinegar to the sauce and use as a dressing for a cold pasta salad, if you wish.

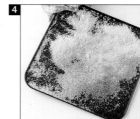

2 Remove the skin from the bell peppers and chiles and slice the flesh into strips, using a sharp knife.

3 Peel the garlic, and peel and seed the tomatoes.

4 Place the almonds on a cookie sheet and place under the broiler for 2–3 minutes, or until golden.

5 Using a food processor, blend the bell pepper, chile, garlic, and tomatoes to make a purée. Keep the motor running and slowly add the olive oil to form a thick sauce. Alternatively, mash the mixture

with a fork and beat in the olive oil, drop by drop.

6 Stir the toasted ground almonds into the mixture.

7 Warm the sauce in a pan until it is heated through.

8 Cook the pasta in a pan of boiling water for 8–10 minutes if using dried, or 3–5 minutes if using fresh. Drain the pasta thoroughly and transfer to a serving dish. Pour over the sauce and toss to mix. Garnish with the fresh oregano leaves.

# Artichoke & Olive Spaghetti

The tasty, distinctive flavors of artichoke hearts and black olives are a winning combination.

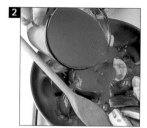

## NUTRITIONAL INFORMATION

| | | | |
|---|---|---|---|
| Calories | .......393 | Sugars | ........11g |
| Protein | ........14g | Fat | ...........11g |
| Carbohydrate | ...63g | Saturates | .......2g |

20 MINS        35 MINS

### SERVES 4

## I N G R E D I E N T S

2 tbsp olive oil

1 large red onion, chopped

2 garlic cloves, crushed

1 tbsp lemon juice

4 baby eggplants, cut into fourths

2½ cups crushed tomatoes

2 tsp superfine sugar

2 tbsp tomato paste

14 oz/400 g canned artichoke hearts,
    drained and halved

¾ cup pitted black olives

12 oz/350 g whole-wheat dried spaghetti

salt and pepper

sprigs of fresh basil, to garnish

olive bread, to serve

1 Heat 1 tablespoon of the oil in a large skillet and gently cook the onion, garlic, lemon juice, and eggplants for 4–5 minutes, or until lightly browned.

2 Pour in the crushed tomatoes, then season with salt and pepper to taste and add the sugar and tomato paste. Bring to a boil, then reduce the heat and simmer for 20 minutes.

3 Gently stir in the artichoke halves and olives and cook for 5 minutes.

4 Meanwhile, bring a large pan of lightly salted water to a boil, and cook the spaghetti for 8–10 minutes or until just tender. Drain well, then toss in the remaining olive oil and season with salt and pepper to taste.

5 Transfer the spaghetti to a warmed serving bowl and top with the vegetable sauce. Garnish with basil sprigs and serve with olive bread.

# Pasta & Cheese Puddings

These delicious pasta puddings are served with a tasty tomato and bay leaf sauce.

## NUTRITIONAL INFORMATION

Calories . . . . . . . . .517  Sugars . . . . . . . . .8g
Protein . . . . . . . .19g  Fat . . . . . . . . . .27g
Carbohydrate . . .47g  Saturates . . . . . .13g

45 MINS      50 MINS

### SERVES 4

## I N G R E D I E N T S

1 tbsp butter or margarine, softened

scant ½ cup dried white bread crumbs

6 oz/175 g tricolour spaghetti

1¼ cups Béchamel Sauce (see page 28)

1 egg yolk

generous 1 cup grated Gruyère cheese

salt and pepper

fresh flat-leaf parsley, to garnish

### T O M A T O   S A U C E

2 tsp olive oil

1 onion, chopped finely

1 bay leaf

⅔ cup dry white wine

⅔ cup crushed tomatoes

1 tbsp tomato paste

1 Grease four ¾ cup molds or ramekins with the butter or margarine. Evenly coat the insides with half of the bread crumbs.

2 Break the spaghetti into 2-inch/5-cm lengths. Bring a pan of lightly salted water to a boil and cook the spaghetti for 5–6 minutes, or until just tender. Drain well and put in a bowl.

3 Mix the Béchamel Sauce, egg yolk, cheese, and seasoning into the cooked pasta and pack into the molds.

4 Sprinkle with the remaining bread crumbs and place the molds on a cookie sheet. Bake in a preheated oven, 425°F/220°C, for 20 minutes, or until golden. Leave to stand for 10 minutes.

5 Meanwhile, make the sauce. Heat the oil in a pan and cook the onion and bay leaf for 2–3 minutes, or until just softened.

6 Stir in the wine, strained tomatoes, tomato paste, and seasoning. Bring to a boil and simmer for 20 minutes, or until thickened. Discard the bay leaf.

7 Run a spatula around the inside of the molds. Turn onto serving plates, then garnish and serve with the tomato sauce.

# Pasta & Bean Casserole

A satisfying winter dish, this is a slow-cooked, one-pot meal. The Great Northern beans need to be soaked overnight, so prepare well in advance.

## NUTRITIONAL INFORMATION

| | | | |
|---|---|---|---|
| Calories | .......323 | Sugars | .........5g |
| Protein | ........13g | Fat | ..........12g |
| Carbohydrate | ...41g | Saturates | .......2g |

  25 MINS  3¹/₂ HOURS

### SERVES 6

### INGREDIENTS

generous 1 cup dried Great Northern beans, soaked overnight and drained

2 cups penne, or other short pasta shapes

6 tbsp olive oil

3¾ cups vegetable stock

2 large onions, sliced

2 cloves garlic, chopped

2 bay leaves

1 tsp dried oregano

1 tsp dried thyme

5 tbsp red wine

2 tbsp tomato paste

2 celery stalks, sliced

1 fennel bulb, sliced

generous 2 cups sliced mushrooms

8 oz/225 g tomatoes, sliced

1 tsp dark muscovado sugar

4 tbsp dry white bread crumbs

salt and pepper

### TO SERVE

salad greens

crusty bread

1 Put the beans in a large pan, then cover them with water and bring to a boil. Boil the beans rapidly for 20 minutes, then drain.

2 Cook the pasta for only 3 minutes in a large pan of boiling salted water, adding 1 tablespoon of the oil. Drain in a colander and set aside.

3 Put the beans in a large flameproof casserole, then pour on the vegetable stock and stir in the remaining olive oil, the onions, garlic, bay leaves, herbs, wine, and tomato paste.

4 Bring to a boil, then cover the casserole and cook in a preheated oven, 350°F/180°C, for 2 hours.

5 Add the reserved pasta, the celery, fennel, mushrooms, and tomatoes, and season with salt and pepper.

6 Stir in the sugar and sprinkle on the bread crumbs. Cover the casserole and continue cooking for 1 hour. Serve hot, with salad greens and crusty bread.

# Pasta with Cheese & Broccoli

Some of the simplest and most satisfying dishes are made with pasta, such as this delicious combination of tagliatelle with two-cheese sauce.

## NUTRITIONAL INFORMATION

| | | | |
|---|---|---|---|
| Calories | .......624 | Sugars | .........2g |
| Protein | ........22g | Fat | ..........45g |
| Carbohydrate | ...34g | Saturates | ......28g |

 5 MINS   15 MINS

### SERVES 4

### I N G R E D I E N T S

10½ oz/300 g dried tagliatelle tricolore
(plain, spinach-, and tomato-flavored
noodles)

8 oz/225 g broccoli, broken into small
florets

1½ cups mascarpone cheese

1 cup chopped blue cheese

1 tbsp chopped fresh oregano

2 tbsp butter

salt and pepper

sprigs of fresh oregano, to garnish

freshly grated Parmesan cheese, to serve

1 Cook the tagliatelle in plenty of boiling salted water for 8–10 minutes, or until just tender.

2 Meanwhile, cook the broccoli florets in a small amount of lightly salted, boiling water. Avoid overcooking the broccoli, so that it retains much of its color and texture.

3 Heat the mascarpone and blue cheeses together gently in a large pan until they are melted. Stir in the oregano and season with salt and pepper to taste.

4 Drain the pasta thoroughly. Return it to the pan and add the butter, tossing the tagliatelle to coat it. Drain the broccoli well and add to the pasta with the sauce, tossing gently to mix.

5 Divide the pasta between 4 warmed serving plates. Garnish with sprigs of fresh oregano and serve with freshly grated Parmesan.

# Pasta Provençale

A Mediterranean mixture of red bell peppers, garlic, and zucchini cooked in olive oil and tossed with pasta.

## NUTRITIONAL INFORMATION

| | | | |
|---|---|---|---|
| Calories | .341 | Sugars | .8g |
| Protein | 13g | Fat | 20g |
| Carbohydrate | 30g | Saturates | .8g |

15 MINS   20 MINS

### SERVES 4

## INGREDIENTS

3 tbsp olive oil

1 onion, sliced

2 garlic cloves, chopped

3 red bell peppers, seeded and cut
  into strips

3 zucchini, sliced

14 oz/400 g canned chopped tomatoes

3 tbsp sun-dried tomato paste

2 tbsp chopped fresh basil

8 oz/225 g fresh pasta spirals

1 cup grated Gruyère cheese

salt and pepper

fresh basil sprigs, to garnish

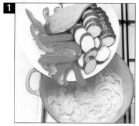  

1 Heat the oil in a heavy-based pan or flameproof casserole. Add the onion and garlic and cook, stirring occasionally, until softened. Add the bell peppers and zucchini and cook for 5 minutes, stirring occasionally.

2 Add the tomatoes, sun-dried tomato paste, basil, and seasoning, then cover and cook for 5 minutes.

3 Meanwhile, bring a large pan of salted water to a boil and add the pasta. Stir and bring back to a boil. Reduce the heat slightly and cook, uncovered, for 3 minutes, or until just tender. Drain thoroughly and add to the vegetables. Toss gently to mix well.

4 Put the mixture into a shallow ovenproof dish and sprinkle over the grated cheese.

5 Cook under a preheated broiler for 5 minutes, or until the cheese is golden. Garnish with basil sprigs and serve.

## COOK'S TIP

Be careful not to overcook fresh pasta—it should be *al dente* (retaining some "bite"). It takes only a few minutes to cook as it is still full of moisture.

# Tagliatelle with Pumpkin

This unusual pasta dish comes from the Emilia Romagna region of Italy.

## NUTRITIONAL INFORMATION

Calories . . . . . . . .454   Sugars . . . . . . . . .4g
Protein . . . . . . . . .9g   Fat . . . . . . . . . .33g
Carbohydrate . . .33g   Saturates . . . . . .12g

15 MINS        35 MINS

### SERVES 4

### INGREDIENTS

1 lb 2 oz/500 g pumpkin or butternut
   squash

2 tbsp olive oil

1 onion, chopped finely

2 garlic cloves, crushed

4–6 tbsp chopped fresh parsley

good pinch of ground or freshly grated
   nutmeg

about 1 cup chicken or vegetable stock

4½ oz/125 g prosciutto, cut into
   narrow strips

9 oz/275 g tagliatelle, green or white (fresh
   or dried)

⅔ cup heavy cream

salt and pepper

freshly grated Parmesan cheese, to serve

1 Peel the pumpkin or squash and scoop out the seeds and membrane. Cut the flesh into ½-inch/1-cm dice.

2 Heat the olive oil in a pan and gently cook the onion and garlic until softened. Add half of the parsley and cook for 1–2 minutes.

3 Add the pumpkin or squash and continue to cook for 2–3 minutes. Season well with salt, pepper, and nutmeg.

4 Add half the stock and bring to a boil, then cover and simmer for 10 minutes or until the pumpkin is tender, adding more stock as necessary. Add the prosciutto and continue to cook for 2 minutes, stirring frequently.

5 Meanwhile, cook the tagliatelle in a large pan of boiling salted water, allowing 3–4 minutes for fresh pasta or 8–10 minutes for dried. Drain thoroughly and turn into a warmed dish.

6 Add the cream to the ham mixture and heat gently. Season and spoon over the pasta. Sprinkle with the remaining parsley and grated Parmesan separately.

# Basil & Pine Nut Pesto

Delicious stirred into pasta, soups, and salad dressings, pesto is available in most supermarkets, but making your own gives a concentrated flavor.

## NUTRITIONAL INFORMATION

| | | |
|---|---|---|
| Calories . . . . . . . .321 | Sugars . . . . . . . . .1g |
| Protein . . . . . . . .11g | Fat . . . . . . . . . .17g |
| Carbohydrate . . .32g | Saturates . . . . . . .4g |

🍲 15 MINS    🕐 10 MINS

### SERVES 4

## I N G R E D I E N T S

about 40 fresh basil leaves,
   washed and dried

3 garlic cloves, crushed

¼ cup pine nuts

½ cup finely grated Parmesan cheese

2–3 tbsp extra virgin olive oil

salt and pepper

1 lb 8 oz/675 g fresh pasta or
   12 oz/350 g dried pasta

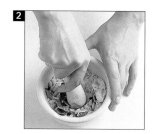

1 Rinse the basil leaves and pat them dry with paper towels.

2 Put the basil leaves, garlic, pine nuts, and grated Parmesan into a food processor and blend for about 30 seconds, or until smooth. Alternatively, pound all of the ingredients by hand, using a mortar and pestle.

3 If you are using a food processor, keep the motor running and slowly add the olive oil. Alternatively, add the oil drop by drop while stirring briskly. Season with salt and pepper to taste.

4 Cook the pasta in a pan of boiling water allowing 3–4 minutes for fresh pasta or 8–10 minutes for dried, or until it is cooked through, but still has "bite." Drain the pasta thoroughly in a colander.

5 Transfer the pasta to a serving plate and serve with the pesto. Toss to mix well and serve hot.

## COOK'S TIP

You can store pesto in the refrigerator for about 4 weeks. Cover the surface of the pesto with olive oil before sealing the container or bottle, to prevent the basil from oxidizing and turning black.

# Italian Tomato Sauce & Pasta

Fresh tomatoes make a delicious Italian-style sauce that goes particularly well with pasta.

## NUTRITIONAL INFORMATION

| | | | |
|---|---|---|---|
| Calories | .......304 | Sugars | .........8g |
| Protein | ........15g | Fat | ..........14g |
| Carbohydrate | ...31g | Saturates | .......5g |

  10 MINS     25 MINS

### SERVES 2

## INGREDIENTS

1 tbsp olive oil

1 small onion, chopped finely

1–2 cloves garlic, crushed

12 oz/350 g tomatoes, peeled and chopped

2 tsp tomato paste

2 tbsp water

2½–3 cups dried pasta shapes

⅓ cup lean bacon, derinded and diced

scant 1 cup sliced mushrooms

1 tbsp chopped fresh parsley or 1 tsp
    chopped fresh cilantro

2 tbsp sour cream or mascarpone
    (optional)

salt and pepper

## COOK'S TIP

Sour cream contains
18–20% fat, so if you are
following a lowfat diet you can leave
it out of this recipe or substitute a
lowfat alternative.

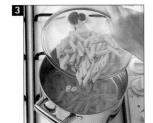

1 To make the tomato sauce, heat the oil in a pan and cook the onion and garlic gently until soft.

2 Add the tomatoes, tomato paste, water, and salt and pepper to taste to the mixture in the pan and bring to a boil. Cover and simmer gently for 10 minutes.

3 Meanwhile, cook the pasta in a pan of boiling salted water for 8–10 minutes, or until just tender. Drain the pasta and transfer to warm serving dishes.

4 Heat the bacon gently in a skillet until the fat runs, then add the mushrooms and continue cooking for 3–4 minutes. Drain off any excess oil.

5 Add the bacon and mushrooms to the tomato mixture, together with the parsley and the sour cream or mascarpone, if using. Reheat and serve with the pasta.

# Mushroom & Pasta Flan

Lightly cooked vermicelli is pressed into a flan ring and baked with a creamy mushroom filling.

## NUTRITIONAL INFORMATION

| | | |
|---|---|---|
| Calories | ......557 | Sugars ..........5g |
| Protein | ........15g | Fat ..........36g |
| Carbohydrate | ...47g | Saturates ......19g |

 10 MINS    1 HR 10 MINS

### SERVES 4

## I N G R E D I E N T S

8 oz/225 g vermicelli or spaghetti

1 tbsp olive oil

2 tbsp butter, plus extra for

greasing

salt and pepper

tomato and basil salad, to serve

### S A U C E

¼ cup butter

1 onion, chopped

3 cups white mushrooms, trimmed

1 green bell pepper, cored, seeded, and

sliced into thin rings

⅔ cup milk

3 eggs, beaten lightly

2 tbsp heavy cream

1 tsp dried oregano

pinch of finely grated nutmeg

1 tbsp freshly grated Parmesan cheese

1 Cook the pasta in a large pan of salted boiling water, adding the olive oil, for 8–10 minutes, or until tender. Drain the pasta in a colander and return to the pan, then add the butter and shake the pan well.

2 Grease a 8-inch/20-cm loose-bottomed flan pan. Press the pasta onto the base and around the sides to form a case.

3 Heat the butter in a skillet over medium heat and cook the onion until it is translucent. Remove with a slotted spoon and spread in the flan base.

4 Add the mushrooms and bell pepper rings to the pan and turn them in the fat until glazed. Cook for 2 minutes on each side, then arrange in the flan base.

5 Beat together the milk, eggs, and cream and stir in the oregano, then season with nutmeg and pepper. Pour the mixture carefully over the vegetables and sprinkle on the cheese.

6 Bake the flan in the preheated oven, 350°F/180°C, for 40–45 minutes, or until the filling is set. Slide on to a serving plate and serve warm.

# Three-Cheese Macaroni

Based on a traditional family favorite, this pasta bake has plenty of flavor. Serve with a crisp salad for a quick, tasty supper.

## NUTRITIONAL INFORMATION

| | | | |
|---|---|---|---|
| Calories | .......672 | Sugars | ........10g |
| Protein | ........31g | Fat | ..........44g |
| Carbohydrate | ...40g | Saturates | ......23g |

🍲 30 MINS   🕙 45 MINS

### SERVES 4

## INGREDIENTS

2½ cups Béchamel Sauce (see page 28)

2 cups macaroni

1 egg, beaten

1 cup grated Cheddar cheese

1 tbsp whole-grain mustard

2 tbsp chopped fresh chives

4 tomatoes, sliced

1 cup grated brick cheese

½ cup grated blue cheese

2 tbsp sunflower seeds

salt and pepper

snipped fresh chives, to garnish

1 Make the Béchamel Sauce, put into a bowl and cover with plastic wrap to prevent a skin forming. Set aside.

2 Bring a pan of salted water to a boil and cook the macaroni for 8–10 minutes, or until just tender. Drain well and place in an ovenproof dish.

3 Stir the beaten egg, Cheddar, mustard, chives, and seasoning into the Béchamel Sauce and spoon over the macaroni, making sure it is well covered. Top with a layer of sliced tomatoes.

4 Sprinkle over the brick and blue cheeses, and sunflower seeds. Put on a cookie sheet and bake in a preheated oven, 375°F/190°C, for 25–30 minutes, or until bubbling and golden. Garnish with chives and serve immediately.

# Vegetable & Pasta Pockets

These small pockets are very easy to make and have the advantage of being filled with your favorite mixture of succulent mushrooms.

## NUTRITIONAL INFORMATION

Calories .......333    Sugars .........1g
Protein .........7g    Fat ..........30g
Carbohydrate ...10g    Saturates ......13g

20 MINS    20 MINS

### SERVES 4

## INGREDIENTS

### FILLING

2 tbsp butter or margarine

2 garlic cloves, crushed

1 small leek, chopped

2 celery stalks, chopped

2⅓ cups open-cup mushrooms, chopped

1 egg, beaten

2 tbsp freshly grated Parmesan cheese

salt and pepper

### POCKETS

4 sheets phyllo pastry

2 tbsp margarine

oil, for deep-frying

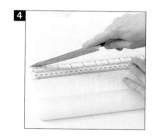

1 To make the filling, melt the butter in a skillet and sauté the garlic and leek for 2–3 minutes, or until softened.

2 Add the celery and mushrooms and cook for an additional 4–5 minutes until all of the vegetables are tender.

3 Turn off the heat and stir in the egg and grated Parmesan cheese. Season with salt and pepper to taste.

4 Lay the phyllo sheets on a chopping board and cut each into 9 squares.

5 Spoon a little of the filling into the center half of the squares and brush the edges of the pastry with butter. Lay another square on top and seal the edges to make a pocket.

6 Heat the oil for deep-frying to 350°F/180°C, or until a cube of bread browns in 30 seconds. Fry the pockets, in batches, for 2–3 minutes, or until golden brown. Remove from the oil with a slotted spoon and pat dry on absorbent paper towels. Transfer to a warm serving plate and serve.

# Rice & Grains

Rice dishes are particularly popular in the north of Italy as the people in this area are very fond of risottos. Milanese and other risottos are made with short-grain Italian rice, the best of which is arborio rice. An Italian risotto is far moister than a pilaf or other savory rice dish, but it should not be soggy or sticky. Gnocchi are made with maize flour, cornmeal, potatoes, or semolina, often combined with spinach or some sort of cheese. Gnocchi resemble dumplings and are either poached or baked. Polenta is made with cornmeal or polenta flour and can be served either as a soft porridge or a firmer cake that is then fried until crisp.

# Golden Chicken Risotto

Long-grain rice can be used instead of risotto rice, but it won't give you the traditional, creamy texture that is typical of Italian risottos.

## NUTRITIONAL INFORMATION

| | | | |
|---|---|---|---|
| Calories | . . . . . . . .701 | Sugars | . . . . . . . . .7g |
| Protein | . . . . . . . .35g | Fat | . . . . . . . . . .26g |
| Carbohydrate | . . .88g | Saturates | . . . . . . . .8g |

10 MINS     30 MINS

SERVES 4

## I N G R E D I E N T S

2 tbsp corn oil

1 tbsp butter or margarine

1 medium leek, thinly sliced

1 large yellow bell pepper, diced

3 skinless, boneless chicken breasts, diced

1½ cups risotto rice

a few strands of saffron

6¼ cups chicken stock

scant 1 cup canned corn

½ cup toasted unsalted peanuts

½ cup freshly grated Parmesan cheese

salt and pepper

1 Heat the corn oil and butter in a large pan. Cook the leek and bell pepper for 1 minute, then stir in the chicken and cook, stirring until golden brown.

2 Stir in the risotto rice and cook for 2–3 minutes.

3 Stir in the saffron strands and salt and pepper to taste. Add the chicken stock, a little at a time, then cover and cook over a low heat, stirring occasionally, for 20 minutes, or until the rice is tender and most of the liquid has been absorbed. Do not let the risotto dry out—add more stock if necessary.

4 Stir in the corn, peanuts, and Parmesan cheese until evenly distributed, then season with salt and pepper to taste. Serve hot.

## COOK'S TIP

Risottos can be frozen, before adding the Parmesan cheese, for up to 1 month, but remember to reheat this risotto thoroughly as it contains chicken.

# Sun-Dried Tomato Risotto

A Milanese risotto can be cooked in a variety of ways—but always with saffron. This version with sun-dried tomatoes has a lovely tangy flavor.

## NUTRITIONAL INFORMATION

| | | |
|---|---|---|
| Calories .......558 | Sugars .........2g | |
| Protein ........16g | Fat ..........19g | |
| Carbohydrate ...80g | Saturates .......9g | |

 10 MINS  30 MINS

### SERVES 4

## INGREDIENTS

1 tbsp olive oil

2 tbsp butter

1 large onion, finely chopped

1⅞ cups risotto rice, washed

about 15 strands of saffron

⅔ cup white wine

3¾ cup hot vegetable or chicken stock

8 sun-dried tomatoes, cut into strips

scant 1 cup frozen peas, defrosted

1¾ oz/50 g prosciutto, shredded

¾ cup freshly grated Parmesan cheese

1 Heat the oil and butter in a large skillet. Add the onion and cook for 4–5 minutes, or until softened.

2 Add the rice and saffron to the skillet, stirring well to coat the rice in the oil, and cook for 1 minute.

3 Add the wine and stock slowly to the rice mixture in the pan, a ladleful at a time, stirring and making sure that all the liquid is absorbed before adding the next ladleful of liquid.

4 About half-way through adding the stock, stir in the sun-dried tomatoes.

5 When all of the wine and stock has been absorbed, the rice should be cooked. Test by tasting a grain—if it is still crunchy, add a little more water and continue cooking. It should take 15–20 minutes to cook.

6 Stir in the peas, prosciutto, and cheese. Cook for 2–3 minutes, stirring, until hot. Serve with extra Parmesan.

## COOK'S TIP

The finished risotto should have moist but separate grains. This is achieved by adding the hot stock a little at a time, adding more only when the last addition has been absorbed. Don't leave the risotto to cook by itself: it needs constant checking to see when more liquid is required.

# Green Risotto

A simple rice dish cooked with green vegetables and herbs.
This recipe has been adapted for the microwave.

## NUTRITIONAL INFORMATION

| | | | |
|---|---|---|---|
| Calories | .......344 | Sugars | ........4g |
| Protein | ........13g | Fat | ..........10g |
| Carbohydrate | ...54g | Saturates | .......4g |

🍲 15 MINS    🕙 20 MINS

### SERVES 4

## I N G R E D I E N T S

1 onion, chopped

2 tbsp olive oil

generous 1 cup risotto rice

3 cups hot vegetable stock

12 oz/350 g mixed green vegetables,
  such as asparagus, thin green beans,
  snow peas, zucchini, broccoli florets,
  frozen peas

2 tbsp chopped fresh parsley

2 oz/55g fresh Parmesan cheese,
  shaved thinly

salt and pepper

1 Place the onion and oil in a large bowl. Cover and cook on High power for 2 minutes.

2 Add the rice and stir until thoroughly coated in the oil. Pour in about ⅓ cup of the hot stock. Cook, uncovered, for 2 minutes, until the liquid has been absorbed. Pour in another ⅓ cup of the stock and cook, uncovered, on High power for 2 minutes. Repeat once more.

3 Chop or slice the vegetables into even-size pieces. Stir into the rice with the remaining stock. Cover and cook on High power for 8 minutes, stirring occasionally, until most of the liquid has been absorbed and the rice is just tender.

4 Stir in the parsley and season generously. Leave to stand, covered, for almost 5 minutes. The rice should be tender and creamy.

5 Scatter the Parmesan cheese over the risotto before serving.

## COOK'S TIP

For extra texture, stir in a
few toasted pine nuts or
coarsely chopped cashew nuts at
the end of the cooking time.

# Genoese Seafood Risotto

This is cooked in a different way from any of the other risottos. First, you cook the rice, then you prepare a sauce, then you mix the two together.

## NUTRITIONAL INFORMATION

| | | |
|---|---|---|
| Calories .......424 | Sugars .........0g | |
| Protein ........23g | Fat ..........17g | |
| Carbohydrate ...46g | Saturates ......10g | |

10 MINS     25 MINS

### SERVES 4

## I N G R E D I E N T S

5 cups hot fish or chicken stock

1½ cups risotto rice, washed

3 tbsp butter

2 garlic cloves, chopped

9 oz/250 g mixed seafood, preferably raw,
  such as shrimp, squid, mussels, and
  clams

2 tbsp chopped oregano, plus extra
  for garnishing

½ cup freshly grated Romano or Parmesan
  cheese

1 In a large pan, bring the stock to a boil. Add the rice and cook for about 12 minutes, stirring, or until the rice is tender. Drain thoroughly, reserving any excess liquid.

2 Heat the butter in a large skillet and add the garlic, stirring.

3 Add the raw mixed seafood to the skillet and cook for 5 minutes. If you are using cooked seafood, cook for 2–3 minutes.

4 Stir the oregano into the seafood mixture in the skillet.

5 Add the cooked rice to the skillet and cook for 2–3 minutes, stirring, or until hot. Add the reserved stock if the mixture gets too sticky.

6 Add the Romano or Parmesan cheese and mix well.

7 Transfer the risotto to warm serving dishes and serve immediately.

## COOK'S TIP

The Genoese are excellent cooks, and they make particularly delicious fish dishes flavored with the local olive oil.

# Mushroom & Cheese Risotto

Make this creamy risotto with Italian arborio rice and freshly grated Parmesan cheese for the best results.

## NUTRITIONAL INFORMATION

| | | | |
|---|---|---|---|
| Calories | .......358 | Sugars | ........3g |
| Protein | ........11g | Fat | ..........14g |
| Carbohydrate | ...50g | Saturates | .......5g |

 20 MINS    40 MINS

### SERVES 4

## I N G R E D I E N T S

2 tbsp olive or vegetable oil

generous 1 cup risotto rice

2 garlic cloves, crushed

1 onion, chopped

2 celery stalks, chopped

1 red or green bell pepper, seeded
  and chopped

4 cups sliced mushrooms

1 tbsp chopped fresh oregano or
  1 tsp dried oregano

4 cups vegetable stock

⅓ cup sun-dried tomatoes in olive oil,
  drained and chopped (optional)

½ cup finely grated Parmesan cheese

salt and pepper

### TO GARNISH

fresh flatleaf parsley sprigs

fresh bay leaves

1 Heat the oil in a wok or large skillet. Add the rice and cook, stirring, for 5 minutes.

2 Add the garlic, onion, celery, and bell pepper and cook, stirring, for 5 minutes. Add the mushrooms and cook for 3–4 minutes.

3 Stir in the oregano and stock. Heat until just boiling, then reduce the heat and simmer gently, covered, for 20 minutes, or until the rice is tender and creamy.

4 Add the sun-dried tomatoes, if using, and season to taste. Stir in half of the Parmesan cheese. Top with the remaining cheese, then garnish with the flatleaf parsley and bay leaves and serve.

# Chicken Risotto Milanese

This famous dish is known throughout the world, and it is perhaps the best known of all Italian risottos, although there are many variations.

## NUTRITIONAL INFORMATION

| Calories | .......857 | Sugars | .........1g |
| Protein | ........57g | Fat | .........38g |
| Carbohydrate | ...72g | Saturates | ......21g |

5 MINS    55 MINS

### SERVES 4

## INGREDIENTS

generous ½ cup butter

2 lb/900 g chicken meat, sliced thinly

1 large onion, chopped

2½ cups risotto rice

2½ cups chicken stock

⅔ cup white wine

1 tsp crumbled saffron

salt and pepper

½ cup freshly grated Parmesan cheese,
  to serve

1 Heat 4 tablespoons butter in a deep skillet, and cook the chicken and onion until golden brown.

2 Add the rice and stir well, then cook for 15 minutes.

3 Heat the stock until boiling and gradually add to the rice. Add the white wine, saffron, and salt and pepper to taste and mix well. Simmer gently for 20 minutes, stirring occasionally, and adding more stock if the risotto becomes too dry.

4 Leave to stand for 2–3 minutes. Just before serving, add a little more stock and simmer for 10 minutes. Serve the risotto, sprinkled with the grated Parmesan cheese and the remaining butter.

# Rice & Peas

If you can get fresh peas (and willing helpers to shell them), do use them: you will need 2 lb 4 oz/1 kg. Add them to the pan with the stock.

## NUTRITIONAL INFORMATION

| | |
|---|---|
| Calories .......409 | Sugars .........2g |
| Protein ........15g | Fat ..........23g |
| Carbohydrate ...38g | Saturates ......12g |

10 MINS     50 MINS

### SERVES 4

### INGREDIENTS

1 tbsp olive oil

¼ cup butter

scant ¼ cup pancetta (Italian unsmoked bacon), chopped

1 small onion, chopped

scant 6 cups hot chicken stock

scant 1 cup risotto rice

3 tbsp chopped fresh parsley

2 cups frozen or canned baby peas

½ cup freshly grated Parmesan

pepper

1 Heat the oil and half of the butter in a pan.

2 Add the pancetta and onion to the pan and cook for 5 minutes.

3 Add the stock (and fresh peas if using) to the pan and bring to a boil.

4 Stir in the rice and season to taste with pepper. Cook until the rice is tender, about 20–30 minutes, stirring occasionally.

5 Add the parsley and baby peas and cook for 8 minutes, or until the peas are thoroughly heated.

6 Stir in the remaining butter and the Parmesan cheese. Serve immediately, with freshly ground black pepper.

# Pesto Rice with Garlic Bread

Try this combination of two types of rice with the richness of pine nuts, basil, and freshly grated Parmesan.

## NUTRITIONAL INFORMATION

| | | |
|---|---|---|
| Calories . . . . . . . .918 | Sugars . . . . . . . . .2g |
| Protein . . . . . . . .18g | Fat . . . . . . . . . .64g |
| Carbohydrate . . .73g | Saturates . . . . . .19g |

20 MINS          40 MINS

### SERVES 4

## INGREDIENTS

1½ cups mixed long-grain and wild rice

fresh basil sprigs, to garnish

tomato and orange salad, to serve

### PESTO DRESSING

½ oz/15 g fresh basil

generous ⅔ cup pine nuts

2 garlic cloves, crushed

6 tbsp olive oil

½ cup freshly grated Parmesan cheese

salt and pepper

### GARLIC BREAD

2 small granary or whole-wheat
   French bread sticks

scant ½ cup butter or margarine, softened

2 garlic cloves, crushed

1 tsp dried mixed herbs

1 Place the rice in a pan and cover with water. Bring to a boil and cook for 15–20 minutes. Drain well and keep the rice warm.

2 Meanwhile, make the pesto dressing. Remove the basil leaves from the stems and finely chop the leaves. Reserve scant ¼ cup of the pine nuts and finely chop the remainder. Mix with the chopped basil and the rest of the dressing ingredients. Alternatively, put all the ingredients in a food processor or blender and blend for a few seconds until smooth. Set aside.

3 To make the garlic bread, slice the bread at 1-inch/2.5-cm intervals, taking care not to slice all the way through. Mix the butter with the garlic, herbs, and seasoning. Spread thickly between each slice.

4 Wrap the bread in foil and bake in a preheated oven, 400°F/200°C, for 10–15 minutes.

5 To serve, toast the reserved pine nuts under a preheated medium broiler for 2–3 minute, or until golden. Toss the pesto dressing into the hot rice and pile into a warmed serving dish. Sprinkle with toasted pine nuts and garnish with basil sprigs. Serve with the garlic bread and a tomato and orange salad.

# Green Easter Pie

This traditional Easter risotto pie is from Piedmont in northern Italy. Serve it warm or chilled in slices.

## NUTRITIONAL INFORMATION

| | | | |
|---|---|---|---|
| Calories | .......392 | Sugars | .........3g |
| Protein | ........17g | Fat | ..........17g |
| Carbohydrate | ...41g | Saturates | .......5g |

25 MINS     50 MINS

### SERVES 4

## I N G R E D I E N T S

3 oz/85 g arugula

2 tbsp olive oil

1 onion, chopped

2 garlic cloves, chopped

scant 1 cup risotto rice

scant 3 cups hot chicken or vegetable stock

scant ½ cup white wine

scant ½ cup freshly grated Parmesan
cheese

1 cup frozen peas, defrosted

2 tomatoes, diced

4 eggs, beaten

3 tbsp fresh marjoram, chopped

scant 1 cup fresh bread crumbs

salt and pepper

1 Lightly grease and then line the base of a 9-inch/23-cm deep cake pan.

2 Using a sharp knife, coarsely chop the arugula.

3 Heat the oil in a large skillet. Add the onion and garlic and cook for 4–5 minutes, or until softened.

4 Add the rice to the mixture in the skillet and mix well to combine, then begin adding the stock a ladleful at a time. Wait until all of the stock has been absorbed before adding another ladleful of liquid.

5 Continue to cook the mixture, adding the wine, until the rice is tender. This will take at least 15 minutes.

6 Stir in the Parmesan cheese, peas, arugula, tomatoes, eggs, and 2 tablespoons of the marjoram. Season to taste with salt and pepper.

7 Spoon the risotto into the pan and level the surface by pressing down with the back of a wooden spoon.

8 Top with the bread crumbs and the remaining marjoram.

9 Bake in a preheated oven, at 350°F/180°C, for 30 minutes, or until set. Cut into slices and serve immediately.

# Eggplant & Rice Rolls

Slices of eggplant are blanched and stuffed with a savory rice and nut mixture, and baked in a piquant tomato and wine sauce.

## NUTRITIONAL INFORMATION

| | | | |
|---|---|---|---|
| Calories | .......142 | Sugars | .........3g |
| Protein | .........6g | Fat | ...........9g |
| Carbohydrate | ....9g | Saturates | .......3g |

30 MINS     1HR 5 MINS

### SERVES 8

## I N G R E D I E N T S

3 eggplants (total weight about
  1 lb 10 oz/750 g)

scant ⅓ cup mixed long-grain and wild rice

4 scallions, trimmed and thinly sliced

3 tbsp chopped cashew nuts or toasted
  chopped hazelnuts

2 tbsp capers

1 garlic clove, crushed

2 tbsp freshly grated Parmesan cheese

1 egg, beaten

1 tbsp olive oil

1 tbsp balsamic vinegar

2 tbsp tomato paste

⅔ cup water

⅔ cup white wine

salt and pepper

cilantro sprigs, to garnish

1 Using a sharp knife, cut off the stem end of each eggplant, then cut off and discard a strip of skin from alternate sides of each eggplant. Cut each eggplant into thin slices to give a total of 16 slices.

2 Blanch the eggplant slices in boiling water for 5 minutes, then drain on paper towels.

3 Cook the rice in boiling salted water for about 12 minutes or until just tender. Drain and place in a bowl. Add the scallions, nuts, capers, garlic, cheese, egg, and salt and pepper to taste, and mix well.

4 Spread a thin layer of rice mixture over each slice of eggplant and roll up carefully, securing with a wooden toothpick. Place the rolls in a greased ovenproof dish and brush each one with the olive oil.

5 Combine the vinegar, tomato paste, and water, and pour over the eggplant rolls. Cook in a preheated oven, at 350°F/180°C, for about 40 minutes, or until tender and most of the liquid has been absorbed. Transfer the rolls to a serving dish.

6 Add the wine to the pan juices and heat gently until the sediment loosens and then simmer gently for 2–3 minutes. Adjust the seasoning and strain the sauce over the eggplant rolls. Leave until cold and then chill thoroughly. Garnish with sprigs of cilantro and serve.

# Polenta

Polenta is prepared and served in a variety of ways and can be served hot or cold, sweet or savory.

## NUTRITIONAL INFORMATION

Calories . . . . . . . .661  Sugars . . . . . . . . .5g
Protein . . . . . . . .15g  Fat . . . . . . . . . .34g
Carbohydrate . . .68g  Saturates . . . . . .12g

1¼ HOURS     1 HOUR

### SERVES 4

### INGREDIENTS

6¼ cups water

1½ tsp salt

2 cups polenta or cornmeal flour

2 beaten eggs (optional)

2 cups fresh fine white bread crumbs
   (optional)

vegetable oil, for frying and oiling

2 quantities Basic Tomato Sauce (see
   page 28)

#### MUSHROOM SAUCE

3 tbsp olive oil

4 cups sliced mushrooms

2 garlic cloves, crushed

⅔ cup dry white wine

4 tbsp heavy cream

2 tbsp chopped fresh mixed herbs

salt and pepper

1 Bring the water and salt to a boil in a large pan and gradually sprinkle in the polenta or cornmeal flour, stirring all the time to prevent lumps forming. Simmer the mixture very gently, stirring frequently, until the polenta becomes very thick and starts to draw away from the sides of the pan, about 30–35 minutes. It is likely to splatter, in which case partially cover the pan with a lid.

2 Thoroughly oil a shallow pan, about 11 x 7 inches/28 x 18 cm, and spoon in the polenta. Spread out evenly, using a wet wooden spoon or spatula. Leave to cool, then leave to stand for a few hours at room temperature, if possible.

3 Cut the polenta into 30–36 squares. Heat the oil in a skillet and cook the pieces for about 5 minutes, turning several times, until they are golden brown all over. Alternatively, dip each piece of polenta in beaten egg and coat in bread crumbs before cooking in the hot oil.

4 To make the mushroom sauce: heat the oil in a pan and cook the mushrooms with the crushed garlic for 3–4 minutes. Add the wine, then season well and simmer for 5 minutes. Add the cream and chopped herbs and simmer for 1–2 minutes.

5 Serve the polenta with either the tomato sauce or mushroom sauce.

# Smoked Cod Polenta

Using polenta as a crust for a gratin dish gives a lovely crispy outer texture and a smooth inside. It works well with smoked fish and chicken.

## NUTRITIONAL INFORMATION

| | | | |
|---|---|---|---|
| Calories | 616 | Sugars | 3g |
| Protein | 41g | Fat | 24g |
| Carbohydrate | 58g | Saturates | 12g |

30 MINS     1¼ HOURS

### SERVES 4

## I N G R E D I E N T S

2 cups instant polenta

6¼ cups water

7 oz/200 g chopped frozen
   spinach, defrosted

3 tbsp butter

½ cup freshly grated pecorino cheese

generous ¾ cup milk

1 lb/450 g smoked cod fillet,
   skinned and boned

4 eggs, beaten

salt and pepper

1 Cook the polenta, using 6¼ cups of water to 12 oz/350 g polenta, stirring, for 30–35 minutes.

2 Stir the spinach, butter, and half of the pecorino cheese into the polenta. Season to taste with salt and pepper.

3 Divide the polenta among 4 individual ovenproof dishes, spreading the polenta evenly across the bottom and up the sides of the dishes.

4 In a skillet, bring the milk to a boil. Add the fish and cook for 8–10 minutes, turning once, or until tender. Remove the fish with a perforated spoon.

5 Remove the pan from the heat. Pour the eggs into the milk in the pan and mix together.

6 Using a fork, flake the fish into smaller pieces and place it in the center of the dishes.

7 Pour the milk and egg mixture over the fish.

8 Sprinkle with the remaining cheese and bake in a preheated oven, at 375°F/190°C, for 25–30 minutes. or until set and golden. Serve hot.

## VARIATION

Try using 12 oz/350 g cooked chicken breast with 2 tablespoons of chopped tarragon, instead of the smoked cod, if you prefer.

# Polenta with Rabbit Stew

Polenta can be served fresh, as in this dish, or it can be cooled, then sliced and broiled.

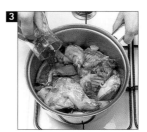

### NUTRITIONAL INFORMATION

Calories .......726    Sugars .........2g
Protein ........61g    Fat ..........25g
Carbohydrate ...55g    Saturates .......6g

20 MINS    1³/₄ MINUTES

## SERVES 4

## I N G R E D I E N T S

2 cups polenta or cornmeal

1 tbsp coarse sea salt

5 cups water

4 tbsp olive oil

4 lb 8 oz/2 kg rabbit joints (pieces)

3 garlic cloves, peeled

3 shallots, sliced

²/₃ cup red wine

1 carrot, sliced

1 celery stalk, sliced

2 bay leaves

1 sprig rosemary

3 tomatoes, skinned and diced

½ cup pitted black olives

salt and pepper

1 Butter a large ovenproof dish. Mix the polenta, salt, and water in a large pan, whisking well to prevent lumps forming. Bring to a boil and boil for 10 minutes, stirring vigorously. Turn into the buttered dish and bake in a preheated oven, 375°F/190°C, for 40 minutes.

2 Meanwhile, heat the oil in a large pan and add the rabbit pieces, garlic, and shallots. Cook for 10 minutes, or until browned.

3 Stir in the wine and cook for an additional 5 minutes.

4 Add the carrot, celery, bay leaves, rosemary, tomatoes, olives and 1¼ cups water. Cover the pan and simmer for about 45 minutes, or until the rabbit is very tender. Season with salt and pepper to taste.

5 To serve, spoon or cut a portion of polenta and place on each serving plate. Top with a ladleful of rabbit stew. Serve immediately.

# Chili Polenta Chips

Polenta is used in Italy in the same way as potatoes and rice. It has little flavor, but combined with butter, garlic, and herbs, it is transformed.

## NUTRITIONAL INFORMATION

Calories . . . . . . .365   Sugars . . . . . . . . .1g
Protein . . . . . . . . .8g   Fat . . . . . . . . . .12g
Carbohydrate . . .54g   Saturates . . . . . . .5g

 5 MINS      20 MINS

### SERVES 4

## I N G R E D I E N T S

2 cups instant polenta

2 tsp chili powder

1 tbsp olive oil or melted butter

⅔ cup sour cream

1 tbsp chopped parsley

salt and pepper

1 Place 6¼ cups of water in a pan and bring to a boil. Add 2 teaspoons of salt and then add the polenta in a steady stream, stirring constantly.

2 Reduce the heat slightly and continue stirring for about 5 minutes. It is essential to stir the polenta, otherwise it will stick and burn. The polenta should have a thick consistency at this point and should be stiff enough to hold the spoon upright in the pan.

3 Add the chili powder to the polenta mixture and stir well. Season to taste with a little salt and pepper.

4 Spread the polenta out on to a board or cookie sheet to about 1½ inch/4 cm thick. Leave to cool and set.

5 Cut the cooled polenta mixture into thin wedges.

6 Heat 1 tablespoon of oil in a pan. Add the polenta wedges and cook for 3–4 minutes on each side or until golden and crispy. Alternatively, brush with melted butter and broil for 6–7 minutes, or until golden. Drain the cooked polenta on paper towels.

7 Mix the sour cream with parsley and place in a bowl.

8 Serve the polenta with the sour cream and parsley dip.

## COOK'S TIP

Easy-cook instant polenta is widely available in supermarkets and is quick to make. It will keep for up to one week in the refrigerator. The polenta can also be baked in a preheated oven, at 400°F/200°C, for 20 minutes.

# Spinach Gnocchi

These gnocchi or small dumplings are made with potato and flavored with spinach and nutmeg and served in a tomato and basil sauce.

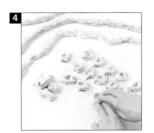

## NUTRITIONAL INFORMATION

| | | | |
|---|---|---|---|
| Calories | .......337 | Sugars | .........4g |
| Protein | .........9g | Fat | ..........10g |
| Carbohydrate | ...52g | Saturates | .......4g |

 25 MINS      1 HOUR

### SERVES 4

## INGREDIENTS

1 lb/450 g baking potatoes

2¾ oz/75 g spinach

1 tsp water

2 tbsp butter or margarine

1 small egg, beaten

1 cup all-purpose flour

fresh basil sprigs, to garnish

### TOMATO SAUCE

1 tbsp olive oil

1 shallot, chopped

1 tbsp tomato paste

8 oz/225 g canned chopped tomatoes

2 tbsp chopped basil

⅓ cup red wine

1 tsp superfine sugar

salt and pepper

1 Cook the potatoes in their skins in a pan of boiling salted water for 20 minutes. Drain well and press through a strainer into a bowl.

2 Cook the spinach in 1 teaspoon of water for 5 minutes, or until wilted. Drain and pat dry with paper towels. Chop and stir into the potatoes.

3 Add the butter, egg, and half of the flour to the spinach mixture, mixing well. Turn out onto a counter, gradually kneading in the remaining flour to form a soft dough.

4 With floured hands, roll the dough into thin ropes and cut off ¾-inch/ 2-cm pieces. Press the center of each dumpling with your finger, drawing it toward you to curl the sides of the gnocchi. Cover the gnocchi and leave to chill.

5 Heat the oil for the sauce in a pan and sauté the chopped shallot for 5 minutes. Add the tomato paste, tomatoes, basil, red wine, and sugar and season well. Bring to a boil and then simmer for 20 minutes.

6 Bring a pan of salted water to a boil and cook the gnocchi for 2–3 minutes, or until they rise to the top of the pan. Drain well and transfer to serving dishes. Spoon the tomato sauce over the gnocchi. Garnish and serve.

# Gnocchi Romana

This is a traditional Italian recipe but, for a less rich version, simply omit the eggs.

## NUTRITIONAL INFORMATION

| | | |
|---|---|---|
| Calories . . . . . . . .709 | Sugars . . . . . . . .9g | |
| Protein . . . . . . .32g | Fat . . . . . . . . .41g | |
| Carbohydrate . . .58g | Saturates . . . . .25g | |

🍲 1¼ HOURS 🕐 45 MINS

### SERVES 4

## INGREDIENTS

3 cups milk

pinch of freshly grated nutmeg

6 tbsp butter, plus extra
   for greasing

1¼ cups semolina

generous 1 cup freshly grated Parmesan
   cheese

2 eggs, beaten

½ cup grated Gruyère cheese

salt and pepper

fresh basil sprigs, to garnish

1 Pour the milk into a pan and bring to a boil. Remove the pan from the heat and stir in the nutmeg, 2 tablespoons of butter, and salt and pepper.

2 Gradually stir the semolina into the milk, whisking to prevent lumps forming, and return the pan to low heat. Simmer, stirring constantly, for about 10 minutes, or until very thick.

3 Beat ½ cup of Parmesan cheese into the semolina mixture, then beat in the eggs. Continue beating the mixture until smooth. Set the mixture aside for a few minutes to cool slightly.

4 Spread out the cooled semolina mixture in an even layer on a sheet of baking parchment or in a large, oiled baking pan, smoothing the surface with a damp spatula—it should be ½ inch/1 cm thick. Set aside to cool completely, then chill in the refrigerator for 1 hour.

5 Once chilled, cut out rounds of gnocchi, measuring about 1½ inches/ 4 cm in diameter, using a plain, greased pastry cutter.

6 Grease a shallow ovenproof dish or 4 individual dishes. Lay the gnocchi trimmings in the base of the dish or dishes and cover with overlapping rounds of gnocchi.

7 Melt the remaining butter and drizzle over the gnocchi. Sprinkle over the remaining Parmesan cheese, then sprinkle over the Gruyère cheese.

8 Bake in a preheated oven, at 400°F/200°C, for 25-30 minutes, or until the top is crisp and golden brown. Serve hot, garnished with the basil.

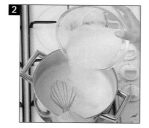

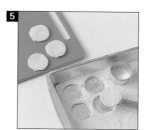

# Gnocchi Piedmontese

Gnocchi, a specialty from northern Italy, are small dumplings that are either poached or baked. Prepare the Espagnole Sauce well in advance.

## NUTRITIONAL INFORMATION

| | | |
|---|---|---|
| Calories .......643 | Sugars .........4g | |
| Protein ........25g | Fat ..........44g | |
| Carbohydrate ...34g | Saturates ......21g | |

  4³/₄ HOURS    15 MINS

### SERVES 4

## I N G R E D I E N T S

1 lb/450 g warm mashed potato

½ cup self-rising flour

1 egg

2 egg yolks

1 tbsp olive oil

²/₃ cup Espagnole Sauce (see page 29)

4 tbsp butter

1½ cups freshly grated Parmesan cheese

salt and pepper

freshly chopped herbs, to garnish

1 In a large bowl, mix together the mashed potato and flour. Add the egg and egg yolks, then season with salt and pepper and mix together to form a dough.

## VARIATION

Serve with a tomato sauce. Mix 2 cups chopped sun-dried tomatoes, 1 sliced celery stalk, 1 crushed garlic clove and ⅓ cup red wine in a pan. Cook over low heat for 15–20 minutes. Stir in 8 skinned, chopped plum tomatoes, season, and simmer for 10 minutes.

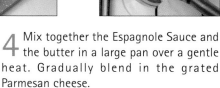

2 Break off pieces of the dough and roll between the palms of your hands to form small balls the size of a walnut. Flatten the balls with a fork into the shape of small cylinders.

3 Bring a large pan of lightly salted water to a boil. Add the gnocchi and olive oil and poach for 10 minutes.

4 Mix together the Espagnole Sauce and the butter in a large pan over a gentle heat. Gradually blend in the grated Parmesan cheese.

5 Remove the gnocchi from the pan with a slotted spoon. Toss the gnocchi in the sauce, then transfer to 4 serving plates. Garnish and serve immediately.

# Potato & Spinach Gnocchi

These small potato dumplings are flavored with spinach and cooked in boiling water, then served with a simple tomato sauce.

## NUTRITIONAL INFORMATION

| | | | |
|---|---|---|---|
| Calories | .......315 | Sugars | .........7g |
| Protein | .........8g | Fat | ...........8g |
| Carbohydrate | ...56g | Saturates | .......1g |

20 MINS    30 MINS

### SERVES 4

## INGREDIENTS

10½ oz/300 g mealy potatoes, diced

6 oz/175 g spinach

1 egg yolk

1 tsp olive oil

scant 1 cup all-purpose flour

salt and pepper

spinach leaves, to garnish

### SAUCE

1 tbsp olive oil

2 shallots, chopped

1 garlic clove, crushed

1¼ cups crushed tomatoes

2 tsp soft light brown sugar

1 Cook the diced potatoes in a pan of boiling water for 10 minutes, or until cooked through. Drain and mash the potatoes.

2 Meanwhile, in a separate pan, blanch the spinach in a little boiling water for 1-2 minutes. Drain the spinach and shred the leaves.

3 Transfer the mashed potato to a lightly floured cutting board and make a well in the center. Add the egg yolk, olive oil, spinach, and a little of the flour, then quickly mix the ingredients into the potato, adding more flour as you go, until you have a firm dough. Divide the mixture into very small dumplings.

4 Cook the gnocchi, in batches, in a pan of boiling salted water for about 5 minutes, or until they rise to the surface.

5 Meanwhile, make the sauce. Put the oil, shallots, garlic, crushed tomatoes, and sugar into a pan and cook over a low heat for 10-15 minutes, or until the sauce has thickened.

6 Drain the gnocchi using a perforated spoon and transfer to warm serving dishes. Spoon the sauce over the gnocchi and garnish with the fresh spinach leaves.

## VARIATION

Add chopped fresh herbs and cheese to the gnocchi dough instead of the spinach, if you prefer.

# Baked Semolina Gnocchi

Semolina has a similar texture to polenta, but is slightly grainier. These gnocchi, which are flavored with cheese and thyme, are easy to make.

## NUTRITIONAL INFORMATION

| | | | |
|---|---|---|---|
| Calories | ..... .259 | Sugars | ......... .0g |
| Protein | ..... ....9g | Fat | ......... .16g |
| Carbohydrate | ...20g | Saturates | ..... .10g |

15 MINS     30 MINS

### SERVES 4

### I N G R E D I E N T S

generous 1¾ cups vegetable stock

1¼ cups semolina

1 tbsp thyme, stems removed

1 egg, beaten

½ cup freshly grated Parmesan cheese

¼ cup butter

2 garlic cloves, crushed

salt and pepper

1 Place the stock in a large pan and bring to a boil. Add the semolina in a steady trickle, stirring continuously. Keep stirring for 3–4 minutes, or until the mixture is thick enough to hold a spoon upright. Set aside and leave to cool slightly.

2 Add the thyme, egg, and half of the cheese to the semolina mixture, and season to taste with salt and pepper.

3 Spread the semolina mixture onto a board to about ½ inch/12 mm thick. Set aside to cool and set.

4 When the semolina is cold, cut it into 1-inch/2.5-cm squares, reserving any offcuts.

5 Grease an ovenproof dish, placing the reserved offcuts in the bottom. Arrange the semolina squares on top and sprinkle with the remaining cheese.

6 Melt the butter in a pan, then add the garlic and season with pepper to taste. Pour the butter mixture over the gnocchi. Bake in a preheated oven, at 425°F/220°C, for 15–20 minutes, or until puffed up and golden. Serve hot.

## VARIATION

Try adding ½ tablespoon of sun-dried tomato paste or scant 1 cup finely chopped mushrooms, fried in butter, to the semolina mixture in step 2. Follow the same cooking method.

# Potato Noodles

Potatoes are used to make a "pasta" dough that is cut into thin noodles and boiled. The noodles are served with a bacon and mushroom sauce.

## NUTRITIONAL INFORMATION

| | | | |
|---|---|---|---|
| Calories | .......810 | Sugars | .........5g |
| Protein | ........21g | Fat | ..........47g |
| Carbohydrate | ...81g | Saturates | ......26g |

 30 MINS     25 MINS

### SERVES 4

## I N G R E D I E N T S

1 lb/450 g mealy potatoes, diced

1¾ cups all-purpose flour

1 egg, beaten

1 tbsp milk

salt and pepper

parsley sprig, to garnish

### S A U C E

1 tbsp vegetable oil

1 onion, chopped

1 garlic clove, crushed

generous 2 cups sliced open-capped
   mushrooms

3 smoked bacon slices, chopped

½ cup freshly grated Parmesan cheese

1¼ cups heavy cream

2 tbsp chopped fresh parsley

1 Cook the diced potatoes in a pan of boiling water for 10 minutes, or until cooked through. Drain well. Mash the potatoes until smooth, then beat in the flour, egg, and milk. Season with salt and pepper to taste and bring together to form a stiff paste.

2 On a lightly floured counter, roll out the paste to form a thin sausage shape. Cut the sausage into 1-inch/2.5-cm lengths. Bring a large pan of salted water to a boil, then drop in the dough pieces and cook for 3-4 minutes. They will rise to the surface when cooked.

3 To make the sauce, heat the oil in a pan and sauté the onion and garlic for 2 minutes. Add the mushrooms and bacon and cook for 5 minutes. Stir in the cheese, cream, and parsley, and season.

4 Drain the noodles and transfer to a warm pasta bowl. Spoon the sauce over the top and toss to mix. Garnish with a parsley sprig and serve.

### COOK'S TIP

Make the dough in advance, then wrap and store the noodles in the refrigerator for up to 24 hours.

# Pizzas & Breads

There is little to beat the irresistible aroma and taste of a freshly made pizza cooked in a wood-fired oven. The recipes for the homemade dough base and freshly made tomato sauce in this chapter will give you the closest thing possible to an authentic Italian pizza. You can add any type of topping, from salamis and cooked meats, to vegetables and fragrant herbs—the choice is yours! The Italians make delicious bread, combining all of the flavors of the Mediterranean. You can use the breads in this chapter to mop up the juices from a range of Italian dishes, or you can eat them on their own as a tasty snack.

# Bread Dough Base

Traditionally, pizza bases are made from bread dough; this recipe will give you a base similar to an Italian pizza.

### NUTRITIONAL INFORMATION

| | | |
|---|---|---|
| Calories .......182 | Sugars .........2g |
| Protein .........5g | Fat ...........3g |
| Carbohydrate ...36g | Saturates .....0.5g |

  1½ HOURS    0 MINS

### SERVES 4

## INGREDIENTS

½ oz/15 g fresh yeast or 1 tsp dry
   active yeast

scant ⅓ cup tepid water

½ tsp sugar

1 tbsp olive oil

scant 1¼ cups all-purpose flour

1 tsp salt

1 Combine the fresh yeast with the water and sugar in a bowl. If using dry yeast, sprinkle it over the surface of the water and whisk in until dissolved.

2 Leave the mixture to rest in a warm place for 10–15 minutes, or until frothy on the surface. Stir in the olive oil.

3 Sift the flour and salt into a large bowl. If using active dry yeast, stir it in at this point. Make a well in the center and pour in the yeast liquid, or water and oil (without the sugar for active dry yeast).

4 Using either floured hands or a wooden spoon, mix together to form a dough. Turn out on to a floured counter and knead for 5 minutes, or until smooth and elastic.

5 Place the dough in a large greased plastic bag and leave in a warm place for about 1 hour, or until doubled in size. Airing cupboards are often the best places for this process, as the temperature remains constant.

6 Turn out on to a lightly floured counter and "knock back" by punching the dough. This releases any air bubbles which would make the pizza uneven. Knead 4 or 5 times. The dough is now ready to use.

# Biscuit Base

This is a quicker alternative to the bread dough base. If you do not have time to wait for bread dough to rise, a biscuit base is ideal.

## NUTRITIONAL INFORMATION

Calories . . . . . . . .215    Sugars . . . . . . . . .3g
Protein . . . . . . . . .5g    Fat . . . . . . . . . . .7g
Carbohydrate . . .35g    Saturates . . . . . . .4g

20 MINS    0 MINS

### SERVES 4

## I N G R E D I E N T S

scant 1¼ cups self-rising flour

½ tsp salt

2 tbsp butter

½ cup milk

1 Sift the flour and salt into a large mixing bowl.

2 Rub in the butter with your fingertips until it resembles fine bread crumbs.

3 Make a well in the center of the flour and butter mixture and pour in nearly all of the milk at once. Mix in quickly with a knife. Add the remaining milk only if necessary to mix to a soft dough.

4 Turn the dough out on to a floured counter and knead by turning and pressing with the heel of your hand 3 or 4 times.

5 Either roll out or press the dough into a 10-inch/25-cm circle on a lightly greased cookie sheet or pizza pan. Push up the edge slightly all round to form a ridge and use immediately.

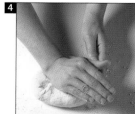

# Potato Base

This is an unusual pizza base made from mashed potatoes and flour and is a great way to use up any leftover boiled potatoes.

## NUTRITIONAL INFORMATION

| | | |
|---|---|---|
| Calories . . . . . . . .170 | Sugars . . . . . . . . .1g | |
| Protein . . . . . . . . .4g | Fat . . . . . . . . . . .3g | |
| Carbohydrate . . .34g | Saturates . . . . . . .1g | |

2¼ HOURS    0 MINS

### SERVES 4

## INGREDIENTS

8 oz/225 g boiled potatoes

¼ cup butter or margarine

scant 1 cup self-rising flour

½ tsp salt

1  If the potatoes are hot, mash them, then stir in the butter until it has melted and is distributed evenly throughout the potatoes. Leave to cool.

2  Sift the flour and salt together and stir into the mashed potato to form a soft dough.

3  If the potatoes are cold, mash them without adding the butter. Sift the flour and salt into a bowl.

4  Rub in the butter with your fingertips until the mixture resembles fine bread crumbs, then stir the flour and butter mixture into the mashed potatoes to form a soft dough.

5  Either roll out or press the dough into a 10-inch/25-cm round on a lightly greased cookie sheet or pizza pan, pushing up the edge slightly all round to form a ridge before adding the topping of your choice. This potato base is rather tricky to

lift before it is cooked, so you will find it much easier to handle if you roll it out directly onto the cookie sheet.

6  If the base is not required for cooking immediately, cover it with plastic wrap and chill it for up to 2 hours.

# Tomato Sauce

This is a basic topping sauce for pizzas. Using canned chopped tomatoes for this dish saves time.

## NUTRITIONAL INFORMATION

| | | | |
|---|---|---|---|
| Calories | .........41 | Sugars | .........3g |
| Protein | .........1g | Fat | ..........3g |
| Carbohydrate | ....3g | Saturates | .....0.4g |

 5 MINS 🕐 25 MINS

### SERVES 4

## I N G R E D I E N T S

1 small onion, chopped

1 garlic clove, crushed

1 tbsp olive oil

7 oz/200 g canned chopped tomatoes

2 tsp tomato paste

½ tsp sugar

½ tsp dried oregano

1 bay leaf

salt and pepper

1 Cook the onion and garlic gently in the oil for 5 minutes, or until softened but not browned.

2 Add the tomatoes, tomato paste, sugar, oregano, bay leaf, and salt and pepper to taste. Stir well.

3 Bring the sauce to a boil, then cover and leave to simmer gently for 20 minutes, stirring occasionally, until you have a thickish sauce.

4 Remove the bay leaf and season to taste. Leave to cool completely before using. This sauce keeps well in a screw-top jar in the refrigerator for up to 1 week.

# Special Tomato Sauce

This sauce is made with fresh tomatoes. Use the plum variety whenever available and always choose the reddest ones for the best flavor.

## NUTRITIONAL INFORMATION

| | |
|---|---|
| Calories . . . . . . . . .81 | Sugars . . . . . . . . .6g |
| Protein . . . . . . . . .1g | Fat . . . . . . . . . . .6g |
| Carbohydrate . . . .6g | Saturates . . . . . . .1g |

10 MINS    35 MINS

### SERVES 4

## INGREDIENTS

1 small onion, chopped

1 small red bell pepper, chopped

1 garlic clove, crushed

2 tbsp olive oil

8 oz/225 g tomatoes

1 tbsp tomato paste

1 tsp soft brown sugar

2 tsp chopped fresh basil

½ tsp dried oregano

1 bay leaf

salt and pepper

1 Cook the onion, bell pepper, and garlic gently in the oil for 5 minutes, or until softened but not browned.

2 Cut a cross in the base of each tomato and place them in a bowl. Pour on boiling water and leave for about 45 seconds. Drain, and then plunge in cold water. The skins will slide off easily.

3 Chop the tomatoes, discarding any hard cores.

4 Add the tomatoes to the onion mixture with the tomato paste, sugar, herbs, and seasoning. Stir well. Bring to a boil, then cover and leave to simmer gently for 30 minutes, stirring occasionally, or until you have a thickish sauce.

5 Remove the bay leaf and adjust the seasoning to taste. Leave to cool completely before using.

6 This sauce will keep well in a screw-top jar in the refrigerator for up to 1 week.

# Pizza Margherita

Pizza means "pie" in Italian. The fresh bread dough is not difficult to make but it does take a little time.

## NUTRITIONAL INFORMATION

| | | |
|---|---|---|
| Calories .......456 | Sugars .........7g |
| Protein ........16g | Fat ..........13g |
| Carbohydrate ...74g | Saturates .......5g |

1 HOUR    45 MINS

### SERVES 4

## INGREDIENTS

### BASIC PIZZA DOUGH

¼ oz/7 g active yeast

1 tsp sugar

1 cup hand-hot water

3 cups bread flour

1 tsp salt

1 tbsp olive oil

### TOPPING

14 oz/400 g canned tomatoes, chopped

2 garlic cloves, crushed

2 tsp dried basil

1 tbsp olive oil

2 tbsp tomato purée

scant 1 cup chopped mozzarella cheese

2 tbsp freshly grated Parmesan cheese

salt and pepper

1 Place the yeast and sugar in a measuring cup and mix with 4 tablespoons of the water. Leave the yeast mixture in a warm place for 15 minutes, or until frothy.

2 Mix the flour with the salt and make a well in the center. Add the oil, the yeast mixture, and the remaining water. Using a wooden spoon, mix to form a smooth dough.

3 Turn the dough out onto a floured counter and knead for 4–5 minutes, or until smooth.

4 Return the dough to the bowl, then cover with an oiled sheet of plastic wrap and leave to rise for 30 minutes, or until doubled in size.

5 Knead the dough for 2 minutes. Stretch the dough with your hands, then place it on an oiled cookie sheet, pushing out the edges until even. The dough should be no more than ¼ inch/5 mm thick because it will rise during cooking.

6 To make the topping, place the tomatoes, garlic, dried basil, olive oil, and salt and pepper to taste in a large skillet and leave to simmer for 20 minutes or until the sauce has thickened. Stir in the tomato paste and leave to cool slightly.

7 Spread the topping evenly over the pizza base. Top with the mozzarella and Parmesan cheeses and bake in a preheated oven, at 400°F/200°C, for 20–25 minutes. Serve hot.

# Vegetable Calzone

These pizza base pockets are great for making in advance and freezing—they can be defrosted when required for a quick snack.

## NUTRITIONAL INFORMATION

| | | | |
|---|---|---|---|
| Calories | .......499 | Sugars | .........7g |
| Protein | ........16g | Fat | ...........9g |
| Carbohydrate | ...95g | Saturates | .......2g |

1¹/₂ HOURS     40 MINS

### SERVES 4

## INGREDIENTS

### DOUGH

4 cups white bread flour

2 tsp easy-blend dried yeast

1 tsp superfine sugar

¾ cup vegetable stock

¾ cup crushed tomatoes

beaten egg

### FILLING

1 tbsp vegetable oil

1 onion, chopped

1 garlic clove, crushed

2 tbsp chopped sun-dried tomatoes

3¹/₂ oz/100 g spinach, chopped

3 tbsp canned and drained corn

scant ¼ cup green beans, cut into 3

1 tbsp tomato paste

1 tbsp chopped oregano

¹/₂ cup sliced mozzarella cheese

salt and pepper

1 Sieve the flour into a bowl. Add the yeast and sugar and beat in the stock and crushed tomatoes to make a smooth dough.

2 Knead the dough on a lightly floured counter for 10 minutes, then place in a clean, lightly oiled bowl and leave to rise in a warm place for 1 hour.

3 Heat the oil in a skillet and sauté the onion for 2–3 minutes.

4 Stir in the garlic, tomatoes, spinach, corn, and beans and cook for 3–4 minutes. Add the tomato paste and oregano and season with salt and pepper to taste.

5 Divide the risen dough into 4 equal portions and roll each on to a floured surface to form a 7 inch/18 cm round.

6 Spoon one fourth of the filling on to one half of each round and top with cheese. Fold the dough over to encase the filling, sealing the edge with a fork. Glaze with beaten egg. Put the calzone on a lightly greased cookie sheet and cook in a preheated oven, at 425°F/220°C, for 25–30 minutes, or until risen and golden. Serve warm.

# Mushroom Pizza

Juicy mushrooms and stringy mozzarella top this tomato-based pizza. Use exotic mushrooms or a combination of wild and cultivated.

## NUTRITIONAL INFORMATION

| | | |
|---|---|---|
| Calories . . . . . . .302 | Sugars . . . . . . . . .7g | |
| Protein . . . . . . . .10g | Fat . . . . . . . . . .12g | |
| Carbohydrate . . .41g | Saturates . . . . . . .4g | |

 1¼ HOURS　　45 MINS

### SERVES 4

## I N G R E D I E N T S

1 portion Basic Pizza Dough (see page 319)

### T O P P I N G

1½ cups grated mozzarella cheese

14 oz/400 g canned chopped tomatoes

2 garlic cloves, crushed

1 tsp dried basil

1 tbsp olive oil

2 tbsp tomato paste

7 oz/200 g mushrooms

salt and pepper

basil leaves, to garnish

1 Place the yeast and sugar in a measuring cup and mix with 4 tablespoons of the water. Leave the yeast mixture in a warm place for 15 minutes. or until frothy.

2 Mix the flour with the salt and make a well in the center. Add the oil, the yeast mixture. and the remaining water. Using a wooden spoon, mix to form a smooth dough.

3 Turn the dough out on to a floured counter and knead for 4–5 minutes, or until smooth. Return the dough to the bowl, then cover with an oiled sheet of plastic wrap and leave to rise for 30 minutes, or until doubled in size.

4 Remove the dough from the bowl. Knead the dough for 2 minutes. Using a rolling pin, roll out the dough to form an oval or a circular shape, then place it on an oiled cookie sheet, pushing out the edges until even. The dough should be no more than ¼ inch /5 mm thick because it will rise during cooking.

5 Using a sharp knife, chop the mushrooms into slices.

6 To make the topping, place the tomatoes, garlic, dried basil, olive oil, and salt and pepper in a large skillet and simmer for 20 minutes, or until the sauce has thickened. Stir in the tomato paste and leave to cool slightly.

7 Spread the sauce over the base of the pizza, then top with the mushrooms and scatter over the mozzarella. Bake in a preheated oven, at 400°F/200°C, for 25 minutes. Garnish with basil leaves.

# Giardiniera Pizza

As the name implies, this colorful pizza should be topped with fresh vegetables from the garden, especially in the summer months.

## NUTRITIONAL INFORMATION

| | | | |
|---|---|---|---|
| Calories | .......362 | Sugars | ........10g |
| Protein | ........13g | Fat | ..........15g |
| Carbohydrate | ...48g | Saturates | .......5g |

  3¹/₂ HOURS   20 MINS

### SERVES 4

## I N G R E D I E N T S

6 spinach leaves

Potato Base (see page 316)

Special Tomato Sauce (see page 318)

1 tomato, sliced

1 celery stalk, sliced thinly

½ green bell pepper, sliced thinly

1 baby zucchini, sliced

1 oz/25 g asparagus tips

¼ cup corn, defrosted if frozen

¼ cup peas, defrosted if frozen

4 scallions, trimmed and chopped

1 tbsp chopped fresh mixed herbs

½ cup grated mozzarella cheese

2 tbsp freshly grated Parmesan cheese

1 artichoke heart

olive oil, for drizzling

salt and pepper

1 Remove any tough stems from the spinach and wash the leaves in cold water. Pat dry with paper towels.

2 Roll out or press the potato base, using a rolling pin or your hands, into a large 10-inch/25-cm round on a lightly floured counter. Place the round on a large greased cookie sheet or pizza pan and push up the edge a little. Spread with the tomato sauce.

3 Arrange the spinach leaves on the sauce, followed by the tomato slices. Top with the remaining vegetables and the herbs.

4 Mix together the cheeses and sprinkle over. Place the artichoke heart in the center. Drizzle the pizza with a little olive oil and season.

5 Bake in a preheated oven, at 400°F/200°C, for 18–20 minutes, or until the edges are crisp and golden brown. Serve immediately.

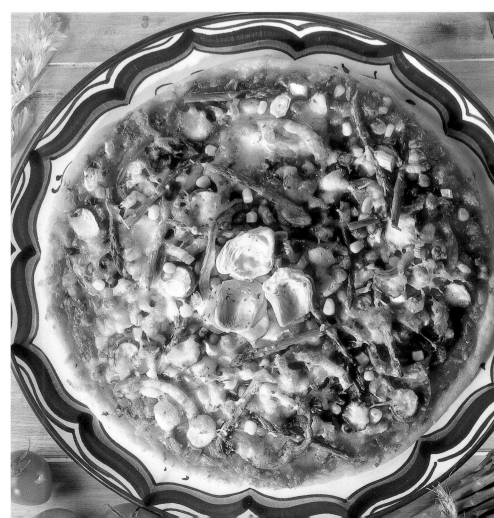

# Tomato & Ricotta Pizza

This is a traditional dish from the Calabrian Mountains in southern Italy, where it is made with naturally sun-dried tomatoes and ricotta cheese.

## NUTRITIONAL INFORMATION

| | | |
|---|---|---|
| Calories .......274 | Sugars .........4g | |
| Protein .........8g | Fat ...........11g | |
| Carbohydrate ...38g | Saturates .......4g | |

  1¼ HOURS  30 MINS

### SERVES 4

## INGREDIENTS

1 portion Basic Pizza Dough (see page 319)

### TOPPING

4 tbsp sun-dried tomato paste

5½ oz/150 g ricotta cheese

10 sun-dried tomatoes

1 tbsp fresh thyme

salt and pepper

1 Place the yeast and sugar in a measuring cup and mix with 4 tablespoons of the water. Leave the yeast mixture in a warm place for 15 minutes, or until frothy.

2 Mix the flour with the salt and make a well in the center. Add the oil, the yeast mixture, and the remaining water. Using a wooden spoon, mix to form a dough.

3 Turn the dough out onto a floured surface and knead for 4–5 minutes. or until smooth.

4 Return the dough to the bowl, then cover with an oiled sheet of plastic wrap and leave to rise for 30 minutes, or until doubled in size.

5 Remove the dough from the bowl. Knead the dough for 2 minutes.

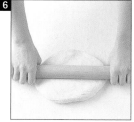  

6 Using a rolling pin, roll out the dough to form a round, then place it on an oiled cookie sheet, pushing out the edges until even. The dough should be no more than ¼ inch/5 mm thick because it will rise during cooking.

7 Spread the sun-dried tomato paste over the dough, then add spoonfuls of ricotta cheese.

8 Cut the sun-dried tomatoes into strips and arrange these on top of the pizza.

9 Sprinkle the thyme, and salt and pepper to taste over the top of the pizza. Bake in a preheated oven, at 400°F/200°C, for 30 minutes, or until the crust is golden. Serve hot.

# Florentine Pizza

A pizza adaptation of Eggs Florentine—sliced hard-cooked eggs on freshly cooked spinach, with a crunchy almond topping.

## NUTRITIONAL INFORMATION

| | | | |
|---|---|---|---|
| Calories | .......462 | Sugars | .........6g |
| Protein | ........18g | Fat | ..........26g |
| Carbohydrate | ...41g | Saturates | .......8g |

3 HOURS     20 MINS

### SERVES 4

## I N G R E D I E N T S

2 tbsp freshly grated Parmesan cheese

Potato Base (see page 316)

Tomato Sauce (see page 317)

6 oz/175 g spinach

1 small red onion, sliced thinly

2 tbsp olive oil

¼ tsp freshly grated nutmeg

2 hard-cooked eggs

¼ cup fresh white bread crumbs

½ cup grated Jarlsberg cheese(or Cheddar
    or Gruyère, if not available)

2 tbsp slivered almonds

olive oil, for drizzling

salt and pepper

1 Mix the Parmesan with the Potato Base. Roll out or press the dough, using a rolling pin or your hands, into a 10-inch/25-cm round on a lightly floured counter. Place on a large greased cookie sheet or pizza pan and push up the edge slightly. Spread the tomato sauce almost to the edge.

2 Remove the stems from the spinach and wash the leaves thoroughly in plenty of cold water. Drain well and pat off the excess water with paper towels.

3 Cook the onion gently in the oil for 5 minutes, or until softened. Add the spinach and continue to cook until just wilted. Drain off any excess liquid. Arrange on the pizza and sprinkle over the nutmeg.

4 Remove the shells from the eggs and slice. Arrange the slices of egg on top of the spinach.

5 Mix together the bread crumbs, cheese, and almonds, and sprinkle over. Drizzle with a little olive oil and season with salt and pepper to taste.

6 Bake in a preheated oven, at 400°F/ 200°C, for 18–20 minutes, or until the edge is crisp and golden. Serve immediately.

# Potato & Tomato Calzone

These pizza dough Italian pasties are best served hot with a salad as a delicious lunch or supper dish.

## NUTRITIONAL INFORMATION

| | |
|---|---|
| Calories . . . . . . .508 | Sugars . . . . . . . . .8g |
| Protein . . . . . . . .14g | Fat . . . . . . . . . . .7g |
| Carbohydrate . .104g | Saturates . . . . . . .2g |

1½ HOURS     35 MINS

### SERVES 4

## I N G R E D I E N T S

### D O U G H

4 cups white bread flour

1 tsp easy blend dried yeast

1¼ cups vegetable stock

1 tbsp clear honey

1 tsp caraway seeds

milk, for glazing

### F I L L I N G

8 oz/225 g waxy potatoes, diced

1 tbsp vegetable oil

1 onion, halved and sliced

2 garlic cloves, crushed

¾ cup sun-dried tomatoes

2 tbsp chopped fresh basil

2 tbsp tomato paste

2 celery stalks, sliced

½ cup grated mozzarella cheese

1 To make the dough, sift the flour into a large bowl and stir in the yeast. Make a well in the center of the mixture.

2 Stir in the vegetable stock, honey, and caraway seeds and bring the mixture together to form a dough.

3 Turn the dough out onto a lightly floured surface and knead for 8 minutes, or until smooth. Place the dough in a lightly oiled mixing bowl, then cover and leave to rise in a warm place for 1 hour, or until it has doubled in size.

4 Meanwhile, make the filling. Heat the oil in a skillet and add all of the remaining ingredients except for the cheese. Cook for 5 minutes, stirring.

5 Divide the risen dough into 4 pieces. On a lightly floured counter, roll them out to form four 7-inch/18-cm rounds. Spoon equal amounts of the filling on to one half of each round.

6 Sprinkle the cheese over the filling. Brush the edge of the dough with milk and fold the dough over to form 4 semi-rounds, pressing to seal the edges.

7 Place on a non-stick cookie tray and brush with milk. Cook in a preheated oven, at 425°F/220°C, for 30 minutes, or until golden and risen. Serve hot.

# Cheese & Garlic Mushroom

This pizza dough is flavored with garlic and herbs and topped with mixed mushrooms and melting cheese for a really delicious pizza.

## NUTRITIONAL INFORMATION

| | | |
|---|---|---|
| Calories . . . . . . . .541 | Sugars . . . . . . . . .5g | |
| Protein . . . . . . . .16g | Fat . . . . . . . . . .15g | |
| Carbohydrate . . .91g | Saturates . . . . . . .6g | |

45 MINS    30 MINS

### SERVES 4

## I N G R E D I E N T S

### D O U G H

4 cups white bread flour

2 tsp active dry yeast

2 garlic cloves, crushed

2 tbsp chopped thyme

2 tbsp olive oil

1¼ cups tepid water

### T O P P I N G

2 tbsp butter or margarine

12 oz/350 g mixed mushrooms, sliced

2 garlic cloves, crushed

2 tbsp chopped parsley

2 tbsp tomato paste

6 tbsp crushed tomatoes

¾ cup grated mozzarella cheese

salt and pepper

chopped parsley, to garnish

1 Put the flour, yeast, garlic, and thyme in a bowl. Make a well in the center and gradually stir in the oil and water. Bring together to form a soft dough.

2 Turn the dough onto a floured surface and knead for 5 minutes, or until smooth. Roll into a 14 inch /35 cm round and place on a greased cookie sheet. Leave in a warm place for 20 minutes, or until the dough puffs up.

3 Meanwhile, make the topping. Melt the butter in a skillet and sauté the mushrooms, garlic, and parsley for 5 minutes.

4 Mix the tomato paste and crushed tomatoes and spoon on to the pizza base, leaving a ½-inch/1-cm edge of dough. Spoon the mushroom mixture on top. Season well and sprinkle the cheese on top.

5 Cook the pizza in a preheated oven, at 375°F/190°C, for 20–25 minutes, or until the base is crisp and the cheese has melted. Garnish with chopped parsley and serve.

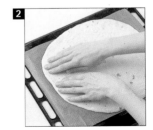

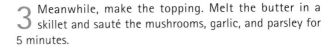

# Bean Curd, Corn & Peas

Chunks of bean curd marinated in ginger and soy sauce impart something of an Eastern flavor to this pizza.

## NUTRITIONAL INFORMATION

| | | |
|---|---|---|
| Calories .......596 | Sugars ........17g | |
| Protein ........33g | Fat ..........23g | |
| Carbohydrate ...66g | Saturates .......9g | |

🍋 1 HOUR  🕐 35 MINS

### SERVES 4

## I N G R E D I E N T S

4 cups milk

1 tsp salt

2¾ cups semolina

1 tbsp soy sauce

1 tbsp dry sherry

½ tsp grated fresh ginger root

9 oz/250 g bean curd, cut into chunks

2 eggs

½ cup freshly grated Parmesan cheese

Tomato Sauce (see page 317)

3 baby corns, each cut into 4

¼ cup snow peas, trimmed and cut into 4

4 scallions, trimmed and cut into 1-inch/
    2.5-cm strips

½ cup thinly sliced mozzarella cheese

2 tsp sesame oil

salt and pepper

1 Bring the milk to a boil with the salt. Sprinkle the semolina over the surface, stirring all the time. Cook for 10 minutes over low heat, stirring occasionally, taking care not to let it burn. Remove from the heat and leave to cool until tepid.

2 Mix the soy sauce, sherry, and ginger together in a bowl, then add the bean curd and stir gently to coat. Leave to marinate in a cool place for 20 minutes.

3 Beat the eggs with a little pepper. Add to the semolina with the Parmesan and mix well. Place on a large greased cookie sheet or pizza pan and pat into a 10-inch/25-cm round, using the back of a metal spoon. Spread the tomato sauce almost to the edge.

4 Blanch the corn and snow peas in a pan of boiling water for 1 minute, then drain and place on the pizza with the drained bean curd. Top with the scallions and slices of cheese. Drizzle over the sesame oil and season with salt and pepper.

5 Bake in a preheated oven, at 400°F/ 200°C, for 18–20 minutes, or until the edge is crisp and golden. Serve immediately.

# Exotic Mushroom & Walnut

Exotic mushrooms make a delicious pizza topping when mixed with walnuts and Roquefort cheese.

## NUTRITIONAL INFORMATION

Calories . . . . . . .499   Sugars . . . . . . . . .9g
Protein . . . . . . . .13g   Fat . . . . . . . . . .32g
Carbohydrate . . .42g   Saturates . . . . . .11g

  1¼ HOURS    25 MINS

### SERVES 4

## INGREDIENTS

Biscuit Base (see page 315)

Special Tomato Sauce (see page 318)

4¼ oz/125 g soft cheese

1 tbsp chopped fresh mixed herbs, such as
    parsley, oregano, and basil

8 oz/225 g exotic mushrooms, such as
    oyster, shiitake, or cèpes, or 4½ oz/125 g
    each exotic and white mushrooms

2 tbsp olive oil

¼ tsp fennel seeds

scant ¼ cup walnuts, chopped coarsely

½ cup crumbled blue cheese

olive oil, for drizzling

salt and pepper

sprig of flat-leaf parsley, to garnish

1 Roll out or press the biscuit base, using a rolling pin or your hands, into a 10-inch/25-cm round on a lightly floured counter. Place on a large greased cookie sheet or pizza pan and push up the edge a little with your fingers to form a rim.

2 Carefully spread the tomato sauce almost to the edge of the pizza base. Dot with the soft cheese and chopped fresh herbs.

3 Wipe and slice the mushrooms. Heat the oil in a large skillet or wok and stir-fry the mushrooms and fennel seeds for 2–3 minutes. Spread over the pizza with the walnuts.

4 Sprinkle the blue cheese over the pizza, then drizzle with a little olive oil and season with salt and pepper to taste.

5 Bake in a preheated oven, at 400°F/ 200°C, for 18–20 minutes, or until the edge is crisp and golden. Serve immediately, garnished with a sprig of flat-leaf parsley.

# Tomato & Olive Pizzas

Halved ciabatta bread or baguettes are a ready-made pizza base.
The colors of the tomatoes and cheese contrast beautifully on top.

## NUTRITIONAL INFORMATION

Calories . . . . . . . .181  Sugars . . . . . . . . .4g
Protein . . . . . . . . .7g  Fat . . . . . . . . . .10g
Carbohydrate . . .18g  Saturates . . . . . . .4g

45 MINS     25 MINS

### SERVES 4

## I N G R E D I E N T S

2 ciabatta loaves or 2 baguettes

Tomato Sauce (see page 317)

4 plum tomatoes, sliced thinly lengthwise

1½ cups thinly sliced mozzarella cheese

10 black olives, cut into rings

8 fresh basil leaves, shredded

olive oil, for drizzling

salt and pepper

1 Cut the bread in half lengthwise and toast the cut side of the bread lightly. Carefully spread the toasted bread with the tomato sauce.

2 Arrange the tomato and mozzarella slices alternately along the length.

3 Top with the olive rings and half of the basil. Drizzle over a little olive oil and season with salt and pepper.

4 Either place under a preheated medium broiler and cook until the cheese is melted and bubbling or bake in a preheated oven, 400°F/200°C, for 15–20 minutes.

5 Sprinkle over the remaining basil and serve immediately.

# Marinara Pizza

This pizza is topped with a cocktail of mixed seafood, such as shrimp, mussels, baby clams, and squid rings.

## NUTRITIONAL INFORMATION

| | | | |
|---|---|---|---|
| Calories | .......359 | Sugars | .........9g |
| Protein | ........19g | Fat | ..........14g |
| Carbohydrate | ...42g | Saturates | .......4g |

  3¹/₄ HOURS    20 MINS

### SERVES 4

## I N G R E D I E N T S

Potato Base (see page 316)

Special Tomato Sauce (see page 318)

7 oz/200 g frozen seafood cocktail, defrosted

1 tbsp capers

1 small yellow bell pepper, chopped

1 tbsp chopped fresh marjoram

½ tsp dried oregano

½ cup grated mozzarella cheese

1 tbsp freshly grated Parmesan cheese

12 black olives

olive oil, for drizzling

salt and pepper

sprig of fresh marjoram or oregano, to garnish

1 Roll out or press out the potato dough, using a rolling pin or your hands, into a 10-inch/25-cm round on a lightly floured counter.

2 Place the dough on a large greased cookie sheet or pizza pan and push up the edge a little with your fingers to form a rim.

3 Spread the tomato sauce evenly over the base almost to the edge.

4 Arrange the seafood cocktail, capers, and yellow bell pepper on top of the tomato sauce.

5 Sprinkle over the herbs and cheeses. Arrange the olives on top. Drizzle over a little olive oil and season with salt and pepper to taste.

6 Bake in a preheated oven, at 400°F/200°C, for 18–20 minutes, or until the edge of the pizza is crisp and golden brown.

7 Transfer to a warmed serving plate, then garnish with a sprig of marjoram and serve immediately.

# Onion & Anchovy Pizza

This tasty onion pizza is topped with a lattice pattern of anchovies and black olives. Cut the pizza into squares to serve.

## NUTRITIONAL INFORMATION

| | | | |
|---|---|---|---|
| Calories | .......373 | Sugars | .........5g |
| Protein | ........12g | Fat | ..........20g |
| Carbohydrate | ...39g | Saturates | .......4g |

1¾ HOURS        30 MINS

### MAKES 6

## INGREDIENTS

4 tbsp olive oil

3 onions, sliced thinly

1 garlic clove, crushed

1 tsp soft brown sugar

½ tsp crushed fresh rosemary

7 oz/200 g canned chopped tomatoes

Bread Dough Base (see page 314)

2 tbsp freshly grated Parmesan cheese

1¾ oz/50 g canned anchovies

12–14 black olives

salt and pepper

1 Heat 3 tablespoons of the oil in a large pan and add the onions, garlic, sugar, and rosemary. Cover and cook gently, stirring occasionally, for 10 minutes, or until the onions are soft but not brown.

2 Add the tomatoes to the pan, then stir and season with salt and pepper to taste. Leave to cool slightly.

3 Roll out or press the dough, using a rolling pin or your hands, on a lightly floured counter to fit a 12 x 7 inch/ 30 x 18 cm greased jelly roll pan. Place in the pan and push up the edges slightly to form a rim.

4 Brush the remaining oil over the dough and sprinkle with the cheese. Cover and leave to rise slightly in a warm place for 10 minutes.

5 Spread the onion and tomato topping over the base. Drain the anchovies, reserving the oil. Split each anchovy in half lengthwise and arrange on the pizza in a lattice pattern. Place olives in between the anchovies and drizzle over a little of the reserved oil. Season to taste.

6 Bake in a preheated oven, at 400°F/ 200°C, for 18–20 minutes, or until the edges are crisp and golden. Cut the pizza into 6 squares and serve immediately.

# Salmon Pizza

You can use either red or pink salmon for this tasty pizza. Red salmon will give a better color and flavor, but it can be expensive.

## NUTRITIONAL INFORMATION

| | | | |
|---|---|---|---|
| Calories | .321 | Sugars | .6g |
| Protein | .12g | Fat | .14g |
| Carbohydrate | .39g | Saturates | .6g |

  1¼ HOURS  20 MINS

### SERVES 4

## INGREDIENTS

1 quantity Biscuit Base (see page 315)

1 quantity Tomato Sauce (see page 317)

1 zucchini, grated

1 tomato, sliced thinly

3½ oz/100 g canned red or pink salmon

½ cup white mushrooms, wiped and sliced

1 tbsp chopped fresh dill

½ tsp dried oregano

Scant ½ cup grated mozzarella cheese

olive oil, for drizzling

salt and pepper

sprig of fresh dill, to garnish

1 Roll out or press the dough, using a rolling pin or your hands, into a 10-inch/25-cm round on a lightly floured counter. Place on a large greased cookie sheet or pizza pan and push up the edge a little with your fingers to form a rim.

2 Spread the tomato sauce over the pizza base, almost to the edge.

3 Top the tomato sauce with the grated zucchini, then lay the tomato slices on top.

4 Drain the canned salmon. Remove any bones and skin and flake the fish. Arrange on the pizza with the mushrooms. Sprinkle over the herbs and cheese. Drizzle with a little olive oil and season with salt and pepper.

5 Bake in a preheated oven, at 400°F/200°C, for 18–20 minutes, or until the edge is golden and crisp.

6 Transfer to a warmed serving plate and serve immediately, garnished with a sprig of dill.

## COOK'S TIP

If salmon is too pricy, use either canned tuna or sardines to make a delicious everyday fish pizza. Choose canned fish in brine for a healthier topping. If fresh dill is unavailable, you can use parsley instead.

# Pissaladière

This is a variation of a classic pizza but is made with ready-made puff pastry. It is perfect for outdoor eating.

## NUTRITIONAL INFORMATION

| | | | |
|---|---|---|---|
| Calories | 612 | Sugars | 13g |
| Protein | 12g | Fat | 43g |
| Carbohydrate | 47g | Saturates | 11g |

20 MINS    55 MINS

### SERVES 8

## INGREDIENTS

4 tbsp olive oil

1 lb 9 oz/700 g red onions, sliced thinly

2 garlic cloves, crushed

2 tsp superfine sugar

2 tbsp red wine vinegar

12 oz/350 g fresh ready-made puff pastry

salt and pepper

### TOPPING

3½ oz/100 g canned anchovy fillets

12 green pitted olives

1 tsp dried marjoram

1 Lightly grease a jelly roll pan. Heat the olive oil in a large pan. Add the red onions and garlic and cook over low heat for 30 minutes, stirring occasionally.

2 Add the sugar and red wine vinegar to the pan and season with plenty of salt and pepper.

3 On a lightly floured surface, roll out the pastry to a rectangle, about 13 x 9 inches/33 x 23 cm. Place the pastry rectangle on to the prepared pan, pushing the pastry into the corners of the pan.

4 Spread the onion mixture over the pastry.

5 Arrange the anchovy fillets and green olives on top, then sprinkle with the marjoram.

6 Bake in a preheated oven, at 425°F/ 220°C, for 20–25 minutes, or until the pissaladière is lightly golden. Serve the pissaladière piping hot, straight from the oven.

## VARIATION

Cut the pissaladière into squares or triangles for easy finger food at a party or barbecue.

# Mini Pizzas

*Pizette*, as they are known in Italy, are tiny pizzas. This quantity will make 8 individual pizzas, or 16 cocktail pizzas to go with drinks.

## NUTRITIONAL INFORMATION

| | | | |
|---|---|---|---|
| Calories | .......139 | Sugars | .........1g |
| Protein | .........4g | Fat | ...........6g |
| Carbohydrate | ...18g | Saturates | .......1g |

1¼ HOURS     15 MINS

### SERVES 8

## INGREDIENTS

1 portion Basic Pizza Dough (see page 319)

### TOPPING

2 zucchini

3½ oz/100 g crushed tomatoes

scant ⅓ cup diced pancetta

scant ⅓ cup black olives, pitted and
   chopped

1 tbsp mixed dried herbs

2 tbsp olive oil

1 Place the yeast and sugar in a measuring cup and mix with 4 tablespoons of the water. Leave the yeast mixture in a warm place for 15 minute, or until frothy.

2 Mix the flour with the salt and make a well in the center. Add the oil, the yeast mixture, and the remaining water. Using a wooden spoon, mix to form a smooth dough.

3 Turn the dough out onto a floured counter and knead for 4–5 minutes< or until smooth. Return the dough to the bowl, then cover with an oiled sheet of plastic wrap and leave to rise for 30 minutes, or until the dough has doubled in size.

4 Knead the dough for 2 minutes and divide it into 8 balls.

5 Roll out each portion thinly to form rounds or squares, then place them on an oiled cookie sheet, pushing out the edges until even. The dough should be no more than ¼ inch/5 mm thick because it will rise during cooking.

6 To make the topping, grate the zucchini finely. Cover with paper towels and leave to stand for 10 minutes to absorb some of the juices.

7 Spread 2–3 teaspoons of the crushed tomatoes over the pizza bases and top each with the grated zucchini, pancetta, and olives. Season with pepper to taste and a sprinkling of mixed dried herbs, then drizzle with olive oil.

8 Bake in a preheated oven at 400°F/ 200°C, for 15 minutes, or until crispy. Season with salt and pepper to taste and serve hot.

# Four Seasons Pizza

This is a traditional pizza on which the toppings are divided into four sections, each of which is supposed to depict a season of the year.

## NUTRITIONAL INFORMATION

Calories . . . . . . . .313   Sugars . . . . . . . . .8g
Protein . . . . . . . . .8g   Fat . . . . . . . . . .13g
Carbohydrate . . .44g   Saturates . . . . . . .3g

2³/₄ HOURS    20 MINS

### SERVES 4

## INGREDIENTS

Bread Dough Base (see page 314)

Special Tomato Sauce (see page 318)

1 oz/25 g chorizo sausage, sliced thinly

¼ cup white mushrooms, wiped and
  sliced thinly

1½ oz/45 g artichoke hearts, sliced thinly

¼ cup thinly sliced mozzarella cheese

3 anchovies, halved lengthwise

2 tsp capers

4 pitted black olives, sliced

4 fresh basil leaves, shredded

olive oil, for drizzling

salt and pepper

1 Roll out or press the dough, using a rolling pin or your hands, into a 10-inch/25-cm round on a lightly floured surface. Place on a large greased cookie sheet or pizza pan and push up the edge a little.

2 Cover and leave to rise slightly for 10 minutes in a warm place. Spread the tomato sauce over the pizza base, almost to the edge.

3 Put the sliced chorizo onto one fourth of the pizza, the sliced mushrooms on another, the artichoke hearts on a third, and the mozzarella and anchovies on the fourth.

4 Dot with the capers, olives, and basil leaves. Drizzle with a little olive oil and season. Do not put any salt on the anchovy section as the fish are very salty.

5 Bake in a preheated oven, at 400°F/ 200°C, for 18–20 minutes, or until the crust is golden and crisp. Serve immediately.

# Eggplant & Lamb

An unusual fragrant, spiced pizza topped with ground lamb and eggplant on a bread base.

## NUTRITIONAL INFORMATION

| | | | |
|---|---|---|---|
| Calories | .......430 | Sugars | ........10g |
| Protein | ........18g | Fat | .........22g |
| Carbohydrate | ...44g | Saturates | .......7g |

🥩 3 HOURS     🕐 30 MINS

### SERVES 4

## I N G R E D I E N T S

1 small eggplant, diced

Bread Dough Base (see page 314)

1 small onion, sliced thinly

1 garlic clove, crushed

1 tsp cumin seeds

1 tbsp olive oil

¾ cup ground lamb

1 oz/25 g canned pimiento, thinly sliced

2 tbsp chopped fresh cilantro

Special Tomato Sauce (see page 318)

¾ cup thinly sliced mozzarella cheese

olive oil, for drizzling

salt and pepper

1 Place the diced eggplant in a colander, then sprinkle with the salt and let the bitter juices drain for about 20 minutes. Rinse thoroughly, then pat dry with paper towels.

2 Roll out or press the dough, using a rolling pin or your hands, into a 10-inch/25-cm round on a lightly floured counter. Place on a large greased cookie sheet or pizza pan and push up the edge to form a rim.

3 Cover and leave to rise slightly for 10 minutes in a warm place.

4 Cook the onion, garlic, and cumin seeds gently in the oil for 3 minutes. Increase the heat slightly and add the lamb, eggplant, and pimiento. Cook for 5 minutes, stirring occasionally. Add the cilantro and season with salt and pepper to taste.

5 Spread the tomato sauce over the dough base, almost to the edge. Top with the lamb mixture.

6 Arrange the mozzarella slices on top. Drizzle over a little olive oil and season with salt and pepper.

7 Bake in a preheated oven, at 400°F/ 200°C, for 18–20 minutes, or until the crust is crisp and golden. Serve at once.

# Onion, Ham & Cheese Pizza

This pizza was a favorite of the Romans. It is slightly unusual because the topping is made without a tomato sauce base.

## NUTRITIONAL INFORMATION

Calories .......333  Sugars .........8g
Protein ........12g  Fat ..........14g
Carbohydrate ...43g  Saturates .......4g

🍴 1 HOUR   🕐 40 MINS

### SERVES 4

## INGREDIENTS

1 portion of Basic Pizza Dough (see page 319)

### TOPPING

2 tbsp olive oil

9 oz/250 g onions, sliced into rings

2 garlic cloves, crushed

1 red bell pepper, diced

3½ oz/100 g prosciutto, cut into strips

1 cup sliced mozzarella cheese

2 tbsp rosemary, stems removed and coarsely chopped

**1** Place the yeast and sugar in a measuring cup and mix with 4 tablespoons of the water. Leave in a warm place for 15 minutes, or until frothy.

**2** Mix the flour with the salt and make a well in the center. Add the oil, the yeast mixture, and the remaining water. Using a wooden spoon, mix to form a smooth dough.

**3** Turn the dough out onto a floured surface and knead for 4–5 minutes, or until smooth. Return the dough to the bowl, then cover with an oiled sheet of plastic wrap and leave to rise for 30 minutes, or until doubled in size.

**4** Remove the dough from the bowl. Knead the dough for 2 minutes. Using a rolling pin, roll out the dough to form a square shape, then place it on an oiled cookie sheet, pushing out the edges until even. The dough should be no more than ¼ inch/5 mm thick because it will rise during cooking.

**5** To make the topping, heat the oil in a pan. Add the onions and garlic and cook for 3 minutes. Add the bell pepper and cook for 2 minutes.

**6** Cover the pan and cook the vegetables over low heat for 10 minutes, stirring occasionally, until the onions are slightly caramelized. Leave to cool slightly.

**7** Spread the topping evenly over the pizza base. Arrange the prosciutto, mozzarella, and rosemary over the top.

**8** Bake in a preheated oven, at 400°F/ 200°C, for 20–25 minutes. Serve hot.

# Tomato & Chorizo Pizza

Spicy chorizo sausage blends beautifully with juicy tomatoes and mild, melting mozzarella cheese. This pizza makes a delicious light lunch.

## NUTRITIONAL INFORMATION

| | | | |
|---|---|---|---|
| Calories | .......574 | Sugars | .........8g |
| Protein | ........17g | Fat | ..........38g |
| Carbohydrate | ...43g | Saturates | .......8g |

 15 MINS   15 MINS

### SERVES 2

## INGREDIENTS

9-inch/23-cm ready-made pizza base

1 tbsp black olive paste

1 tbsp olive oil

1 onion, sliced

1 garlic clove, crushed

4 tomatoes, sliced

3 oz/85 g chorizo sausages, sliced

1 tsp fresh oregano

1 cup sliced mozzarella cheese

6 black olives, pitted and halved

pepper

1 Put the pizza base on a cookie sheet and spread the black olive paste to within ½ inch/1 cm of the edge.

2 Heat the oil in a skillet and cook the onion for 2 minutes. Add the garlic and cook for 1 minute.

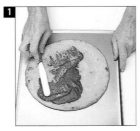  

## COOK'S TIP

There are several varieties of pizza base available. Those with added olive oil are preferable because the dough is much lighter and tastier.

3 Spread the onion mixture over the pizza base and arrange the tomato and chorizo slices on top. Sprinkle with the oregano, then season with pepper to taste and arrange the mozzarella cheese and olives on top.

4 Bake in a preheated oven, at 450°F/ 230°C, for 10 minutes, or until the cheese is melted and golden. Serve immediately.

# Smoky Bacon & Pepperoni

This more traditional kind of pizza is topped with pepperoni, smoked bacon, and bell peppers covered in a smoked cheese.

## NUTRITIONAL INFORMATION

| | | | |
|---|---|---|---|
| Calories | .......450 | Sugars | .........6g |
| Protein | ........19g | Fat | ..........24g |
| Carbohydrate | ...41g | Saturates | .......6g |

1½ HOURS    20 MINS

### SERVES 4

## I N G R E D I E N T S

Bread Dough Base (see page 314)

1 tbsp olive oil

1 tbsp freshly grated Parmesan

Tomato Sauce (see page 317)

½ cup diced lightly smoked bacon

½ green bell pepper, sliced thinly

½ yellow bell pepper, sliced thinly

2 oz/55 g pepperoni-style sliced spicy
    sausage

½ cup grated smoked Bavarian cheese

½ tsp dried oregano

olive oil, for drizzling

salt and pepper

1 Roll out or press the dough, using a rolling pin or your hands, into a 10-inch/25-cm round on a lightly floured counter.

2 Place the dough base on a large greased cookie sheet or pizza pan and push up the edge a little with your fingers, to form a rim.

3 Brush the base with the olive oil and sprinkle with the Parmesan. Cover and leave to rise slightly in a warm place for 10 minutes.

4 Spread the tomato sauce over the base almost to the edge. Top with the bacon and bell peppers. Arrange the pepperoni on top and sprinkle with the smoked cheese.

5 Sprinkle over the oregano and drizzle with a little olive oil. Season well.

6 Bake in a preheated oven, at 400°F/ 200°C, for 18–20 minutes, or until the crust is golden and crisp around the edge. Cut the pizza into wedges and serve immediately.

# Potato & Pepperoni Pizza

Potatoes make a great pizza base and this recipe is well worth making, rather than using a ready-made base, both for texture and flavor.

## NUTRITIONAL INFORMATION

Calories .......234  Sugars .........5g
Protein .........4g  Fat ..........12g
Carbohydrate ...30g  Saturates .......1g

20 MINS    45 MINS

### SERVES 4

## I N G R E D I E N T S

2 lb/900 g mealy potatoes, diced

1 tbsp butter

2 garlic cloves, crushed

2 tbsp mixed chopped fresh herbs

1 egg, beaten

$\frac{1}{3}$ cup crushed tomatoes

2 tbsp tomato paste

1$\frac{3}{4}$ oz/50 g pepperoni slices

1 green bell pepper, cut into strips

1 yellow bell pepper, cut into strips

2 large open-cup mushrooms, sliced

1 oz/25 g pitted black olives,
    cut into fourths

1 cup sliced mozzarella cheese

1 Grease and flour a 9 inch/23-cm pizza pan.

2 Cook the diced potatoes in a pan of boiling water for 10 minutes, or until cooked through. Drain and mash until smooth. Transfer the mashed potato to a mixing bowl and stir in the butter, garlic, herbs, and egg.

3 Spread the mixture into the prepared pizza pan. Cook in a preheated oven, at 425°F/220°C, for 7-10 minutes, or until the pizza base begins to set.

4 Mix the crushed tomatoes and tomato paste together and spoon it over the pizza base, to within $\frac{1}{2}$ inch/1 cm of the edge of the base.

5 Arrange the pepperoni, bell peppers, mushrooms, and olives on top of the strained tomatoes.

6 Arrange the mozzarella cheese on top of the pizza. Return to the oven for 20 minutes, or until the base is cooked through and the cheese has melted on top. Serve hot.

## COOK'S TIP

This pizza base is softer in texture than a normal bread dough and is ideal served from the pan. Top with any of your favorite pizza ingredients that you have to hand.

# Hot Chile Beef Pizza

This deep-pan pizza is topped with ground beef, red kidney beans, and jalapeño chiles, which are small, green and very hot.

## NUTRITIONAL INFORMATION

Calories .......550    Sugars .........5g
Protein ........24g    Fat ..........26g
Carbohydrate ...60g    Saturates .......9g

1½ HOURS    30 MINS

### SERVES

## INGREDIENTS

1½ tsp dried or active dry yeast

½ cup tepid water

1 tsp sugar

3 tbsp olive oil

scant 1⅔ cups all-purpose flour

1 tsp salt

### TOPPING

1 small onion, sliced thinly

1 garlic clove, crushed

½ yellow bell pepper, chopped

1 tbsp olive oil

6 oz/175 g lean ground beef

¼ tsp chili powder

¼ tsp ground cumin

7 oz/200 g canned red kidney beans,
    drained

Tomato Sauce (see page 317)

1 oz/25 g jalapeño chiles, sliced

½ cup thinly sliced mozzarella cheese

½ cup grated sharp Cheddar cheese or
    Monterey Jack

olive oil, for drizzling

salt and pepper

chopped parsley, to garnish

1 For the deep-pan dough base, use the same method as the Bread Dough Base recipe.

2 Roll out or press the dough, using a rolling pin or your hands, into a 9-inch/23-cm round on a lightly floured counter. Place on a large greased cookie sheet or pizza pan and push up the edge to form a small rim. Cover and leave to rise slightly for 10 minutes.

3 Cook the onion, garlic, and bell pepper gently in the oil for 5 minutes, or until soft but not browned. Increase the heat slightly and add the beef, chili powder, and cumin. Cook for 5 minutes, stirring occasionally. Remove from the heat and stir in the kidney beans. Season well.

4 Spread the tomato sauce over the dough, almost to the edge. Top with the meat mixture.

5 Top with the sliced chiles and mozzarella and sprinkle over the grated cheese. Drizzle with a little olive oil and season with salt and pepper to taste.

6 Bake in a preheated oven, at 400°F/200°C, for 18–20 minutes, or until the crust is golden. Serve immediately sprinkled with chopped parsley.

# Folded-Over Pizza

This recipe makes 4 large *calzones* (as these pizzas are known) or 8 small *calzones*.

## NUTRITIONAL INFORMATION

| | |
|---|---|
| Calories .......402 | Sugars .........3g |
| Protein ........16g | Fat ..........22g |
| Carbohydrate ...37g | Saturates .......5g |

🍲 1¼ HOURS   🕐 15 MINS

### SERVES 4

## I N G R E D I E N T S

1 portion of Basic Pizza Dough (see page 319)

freshly grated Parmesan cheese, to serve

### T O P P I N G

scant ⅓ cup chopped mortadella or other Italian pork sausage

scant ¼ cup chopped Italian sausage

½ cup sliced Parmesan cheese

1 cup diced mozzarella cheese

2 tomatoes, diced

4 tbsp fresh oregano

salt and pepper

1 Place the yeast and sugar in a measuring cup and mix with 4 tablespoons of the water. Leave the yeast mixture in a warm place for 15 minutes, or until frothy.

2 Mix the flour with the salt and make a well in the center. Add the oil, yeast mixture, and remaining water. Using a wooden spoon, mix to form a dough.

3 Turn the dough out on to a floured counter and knead for 4–5 minutes, or until smooth. Return the dough to the bowl, then cover with an oiled sheet of plastic wrap and leave to rise for 30 minutes, or until doubled in size.

4 Knead the dough for 2 minutes and divide it into 4 pieces. Roll out each portion thinly to form rounds. Place them on an oiled cookie sheet. The dough should be no more than ¼ inch/5 mm thick because it will rise during the cooking time.

5 To make the topping, place both Italian sausages and the Parmesan and mozzarella on one side of each round. Top with the tomatoes and oregano. Season to taste with salt and pepper.

6 Brush around the edges of the dough with a little water then fold over the round to form a "pasty" shape. Squeeze the edges together to seal so that none of the filling leaks out during cooking.

7 Bake in a preheated oven, at 400°F/ 200°C, for 10–15 minutes, or until golden. If you are making the smaller pizzas, reduce the cooking time to 8–10 minutes. Garnish with freshly grated Parmesan cheese and serve with salad greens, if liked.

# English Muffin Pizzas

Toasted muffins are topped with pineapple and prosciutto.
Plain, whole-wheat, or cheese muffins will all make great pizza bases.

## NUTRITIONAL INFORMATION

| | | |
|---|---|---|
| Calories .......259 | Sugars .........7g | |
| Protein .........9g | Fat ..........15g | |
| Carbohydrate ...24g | Saturates .......3g | |

45 MINS     5 MINS

### SERVES 4

## I N G R E D I E N T S

4 muffins

1 quantity Tomato Sauce (see page 317)

2 sun-dried tomatoes in oil, chopped

2 oz/55 g prosciutto

2 rings canned pineapple, chopped

½ green bell pepper, chopped

1 cup thinly sliced mozzarella cheese

olive oil, for drizzling

salt and pepper

fresh basil leaves, to garnish

1 Cut the muffins in half and toast the cut side lightly.

2 Spread the tomato sauce evenly over the muffins.

3 Sprinkle the sun-dried tomatoes on top of the tomato sauce.

4 Cut the ham into thin strips and place on the muffins with the pineapple and green bell pepper.

5 Carefully arrange the mozzarella slices on top.

6 Drizzle a little olive oil over each pizza, and season.

7 Place under a preheated medium broiler and cook until the cheese melts and bubbles.

8 Serve immediately garnished with small basil leaves.

## COOK'S TIP

You don't have to use plain muffins for your base; whole-wheat or cheese muffins will also make ideal pizza bases. Muffins freeze well, so always keep some in the freezer for an instant pizza.

# Avocado & Ham Pizza

A smoked ham and avocado salad is served on a pizza with a base enriched with chopped sun-dried tomatoes and black olives.

## NUTRITIONAL INFORMATION

| | | |
|---|---|---|
| Calories .......397 | Sugars .........9g | |
| Protein ........10g | Fat ..........22g | |
| Carbohydrate ...43g | Saturates .......5g | |

  2³/₄ HOURS    20 MINS

### SERVES 4

## INGREDIENTS

Bread Dough Base (see page 314)

4 sun-dried tomatoes, chopped

9–10 black olives, chopped

Special Tomato Sauce (see page 318)

4 small endive leaves, shredded

4 small radicchio leaves, shredded

1 avocado, peeled, pitted, and sliced

2 oz/55 g wafer-thin smoked ham

½ cup crumbled blue cheese

olive oil, for drizzling

salt and pepper

chopped fresh chervil, to garnish

1 Make the dough according to the instructions on page 314. Knead the dough gently with the sun-dried tomatoes and olives until well mixed.

2 Roll out or press the dough, using a rolling pin or your hands, into a 10-inch/25-cm round on a lightly floured counter. Place on a greased cookie sheet or pizza pan and push up the edge a little to form a rim.

3 Cover the dough and leave to rise slightly in a warm place for 10 minutes. Spread the tomato sauce almost to the edge of the pizza base.

4 Top the pizza with shredded lettuce leaves and avocado slices. Scrunch up the ham and add together with the blue cheese.

5 Drizzle with a little olive oil and season with salt and pepper to taste.

6 Bake in a preheated oven, at 400°F/ 200°C, for 18–20 minutes, or until the edge is crisp and a golden brown color.

7 Sprinkle with chervil to garnish and serve immediately.

# Creamy Ham & Cheese Pizza

This traditional pizza uses a pastry case and Béchamel Sauce to make a type of savory flan. Grating the pastry gives it a lovely nutty texture.

## NUTRITIONAL INFORMATION

| | | | |
|---|---|---|---|
| Calories | . . . . . . .628 | Sugars | . . . . . . . . .5g |
| Protein | . . . . . . . .19g | Fat | . . . . . . . . . .47g |
| Carbohydrate | . . .35g | Saturates | . . . . . .16g |

 20 MINS     40 MINS

### SERVES 4

## I N G R E D I E N T S

9 oz/250 g flaky pastry, well chilled

3 tbsp butter

1 red onion, chopped

1 garlic clove, chopped

3 tbsp bread flour

1¼ cups milk

scant ½ cup finely grated Parmesan cheese, plus extra for sprinkling

2 eggs, hard-cooked, cut into fourths

3½ oz/100 g Italian pork sausage, such as feline salame, cut into strips

salt and pepper

sprigs of fresh thyme, to garnish

1 Fold the pastry in half and grate it into 4 individual flan pans, measuring 4 inches/10 cm across. Using a floured fork, press the pastry flakes down so they are even, there are no holes, and the pastry comes up the sides of the pan.

2 Line with foil and bake blind in a preheated oven, at 425°F/220°C, for 10 minutes. Reduce the heat to 400°F/200°C, then remove the foil and cook for 15 minutes, or until golden and set.

3 Heat the butter in a skillet. Add the onion and garlic and cook for 5–6 minutes, or until softened.

4 Add the flour, stirring well to coat the onions. Gradually stir in the milk to make a thick sauce.

5 Season the sauce with salt and pepper to taste and then stir in the Parmesan cheese. Do not reheat once the cheese has been added or the sauce will become too stringy.

6 Spread the sauce over the pastry cases. Decorate with the egg and strips of sausage.

7 Sprinkle with a little extra Parmesan cheese, then return to the oven and bake for 5 minutes, just to heat through.

8 Serve immediately, garnished with sprigs of fresh thyme.

### COOK'S TIP

This pizza is just as good cold, but do not prepare it too far in advance as the pastry will turn soggy.

# Spicy Meatball Pizza

Small ground beef meatballs, spiced with chiles and cumin seeds, are baked on a biscuit base.

## NUTRITIONAL INFORMATION

| | | | |
|---|---|---|---|
| Calories | .......568 | Sugars | .........5g |
| Protein | ........24g | Fat | ..........37g |
| Carbohydrate | ...38g | Saturates | ......15g |

 2¼ HOURS   25 MINS

### SERVES 4

## INGREDIENTS

8 oz/225 g ground lean beef

1 oz/25 g jalapeño chiles in brine, chopped

1 tsp cumin seeds

1 tbsp chopped fresh parsley

1 tbsp beaten egg

3 tbsp olive oil

Biscuit Base (see page 315)

Tomato Sauce (see page 317)

1 oz/25 g canned pimiento, sliced

2 slices lean bacon, cut into strips

½ cup sharp grated Cheddar cheese

olive oil, for drizzling

salt and pepper

chopped fresh parsley, to garnish

1 Mix the beef, chiles, cumin seeds, parsley, and egg together in a bowl and season. Form into 12 small meatballs. Cover and chill for 1 hour.

2 Heat the oil in a large skillet. Add the meatballs and brown all over. Remove with a perforated spoon or spatula and drain on paper towels.

3 Roll out or press the dough into a 10-inch/25-cm round on a lightly floured counter. Place on a greased cookie sheet or pizza pan and push up the edge slightly to form a rim. Spread with the tomato sauce, almost to the edge.

4 Arrange the meatballs on the pizza with the pimiento and bacon. Sprinkle over the cheese and drizzle with a little olive oil. Season with salt and pepper.

5 Bake in a preheated oven, at 400°F/ 200°C, for 18–20 minutes, or until the edge is crisp and a golden brown color.

6 Serve immediately, garnished with chopped parsley.

# Mini Pita Bread Pizzas

Smoked salmon and asparagus make extra-special party pizza canapés.
Mini pita breads make great bases and are really quick to cook.

## NUTRITIONAL INFORMATION

Calories . . . . . . . . .518  Sugars . . . . . . . .10g
Protein . . . . . . . .21g  Fat . . . . . . . . . .12g
Carbohydrate . . .87g  Saturates . . . . . . .4g

 55 MINS     15 MINS

### SERVES 4

## I N G R E D I E N T S

8 thin asparagus spears

16 mini pita breads

1 quantity Special Tomato Sauce (see
    page 318)

¼ cup mild Cheddar cheese, grated

1 oz/25 g ricotta cheese

2 oz/55 g smoked salmon

olive oil, for drizzling

pepper

1 Cut the asparagus spears into 1-inch/
2.5-cm lengths; then cut each piece
in half lengthwise.

2 Blanch the asparagus in a pan of
boiling water for 1 minute. Drain the
asparagus, then plunge into cold water
and drain again.

3 Place the pita breads on to
2 cookie sheets. Spread about
1 teaspoon of tomato sauce on each pita
bread.

4 Mix the cheeses together and divide
between the 16 pita breads.

5 Cut the smoked salmon into 16 long
thin strips. Arrange one strip on each
pita bread with the asparagus spears.

6 Drizzle over a little olive oil and
season with pepper to taste.

7 Bake in a preheated oven, at 400°F/
200°C, for 8–10 minutes. Serve
immediately.

## COOK'S TIP

Smoked salmon is expensive,
so for a cheaper version, use
smoked trout. It is often half the
price of smoked salmon, and tastes
just as good. Try experimenting with
other smoked fish, such as smoked
mackerel, with its strong, distinctive
flavor, for a bit of variety.

# Roman Focaccia

Roman focaccia makes a delicious snack on its own or can be served with cured meats and salad for a quick supper.

## NUTRITIONAL INFORMATION

| | | | |
|---|---|---|---|
| Calories | ........119 | Sugars | .........2g |
| Protein | .........3g | Fat | ..........2g |
| Carbohydrate | ...24g | Saturates | .....0.3g |

🍲 1 HOUR    🕐 45 MINS

### Makes 16 squares

## INGREDIENTS

¼ oz/7 g active dry yeast

1 tsp sugar

1¼ cups hand-hot water

3 cups strong white flour

2 tsp salt

3 tbsp rosemary, chopped

2 tbsp olive oil

1 lb/450 g mixed red and white onions,
  sliced into rings

4 garlic cloves, sliced

1 Place the yeast and the sugar in a small bowl and mix with scant ½ cup of the water. Leave to ferment in a warm place for 15 minutes.

2 Mix the flour with the salt in a large bowl. Add the yeast mixture, half of the rosemary, and the remaining water and mix to form a smooth dough. Knead the dough for 4 minutes.

3 Cover the dough with oiled plastic wrap and leave to rise for 30 minutes, or until doubled in size.

4 Meanwhile, heat the oil in a large pan. Add the onions and garlic and cook for 5 minutes, or until softened. Cover the pan and continue to cook for 7–8 minutes, or until the onions are lightly caramelized.

5 Remove the dough from the bowl and knead it again for 1–2 minutes.

6 Roll the dough out to form a square shape. The dough should be no more than ¼ inch/5 mm thick because it will rise during cooking. Place the dough on to a large cookie sheet, pushing out the edges until even.

7 Spread the onions over the dough, and sprinkle with the remaining rosemary.

8 Bake in a preheated oven, at 400°F/200°C, for 25–30 minutes, or until a golden brown color. Cut the focaccia into 16 squares and serve immediately.

# Mini Focaccia

This is a delicious Italian bread made with olive oil.
The topping of red onions and thyme is particularly flavorsome.

## NUTRITIONAL INFORMATION

| | | | |
|---|---|---|---|
| Calories | .......439 | Sugars | .........3g |
| Protein | .........9g | Fat | ..........15g |
| Carbohydrate | ....71g | Saturates | .......2g |

  2¼ HOURS  25 MINS

### SERVES 4

## I N G R E D I E N T S

3 cups white bread flour

½ tsp salt

1 x ¼ oz envelope easy-blend dried yeast

2 tbsp olive oil

1 cup tepid water

generous ½ cup green or black olives, halved

### T O P P I N G

2 red onions, sliced

2 tbsp olive oil

1 tsp sea salt

1 tbsp thyme leaves

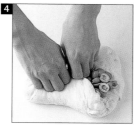  

1 Lightly oil several cookie sheets. Sift the flour and salt into a large mixing bowl, then stir in the yeast. Pour in the olive oil and tepid water and mix everything together to form a dough.

2 Turn the dough out on to a lightly floured counter and knead it for about 5 minutes (alternatively, use an electric mixer with a dough hook and knead for 7–8 minutes).

3 Place the dough in a greased bowl, then cover and leave in a warm place for about 1–1½ hours, or until it has doubled in size. Knock back (punch down) the dough by kneading it again for 1–2 minutes.

4 Knead half of the olives into the dough. Divide the dough into fourths and then shape the fourths into rounds. Place them on the cookie sheets and push your fingers into the dough to achieve a dimpled effect.

5 To make the topping, sprinkle the red onions and remaining olives over the rounds. Drizzle the oil over the top and sprinkle with the sea salt and thyme leaves. Cover and leave to rise for 30 minutes.

6 Bake in a preheated oven, at 375°F/190°C, for 20–25 minutes, or until the focaccia are golden.

7 Transfer to a wire rack and leave to cool before serving.

## VARIATION

Use this quantity of dough to make 1 large focaccia, if you prefer.

# Italian Bruschetta

It is important to use a good quality olive oil for this recipe.
Serve the bruschetta with kabobs or fish for a really summery taste.

## NUTRITIONAL INFORMATION

| | |
|---|---|
| Calories . . . . . . . . .415 | Sugars . . . . . . . . .2g |
| Protein . . . . . . . . .8g | Fat . . . . . . . . . .24g |
| Carbohydrate . . .45g | Saturates . . . . . . .4g |

10 MINS    10 MINS

### Makes 1 loaf

## I N G R E D I E N T S

1 ciabatta loaf or small stick of
  French bread

1 plump clove garlic

extra virgin olive oil

freshly grated Parmesan cheese (optional)

1 Slice the bread in half crossways and
  again lengthwise to give 4 portions.

2 Do not peel the garlic clove, but cut it
  in half.

3 Grill the bread over hot coals for
  2–3 minutes on both sides, or until
golden brown.

4 Rub the garlic, cut side down, all over
  the toasted surface of the bread.

## COOK'S TIP

As ready-grated Parmesan
quickly loses its pungency and
"bite," it is better to buy small
quantities of the cheese in one
piece and grate it yourself as
needed. Tightly wrapped in plastic
wrap or foil, it will keep in the
refrigerator for several months.

5 Drizzle the olive oil over the bread and
  serve hot as an accompaniment.

6 If using Parmesan cheese, sprinkle the
  cheese over the bread.

7 Return the bread to the grill, cut side
  up, for 1–2 minutes, or until the
cheese just begins to melt. Serve hot.

# Roasted Bell Pepper Bread

Bell peppers become sweet and mild when they are roasted and make this bread delicious.

## NUTRITIONAL INFORMATION

| | | | |
|---|---|---|---|
| Calories | .......426 | Sugars | ........4g |
| Protein | ........12g | Fat | ...........4g |
| Carbohydrate | ...90g | Saturates | .......1g |

  1¾ HOURS    1 HR 5 MINS

### SERVES 4

## I N G R E D I E N T S

1 red bell pepper, halved and seeded

1 yellow bell pepper, halved and seeded

2 sprigs of rosemary

1 tbsp olive oil

¼ oz/7 g active dry yeast

1 tsp sugar

1¼ cups hand-hot water

3 cups white bread flour

1 tsp salt

1 Grease a 9-inch/23-cm deep round cake pan.

2 Place the bell peppers and rosemary in a shallow roasting pan. Pour over the oil and roast in a preheated oven, at 400°F/200°C, for 20 minutes, or until slightly charred. Remove the skin from the bell peppers and cut the flesh into slices.

3 Place the yeast and sugar in a small bowl and mix with scant ½ cup of hand-hot water. Leave to ferment in a warm place for 15 minutes.

4 Mix the flour and salt together in a large bowl. Stir in the yeast mixture and the remaining water and mix to form a smooth dough.

5 Knead the dough for 5 minutes, or until smooth. Cover with oiled plastic wrap and leave to rise for 30 minutes, or until doubled in size.

6 Cut the dough into 3 equal portions. Roll the portions into rounds slightly larger than the cake pan.

7 Place 1 round in the base of the pan so that it reaches up the sides of the pan by about ¾ inch/2 cm. Top with half of the bell pepper mixture.

8 Place the second round of dough on top, followed by the remaining bell pepper mixture. Place the last round of dough on top, pushing the edges of the dough down the sides of the pan.

9 Cover the dough with oiled plastic wrap and leave to rise for 30–40 minutes. Return to the oven and bake for 45 minutes until golden, or the base sounds hollow when lightly tapped. Serve warm.

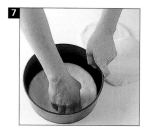

# Sun-Dried Tomato Rolls

These white rolls have the addition of finely chopped sun-dried tomatoes. The tomatoes are sold in jars and are available at most supermarkets.

## NUTRITIONAL INFORMATION

| | | |
|---|---|---|
| Calories . . . . . . . .214 | Sugars . . . . . . . . .1g | |
| Protein . . . . . . . . .5g | Fat . . . . . . . . . .12g | |
| Carbohydrate . . .22g | Saturates . . . . . . .7g | |

2¼ HOURS    15 MINS

### SERVES 8

## I N G R E D I E N T S

generous 1⅔ cups strong white bread flour

½ tsp salt

1 x ¼ envelope active dry yeast

⅓ cup butter, melted and cooled slightly

3 tbsp milk, warmed

2 eggs, beaten

scant ⅓ cup sun-dried tomatoes, well
    drained and chopped finely

milk, for brushing

1 Lightly grease a cookie sheet.

2 Sift the flour and salt into a large mixing bowl. Stir in the yeast, then pour in the butter, milk, and eggs. Mix together to form a dough.

## VARIATION

Add some finely chopped anchovies or olives to the dough in step 5 for extra flavor, if wished.

3 Turn the dough on to a lightly floured counter and knead for 5 minutes (alternatively, use an electric mixer with a dough hook).

4 Place the dough in a greased bowl, cover and leave to rise in a warm place for 1-1½ hours, or until the dough has doubled in size. Knock back (punch down) the dough for 2–3 minutes.

5 Knead the sun-dried tomatoes into the dough, sprinkling the counter with extra flour as the tomatoes are quite oily.

6 Divide the dough into 8 balls and place them on to the cookie sheet. Cover and leave to rise for 30 minutes. or until the rolls have doubled in size.

7 Brush the rolls with milk and bake in a preheated oven, at 450°F/230°C, for 10-15 minutes, or until the rolls are golden brown.

8 Transfer the rolls to a wire rack and leave to cool slightly before serving.

# Garlic Bread

A perennial favorite, garlic bread is perfect with a range of grill meals or as an appetizer with drinks.

## NUTRITIONAL INFORMATION

| | | | |
|---|---|---|---|
| Calories | .......261 | Sugars | .........1g |
| Protein | .........3g | Fat | ..........22g |
| Carbohydrate | ...15g | Saturates | ......14g |

 10 MINS     15 MINS

### SERVES 6

## I N G R E D I E N T S

scant ¾ cup butter, softened

3 garlic cloves, crushed

2 tbsp chopped, fresh parsley

pepper

1 large or 2 small sticks of French bread

1 Mix together the butter, garlic, and parsley in a bowl until well combined. Season with pepper to taste and mix well.

2 Cut the French bread into thick slices.

3 Spread the flavored butter over one side of each slice and reassemble the loaf on a large sheet of thick kitchen foil.

4 Wrap the bread well and grill over hot coals for 10–15 minutes, or until the butter melts and the bread is piping hot.

5 Serve as an accompaniment to a wide range of dishes.

# Desserts

The Italians love their desserts, but when there is an important gathering or celebration, then an extra-special effort is made and a wide range of exquisite delicacies appear. The Sicilians are said to have the sweetest tooth of all, and many Italian desserts are thought to have originated there. Indeed, you have to go a very long way to

beat a Sicilian ice cream—they truly are the best in the world! Fresh fruit also features in many Italian desserts— oranges are often peeled and served whole, marinated in a fragrant syrup and liqueur. Chocolate, too, is very popular in Italy—try the different varieties of the classic Tiramisu that are included in this chapter. Whatever your dessert preference, there is sure to be an Italian dessert to tempt and satisfy you—you'll never be disappointed!

# Tuscan Pudding

These baked mini-ricotta puddings are delicious served warm or chilled and will keep in the refrigerator for three or four days.

## NUTRITIONAL INFORMATION

Calories .......293  Sugars ........28g
Protein .........9g  Fat ..........17g
Carbohydrate ...28g  Saturates .......9g

 20 MINS   15 MINS

## SERVES 4

### INGREDIENTS

1 tbsp butter

scant ½ cup mixed dried fruit

1 cup ricotta cheese

3 egg yolks

¼ cup superfine sugar

1 tsp cinnamon

finely grated rind of 1 orange,
   plus extra to decorate

crème fraîche or sour cream, to serve

1 Lightly grease 4 mini pudding basins or ramekin dishes with the butter.

2 Put the dried fruit in a bowl and cover with warm water. Leave to soak for 10 minutes.

## COOK'S TIP

Crème fraîche has a slightly sour, nutty taste and is very thick. It is suitable for cooking, but has the same fat content as heavy cream. It can be made by stirring cultured buttermilk into heavy cream and refrigerating overnight.

3 Beat the ricotta cheese with the egg yolks in a bowl. Stir in the superfine sugar, cinnamon, and orange rind and mix to combine.

4 Drain the dried fruit in a strainer set over a bowl. Mix the drained fruit with the ricotta cheese mixture.

5 Spoon the mixture into the basins or ramekin dishes.

6 Bake in a preheated oven, at 350°F/180°C, for 15 minutes. The tops should be firm to the touch but not brown.

7 Decorate the puddings with grated orange rind. Serve warm or chilled with a spoonful of crème fraîche or sour cream, if liked.

# Tiramisu Layers

This is a modern version of the well-known and very tempting chocolate dessert from Italy.

## NUTRITIONAL INFORMATION

| | | |
|---|---|---|
| Calories .......798 | Sugars ........60g | |
| Protein ........12g | Fat ..........50g | |
| Carbohydrate ...76g | Saturates ......25g | |

🍰 🍰

❄ 1¼ HOURS    🕐 5 MINS

### SERVES 6

## I N G R E D I E N T S

10½ oz/300 g dark chocolate

1¾ cups mascarpone cheese

⅔ cup heavy cream, whipped until it just holds its shape

1¼ cups black coffee with ¼ cup superfine sugar, cooled

6 tbsp dark rum or brandy

36 lady-fingers, about 14 oz/400 g

unsweetened cocoa, to dust

1 Melt the chocolate in a bowl set over a pan of simmering water, stirring occasionally. Leave the chocolate to cool slightly, then stir it into the mascarpone and cream.

2 Mix the coffee and rum together in a bowl. Dip the lady-fingers into the mixture briefly so that they absorb the coffee and rum liquid but do not become soggy.

3 Place 3 lady-fingers on 3 serving plates.

4 Spoon a layer of the mascarpone and chocolate mixture over the lady-fingers.

5 Place 3 more lady-fingers on top of the mascarpone layer. Spread another layer of mascarpone and chocolate mixture and place 3 more lady-fingers on top.

6 Leave the tiramisu to chill in the refrigerator for at least 1 hour. Dust all over with a little unsweetened cocoa just before serving.

## VARIATION

Try adding ⅓ cup toasted, chopped filberts to the chocolate cream mixture in step 1, if you prefer.

# Orange & Almond Cake

This light and tangy citrus cake from Sicily is better eaten as a dessert than as a cake. It is especially good served after a large meal.

## NUTRITIONAL INFORMATION

Calories .......399  Sugars ........20g
Protein .........8g  Fat ..........31g
Carbohydrate ...23g  Saturates ......13g

30 MINS     40 MINS

### SERVES 8

## I N G R E D I E N T S

4 eggs, separated

scant ⅔ cup superfine sugar, plus
  2 tsp for the cream

finely grated rind and juice of 2 oranges

finely grated rind and juice of 1 lemon

scant 1⅛ cups ground almonds

2 tbsp self-rising flour

¾ cup whipping cream

1 tsp cinnamon

¼ cup slivered almonds, toasted

confectioners' sugar, to dust

1 Grease and line the base of a 7-inch/18 cm round deep cake pan.

2 Blend the egg yolks with the sugar until the mixture is thick and creamy. Whisk half of the orange rind and all of the lemon rind into the egg yolks.

## VARIATION

You could serve this cake with a syrup. Boil the juice and finely grated rind of 2 oranges, scant ⅓ cup superfine sugar and 2 tablespoons water for 5–6 minutes, or until slightly thickened. Stir in 1 tablespoon orange liqueur just before serving.

3 Mix the juice from both oranges and the lemon with the ground almonds and stir into the egg yolks. The mixture will become quite runny at this point. Fold in the flour.

4 Whisk the egg whites until stiff and gently fold into the egg yolk mixture.

5 Pour the mixture into the pan and bake in a preheated oven, at 350°F/180°C, for 35–40 minutes, or until golden

and springy to the touch. Leave to cool in the pan for 10 minutes and then turn out. It is likely to sink slightly at this stage.

6 Whip the cream to form soft peaks. Stir in the remaining orange rind, cinnamon, and sugar.

7 Once the cake is cold, cover with the almonds, dust with confectioners' sugar and serve with the cream.

# Panforte di Siena

This famous Tuscan honey and nut cake is a Christmas specialty.
In Italy it is sold in pretty boxes, and served in very thin slices.

## NUTRITIONAL INFORMATION

Calories . . . . . . .257  Sugars . . . . . . . .29g
Protein . . . . . . . . .5g  Fat . . . . . . . . . .13g
Carbohydrate . . .33g  Saturates . . . . . . .1g

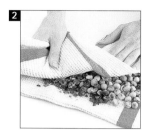

🍯 10 MINS   🕐 1¼ HOURS

### SERVES 12

## I N G R E D I E N T S

scant 1 cup split whole almonds

¾ cup filberts

½ cup cut candied peel

⅓ cup no-soak dried apricots

2 oz/55 g candied pineapple

grated rind of 1 large orange

scant ½ cup all-purpose flour

2 tbsp unsweetened cocoa

2 tsp ground cinnamon

½ cup superfine sugar

½ cup honey

confectioners' sugar, for dredging

1 Toast the almonds under the broiler until lightly browned and place in a bowl.

2 Toast the filberts until the skins split. Place on a dry dish cloth and rub off the skins. Coarsely chop the nuts and add to the almonds with the candied peel.

3 Chop the apricots and pineapple fairly finely, then add to the nuts with the orange rind and mix well.

4 Sift the flour with the cocoa and cinnamon, add to the nut mixture; mix.

5 Line a round 20 cm/8 inch cake tin or deep loose-based flan pan with baking parchment.

6 Put the sugar and honey in a pan and heat until the sugar dissolves, then boil gently for 5 minutes, or until the mixture thickens and begins to turn a deeper shade of brown. Quickly add to the nut mixture and mix evenly. Turn into the prepared cake tin and level the top with the back of a damp spoon.

7 Cook in a preheated oven, at 300°F/ 150°C, for 1 hour. Remove from the oven and leave in the pan until cold. Take out of the pan and carefully peel off the paper. Before serving, dredge the cake heavily with sifted confectioners' sugar. Serve in very thin slices.

# Pear Cake

This is a really moist cake, deliciously flavored with chopped pears and cinnamon.

## NUTRITIONAL INFORMATION

Calories . . . . . . . .119   Sugars . . . . . . . .16g
Protein . . . . . . . . .2g   Fat . . . . . . . . . .0.3g
Carbohydrate . . .29g   Saturates . . . . . . .0g

 25 MINS   🕐 1½ HOURS

### SERVES 12

## I N G R E D I E N T S

4 pears, peeled and cored

margarine, for greasing

2 tbsp water

1⅓ cups all-purpose flour

2 tsp baking powder

½ cup soft light brown sugar

4 tbsp milk

2 tbsp clear honey, plus extra to drizzle

2 tsp ground cinnamon

2 egg whites

1 Grease and line the base of a 8-inch/20-cm cake pan.

2 Put 1 pear in a food processor with the water and blend until almost smooth. Transfer to a mixing bowl.

3 Sift in the all-purpose flour and baking powder. Beat in the sugar, milk, honey, and cinnamon and mix well.

4 Chop all but one of the remaining pears and add to the mixture.

5 Whisk the egg whites until peaking and gently fold into the mixture until fully blended.

6 Slice the remaining pear and arrange in a fan pattern on the base of the cake pan.

7 Spoon the cake mixture into the pan and cook in a preheated oven, at 300°F/150°C, for 1¼ –1½ hours, or until cooked through.

8 Remove the cake from the oven and leave to cool in the pan for 10 minutes.

9 Turn the cake out on to a wire cooling rack and drizzle with honey. Leave to cool completely, then cut into slices to serve.

## COOK'S TIP

To test if the cake is cooked through, insert a skewer into the center—if it comes out clean the cake is cooked. If not, return the cake to the oven and test at frequent intervals.

# Pear & Ginger Cake

This deliciously buttery pear and ginger cake is ideal for tea-time or you can serve it with cream for a delicious dessert.

## NUTRITIONAL INFORMATION

| | | | |
|---|---|---|---|
| Calories | .531 | Sugars | .41g |
| Protein | .6g | Fat | .30g |
| Carbohydrate | .62g | Saturates | .19g |

15 MINS     40 MINS

### SERVES 6

## INGREDIENTS

scant 1 cup unsalted butter, softened

scant 1 cup superfine sugar

generous 1 cup self-rising flour, sifted

3 tsp ground ginger

3 eggs, beaten

1 lb/450 g dessert (eating) pears, peeled, cored, and thinly sliced

1 tbsp soft brown sugar

1 Lightly grease and line the base of a deep 8-inch/20-cm cake pan.

2 Using a whisk, combine ¾ cup of the butter with the sugar, flour, ginger, and eggs and mix to form a smooth consistency.

3 Spoon the cake mixture into the prepared pan, leveling out the surface.

4 Arrange the pear slices over the cake mixture. Sprinkle with the brown sugar and dot with the remaining butter.

5 Bake in a preheated oven, at 350°F/ 180°C, for 35–40 minutes, or until the cake is golden and feels springy to the touch.

6 Serve the pear and ginger cake warm, with ice cream or cream, if you wish.

## COOK'S TIP

Soft brown sugar is often known as Barbados sugar. It is a darker form of light brown soft sugar.

# Mascarpone Cheesecake

The mascarpone gives this baked cheesecake a wonderfully tangy flavor. Ricotta cheese could be used as an alternative.

## NUTRITIONAL INFORMATION

| | | |
|---|---|---|
| Calories . . . . . . .327 | Sugars . . . . . . . .25g | |
| Protein . . . . . . . . .9g | Fat . . . . . . . . . .18g | |
| Carbohydrate . . .33g | Saturates . . . . . .11g | |

 15 MINS     50 MINS

### SERVES 8

## INGREDIENTS

scant ¼ cup unsalted butter

5½ oz/150 g ginger cookies, crushed

1 oz/25 g preserved ginger, chopped

1 lb 2 oz/500 g mascarpone cheese

finely grated rind and juice of 2 lemons

½ cup superfine sugar

2 large eggs, separated

fruit coulis (see Cook's Tip), to serve

1 Grease and line the base of a 10-inch/25-cm spring-form cake pan or loose-bottomed pan.

2 Melt the butter in a pan and stir in the crushed cookies and chopped ginger. Use the mixture to line the pan, pressing the mixture about ¼ inch/5 mm up the sides.

## COOK'S TIP

Fruit coulis can be made by cooking 14 oz/400 g fruit, such as blueberries or raspberries, for 5 minutes with 2 tablespoons of water. Blend and strain the mixture, then stir in 1 tablespoon (or more to taste) of sifted confectioners' sugar. Leave to cool before serving.

3 Beat together the cheese, lemon rind and juice, sugar, and egg yolks until quite smooth.

4 Whisk the egg whites until they are stiff and fold into the cheese and lemon mixture.

5 Pour the mixture into the pan and bake in a preheated oven, at 350°F/180°C, for 35–45 minutes, or until just set. Don't worry if it cracks or sinks—this is quite normal.

6 Leave the cheesecake in the pan to cool. Serve with fruit coulis (see Cook's Tip).

# Zabaglione

This well-known dish is really a light but rich egg mousse flavored with Marsala wine.

## NUTRITIONAL INFORMATION

Calories .......158  Sugars ........29g
Protein .........1g  Fat ...........1g
Carbohydrate ...29g  Saturates .....0.2g

 5 MINS   15 MINS

### SERVES 4

## INGREDIENTS

5 egg yolks

½ cup superfine sugar

⅔ cup Marsala or sweet sherry

amaretti cookies, to serve (optional)

1 Place the egg yolks in a large mixing bowl.

2 Add the superfine sugar to the egg yolks and whisk until the mixture is thick and very pale and has doubled in volume.

3 Place the bowl containing the egg yolk and sugar mixture over a pan of gently simmering water.

4 Add the Marsala to the egg yolk and sugar mixture and continue whisking until the foam mixture becomes warm. This process may take as long as 10 minutes.

5 Pour the mixture, which should be frothy and light, into 4 wine glasses.

6 Serve the zabaglione warm with fresh fruit or amaretti cookies, if you wish.

# Chocolate Zabaglione

As this recipe uses only a little chocolate, choose one with a minimum of 70 percent cocoa solids for a good flavor.

## NUTRITIONAL INFORMATION

| | |
|---|---|
| Calories . . . . . . .224 | Sugars . . . . . . . .23g |
| Protein . . . . . . . . .4g | Fat . . . . . . . . . .10g |
| Carbohydrate . . .23g | Saturates . . . . . . .4g |

10 MINS

5 MINS

### SERVES 4

## I N G R E D I E N T S

4 egg yolks

4 tbsp superfine sugar

1¾ oz/50 g dark chocolate

½ cup Marsala wine

unsweetened cocoa, to dust

1 In a large glass mixing bowl, whisk together the egg yolks and superfine sugar until you have a very pale mixture, using electric beaters.

2 Grate the chocolate finely and fold into the egg mixture.

3 Fold the Marsala wine into the chocolate mixture.

4 Place the mixing bowl over a pan of gently simmering water and set the beaters on the lowest speed or swop to a

balloon whisk. Cook gently, whisking continuously until the mixture thickens; take care not to overcook or the mixture will curdle.

5 Spoon the hot mixture into warmed individual glass dishes or coffee cups (as here) and dust with unsweetened cocoa. Serve the zabaglione as soon as possible so that it is warm, light, and fluffy.

## COOK'S TIP

Make the dessert just before serving as it will separate if left to stand. If it begins to curdle, remove it from the heat immediately and place it in a bowl of cold water to stop the cooking. Whisk furiously until the mixture comes together.

# Chocolate Chip Ice Cream

This marvellous frozen dessert offers the best of both worlds, delicious chocolate chip cookies and a rich dairy-flavored ice.

## NUTRITIONAL INFORMATION

Calories . . . . . . .238    Sugars . . . . . . . .23g
Protein . . . . . . . . .9g    Fat . . . . . . . . . .10g
Carbohydrate . . .30g    Saturates . . . . . . .4g

6 HOURS          5 MINS

### SERVES 6

## I N G R E D I E N T S

1¼ cups milk

1 vanilla bean

2 eggs

2 egg yolks

¼ cup superfine sugar

1¼ cups plain yogurt

4½ oz/125 g chocolate chip cookies,
    broken into small pieces

1 Pour the milk into a small pan, add the vanilla bean and bring to a boil over low heat. Remove from the heat, then cover the pan and set aside to cool.

2 Beat the eggs and egg yolks in a double boiler or in a bowl set over a pan of simmering water. Add the sugar and continue beating until the mixture is pale and creamy.

3 Reheat the milk to simmering point and strain it over the egg mixture. Stir continuously until the custard is thick enough to coat the back of a spoon. Remove the custard from the heat and stand the pan or bowl in cold water to prevent any further cooking. Wash and dry the vanilla bean for future use.

4 Stir the yogurt into the cooled custard and beat until it is well blended. When the mixture is thoroughly cold, stir in the broken cookies.

5 Transfer the mixture to a chilled metal cake pan or plastic container, then cover and freeze for 4 hours. Remove from the freezer every hour, then transfer to a chilled bowl and beat vigorously to prevent ice crystals from forming then return to the freezer. Alternatively, freeze the mixture in an ice-cream maker, following the manufacturer's instructions.

6 To serve the ice-cream, transfer it to the main part of the refrigerator for 1 hour to soften. Serve in scoops.

# Honey & Nut Nests

Pistachio nuts and honey are combined with crisp cooked angel hair pasta in this unusual dessert.

## NUTRITIONAL INFORMATION

| | | |
|---|---|---|
| Calories .......802 | Sugars ........53g | |
| Protein ........13g | Fat .........48g | |
| Carbohydrate ...85g | Saturates ......16g | |

10 MINS     1 HOUR

### SERVES 4

## I N G R E D I E N T S

8 oz/225 g angel hair pasta

½ cup butter

scant 1½ cups shelled pistachio nuts
   chopped

½ cup sugar

⅓ cup clear honey

⅔ cup water

2 tsp lemon juice

salt

strained plain yogurt, to serve

1 Bring a large pan of lightly salted water to a boil. Add the angel hair pasta and cook for 8–10 minutes, or until tender but still firm to the bite. Drain the pasta and return to the pan. Add the butter and toss to coat the pasta thoroughly. Set aside to cool.

2 Arrange 4 small flan or poaching rings on a cookie sheet. Divide the angel hair pasta into 8 equal quantities and spoon 4 of them into the rings. Press down lightly. Top the pasta with half of the nuts, then add the remaining pasta.

3 Bake in a preheated oven, at 350°F/180°C, for 45 minutes, or until golden brown.

4 Meanwhile, put the sugar, honey, and water in a pan and bring to a boil over low heat, stirring constantly until the sugar has dissolved completely. Simmer for 10 minutes, then add the lemon juice and simmer for 5 minutes.

5 Using a spatula, carefully transfer the angel hair nests to a serving dish. Pour over the honey syrup, then sprinkle over the remaining nuts and set aside to cool completely before serving. Serve the yogurt separately.

## COOK'S TIP

Angel hair pasta is also known as *capelli d'Angelo*. Long and very fine, it is usually sold in small bunches that already resemble nests.

# Pear Tart

Pears are a very popular fruit in Italy. In this recipe from Trentino they are flavored with almonds, cinnamon, raisins, and apricot jam.

## NUTRITIONAL INFORMATION

Calories . . . . . . .629   Sugars . . . . . . . .70g
Protein . . . . . . . . .7g   Fat . . . . . . . . . .21g
Carbohydrate . .109g   Saturates . . . . . .13g

 1½ HOURS    50 MINS

### SERVES 6

## I N G R E D I E N T S

2¼ cups all-purpose flour

pinch of salt

generous ½ cup superfine sugar

½ cup butter, diced

1 egg

1 egg yolk

few drops of vanilla extract

2–3 tsp water

sifted confectioners' sugar, for
   sprinkling

### F I L L I N G

4 tbsp apricot jam

2 oz/55 g amaretti or ratafia cookies,
   crumbled

1¾–2 lb 4 oz/850–1 kg pears, peeled
   and cored

1 tsp ground cinnamon

generous ½ cup raisins

⅓ cup soft brown or raw sugar

1 Sift the flour and salt on to a flat surface, then make a well in the center and add the sugar, butter, egg, egg yolk, vanilla extract and most of the water.

2 Using your fingers, gradually work the flour into the other ingredients to give a smooth dough, adding more water if necessary. Wrap in plastic wrap and chill for 1 hour, or until firm. Alternatively, put all the ingredients into a food processor and work until smooth.

3 Roll out three-fourths of the dough and use to line a shallow 10-inch/ 25-cm cake pan or deep flan pan. Spread the jam over the base and sprinkle with the crushed cookies.

4 Slice the pears very thinly. Arrange over the cookies in the pastry case.

Sprinkle with cinnamon, then with raisins, and finally with brown sugar.

5 Roll out a thin sausage shape using one-third of the remaining dough, and place around the edge of the pie. Roll the remainder into thin sausages and arrange in a lattice over the pie, 4 or 5 strips in each direction, attaching them to the strip around the edge.

6 Bake in a preheated oven, at 400°F/ 200°C, for 50 minutes, or until golden and cooked through. Leave to cool, then serve warm or chilled, sprinkled with sifted confectioners' sugar.

# Quick Tiramisu

This quick version of one of the most popular Italian desserts is ready in minutes.

## NUTRITIONAL INFORMATION

| | | | |
|---|---|---|---|
| Calories | .......387 | Sugars | ........17g |
| Protein | .........9g | Fat | ..........28g |
| Carbohydrate | ...22g | Saturates | ......15g |

 15 MINS    0 MINS

### SERVES 4

## I N G R E D I E N T S

1 cup mascarpone or full-fat soft cheese

1 egg, separated

2 tbsp plain yogurt

2 tbsp superfine sugar

2 tbsp dark rum

2 tbsp strong black coffee

8 sponge lady-fingers

2 tbsp grated dark chocolate

1 Put the cheese in a large bowl, then add the egg yolk and yogurt and beat until smooth.

2 Whisk the egg white until stiff but not dry, then whisk in the sugar and carefully fold into the cheese mixture.

3 Spoon half of the mixture into 4 sundae glasses.

4 Mix together the rum and coffee in a shallow dish. Dip the lady-fingers into the rum mixture, then break them in half, or into smaller pieces if necessary, and divide among the glasses.

5 Stir any remaining coffee mixture into the remaining cheese and spoon over the top.

6 Sprinkle with grated chocolate. Serve immediately or chill until required.

## COOK'S TIP

Mascarpone is an Italian soft cream cheese made from cow's milk. It has a rich, silky smooth texture and a deliciously creamy flavor. It can be eaten as it is with fresh fruits or flavored with coffee or chocolate.

# Raspberry Fusilli

This is the ultimate in self-indulgence—a truly delicious dessert that tastes every bit as good as it looks.

## NUTRITIONAL INFORMATION

Calories .......235  Sugars ........20g
Protein .........7g  Fat ...........7g
Carbohydrate ...36g  Saturates .......1g

5 MINS  20 MINS

**SERVES 4**

## I N G R E D I E N T S

½ cup fusilli

1 lb 9 oz/700 g raspberries

2 tbsp superfine sugar

1 tbsp lemon juice

4 tbsp slivered almonds

3 tbsp raspberry liqueur

1 Bring a large pan of lightly salted water to a boil. Add the fusilli and cook for 8–10 minutes, or until tender but still firm to the bite. Drain the fusilli thoroughly, then return to the pan and set aside to cool.

2 Using a spoon, firmly press 1⅓ cups of the raspberries through a strainer set over a large mixing bowl to form a smooth purée.

3 Put the raspberry purée and sugar in a small pan and simmer over a low heat, stirring occasionally, for 5 minutes.

4 Stir in the lemon juice and set the sauce aside until required.

5 Add the remaining raspberries to the fusilli in the pan and mix together well. Transfer the raspberry and fusilli mixture to a serving dish.

6 Spread the almonds out on a cookie sheet and toast under the broiler until golden brown. Remove and set aside to cool slightly.

7 Stir the raspberry liqueur into the reserved raspberry sauce and mix together well until very smooth. Pour the raspberry sauce over the fusilli. Sprinkle over the toasted almonds and serve.

## VARIATION

You could use any sweet, ripe berry for making this dessert. Strawberries and blackberries are especially suitable, combined with the correspondingly flavored liqueur. Alternatively, you could use a different berry mixed with the fusilli, but still pour over raspberry sauce.

# Peaches & Mascarpone

If you prepare these in advance, all you have to do is pop the peaches on the grill when you are ready to serve them.

## NUTRITIONAL INFORMATION

Calories . . . . . . . . .301    Sugars . . . . . . . .24g
Protein . . . . . . . . .6g    Fat . . . . . . . . . .20g
Carbohydrate . . .24g    Saturates . . . . . . .9g

  10 MINS    10 MINS

### SERVES 4

## I N G R E D I E N T S

4 peaches

¾ cup mascarpone cheese

scant ⅓ cup chopped pecans or walnuts

1 tsp corn oil

4 tbsp maple syrup

1 Cut the peaches in half and remove the stones. If you are preparing this recipe in advance, press the peach halves together again and wrap them in plastic wrap until required.

2 Mix the mascarpone and pecans together in a small bowl until well combined. Leave to chill in the refrigerator until required.

3 To serve, brush the peaches with a little oil and place on a rack set over medium hot coals. Grill for 5–10 minutes, turning once, until hot.

4 Transfer the peaches to a serving dish and top with the mascarpone mixture.

5 Drizzle the maple syrup over the peaches and mascarpone filling and serve at once.

## VARIATION

You can use nectarines instead of peaches for this recipe. Remember to choose ripe but firm fruit which won't go soft and mushy when it is grilled. Prepare the nectarines in the same way as the peaches and grill for 5–10 minutes.

# Sweet Mascarpone Mousse

A sweet cream cheese dessert that complements the tartness of fresh summer fruits rather well.

## NUTRITIONAL INFORMATION

Calories . . . . . . .542   Sugars . . . . . . . .31g
Protein . . . . . . . .14g   Fat . . . . . . . . . .41g
Carbohydrate . . .31g   Saturates . . . . . .24g

1¹⁄₂ HOURS     0 MINS

### SERVES 4

## INGREDIENTS

1 lb/450 g mascarpone cheese

4 egg yolks

½ cup superfine sugar

14 oz/400 g frozen summer fruits, such as
   raspberries and red currants

red currants, to garnish

amaretti cookies, to serve

1 Place the mascarpone cheese in a large mixing bowl. Using a wooden spoon, beat the mascarpone cheese until quite smooth.

2 Stir the egg yolks and sugar into the mascarpone cheese, mixing well. Leave the mixture to chill in the refrigerator for about 1 hour.

3 Spoon a layer of the mascarpone mixture into the bottom of 4 individual serving dishes. Spoon a layer of the summer fruits on top. Repeat the layers in the same order, reserving some of the mascarpone mixture for the top.

4 Leave the mousses to chill in the refrigerator for about 20 minutes. The fruits should still be slightly frozen.

5 Serve the mascarpone mousses with amaretti cookies.

# Panettone & Strawberries

Panettone is a sweet Italian bread. It is delicious toasted, and when it is topped with mascapone and strawberries it makes a sumptuous dessert.

## NUTRITIONAL INFORMATION

| | |
|---|---|
| Calories .......227 | Sugars ........11g |
| Protein .........5g | Fat ..........13g |
| Carbohydrate ...19g | Saturates .......8g |

35 MINS    2 MINS

### SERVES 4

### I N G R E D I E N T S

8 oz/225 g strawberries

2 tbsp superfine sugar

scant ⅓ cup Marsala wine

½ tsp ground cinnamon

4 slices panettone

4 tbsp mascarpone cheese

1 Hull and slice the strawberries and place them in a bowl. Add the sugar, Marsala, and cinnamon to the strawberries.

2 Toss the strawberries in the sugar and cinnamon mixture until they are well coated. Leave to chill in the refrigerator for at least 30 minutes.

3 When ready to serve, transfer the slices of panettone to a rack set over medium hot coals. Grill the panettone for 1 minute on each side, or until golden brown.

4 Carefully remove the panettone from the grill and transfer to serving plates.

5 Top the panettone with the mascarpone cheese and the marinated strawberries. Serve immediately.

# Orange & Grapefruit Salad

Sliced citrus fruits with a delicious almond and honey dressing make an unusual and refreshing dessert.

## NUTRITIONAL INFORMATION

| | | |
|---|---|---|
| Calories . . . . . . . .217 | Sugars . . . . . . . .33g | |
| Protein . . . . . . . . .4g | Fat . . . . . . . . . . .9g | |
| Carbohydrate . . .33g | Saturates . . . . . . .1g | |

  2¼ HOURS    3 MINS

### SERVES 4

### I N G R E D I E N T S

2 grapefruit, ruby or plain

4 oranges

pared rind and juice of 1 lime

4 tbsp runny honey

2 tbsp warm water

1 sprig of mint, roughly chopped

chopped ⅓ cup chopped walnuts

1 Using a sharp knife, slice the top and bottom from the grapefruits, then slice away the rest of the skin and pith.

2 Cut between each segment of the grapefruit and remove the fleshy part only.

3 Using a sharp knife, slice the top and bottom from the oranges, then slice away the rest of the skin and pith.

4 Cut between each segment of the oranges to remove the fleshy part. Add to the grapefruit.

5 Place the lime rind, 2 tablespoons of lime juice, the honey, and the warm water in a small bowl. Whisk with a fork to mix the dressing.

6 Pour the dressing over the segmented fruit, then add the chopped mint and mix well. Leave to chill in the refrigerator for 2 hours for the flavors to mingle.

7 Place the chopped walnuts on a cookie sheet. Lightly toast the walnuts under a preheated medium broiler for 2–3 minutes, or until browned.

8 Sprinkle the toasted walnuts over the fruit and serve.

# Vanilla Ice Cream

This homemade version of real vanilla ice cream is absolutely delicious and so easy to make. A tutti-frutti variation is also provided.

## NUTRITIONAL INFORMATION

Calories . . . . . . .626  Sugars . . . . . . . .33g

Protein . . . . . . . . .7g  Fat . . . . . . . . . .53g

Carbohydrate . . .33g  Saturates . . . . . .31g

5 MINS        15 MINS

### SERVES 6

## INGREDIENTS

2½ cups heavy cream

1 vanilla bean

pared rind of 1 lemon

4 eggs, beaten

2 egg yolks

scant 1 cup superfine sugar

1 Place the cream in a heavy-based pan and heat gently, whisking.

2 Add the vanilla bean, lemon rind, eggs, and egg yolks to the pan and heat until the mixture reaches just below boiling point.

3 Reduce the heat and cook for 8–10 minutes, whisking the mixture continuously, until thickened.

## VARIATION

For tutti frutti ice cream, soak generous ½ cup mixed dried fruit in 2 tbsp Marsala or sweet sherry for 20 minutes. Follow the method for vanilla ice cream, omitting the vanilla bean, and stir in the Marsala or sherry-soaked fruit in step 6, just before freezing.

4 Stir the sugar into the cream mixture, then set aside and leave to cool.

5 Pass the cream mixture through a strainer.

6 Slit open the vanilla bean, then scoop out the tiny black seeds and stir them into the cream.

7 Pour the mixture into a shallow freezing container with a lid and freeze overnight until set. Serve the ice cream when required.

# Ricotta Ice Cream

The ricotta cheese gives a creamy flavor, while the nuts add a crunchy texture. This ice cream needs to be chilled in the freezer overnight.

## NUTRITIONAL INFORMATION

| | | | |
|---|---|---|---|
| Calories | .......438 | Sugars | ........39g |
| Protein | ........13g | Fat | ..........25g |
| Carbohydrate | ...40g | Saturates | .......9g |

20 MINS    0 MINS

### SERVES 6

## INGREDIENTS

scant ¼ cup pistachio nuts

¼ cup walnuts or pecan nuts

scant ¼ cup toasted chopped hazelnuts

grated rind of 1 orange

grated rind of 1 lemon

2 tbsp stem ginger

2 tbsp candied cherries

scant ¼ cup dried apricots

3 tbsp raisins

1 lb 2 oz/500 g ricotta cheese

2 tbsp Maraschino, Amaretto, or brandy

1 tsp vanilla extract

4 egg yolks

generous ½ cup superfine sugar

### TO DECORATE

whipped cream

a few candied cherries, pistachio nuts, or mint leaves

1 Roughly chop the pistachio nuts and walnuts and mix with the toasted hazelnuts and orange and lemon rind.

2 Finely chop the ginger, cherries, apricots, and raisins, and add to the bowl.

3 Stir the ricotta evenly through the fruit mixture, then beat in the liqueur and vanilla extract.

4 Put the egg yolks and sugar in a bowl and whisk hard until very thick and creamy—they may be whisked over a pan of gently simmering water to speed up the process. Leave to cool if necessary.

5 Carefully fold the ricotta mixture evenly through the beaten eggs and sugar until smooth.

6 Line a 7 x 5 inch/18 x 12 cm loaf pan with a double layer of plastic wrap or baking parchment. Pour in the ricotta mixture and level the top, then cover with more plastic wrap or baking parchment and chill in the freezer until firm—at least overnight.

7 To serve, carefully remove the ice cream from the pan and peel off the paper. Place on a serving dish and decorate with whipped cream, candied cherries, pistachio nuts, and/or mint leaves. Serve in slices.

# Chocolate Biscotti

These dry cookies are delicious served with black coffee after your evening meal.

## NUTRITIONAL INFORMATION

| | | | |
|---|---|---|---|
| Calories | 113 | Sugars | 9g |
| Protein | 2g | Fat | 5g |
| Carbohydrate | 15g | Saturates | 1g |

20 MINS    40 MINS

### MAKES 16

## INGREDIENTS

1 egg

½ cup superfine sugar

1 tsp vanilla extract

1 cup all-purpose flour

½ tsp baking powder

1 tsp ground cinnamon

1¾ oz/50 g dark chocolate, chopped coarsely

½ cup toasted slivered almonds

⅓ cup pine nuts

1 Lightly grease a large cookie sheet.

2 Whisk the egg, sugar and vanilla extract in a mixing bowl with an electric mixer until it is thick and pale—ribbons of mixture should trail from the whisk as you lift it.

3 Sift the flour, baking powder, and cinnamon into a separate bowl, then sift into the egg mixture and fold in gently. Stir in the chocolate, almonds, and pine nuts.

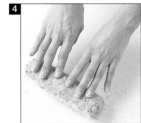

4 Turn onto a lightly floured surface and shape into a flat log, 9 inches/23 cm long and ¾ inch/1.5 cm wide. Transfer to the cookie sheet.

5 Bake in a preheated oven, at 350°F/180°C, for 20-25 minutes, or until golden. Remove from the oven and leave to cool for 5 minutes or until firm.

6 Transfer the log to a cutting board. Using a serrated bread knife, cut the log on the diagonal into slices about ½ inch/1 cm thick and arrange them on the cookie sheet. Cook for 10-15 minutes, turning halfway through the cooking time.

7 Leave to cool for about 5 minutes, then transfer to a wire rack to cool.

# Florentines

These luxury cookies will be popular at any time of the year, but make a particularly wonderful treat at Christmas.

## NUTRITIONAL INFORMATION

Calories .......186   Sugars ........19g
Protein .........2g   Fat ...........11g
Carbohydrate ...22g   Saturates .......5g

   20 MINS   🕐 15 MINS

### MAKES 10

### INGREDIENTS

scant ¼ cup butter

¼ cup superfine sugar

scant ¼ cup all-purpose flour, strained

scant ⅓ cup almonds, chopped

scant ⅓ cup chopped candied peel

scant ¼ cup raisins, chopped

2 tbsp chopped candied cherries

finely grated rind of ½ lemon

4½ oz/125 g dark chocolate, melted

1 Line 2 large cookie sheets with baking parchment.

2 Heat the butter and superfine sugar in a small pan until the butter has just melted and the sugar dissolved. Remove the pan from the heat.

3 Stir in the flour and mix well. Stir in the chopped almonds, candied peel, raisins, cherries, and lemon rind. Place teaspoonfuls of the mixture well apart on the cookie sheets.

4 Bake in a preheated oven, at 350°F/180°C, for 10 minutes, or until lightly golden.

5 As soon as the Florentines are removed from the oven, press the edges into neat shapes while still on the cookie sheets, using a cookie cutter. Leave to cool on the cookie sheets until firm, then transfer to a wire rack to cool.

6 Spread the melted chocolate over the smooth side of each Florentine. As the chocolate begins to set, mark wavy lines in it with a fork. Leave the Florentines until set, chocolate side up.

## VARIATION

Replace the dark chocolate with white chocolate or, for a dramatic effect, cover half of the Florentines in dark chocolate and half in white.

# White Chocolate Florentines

These attractive jewelled cookies are coated with white chocolate to give them a delicious flavor.

## NUTRITIONAL INFORMATION

| | | | |
|---|---|---|---|
| Calories | .......235 | Sugars | ........20g |
| Protein | .........3g | Fat | ..........17g |
| Carbohydrate | ...20g | Saturates | .......7g |

20 MINS    15 MINS

### MAKES 24

## I N G R E D I E N T S

scant 1 cup butter

generous 1 cup superfine sugar

scant 1 cup chopped walnuts

scant 1 cup chopped almonds

⅓ cup golden raisins, chopped

scant ¼ cup candied cherries

scant ¼ cup candied peel, chopped finely

2 tbsp light cream

8 oz/225 g white chocolate

1 Line 3–4 cookie sheets with non-stick baking parchment.

2 Melt the butter over a low heat and then add the sugar, stirring until it has dissolved. Boil the mixture for exactly 1 minute. Remove from the heat.

## COOK'S TIP

A combination of white and dark chocolate Florentines looks very attractive, especially if you are making them as gifts. Pack them in pretty boxes, lined with tissue paper and tied with some ribbon.

3 Add the walnuts, almonds, golden raisins, candied cherries, candied peel, and cream to the pan, stirring well to mix.

4 Drop heaped teaspoonfuls of the mixture on to the cookie sheets, leaving plenty of room for them to spread while cooking. Bake in a preheated oven, at 350°F/180°C, for 10 minutes, or until golden brown.

5 Remove the cookies from the oven and neaten the edges with a knife

while they are still warm. Leave to cool slightly, and then transfer them to a wire rack to cool completely.

6 Melt the chocolate in a bowl placed over a pan of gently simmering water. Spread the underside of the cookies with chocolate and use a fork to make wavy lines across the surface. Leave to cool completely.

7 Store the Florentines in an airtight tin, kept in a cool place.

# Italian Chocolate Truffles

These are flavored with almonds and chocolate, and are simplicity itself to make. Served with coffee, they are the perfect end to a meal.

## NUTRITIONAL INFORMATION

| | | | |
|---|---|---|---|
| Calories | ........82 | Sugars | ........7g |
| Protein | .........1g | Fat | ..........5g |
| Carbohydrate | ....8g | Saturates | .......3g |

 5 MINS       5 MINS

### MAKES 24

## I N G R E D I E N T S

6 oz/175 g dark chocolate

2 tbsp almond-flavored liqueur (amaretto)
    or orange-flavored liqueur

3 tbsp unsalted butter

¼ cup confectioners' sugar

generous ½ cup ground almonds

1¾ oz/50 g milk chocolate, grated

1 Melt the dark chocolate with the liqueur in a bowl set over a pan of hot water, stirring until well combined.

2 Add the butter and stir until it has melted. Stir in the confectioners' sugar and the ground almonds.

3 Leave the mixture in a cool place until firm enough to roll into 24 balls.

4 Place the grated chocolate on a plate and roll the truffles in the chocolate to coat them.

5 Place the truffles in paper candy cases and chill.

# Index